RESTRUCTURING THE CITY

The Political Economy
of Urban Redevelopment

Revised Edition

Susan S. Fainstein
Norman I. Fainstein
Richard Child Hill
Dennis R. Judd
Michael Peter Smith

WITH

P. Jefferson Armistead and Marlene Keller

Longman
New York & London

RESTRUCTURING THE CITY, Revised Edtion

Copyright © 1983, 1986 by Longman Inc.

Longman Inc.
95 Church Street
White Plains, N.Y. 10601

Associated companies:
Longman Group Ltd., London
Longman Cheshire Pty., Melbourne
Longman Paul Pty., Auckland
Copp Clark Pitman, Toronto
Pitman Publishing Inc., New York

Library of Congress Cataloging-in-Publication Data
Main entry under title:
Restructuring the city.
    Includes bibliographies and index.
    1. Urban renewal—United States—Case studies.
2. Urban policy—United States—Case studies.   3. Munici-
pal government—United States—Case studies.   4. Urban
economics—Case studies.   I. Fainstein, Susan S.
HT175.R47 1986   307.3'4'0973   85-23933
ISBN 0-582-28619-0 (pbk.)

Manufactured in the United States of America

86 87 88 89   9 8 7 6 5 4 3 2 1

Contents

Preface   vii

1. **Economic Change, National Policy, and the System of Cities** / *Susan S. Fainstein and Norman I. Fainstein*   1

   The Changing Social Economy of Cities   4
   The Policy Framework   13
   Political Control and the Representation of Low-
     Income Groups   21

2. **New Haven: The Limits of the Local State** /
   Norman I. Fainstein and Susan S. Fainstein   27

   The City and Its People over Three Decades   29
   Change and Continuity in the Politics of
     Development   34
   The Executive-Centered Coalition: 1954–67   36
   Street-Fighting Pluralism: 1967–74   52
   Conserving Clientelism: The Politics of Urban
     Development, 1975–80   55

3. **Crisis in the Motor City: The Politics of Economic Development in Detroit** / *Richard Child Hill*   80

   Detroit's Space Economy   83
   Uneven Development: Popular Rebellion and Elite
     Response   91
   Crisis in the Motor City   98
   The Corporate-Center Strategy   102
   The Politics of Austerity   109
   Car Wars: The Global Reorganization of the Auto
     Industry   113
   Urban Crisis or Urban Renaissance?   116

4. "Managed Growth" and the Politics of Uneven
   Development in New Orleans / *Michael Peter Smith
   and Marlene Keller*   **126**

   Uneven Regional and Intrametropolitan
      Development 128
   Managed Growth and Downtown Boom   132
   Structural Economic Change and Political
      Response 144
   The Social Costs of Uneven Development   159

5. From Cowtown to Sunbelt City: Boosterism and
   Economic Growth in Denver / *Dennis R. Judd*   **167**

   Denver as a Sunbelt City   169
   The Effort to Reclaim the Downtown   177
   Urban Sprawl and the Quality of Life   186
   The Uneven Benefits of Growth   195
   The Uncertain Effects of Growth   197

6. San Francisco: Urban Transformation and the Local
   State / *Susan S. Fainstein, Norman I. Fainstein, and
   P. Jefferson Armistead*   **202**

   Transformation of the City   204
   The Unopposed-Clearance Period: 1950–64   216
   Confrontation with Continued Investment:
      1964–74 219
   Consolidation: 1975–81   226
   Conclusion: The Right to the City   240

7. Regime Strategies, Communal Resistance, and
   Economic Forces / *Norman I. Fainstein and Susan S.
   Fainstein*   **245**

   Interests of State and Capital in Urban
      Redevelopment 246
   The Character of State-Sponsored
      Redevelopment 250
   Political Representation and Redevelopment
      Outcomes 268
   Urban Redevelopment and Capitalist Crisis   274

Epilogue 283

Index 289

Preface

The rapid development of both theoretical and empirical studies of urbanism during the last decade has made it possible to embark on comparative works which build on an established body of knowledge. So far, however, comparative analyses that deal simultaneously with urban economic and political systems have been relatively rare. It is our hope to fill this gap by providing analytic case studies of five quite different American cities, seeking to generalize from them to overarching questions of urban change. We focus on one aspect of urban political economy—redevelopment—because it has been so central an issue in most cities and because it is pivotal in the relationship between local and national forces.

While the need for comparative case studies is readily apparent, the task of generating them is fraught with obstacles, which perhaps explains their rarity. A wholly unified project, with one centrally based team of authors collecting and analyzing data from all the study cities, requires large-scale funding. Such funding is not usually available for an endeavor which is essentially critical in its viewpoint. In fact, the idea for this volume was originated by Norman and Susan Fainstein when they were working on a $12-million, nine-city project funded by the U.S. Department of Housing and Urban Development (HUD). They ended their relationship with that project when the University of Pennsylvania, where the study was housed, prohibited them from publishing findings without prior clearance. In fact, even before a final confrontation over a paper to be presented at the American Political Science Association, the confining nature of government sponsorship had become quite clear.

While funded projects limit scholarly independence, unfunded ones make in-depth research in distant cities prohibitively expensive. Lack of official sponsorship also makes access to important decision makers formidable. The solution which we used in this study—the participation of independent scholars residing in the various cities—overcomes some of these obstacles by placing responsibility in the hands of individuals long familiar with their research sites, with ongoing data files and personal acquaintances among local informants.

The cost of our approach—we seek here to disarm our critics if not to dissuade them—is the lack of precise parallelism in the case studies. Because the authors were not part of a single project team, they had accumulated data based on their own research interests. Consequently, the five city studies stress different elements, although as we explain in greater detail in Chapter 1, they also share an overall outlook. The chapters on New Haven and San Francisco by Norman and Susan Fainstein indicate their concern with the local state, its penetrability by nonelite groups, and the effects of national policy on the local political economy. Richard Hill's analysis of Detroit derives from his ongoing research into the effects of the reorganization of the world economy, in particular the influence of changes in the auto industry on urban systems. Michael Smith has been particularly concerned with the theory of uneven development and thus has explored in detail how that process has unfolded in New Orleans. Dennis Judd has taken a special interest in the conflict between advocates and opponents of growth and the way that has played itself out in Denver. Needless to say, we hope that the richness provided by our somewhat different emphases overweighs the lack of perfect correspondence.

The authors are indebted to many individuals, only some of whom they can acknowledge here. Norman and Susan Fainstein were given able research assistance by Ricky Fain, Douglas Goodfriend, Jerome Groomes, Cynthia Livermore, Hope Melton, Lynn Shields, and Paul Tainsh. They received helpful comments from Robert Beauregard, Susan Bok, Kenneth Fox, George Sternlieb, and Douglas Yates. Chester Hartman deserves special thanks for close reading of a manuscript which benefited greatly from his criticisms and suggestions. As usual, excellent typing was provided by Robert Rivelli at the New School for Social Research and Barbara Swan at Rutgers University. We wish to acknowledge support for part of our research by the Community Development Strategies Evaluation Project at the University of Pennsylvania. This project was funded by HUD, but nothing we have written is an official document, nor does it represent the views of the U.S. government.

Michael Smith is indebted to Clarence Stone, Anthony Giddens, and Manuel Castells for their critical comments and to Pat Smith for her perception, forbearance, and support.

Dennis Judd would like to acknowledge the very important research assistance of Karen Larsen.

Each of the authors assumes responsibility for the contents of his or her respective chapters.

Susan S. Fainstein
Norman I. Fainstein

1

Economic Change, National Policy, and the System of Cities

Susan S. Fainstein
Norman I. Fainstein

Cities have an air of permanence which is both real and illusory. Because they are built of concrete and steel, their physical forms display the layers of time. When cities are old, it takes the violence of the bulldozer to change their faces. But cities have a social and economic dynamism which continually remakes them, sometimes very quickly. Major parts of their population may leave, to be replaced by quite different people. Changing patterns of investment and production continually affect the character of economic life. Their built environments—houses, office buildings, factories, railroad yards—may fall into ruin or take on new uses as a result of technological innovations and large-scale economic shifts that can occur over just a few years. Neither physical nor social fabric simply stay the same without being continually reproduced.

In capitalist societies the reproduction of the physical, social, and economic fabric of cities depends upon the complex interaction of private and public decisions. Most of the critical determinations about the shape of industry, the wages to be paid bosses and workers, the location of investment in the built environment, are made by what is called the private sector—private in the sense that business is not controlled democratically. But government too plays a critical role. For government helps disparate business interests to act collectively. Government also carries out needed functions that are inherently unprofitable, and it frequently subsidizes other activities that turn a profit only because part of the bill is publicly paid. Finally, government mediates conflicts among opposing social groups. Urban redevelopment cannot, therefore, be explained through either a purely economic analysis or a study of local politics divorced from the economic relations that confine it. Our understanding necessarily requires that we reject the traditional antinomies of public and private, plan and market, control and conflict, social composition and physical form.

1

We proceed, then, with an integrated examination of all the factors that interact to define the political economy of urban redevelopment. The particular concerns of this volume are the politics of land use, economic growth, and housing; the efforts by governmental officials and business leaders to transform downtowns and residential neighborhoods in old American cities; and the demands and actions of citizens opposed in various ways to these efforts. The studies that follow address the same basic set of questions:

1. What have been the conditions which have given rise to state activity aimed at restructuring the city?
2. What has been the character of state programs, nationally and locally?
3. How has state activity been shaped by
   a. objective conditions?
   b. the relative capacities of social classes?
   c. specific political mobilizations and conflicts?
4. Which social groups have won and which have lost as a consequence of state activity?

Since issues associated with land use, economic activity, and housing are central to urban politics, their study helps us to capture the more general political transformations of the postwar years. And because cities are so dependent on external economic forces and governmental programs, the history of redevelopment at the local level reveals much about the changing characters of both the U.S. economy and national politics.

The main body of the book is composed of historical case studies of five cities: from east to west, New Haven, Detroit, New Orleans, Denver, and San Francisco. The elements common to these cities are quite typical of older urban areas. They were all originally structured to serve an industrial economy and have tried to reorient themselves to a service economy. They all have substantial minority and lower-income populations, an old housing stock, and little undeveloped land within their boundaries. But these cities also differ in critical ways, including political and programmatic histories, the character of their business classes, and the impact on them of various efforts at redevelopment, marked at the extremes by Denver and Detroit. Thus the cases allow us to distinguish between constant and variable elements and to see their interaction through a relatively long period of time. The last chapter is a theoretical synthesis in which we provide an interpretation of the politics of redevelopment over the last three decades and root the history of U.S. cities in the evolution and contradictions of American capitalism.

While the studies of each city reflect the individuality both of authors and of local histories, the book consistently uses a political economy approach.[1] Put most simply, our analyses of particular processes and events are shaped by three assumptions about urban development in the United States:

1. *The city is not a unitary political community, but rather a site for class and racial conflict.*
   Decisions associated with physical and economic development embody class

and racial interests. There are always distinct social groups who win and lose, regardless of whether political conflict becomes overt.[2]

2. *Class and racial inequality is expressed by the form of the built environment.* This process involves first a spatial dimension. Depending on the historical stage of local and national economic development and on cultural factors, some locations are more desirable than others—these may be the hills rather than the valleys, places near (or far) from transportation routes, neighborhoods proximate (or remote) from the central business district (CBD). In general, upper-income groups use their superior economic and political power to gain valued territories for themselves. Second, and of course related to the spatial aspect, upper-income groups acquire the best packages of housing and ancillary social amenities. Since both these allocations must be continually reproduced in the face of changing circumstances, class and racial conflicts will be structured by the existing character of the built environment, and their outcomes will, in turn, have profound effects on future development of urban form.

3. *Urban development is generally uneven between and within cities.* Instead of moving towards equilibrium, market forces produce cumulative advantages and disadvantages. Profit depends upon segmentation within housing and commercial property markets, whereby lower-income and especially minority groups are presented with a constrained supply of housing, while upper-income and commercial investors pay premium prices for their own territorial monopolies. Furthermore, "improvement" in one city or neighborhood leads to "decline" in another, since the process depends upon the spatial displacement of lower-income and minority groups. Together, these and other factors commonly result in situations whereby a city's economy and real estate values may improve in the aggregate while, at the same time, its lower-income areas expand and become poorer. Only governmental action to channel the benefits of growth and the costs of decline can even out the developmental process. (A more detailed discussion of all three points is provided in Chapter 7.)

The authors of these studies also share a common political perspective: a concern for the political role of the least-well-off people in cities and for how they are affected by governmental programs and market forces. If one question is whether politics can overcome economics, another surely is whether lower-income and minority citizens can make government do their bidding, even in places where they constitute well over half of the population. Since we do not hold the sanguine notion of a unitary political community in an unequal class society, each of us tries to understand not only what happened to "cities," but what happened to the ordinary people who live in them. The last chapter generalizes from the five cases in considering the possibilities of strategies for urban development in the interest of lower- and working-class people. As the reader will see soon enough, however, neither history nor theory leaves much room for optimism.

In the remainder of this introductory chapter we outline the social and economic forces which have affected urban development since the war (and especially the consequences for our five cities); the federal programs which were intended to ameliorate the urban condition; and the situation of lower-income groups in the politics of redevelopment.

THE CHANGING SOCIAL ECONOMY OF CITIES

The social economy of American cities is a product of national trends and their uneven geographic expression. The U.S. grew richer and more populous after World War II. While market income distribution changed little, the great expansion of the welfare state mitigated poverty and improved the relative position of lower-income populations. Most of this equalization occurred prior to the economic stagnation and political conservatism of the seventies, but gains remained essentially intact at least until the onset of the Reagan administration (Plotnick and Smeeding, 1979; Danziger, Haveman, and Plotnick, 1981). Increasing American affluence was accompanied by (and a result of) the restructuring of the economy, especially after the mid-sixties, away from the previously dominant manufacturing industries and toward high-technology production and services. These tendencies of economic growth and redistribution through government programs had geographical expressions which were intensified by the social migration to metropolitan areas of southern blacks, Puerto Ricans, and, most recently, immigrant Hispanics.

The position of older central cities (CCs) changed sharply in the postwar urban geography. Both people and industry suburbanized and moved interregionally in a continuous trend of national decentralization. Central-city population growth first slowed relatively, then declined absolutely in relation to that of the suburbs. Finally, whole metropolitan regions in the "snow belt" began contracting by the seventies (see U.S. Department of Housing and Urban Development (USDHUD), 1980b; Sternlieb and Hughes, 1975, 1978, 1981). Cities became poorer and blacker, albeit smaller, as middle- and working-class whites moved out to be replaced by minority households. Accompanying these well-known social changes was the relative economic decline of CCs unable to replace obsolete industries and the associated disinvestment from their built environments. On the whole, older American cities became vehicles for the encapsulation of minority groups and low-income whites in obsolete sectors of the economy and deteriorating physical environments.

There is strong evidence that urban inequality intensified during recent years for central cities *in the aggregate*. Between 1960 and 1978, CCs lost 9 percent of their white populations, while their black populations grew by about 40 percent (USDHUD, 1980b: 1–14). By 1980, 55 percent of blacks versus 24 percent of whites lived in central cities (USDHUD, 1980b: 1–15), and almost one-third of the entire central city population was black or Hispanic (USDHUD, 1980b: 1–3). During a period (1969–76) in which government-defined poverty dropped for the United States, it increased 6 percent in CCs and 16 percent in CCs larger than 1 million people (USDHUD, 1980b: 4–2); the proportion of CC blacks in poverty rose at similar rates—to the point where 31 percent of blacks living in CCs of any size as of 1976 were defined as poor (USDHUD, 1980b: 4–4). (As of 1979 this figure had increased slightly to more than 31 percent [U.S. Bureau of the Census, 1981: Table 747].)

Central cities became impoverished both relative to their prior condition and to their surrounding suburban municipalities. The difference between the incomes of households exiting versus those entering CCs resulted in an aggregate drop of $94 billion in CC household income between 1970 and 1977 (using constant 1980 dollars): this translated into an average annual withdrawal of almost $13.5 billion in consumption capacity, with perhaps one-quarter to one-third of that decrease in buying power felt in the housing market alone (based on analysis by Sternlieb and Hughes [1981: 55] adjusted to 1980 dollars). Not surprisingly, the gap between CC and suburban family income increased appreciably during the seventies (USDHUD, 1980b: 4–17).

One reason for the relative decline in central city income was the deterioration of CC economies in the seventies, as may be seen by a number of indicators. Private employment for a sample of eight large cities decreased by about 10 percent from 1970 to 1977, wiping out the gains of the previous decade; among the five of these cities with populations experiencing the most social deprivation, private employment contracted by almost 17 percent in the seventies (USDHUD, 1980b: Table 3–7). Using the same cities, Franklin James (1981: 28) found that CC employment declined steadily as a percentage of the metropolitan area figure: from 56 percent in 1962, to 49 percent in 1970, and, finally, to 42 percent in 1976; these trends continued into the eighties.

Suburban shopping centers and use of truck transport significantly reduced the comparative advantages of central cities' retail and wholesale industries. The sharpest losses, however, came in manufacturing, an industry sector upon which the economies of most older CCs had been built. While manufacturing employment changed little in the U.S. as a whole, it dropped in almost two-thirds of large CCs in the early seventies (USDHUD, 1980b: 3–2). Between 1970 and 1975, manufacturing employment contracted 1 percent in metropolitan suburbs, but 17 percent in CCs (James, 1981: 33). Moreover, the gap between CC and suburban wages grew during the same period (USDHUD, 1980b: Table 3–8).

But there were also signs that central cities responded to the positive dynamics of the national economy, though insufficiently to provide CCs in the aggregate with net economic growth (see Sternlieb and Hughes, 1975, 1978; Burchell and Listokin, 1981). Thus a study of the composition of employment change in 28 large cities pointed to the strength of service industries, the growth sector of the U.S. economy since the sixties. As expected, services were the most rapidly expanding industry in the fourteen cities with increased total private employment. More interesting, however, is the finding that even in contracting cities, service employment expanded. Such cities gained 47,000 service jobs while losing a total of 404,000 jobs in manufacturing, retail and wholesale trade (derived from USDHUD, 1980b: Table 3–3). New York City provided a further case in point. Between 1969 and 1978, when the city lost more than 500,000 jobs (334,000 in manufacturing alone), service employment, banking and finance expanded by 74,000 jobs (City of New

York, 1980: 169). Associated with the emergence of the service economy was a great expansion of office space, even in the most economically moribund central cities (USDHUD, 1980b: Table 3–12).

Demographic changes in the seventies provided further growth opportunities for central cities. During the decade the fastest growing cohort was the 25–34 age group (USDHUD, 1980b: Table 12–5). This group helped contribute to a "singles culture" which included delayed parenthood, smaller households, and new patterns of consumption. To the extent that people in this age group were also central city office and service workers, they established a basis for the reorganization of CC retailing, restaurants, hotels, and, most importantly, housing.

The economic trajectories of U.S. cities were far from uniform; the differences stemmed from variation in the ability of particular municipalities to capture growth industries (services, banking and finance, real estate, high-technology manufacturing) and to retain or restructure stable industries (wholesale and retail trade). As the abundant literature on regional shift demonstrates, relatively new cities, which tended to be concentrated in the West and Southwest, were much more successful than older places (cf. Sternlieb and Hughes, 1978; Perry and Watkins, 1977). Yet it became clear by the end of the decade that older cities themselves were taking different paths, with a minority showing signs of reorganized economies, core land use, and social composition. This group of *restructuring cities* (Fainstein and Fainstein, 1982b) had comparative advantages stemming from location, aesthetic appeal, the position of local industries in national corporate hierarchies (Mollenkopf, 1981: 93–96), and other factors, which allowed them to assume nodal positions in flows of investment capital. Cities like San Francisco, Denver, and, to an extent, New Orleans, were changing rapidly in character even while other old CCs stagnated or collapsed (respectively, New Haven and Detroit).

Conditions in Five Study Cities

Figure 1.1 allows us to compare the performance by industry of the five cities in our study with that of the U.S. economy as a whole. Employment gains and losses over the period 1954–77 are expressed in jobs per 1,000 average population. As we have discussed, service employment was the most rapidly expanding sector in the U.S. economy, and showed the best performance in each city, including Detroit where it lost fewer jobs than other industries. In contrast, manufacturing was the most hard-hit urban industry, with very large job losses in New Haven and Detroit, the two cities where it was most important. Detroit looked worst in every sector, followed closely by New Haven, which did expand in service employment, but far below the U.S. average. Denver, at the other extreme, gained in every sector. San Francisco and New Orleans both contained their losses in the traditional industries of manufacturing and wholesale trade, while experiencing small expansions in retailing and sizable growth in service industries, especially in San Francisco which outperformed the U.S. economy as a whole. These data suggest that our study cities may initially be divided into two groups: on the one hand, typical old declining cities (New Haven and Detroit), and on the other, those with restructuring economies

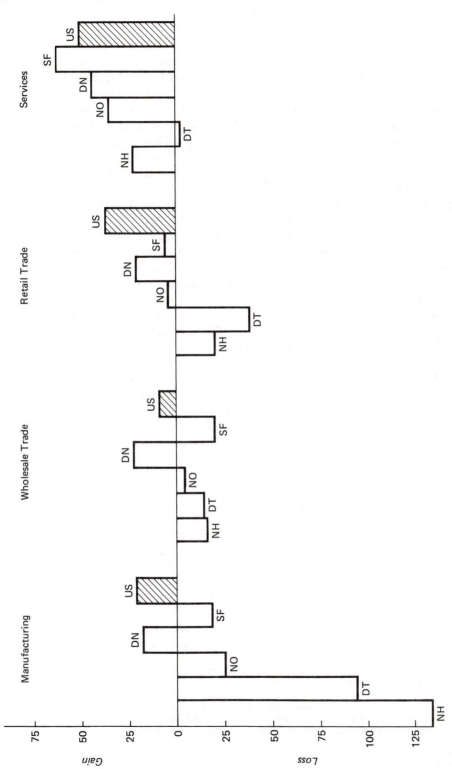

FIGURE 1.1 Relative Employment Gain or Loss by Industry, 1954–77: New Haven (NH), Detroit (DT), New Orleans (NO), Denver (DN), San Francisco (SF), and the United States (US).

Data from U.S. Bureau of the Census, *County and City Data Book*, 1956; *Census of Wholesale Trade, Geographic Area Studies*, 1977; *Statistical Abstract of the United States, 1981*; International City Management Association, *Municipal Yearbook*, 1981.

NOTE: Scale values represent employment gain or loss for each industry and jurisdiction between 1954 and 1977 divided by the average population of that jurisdiction between 1950 and 1980. The resulting figure is then multiplied by 1,000. In effect, then, the scale indicates changes in employment per 1,000 population. We have chosen this method of comparative presentation in order to avoid sharp distortions which result from large percentage increases on small industry bases. Dividing employment changes by average population permits comparisons between jurisdictions of very different sizes (e.g., New Haven, Detroit, U.S.).

(New Orleans, Denver, and San Francisco). It is important to recognize, however, that industry performance may mask the overall unevenness of urban development.

Table 1.1 indicates that the minority proportion of each study city population increased continuously between 1950 and 1980, and the proportion of whites decreased. At the same time, every city but Denver lost population over the three decades, and Denver itself contracted in the 1970s. The shift in racial composition was, however, much greater for the 1970s in New Haven, Detroit, and New Orleans than in San Francisco and Denver. This implies a disjunction between economic performance and social conditions in New Orleans greater than that of the other cities. Such is indeed the case (see Table 1.2). During the 1970s New Orleans had the lowest per capita income of the five cities, ranked worst in percent of its population in poverty, and was neck and neck with Detroit in social hardship. In contrast, Denver and San Francisco showed a high correlation between economic performance and social conditions. The difference may be explained by the tendency of the two western cities (which were initially much whiter and richer than New Orleans) to replace low-income households with those of higher incomes through a process of labor force upgrading and gentrification; while New Orleans exhibits the typical Southern pattern of extreme segmentation of labor markets and great social inequality accompanied by economic growth (Perry and Watkins, 1977: 295–96). In either route to economic expansion, the indigenous low-income population receives relatively few benefits. Neither, of course, does it in cities like New Haven and Detroit, where economic decline is reflected in high levels of social need.

These general impressions are corroborated by a closer examination of economic performance in each city.[3] We begin with New Haven and move westward. From 1954 to 1977, New Haven lost almost 22,000 jobs in the four sectors we have been discussing, with about 19,000 in manufacturing alone (Figure 1.2a). Service expansion

TABLE 1.1
Changes in Population and Racial Composition, Five Cities, 1950–1980

	Population (000s)				Percentage Minority (% Black)			
	1950	1960	1970	1980	1950[a]	1960[b]	1970[c]	1980[c]
New Haven	164	152	138	126	9	15 (13)	30 (26)	42 (30)[d]
Detroit	1854	1670	1514	1203	16	29 (29)	45 (44)	65 (63)
New Orleans	570	628	593	558	32	37 (37)	49 (45)	59 (55)
Denver	416	494	515	491	9	7 (6)	26 (9)	31 (12)
San Francisco	775	740	716	679	11	18 (10)	22 (13)	25 (13)

SOURCE: U.S. Bureau of the Census, *County and City Data Book,* 1956, 1967, 1977; *Census of the Population, Geographic Area Series, Preliminary and Advanced Reports,* 1980.
[a] Defined by the 1950 census as "non-white."
[b] The 1960 census provides two figures, "non-white" and "Negro," which we indicate as "minority" and "black." The census count of Hispanics was probably unreliable at this time.
[c] We define minority as the sum of the census counts of blacks and Hispanics in 1970.
[d] Based on estimates of local officials.

TABLE 1.2
Social Condition of the Population, Five Cities

	Per Capita Income (1974)		Percent of Families Below 125% of Poverty Line (1969)	CBO Index of Social Need[b] (1977)	
	$	Rank[a]		Score	Rank[c]
New Orleans	4029	750	28	61	5
New Haven	4247	650	18	n.a.	n.a.
Detroit	4463	545	15	62	4
Denver	5585	159	13	20	36
San Francisco	5990	154	13	22	33
United States	4572		15		

SOURCE: U.S. Bureau of the Census, *County and City Data Book,* 1977; U.S. Congress, House of Representatives, Committee on Banking, Finance, and Urban Affairs, Subcommittee on the City, *City Need and the Responsiveness of Federal Grants Programs,* 1978.

[a] Rank among all U.S. cities with more than 25,000 population.

[b] Congressional Budget Office Composite Measure of Social Need: updated version of 1970 Brookings Index based on unemployment, income level, poverty, dependency, education, and overcrowded housing.

[c] Range of rank is from 1 (worst off) to 45 (best off).

was sluggish and insufficient. The trend during the seventies (1972–77) was unpromising, as retail and wholesale employment contracted while that of service industries remained unchanged. Detroit paralleled New Haven in most respects, losing half its manufacturing base (Figure 1.2b). But contraction of retailing was sharper and, significantly, service industries actually diminished slightly during the postwar period. Moreover, the slope of decline steepened in the seventies for every industry, with an ominous loss of almost 20 percent of service employment in just a five-year period. And these data did not reflect the collapse of the auto industry at the end of the decade.

New Orleans constitutes an intermediate case. Like New Haven and Detroit it experienced a large drop in manufacturing, but this industry was less important in the local economy, and job losses within it were balanced by a major expansion of service employment; the result was a small net employment gain between 1954 and 1977 (Figure 1.2c). City economic performance in the seventies was mixed and indeterminate. Total employment for the four sectors declined, primarily because of a sharp contraction in manufacturing combined with a slowed-down expansion of service employment. A continued increase in retailing, however, suggests that the local economy was being stabilized by the city's position as a tourist and convention center.

Denver and San Francisco offer examples of urban economies which responded positively to national economic transformations (Figures 1.2d and 1.2e). Unlike our other cities, Denver had a growing population until 1970, so it is not surprising that its economy expanded across the board. In the seventies its population declined

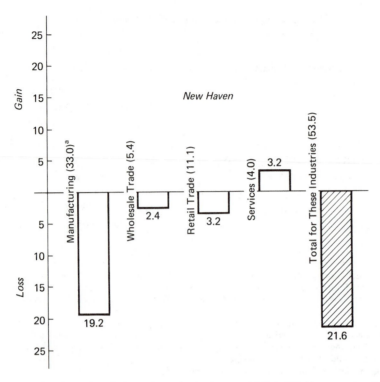

FIGURE 1.2a   Employment Gain or Loss by Industry, 1954–77 (thousands of jobs)

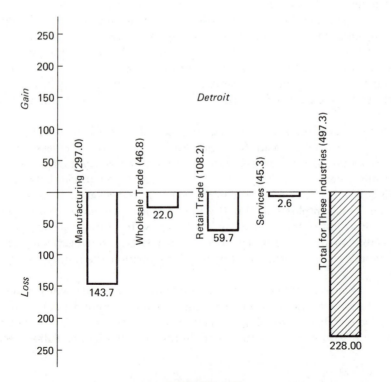

FIGURE 1.2b

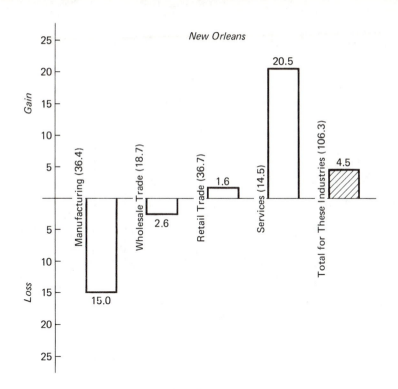

FIGURE 1.2c

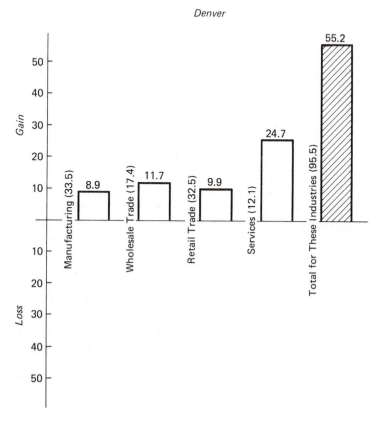

FIGURE 1.2d

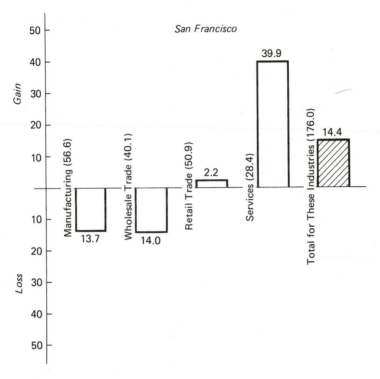

FIGURE 1.2e

Data from U.S. Bureau of the Census, *County and City Data Book,* 1956; *Census of Wholesale Trade, Geographic Area Series,* 1977; International City Management Association, *Municipal Yearbook,* 1981.

NOTE: Figures in parentheses indicate 1954 industry employment.

(see Table 1.1), and so too did manufacturing employment. Nonetheless total employment expanded as a result of growth in the other three sectors. It was at this time that the city established itself as a corporate center for the rising energy industry. Like Denver, San Francisco established a service economy—one based on financial dominance of trans-Pacific capital flows, as well as corporate headquarters functions, conventions, and tourism. Economic reorganization increased in pace at the end of the last decade. Between 1977 and 1980, total employment within the city expanded from 493,000 jobs to 552,000 (California Department of Employment Development, 1981).[4] While growth was exhibited by every industry sector, the most impressive performance was in retailing (10,000 new jobs), services (22,000 new jobs), and finance-insurance-real estate (13,000 new jobs). Combined with changes in core land use and population, sharp employment growth in these sectors indicated that San Francisco was the quintessential restructuring city.

A final piece of evidence completes our sketch of the social economies of the cities to be analyzed in succeeding chapters. The decline—or the reorganization and growth—of local economies is accompanied by varying degrees of investment in the built environment. A useful indicator of trends along this dimension is provided by the gross value of real property (i.e., land, buildings and improvements) within cities. According to this criterion, the five cities performed about as expected from our assessment of the evidence so far (see Table 7.2). During the seventies (1971–76), property values in constant dollars expanded sharply in San Francisco and Denver (respectively by 40 and 35 percent); rose appreciably in New Orleans (14 percent); declined slightly in New Haven (3 percent); and went into a nosedive in Detroit (where they fell by 34 percent). Such differences both reflected the varying socioeconomic trajectories of older cities and had important ramifications for local fiscal capacity and service provision (though the connection was, as we shall see in the case studies, quite complicated). In the next section we consider the character of governmental programs which affected cities during the postwar years.

THE POLICY FRAMEWORK

Redevelopment in individual cities is the result of economic forces, political action, and state policy. We attempt here to describe briefly the important public policy measures that have been specifically aimed at influencing redevelopment. We do not do so because we think that these were necessarily the strongest determinants of urban outcomes. One of the assumptions of this book is that policies not designated as urban, especially national economic policy, may affect cities more profoundly than those ostensibly concerned with functions like housing or transit. The following discussion is therefore intended primarily to supply background information to save repetition in each chapter. We summarize here the national policy areas of transportation, housing, physical redevelopment, and human renewal, as well as the local financing devices that have become increasingly important mechanisms for promoting development.

Highways and Mass Transit

Descriptions of American urban policy are particularly complicated by the nature of the federal system. Not only is policy a mix of decisions at different levels, but the role played by federal, state, and local government varies over time and between functional areas. Government direction of transportation, involved as it is with the interstate commerce system, has, however, tended to be far less under the control of localities than other policies affecting urban land uses.

The Highway Act of 1956, establishing the interstate expressway system, marked the beginning of large-scale federal intervention in urban road systems. Until then state highway departments had been the dominant influence on the construction of major city arteries. Now the federal Bureau of Public Roads would determine routes for the new freeways. Federal intervention greatly increased the tempo of road building and for the first time put priority on urban, as opposed to rural, highways. The federal intrusion, however, did nothing to reorient the preexisting focus on improving traffic flow to the detriment of other considerations such as community preservation and rational land development. City officials at the inception of the 1956 act were mainly concerned with relieving rush-hour traffic congestion and grateful for whatever assistance they could get (Gelfand, 1975: 222–27; Lupo et al., 1971: 79–82).

The scale of federal subsidy, provided on a 90 percent federal, 10 percent local, matching basis proved irresistible to most localities for many years. In 1955 combined federal and state expenditures for urban highway construction totaled $718 million. This figure nearly tripled, to $2.07 billion, by 1962 (Altshuler et al., 1979: 28). Countless households were displaced by the process of urban highway construction—the numbers are unknown since even the minimal requirements of record keeping and relocation assistance that accompanied urban-renewal legislation were absent in the highway acts for many years of their operations. In addition, large areas were removed from the tax rolls, use of urban land for parking facilities grew commensurately, and downtown congestion often increased as the expressways dumped their exponentially increasing users into central business districts (Gelfand, 1975: 228).

The well-known effect of post-1956 transportation policy was to contribute to suburban growth, primarily through the highway system but also through rail networks. Within cities, expressway construction divided neighborhoods, dislocated residents—especially minority groups—and frequently erected "Chinese walls" between cities and their waterfronts. Although the intention of the various highway acts was not urban redevelopment, their consequences were often more far-reaching in terms of urban land uses and residential location than urban renewal and housing programs (see Caro, 1974).

Mounting opposition to urban highways, as well as the increasingly shaky physical and financial state of mass transit, finally created pressure on Congress to subsidize modes of transportation other than the automobile. Federal support for urban public transit, however, never rivaled the highway program in munificence. The Urban Mass Transportation Act of 1964 first authorized the federal government to award capital grants to cities for mass transit programs (Taebel and Cornehls, 1977). The 1975 Highway Act permitted highway trust fund monies to be used for transit, although with a less favorable federal matching grant. Federal funding for mass transit reached $3.3 billion in 1980, in contrast to $8.4 billion allocated in the same year for highway construction (U.S. Bureau of the Census, 1981: Table 1060).

Additions to urban mass transit systems have mainly been intended to provide easier access for commuters to downtown, thereby forming part of the set of programs that identified CBD as the linch pin of redevelopment. Transit subsidies at all governmental levels have consistently been biased toward suburban users of commuter rail and metropolitan subway systems rather than inner-city residents, who generally ride buses. Thus, in 1978, the average per-trip operating subsidy to commuter rail passengers was about four times as large as the per-trip subsidy to bus riders. From 1965 to 1979, 76 percent of the total nationwide capital subsidy was devoted to rail rapid transit and commuter rail, even though these modes accounted for only 27 percent of ridership (Pucher, 1981: 389).

Housing Policy

American transportation policy has frequently been criticized for disregarding the connection between transportation and land use, thereby contributing to urban decay through the encouragement of sprawling development. But even those policies more specifically directed at housing and urban development have reinforced decentralizing tendencies and compounded the problems of low-income urban residents. An examination of housing policy indicates that its principal thrust was toward new construction on the periphery, home ownership, and the creation of homogeneous neighborhoods. This process, while beneficial to those who could profit from it, worsened the position of low- and moderate-income urban residents, particularly renter households.

As in many fields of social policy, the American national government first began significant subsidization and regulation of housing markets during the 1930s. The Housing Act of 1937, along with earlier measures aimed at stabilizing the private mortgage market, provided the framework for all future federal activity in housing. The most important aspects of the Depression-period legislation were the decentralization of responsibility for the construction of public (i.e., government-owned) housing to local housing authorities, whose participation was voluntary; the restriction of public housing occupancy to low-income households; funding at a level well below the amount necessary to provide public housing for all eligible recipients; and subsidies to the private market in the form of mortgage guarantees in order to house the majority of the population.[5]

The first major statute after the war, the 1949 Housing Act, authorized a greatly enlarged public-housing program. Actual annual construction, however, never came close to meeting program goals, and by the mid-1960s over half of the new units built under the program were reserved for the elderly. Until 1969, federal subsidy underwrote only capital costs for new construction and did not contribute to maintenance outlays (Mandelker, 1973).

While subsidies for low-income housing remained modest, vast postwar expansion of the mortgage guarantee programs operated by the Federal Housing Administration (FHA), growth of the federally sponsored secondary mortgage market, and availability of the income tax deduction for home ownership accelerated the exodus to the suburbs. Proliferation of zoning ordinances, which preserved most suburban residential areas for single-family housing, and FHA racial restrictions on its mortgages until the 1960s ensured that the suburban ring would remain primarily white and middle class (Clawson, 1975). Federal policy, which protected lenders against risk and ensured the liquidity of housing investment, resulted in a lowering of interest rates and down-payment requirements so that the majority of households could own their own homes (Aaron, 1972: Chapter 6; Stone, 1977). Easy mortgage terms combined with war-produced savings to promote a huge enlargement of home ownership: by 1979, over 65 percent of United States households owned their own homes, as compared to less than half before the war (U.S. Bureau of the Census, 1981).

During the 1960s, a number of federal programs were directed at making low-income housing profitable for private developers. These involved mortgage guarantees under FHA, mortgage interest rate subsidies to landlords, low-income homeowners, and developers (Sections 235 and 236), subsidies for construction loans, and rent supplements to occupants of privately owned housing (Aaron, 1972). Although authorization took place earlier, major funding of Sections 235 and 236 occurred during the Nixon presidency. For the years 1969 through 1972 more families received federally subsidized housing assistance than throughout the entire 34-year previous history of the national housing program (USDHUD, 1974). The high costs of the programs, various scandals connected with them, and the (unspoken) fear that they could be used to force suburban racial integration caused President Nixon to declare a moratorium on all housing subsidy programs in 1973.

The Housing and Community Development Act (HCDA) of 1974 established Section 8 as the primary instrument for the provision of housing assistance for households too poor to obtain decent housing in the private market (Solomon, 1977; Straszheim, 1980). Its aims were to: avoid segregation of the poor within public housing projects; let supposedly more efficient market processes supply housing in response to demand; and give the poor more choice in accommodations. Section 8 is essentially a rent subsidy that may be used in existing units, units to be rehabilitated, or new construction; it can be applied to privately and publicly owned buildings. Originally tenants paid no more than 25 percent of their income as rent; the amount was to be increased to 30 percent by the Reagan Administration.

Redevelopment and Human Renewal

Housing and redevelopment programs under the 1974 legislation, as in the past, were not integrated with each other and have fluctuated in levels of funding (see Table 1.3). Low-income housing programs were intended to provide shelter to those unable to purchase it in the private market. They have not, however, been funded sufficiently to attain that goal, and they have been seriously undercut by redevelopment policy, which emphasizes the improvement of places rather than assistance to people. In many cities extensive demolition was accompanied by commitments to replacement housing that subsequently never obtained funding. Despite Congressional goals of providing a decent home for every American, far more central-city housing has been destroyed under federal transportation and renewal programs than constructed to replace it (Lineberry and Sharkansky, 1978: 380–82; Sanders, 1980: Tables 4.3 and 4.4). The simultaneous effort to attract urban investment and cope with the social problems of cities ensuing from the low-income status of their inhabitants has produced a variety of program anomalies and reversals. Further examination of nonhousing programs aimed at physical, economic, and social renewal reveals more of the changes of course and conflicting purposes that have characterized U.S. policy.

During the period 1954–74 the federal urban renewal program, established under Title I of the 1949 Housing Act, became the principal weapon used by government to combat urban "blight" (Gelfand, 1975). Under this program, local authorities used the power of eminent domain to acquire privately held land, then, once a

TABLE 1.3

Budgetary Outlays for the U.S. Housing and Home Finance Agency (1959–65) and the Department of Housing and Urban Development (1966–81) (in billions of dollars)

Fiscal Year	Outlay in Current $	Outlay in Constant (1980) $	Fiscal Year	Outlay in Current $	Outlay in Constant (1980) $
1959	1.152	3.249	1971	2.890	5.865
1960	0.309	0.858	1972	3.642	7.167
1961	0.502	1.380	1973	3.592	6.653
1962	0.739	2.009	1974	4.786	7.992
1963	0.410	1.102	1975	7.488	11.453
1964	0.328	0.869	1976	7.079	10.235
1965	0.250	0.651	1977	5.838	7.923
1966	0.767	1.944	1978	7.589	9.570
1967	2.793	6.879	1979	9.213	10.461
1968	4.140	9.789	1980	12.576	12.576
1969	1.529	3.431	1981	13.489[a]	12.359
1970	2.603	5.514			

SOURCE: Derived from U.S. Bureau of the Census, *Statistical Abstract of the United States: 1965, 1967, 1971, 1973, 1976, 1981.*
[a] Estimated.

site appropriate for redevelopment had been aggregated and prepared, they turned the land over to a public agency or private developer at a lower price. The federal government paid for between two-thirds and three-quarters of the net project cost (i.e., the difference between the purchase price and selling price of the land plus costs of demolition and improvements). The local share could be either a cash payment or in-kind contribution—for example, the construction of a police station or school on the project site. Although the act declared that the redevelopment area should be predominantly residential in character and that all displaced families be relocated in suitable accommodations, it included no mechanism to induce private developers to build housing for low-income households.

Implementation of urban renewal resulted in displacement of poor, predominantly minority residents and use of vacated land mainly for commercial, high-rent residential and institutional purposes (Wilson, 1966; Lineberry and Sharkansky, 1978). Often urban-renewal authorities could not attract developers for any land use, and large cleared central city tracts reverted to rubble-strewn vacant lots or parking areas. While the 1954 Housing Act provided incentives for rehabilitation rather than wholesale clearance, demolition remained the mainstay of the program for most of its life span.

Under the Kennedy and Johnson administrations the federal government for a variety of reasons ceased to ignore the situation of poor people in American cities. The principal legislation of the War on Poverty, the Economic Opportunity Act of 1964, aimed at improving cities through affecting the lives of their residents rather than their built environments (Marris and Rein, 1973; Fainstein and Fainstein, 1972; Sundquist, 1969). While the poverty program did not provide funds for physical redevelopment, it did have a geographical focus. Local Community Action Programs (CAPs) sought to coordinate social-service efforts within poverty neighborhoods and create a neighborhood organizational base. After the termination of federally funded CAPs under the Nixon-Ford administrations, the various elements of the poverty program became the responsibilities of different federal departments, local governments, or withered away. Its legacy of community groups and leadership, however, remained.

Within the context of 1960s unrest, neighborhood resistance to urban renewal, along with a crescendo of criticism by intellectuals (Jacobs, 1961; Fried, 1963; Anderson, 1964; Gans, 1965), caused the Johnson Administration to rethink the idea that slums could be eliminated through displacing their occupants. Without terminating the urban renewal program, which continued to be used for downtown redevelopment, Congress passed the Demonstration Cities Act of 1966 (subsequently called Model Cities) to redirect the thrust of activity in poor neighborhoods toward community preservation (Frieden and Kaplan, 1975). The new emphases were on the coordination of physical and social planning; rehabilitation rather than demolition; community participation; and a focus on target neighborhoods. Although the notion of concentrating resources on a few areas dissipated as more and more areas sought to participate in Model Cities, the concept of a multifaceted approach to poor neighborhoods continued.

Both Model Cities and urban renewal terminated with the 1974 passage of the HCDA, which introduced the Community Development Block Grant (CDBG) (USDHUD, 1980a; CDBG Training Advisory Committee, 1979; Dommel et al., 1980; Rosenfeld, 1980). Part of President Nixon's "new federalism" of special revenue sharing and increased authority for local governments, CDBG supplanted seven previous categorical programs. CDBG funds were distributed on a formula rather than a project basis, with the bulk going to approximately 540 entitlement cities larger than 50,000 in population. The allocation formula was originally based on population size and poverty; it was revised in 1977 to provide further assistance to older cities with large stocks of obsolete housing and declining populations. Local elected officials were responsible for setting community priorities in physical improvements and neighborhood-based social services, although the latter were limited by HUD guidelines to first 20 then later 10 percent of the grant.

During the course of the program, the extent of federal involvement shifted from minimal under President Ford to extensive in the Carter administration. Between 1977 and 1980, federal regulations required targeting to low- and moderate-income groups, concentration of grant spending within designated neighborhoods, and a citizen participation plan (Fainstein and Fainstein, 1980). But CDBG could not be used for construction of low-income housing; it offered few benefits to renters who could not take advantage of rehabilitation funds generally limited to owner-occupied housing; and it gave no guarantee that residents would not be displaced from "upgraded" neighborhoods. Most of the Carter regulations were modified or eliminated

under Reagan, and federal oversight lapsed as the application and reporting requirements for cities were drastically curtailed.

The years after 1974 saw an increasing emphasis on using private investment
to redevelop cities. For cities that had drawn heavily on urban renewal financing,
CDBG represented a considerable decline in government funding available to support
redevelopment efforts. Two programs, one operated by HUD and the other by the
Department of Commerce, were aimed at supplying additional funds to support
projects that could induce private investment. The first, the Urban Development
Action Grant (UDAG), like urban renewal, was provided on a discretionary basis
(Gist, 1980). Its sole purpose was economic development, and, as in the earlier program, funds were frequently used for land clearance as well as commercial rehabilitation (Mier, 1982). UDAG differed from urban renewal in that federal money could
only be spent if the private component were committed in advance. Essentially, it
represented a subsidy to business for coming to or remaining in economically distressed areas.

Programs of the Economic Development Administration (EDA) of the Department of Commerce resembled UDAG in their emphasis on economic development.
Rather than tying the federal grant to private commitments, however, they precondi-
tioned funding on the job-creation potential of the project, which could be publicly
or privately operated. Again the objective was not physical redevelopment per se,
but physical improvements for the purpose of promoting economic growth.

Local Investment Incentive Programs

While aggregate national funding for urban programs did not decrease in real terms
after the 1974 HCDA, many large cities saw sharp reductions in their federal aid
as the new allocation formulas dispersed the available appropriation throughout
the country. Southern cities that had not participated in previous federally sponsored
housing and redevelopment programs were now recipients of Section 8 and CDBG.
Cities seeking to make up for lost federal support, as well as many southwestern
municipalities that had pioneered in the use of locally generated inducements to
private investment, devised more and more ways to capture private development
within inner-city jurisdictions.

The mechanisms for doing so are ingenious. In order to raise capital to promote
commercial and industrial investment, cities, under various kinds of state enabling
legislation, have sought to direct tax revenues toward specified ends rather than
the general fund (Mandelker et al., 1980). Usually in the central business district,
but also in industrial and port areas, municipal governments have set up special
assessment and tax districts, whereby a proportion of property taxes levied on structures within the area are returned to it. Funds so raised may be used for further
capital expenditure, as backing for loans, or to pay for services such as special
security forces. Somewhat similarly, tax-increment financing employs any increase
in property taxes resulting from a redevelopment project, such as a hotel or parking
garage, to pay back the bonds used to finance the investment or to reinvest further

in the area (Holcomb and Beauregard, 1981). Tax abatements may be used to reduce
to the owner any tax liability resulting from building or improving a property.
Free trade or enterprise zones offer tax abatements or forgiveness to firms operating
within designated areas (Mier, 1982). All these various measures, justified as producing economic development and employment, undercut what was one of the original
arguments for government-sponsored redevelopment projects—that they would add
to the municipal tax base and thereby support the level of services required by
cities with large dependent groups and fleeing middle-class populations.

Nonprofit community development corporations (CDCs) and economic development corporations (EDCs) permit businesses and neighborhood organizations to em-
ploy various tax advantages, loan funds, and capital grants available within distressed
urban districts (Harrison, 1974: 168–84). In addition to having access to the tax
devices listed above, such corporations, as well as individual firms, may be able to
draw on funds raised through revenue bonds. Monies produced by these tax-free
instruments can be used to finance commercial and industrial development or housing. Since they are tied to revenue streams derived from the development they
create, they are generally exempt from the referendum requirements of general-
obligation bonds.

Yet another method of developing financing for large projects such as sports
arenas is lease financing, whereby a state or city agency leases the facility to an
operator, who usually pledges a percentage of the profits as rent (Hartman and
Kessler, 1978: 156). The difference between the rent and annual debt service is
paid from public funds. Such arrangements may require no initial investment by
the public agency since the original funding comes from private lenders. But if
profits do not in fact reach anticipated levels, the public ends up paying most or
all of the debt.[6]

The effect of this potpourri of financial and legal devices is to turn over various
municipal governmental powers such as taxation, tax-free bonds, zoning, and eminent domain to private business and, to some extent, nonprofit organizations. While
some subsidies may be earmarked for deteriorated areas, they are more often directed
to thriving downtowns and ports. Although legitimized as adding to employment
and producing multiplier effects on general commerce, they tend to encapsulate
their returns, since gains are pledged either for debt service or reinvestment.

Both local and federal programs, as we have shown, increasingly have stressed
the merging of public and private efforts at urban redevelopment. The War on
Poverty and Model Cities represented a brief period in the history of public redevelopment when low-income people were the intended primary beneficiaries of government endeavors. Now policy is mainly constructed to produce economic development, the effects of which are supposed to filter down to the majority of the
population. While present programs do not have the displacing effects of urban
renewal, neither are they aimed principally at improving the environments in which
low-income city residents live. Projects undertaken recently differ from urban renewal in that they are smaller, more ad hoc and piecemeal, and government acts
more as packager than principal. But current urban programs, like those of twenty
years ago, reflect the dominance of the business class over the life of the city.

POLITICAL CONTROL AND THE REPRESENTATION
OF LOW-INCOME GROUPS

Capitalist hegemony has neither gone unchallenged nor escaped modification during the period under consideration. The struggle for control of the city has changed urban political and administrative systems and forced a federal response. Traditional urban patronage excluded the public from governance even while it dispensed discrete material benefits to some of it. The reformed systems grafted onto city governments during the first part of the century further insulated them from popular control (Fainstein and Fainstein, 1974: Chapter 1). But during the 1960s, urban movements pressed for community power and succeeded to some degree in institutionalizing new modes of representation.

The increasing scope of government in the twentieth century has meant that traditional forms of electoral enfranchisement, never very effective in controlling administrative officials, became less and less useful as a mode by which citizens could protect themselves against seemingly arbitrary acts of governmental authority. Client and community groups, seeking to make government more responsive, demanded both administrative jobs for community residents and representation on policy-making bodies. They pressed for *bureaucratic enfranchisement*—for a process wherein they could influence the manner in which agency missions or program objectives were implemented (Fainstein and Fainstein, 1982a).

The federal government, seeking to accommodate itself to the pressure of protest movements and to coopt militant community leaders, established a variety of participatory devices for bureaucratic enfranchisement. These included committees of affected residents in urban renewal areas and, under the Economic Opportunity Act of 1964, "maximum feasible participation" of residents of target neighborhoods in the federal poverty program (Rubin, 1972). Under both urban renewal and the Community Action Program local elected officials were circumvented, as community groups, community action agencies, and urban renewal authorities dealt directly with the federal government.

Congress soon acted to limit the autonomy of these groups and agencies. The pattern that began to emerge by the early days of Model Cities was to give program constituencies only an advisory role defined by local governments themselves. CDBG further increased the discretion of city officials, as it broke the ties that had connected the urban renewal agencies with Washington.[7] While the CDBG legislation mandated citizen participation in the formulation and implementation of each city's community development (CD) program, it was completely vague as to how this process should be set up.

The switch from categorical to block grants limited the leverage of community groups in several ways. They could no longer use the power of the federal government as a resource when pressing demands against the city. Moreover, unlike the poverty program and Model Cities, CDBG allocated no direct federal funding for technical or community staff responsible to neighborhood groups. Equally important, the concentration of the block grant program on physical development lessened its salience to many low-income groups that had been involved with the CAPs and Model

Cities. Although Community Development had become the only significant neigh-
borhood-focused federal program, it did not offer the job and service benefits that
had made the earlier programs particularly important to low-income people (Fainstein
and Fainstein, 1982a).

The decline of militant community activism, the continued growth of community
organizations, the elaboration of citizen participation devices, including citywide
advisory boards, and the increased presence of minority group members on city
councils have established the present framework for the representation of low-income
groups in American cities. Pressure from civil rights groups succeeded in racially
integrating the civil service and placing members of minority groups in some influential administrative positions. A number of cities, including Detroit and New Orleans,
have elected black mayors. But the greater access to government for low-income
and minority groups resulting from these changes has not given them influence
over the entire scope of redevelopment decision making.

The segmentation of redevelopment activity between public and private sectors,
the character of governing coalitions, and the isolation of neighborhood politics
from the major allocation decisions of public bodies all contribute to the limitations
on effective representation of low-income people. Since private interests are the
principal forces in redevelopment, most decisions concerning the location and type
of investment are not subject to popular approval. Even the election of "people's
candidates" cannot change the dependence of public officials on private financial
power—consequently the "governing coalition" differs in composition from the electoral coalition. The segmentation of funds, so that large public investments are
controlled by independent state and regional authorities and much of the CD budget
goes for normal capital expenditures, further restricts the discretionary area for public
redevelopment spending. Within this limited arena, neighborhood representatives
mainly have jurisdiction over the small amounts earmarked for residential areas.
Representatives of low-income constituencies thus comprise only one element in
the complex politics that surround redevelopment.

The economic and political forces described in this chapter are mediated in every
city by the particular nature of its social structure, economic institutions, and political
regime. These factors, however, are themselves mutable, and most cities have changed
significantly over the last thirty years. The case studies that follow are intended
to capture both diachronic and synchronic elements of commonality and difference.
The order of presentation is from east to west, which means also a movement from
declining to expanding cities. The assessment of redevelopment outcomes, however,
stresses the differential effect of aggregate growth and the costs that economically
and politically weak groups have had to pay in the effort for urban redevelopment.

NOTES

1. Extensive citations to the literature of urban political economy are provided in Chapter
   7.
2. We thus reject theoretical paradigms based on a "unitary" model of municipalities such
   as that of Paul Peterson (1981).

3. Where not otherwise indicated, data for the following discussion are drawn from International City Management Association (1981), and U.S. Bureau of the Census (1977a, b).
4. In addition, as James shows (1981: Exhibit 6), city share of metropolitan employment remained stable through the seventies.
5. Histories of federal housing programs are presented in U.S. National Commission on Urban Problems (1969); President's Committee on Urban Housing (1969); Gelfand (1975); and Hartman (1975).
6. A recent article about New Haven described a new "public-private partnership" that employs several of the subsidies and financial devices described here. The project, Shubert Square, is a "multi-purpose entertainment district" combining cultural, retail, housing, and office development. Utilizing $18 million in private financing, $2 million in state and federal financing (the federal share is provided by an EDA grant), and $1.4 million in city funds, the developers also hope to take advantage of 25 percent federal investment tax credits for rehabilitation of historic structures (renovation of the old Shubert Theatre). The city administration guaranteed tax abatement on all but the retail portion of the project. While the city's initial share of development costs is relatively low, it "agreed to guarantee the annual $500,000 in rent for an 18-year lease term, but only in the event the Shubert board can't pay the rent due the partnership. The city also agreed to provide an operating subsidy of up to $2.5 million over a seven-year period, or up to $350,000 a year, and to provide roughly $400,000 for the acquisition of one or more properties to be sold to [the developer]" (*New Haven Register*, 1982: 1, 37).
7. The new federalism of limited bureaucratic enfranchisement has been based on two rationales: first, that the CAPs of the War on Poverty showed the excesses of citizen participation; and second, that block grants are more democratic than categorical programs, which give Washington too much power over local decisions. But, as Yates (1973: 21) points out, despite contrary perceptions, the CAPs produced neither widespread participation nor much radical activity. And while federal decentralization as understood by Nixon meant increasing the power of officials "elected to serve all the people" (Yin, 1980: 118), it also reduced the influence of the poor, of clients of public agencies, and of target-area representatives.

REFERENCES

Aaron, Henry J. 1972. *Shelter and Subsidies*. Washington, D.C.: Brookings Institution.
Altshuler, Alan, James P. Womack, and John R. Pucher. 1979. *The Urban Transportation System: Politics and Policy Innovation*. Cambridge, MA: MIT Press.
Anderson, Martin. 1964. *The Federal Bulldozer*. Cambridge, MA: MIT Press.
Burchell, Robert, and David Listokin, eds. 1981. *Cities Under Stress: The Fiscal Crises of Urban America*. New Brunswick, NJ: Center for Urban Policy Research, Rutgers University.
California Department of Employment Development. 1981. *Annual Planning Information, San Francisco City and County, 1981–82*.
Caro, Robert. 1974. *The Power Broker: Robert Moses and the Fall of New York*. New York: Knopf.
CDBG Training Advisory Committee. 1979. "An advocacy guide to the Community Development Block Grant Program." *Clearinghouse Review* 12 (January supplement): 601–75.
City of New York. 1980. *Comprehensive Annual Report of the Comptroller for the Fiscal Year Ending June 30, 1980*.
Clawson, Marion. 1975. "Factors affecting suburbanization in the postwar years." Pp. 182–88 in Stephen Gale and Eric G. Moore, eds., *The Manipulated City*. Chicago: Maaroufa.
Danziger, Sheldon, Robert Haveman, and Robert Plotnick. 1981. "How income transfer pro-

grams affect work, savings, and the income distribution: a critical review." *Journal of Economic Literature* 19 (September): 975–1028.

Dommel, Paul, Victor E. Bach, Sarah F. Liebschutz, and Leonard S. Rubinowitz. 1980. *Targeting Community Development.* Third report on the Brookings Institution Monitoring Study of the CDBG Program. Washington, D.C.: USDHUD.

Fainstein, Susan S., and Norman I. Fainstein. 1982a. "Neighborhood enfranchisement and urban redevelopment." *Journal of Planning Education and Research* 2 (Autumn).

———. 1982b. "Restructuring the city: a comparative perspective." Pp. 161–90 in *Urban Policy Under Capitalism.* Beverly Hills, CA: Sage.

———. 1980. "Mobility, community, and participation: the American way out." Pp. 242–62 in William A. V. Clark and Eric G. Moore, eds., *Residential Mobility and Public Policy.* Beverly Hills, CA: Sage.

———. 1974. *Urban Political Movements.* Englewood Cliffs, NJ: Prentice-Hall.

———. 1972. "American social policy: beyond progressive analysis." Pp. 212–38 in Dorothy B. James, ed., *Outside Looking In.* New York: Harper & Row.

Fried, Marc. 1963. "Grieving for a lost home: psychological costs of relocation." Pp. 151–71 in Leonard J. Duhl, ed., *The Urban Condition.* New York: Simon and Schuster.

Frieden, Bernard J., and Marshall Kaplan. 1975. *The Politics of Neglect.* Cambridge, MA: MIT Press.

Gans, Herbert J. 1965. "The failure of urban renewal." Reprinted in Wilson, 1966.

Gelfand, Mark I. 1975. *A Nation of Cities.* New York: Oxford University Press.

Gist, John R. 1980. "Urban Development Action Grants: design and implementation." Pp. 237–52 in Donald B. Rosenthal, ed., *Urban Revitalization.* Beverly Hills, CA: Sage.

Harrison, Bennett. 1974. *Urban Economic Development.* Washington, D.C.: Urban Institute.

Hartman, Chester W. 1975. *Housing and Social Policy.* Englewood Cliffs, NJ: Prentice-Hall.

Hartman, Chester, and Rob Kessler. 1978. "The illusion and reality of urban renewal: San Francisco's Yerba Buena Center." Pp. 153–78 in William K. Tabb and Larry Sawers, eds., *Marxism and the Metropolis.* New York: Oxford University Press.

Holcomb, H. Briavel, and Robert A. Beauregard. 1981. *Revitalizing Cities.* Washington, D.C.: Association of American Geographers.

International City Management Association. 1981. *The Municipal Yearbook.* Washington, D.C.

Jacobs, Jane. 1961. *Death and Life of Great American Cities.* New York: Vintage.

James, Franklin. 1981. "Economic distress in central cities." Pp. 19–50 in Burchell and Listokin, 1981.

Lineberry, Robert L., and Ira Sharkansky. 1978. *Urban Politics and Public Policy,* 3rd edition. New York: Harper & Row.

Lupo, Alan, Frank Colcord, and Edmund P. Fowler, 1971. *Rites of Way: The Politics of Transportation in Boston and the U.S. City.* Boston: Little, Brown.

Mandelker, Daniel R. 1973. *Housing Subsidies in the United States and England.* Indianapolis: Bobbs-Merrill.

Mandelker, Daniel R., Gary Feder, and Margaret R. Collins. 1980. *Reviving Cities with Tax Abatement.* New Brunswick, NJ: Center for Urban Policy Research, Rutgers University.

Marris, Peter, and Martin Rein. 1973. *Dilemmas of Social Reform,* 2nd edition. Chicago: Aldine.

Mier, Robert, 1982. "Enterprise zones: a long shot." *Planning* 48 (April): 10–14.

Mollenkopf, John H. 1981. "Paths toward the post-industrial service city: the Northeast and the Southwest." Pp. 77–112 in Burchell and Listokin, 1981.

NCUED (National Council for Urban Economic Development). N.d. (1980?). *CUED's Guide to Federal Economic Development Programs.* Washington, D.C.: NCUED.

New Haven Register. 1982. July 8.

Perry, David C., and Alfred J. Watkins. 1977. "People, profit, and the rise of the sunbelt cities." Pp. 277–306 in *The Rise of the Sunbelt Cities*. Beverly Hills, CA: Sage.

Peterson, Paul. 1981. *City Limits*. Chicago: University of Chicago Press.

Plotnick, Robert, and Timothy Smeeding. 1979. "Poverty and income transfers: past trends and future prospects." *Public Policy* 27 (Summer): 225–72.

President's Committee on Urban Housing (Kaiser Committee). 1969. *A Decent Home*. Washington, D.C.: U.S. Government Printing Office.

Pucher, John. 1981. "Equity in transit finance: distribution of transit subsidy benefits and costs among income classes." *Journal of the American Planning Association* 47 (October): 387–407.

Rosenfeld, Raymond A. 1980. "Who benefits and who decides? The uses of Community Development Block Grants." Pp. 211–35 in Donald B. Rosenthal, ed., *Urban Revitalization*. Beverly Hills, CA: Sage.

Rubin, Lillian B. 1972. "Maximum feasible participation: the origins and implications." Pp. 98–116 in Susan S. Fainstein and Norman I. Fainstein, eds., *The View from Below*. Boston: Little, Brown.

Sanders, Heywood T. 1980. "Urban renewal and the revitalized city: a reconsideration of recent history." Pp. 103–26 in Donald B. Rosenthal, ed., *Urban Revitalization*. Beverly Hills, CA: Sage.

Solomon, Arthur P. 1977. "A national policy and budgetary framework for housing and community development." *Journal of the American Real Estate and Urban Economics Association* 5 (Summer): 147–71.

Sternlieb, George, and James W. Hughes. 1981. "New dimensions of the urban crisis." Pp. 51–77 in Burchell and Listokin, 1981.

———. 1978. *Revitalizing the Northeast*. New Brunswick, NJ: Center for Urban Policy Research, Rutgers University.

———. 1975. *Post-Industrial America: Metropolitan Decline and Inter-Regional Job Shifts*. New Brunswick, NJ: Center for Urban Policy Research, Rutgers University.

Stone, Michael E. 1977. "Mortgage bankers and the politics of housing." Pp. 494–500 in David Gordon, ed., *Problems in Political Economy: An Urban Perspective*, 2nd edition. Lexington, MA: Heath.

Straszheim, Mahlon R. 1980. "The Section 8 rental-assistance program: costs and policy options." Pp. 169–83 in Roger Montgomery and Dale Rogers Marshall, eds., *Housing Policy for the 1980s*. Lexington, MA: Heath.

Sundquist, James L., ed. 1969. *On Fighting Poverty*. New York: Basic Books.

Taebel, Delbert, and James V. Cornehls. 1977. *The Political Economy of Urban Transportation*. Port Washington, N.Y.: Kennikat.

U.S. Bureau of the Census. 1981. *Statistical Abstract of the United States, 1981*. Washington, D.C.: U.S. Government Printing Office.

———. 1977a. *County and City Data Book*. Washington, D.C.: U.S. Government Printing Office.

———. 1977b. *Census of Wholesale Trade*, Geographic Series. Washington, D.C.: U.S. Government Printing Office.

U.S. Department of Housing and Urban Development (USDHUD). 1980a. *Fifth Annual Community Development Block Grant Report*. Washington, D.C.: USDHUD.

———. 1980b. *The President's National Urban Policy Report*. Washington, D.C.: U.S. Government Printing Office.

———. 1974. *Housing in the Seventies*. Washington, D.C.: U.S. Government Printing Office.

U.S. National Commission on Urban Problems (Douglas Commission). 1969. *Building the American City*. New York: Praeger.

Wilson, James Q., ed. 1966. *Urban Renewal: The Record and the Controversy.* Cambridge, MA: MIT Press.

Yates, Douglas. 1973. *Neighborhood Democracy.* Lexington, MA: Heath.

Yin, Robert. 1980. "Decentralizing government agencies." Pp. 113–25 in Carol Weiss and Allen Barton, eds., *Making Bureaucracy Work.* Beverly Hills, CA: Sage.

2

New Haven: The Limits of the Local State

Norman I. Fainstein
Susan S. Fainstein

We in New Haven believe that the goal of a democratic society is the fullest possible development of the individual potentialities of all its people. In urban America, despite great material wealth, there are many obstacles to the achievement of this goal. Most visible are the blight and obsolescence of the environment of a large portion of all but the newest cities. Equally present are social, economic, and cultural obstructions. . . .

We believe that planning and action to renew the central city can remove some of these obstructions. Able and imaginative urban renewal programs are underway in many communities. In this respect New Haven . . . has outstripped other cities in the breadth of its program, the speed of execution, and the quality of the accomplishment.[1]

MAYOR RICHARD LEE

This old, manufacturing city commands an interest far beyond its size. New Haven was a national leader in establishing local programs to combat physical decay and poverty. It took initiatives, created prototypes, trained a generation of program administrators. Edward Logue went from New Haven to reshape Boston and then New York. His successor as development administrator, L. Thomas Appleby, became director of urban renewal in Washington, D.C. Mitchell Sviridoff, who headed Community Progress, Inc., a progenitor of all community action agencies, later originated

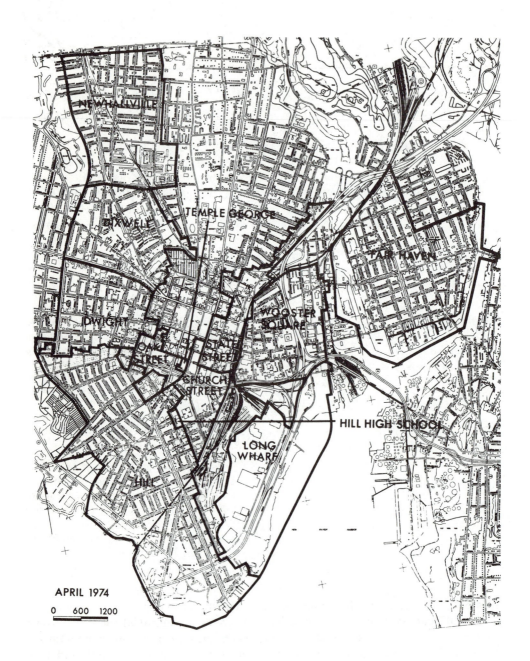

NEWHALLVILLE

BIXWELL

TEMPLE GEORGE

FAIR HAVEN

DWIGHT

WOOSTER SQUARE

STREET

CHURCH STREET

HILL HIGH SCHOOL

LONG WHARF

HILL

APRIL 1974

0   600   1200

NEW HAVEN

the domestic programs of the Ford Foundation. The scale of activity in a municipality of only 150,000 people was impressive. Over the history of the urban renewal program the city expended more than $180 million (U.S. Department of Housing and Urban Development [USDHUD], 1975). Had our national effort been equivalent, instead of amounting to $13.5 billion, public investment in U.S. urban renewal would have exceeded $250 billion.[2] Similar comparisons could be made for subsidized housing and social programs. With so much governmental activity and a corresponding outpouring of publicity about it, New Haven was seen as a test case for the possibilities of planning and public investment to check inner-city decline.

New Haven, for other reasons, is an important city among political scientists and urbanists. From a case study of the city, Robert Dahl (1961) and his students, Raymond Wolfinger (1974) and Nelson Polsby (1963), developed the pluralist model of community power and, beyond that, a theory of the U.S. political system. Later work chronicled the evolution of New Haven's politics (inter alia, Powledge, 1970; Yates, 1973, 1977). That evolution paralleled developments in other cities. The "new convergence of power" (Salisbury, 1964) created during the fifties and early sixties by strong, active mayors like Richard Lee of New Haven did not outlast the decade. In New Haven and elsewhere, riot and black mobilization created a very different politics by 1968; this stage was itself supplanted only a few years later. If New Haven was unusual in the extent of its redevelopment and social programs, it nonetheless typified many cities in its political and programmatic history. The continued scholarly interpretation of the city deserves—with the reader's forgiveness—another chapter. We begin with a sketch of New Haven's physical, social, and economic features, and how these have changed since 1950.

THE CITY AND ITS PEOPLE OVER THREE DECADES

New Haven's present appearance contrasts with its earlier self before the days of urban renewal, but in a familiar way. Run-down, working-class neighborhoods of small brick tenements and frame houses have been cleared for an eight-lane highway (the Oak Street Connector) which forms the southern flank of the central business district (CBD) as it dead-ends unexpectedly—for drivers and planners alike—a mile or two from its inception. Lining the highway are large buildings, some of considerable architectural distinction, strung out in the tradition of the radial city. Walking here is difficult and seemingly unintended. Within the CBD itself, a diversified and dense agglomeration of old office buildings, manufacturers' lofts, movie theaters, five-and-tens, and small retailers have all been demolished. In their place is a redeveloped core typical of dozens of other American cities, as recognizable to the student of urban redevelopment as a face-lift to a plastic surgeon. Two modern department stores, a hotel-shopping mall complex, concrete garages, and several glass and aluminum office buildings constitute the renewed downtown. But now that all the projects are virtually completed, more than twenty-five years since the city started ripping up the deteriorated center of town, distinct signs of shabbiness are visible: the shopping mall does little business; one of the big department stores has gone bankrupt; and downtown is deserted after five. Only the gothic structures of Yale University and the Puritan central Green seem immutable, and it is their juxtaposition that differentiates New Haven's city center from its similarly renewed counterparts elsewhere.

The neighborhoods have changed as well. Here, too, the resemblance to other cities seems to overshadow the differences associated with unusually active governmental intervention. Densities have dropped precipitously since World War II. Thousands of white families have moved away, while the minority ghettos have expanded. In the poorer neighborhoods, much publicly assisted housing is visible, but so are refuse-strewn lots, the end products of arson, abandonment, or urban renewal. The remaining white working- and middle-class neighborhoods struggle to maintain their stability, in part by excluding minority households. The visitor to New Haven would conclude that however much governmental programs may have helped to mitigate the consequences of external social and economic forces, they were not enough to spare the city from the syndrome associated with urban decline.

Demographic and Social Trends

We can see decline another way by examining statistical evidence of demographic, social, and economic change since 1950. In each dimension, New Haven has followed the national trend of central cities in the Northeast and Midwest. From 1920 to 1950 the city maintained a population of 164,000. Since then the suburbs have grown while New Haven has contracted; where previously the central city constituted more than three-fifths of the metropolitan population, it is now less than one-third (Table 2.1). The shrinking city changed dramatically in racial composition, as the black population quadrupled in the two decades after 1950 and the Hispanic population increased considerably in the 1970s. By 1970 the city was at least 31 percent minority, and by 1980, 40–45 percent minority. Except for part of Hamden bordering on the city's main black ghetto and a small piece of West Haven, the suburban towns have managed to exclude minority people almost entirely.

The fact that New Haven has contained the expanding minority population of the area helps explain why the city has gotten progressively poorer over the years compared to its suburban neighbors (Table 2.2). Median income[3] in New Haven rose from $2,717 in 1950 to $5,943 in 1970 and to an estimated $9,449 by 1977. But the comparable incomes for the standard metropolitan statistical area (SMSA) increased much more rapidly, from $3,144 in 1950 to $14,937 by 1977. As a result, metropolitan inequality became much greater. Whereas central city households received 86 percent of the income of the median metropolitan household in 1950, by 1970 they received only 67 percent, and the proportion dropped to 63 percent in 1977. The ratio of New Haven to *suburban* (rather than SMSA) income in 1977 was probably about 55 percent.

Indicators of the social well-being of city residents in 1970 (the last year for which we have reliable data) showed high levels of economic hardship with great interracial inequality. The New Haven profile was similar to other central cities in the region. Black median family income was 75 percent of the median for all families in New Haven. Comparable figures were 80 percent in Bridgeport, 77 percent in

TABLE 2.1
Social Characteristics of New Haven City and Metropolitan Area, 1950–1980

	1950	1960	1970	1980
Population				
New Haven city	164,443	152,048	137,707	125,787
SMSA[a]	264,622	311,681	355,538	416,053
City as percentage of SMSA	62	50	39	30
Racial Composition				
Black population New Haven city	9,605	22,061	36,158	n.a.
Black population as percentage of city population	6	15	26	30[b]
Minority population as percentage of city population	n.a.	n.a.	31[c]	40–45[b]
New Haven city minority population as percentage of SMSA minority population	91	92[d]	88[e]	

SOURCE: U.S. Bureau of the Census, *Census of Population, Population of the States: Connecticut, 1950, 1960, 1970; 1980 Preliminary Report.*

[a] Standard Metropolitan Statistical Area, except Standard Metropolitan Area in 1950, but boundaries unchanged.

[b] Based on informant estimates, New Haven Department of City Planning, 1979.

[c] Includes 4,916 Spanish-speaking and 1,563 members of other minority groups.

[d] Based on SMSA distribution of nonwhite population.

[e] Based on SMSA distribution of black population.

TABLE 2.2
Median Incomes for New Haven City and SMSA, 1950–1977

	1950	1960	1970	1977
Median Income[a]				
City	$2,717	$4,538	5,943	$ 9,449[b]
SMSA	$3,144	$5,630	$8,839	$14,937[c]
City Median as Percentage of SMSA Median	86	80	67	63[d]

SOURCE: U.S. Bureau of the Census, *Census of Population, Population of the States: Connecticut, 1950, 1960, 1970;* International City Managers Association, *The Municipal Yearbook,* 1981.

[a] Families and unrelated individuals.

[b] Projection based on estimated increase of 59 percent in per-capita income between 1970 and 1977 for New Haven.

[c] Projections based on estimated increase of 69 percent in per-capita income between 1970 and 1977 for Connecticut.

[d] Derived from projected city and SMSA median incomes for 1977.

Hartford, 67 percent in Providence, and 69 percent in Boston. Thirteen percent of
New Haven families were below the federally defined poverty line, compared with
9 percent in Bridgeport, 13 percent in Hartford and Providence, 12 percent in Boston
(U.S. Bureau of the Census, 1977), and 15 percent for small cities nationwide
(USDHUD, 1980: Tables 4–1, 4–2). About 30 percent of the city's black population
was poor in 1970. Unemployment, welfare caseload, and similar indicators pointed
to the familiar national pattern of central-city hardship, with minority groups worse
off than whites (USDHUD, 1980: 4–1). By the last years of the decade the relative
income position of minority groups was declining further in New Haven, as in
the nation.

The Changing Economy

For several decades, old U.S. cities have been hit hard by declines in manufacturing
base and retail trade. A few (like San Francisco and Denver) have been able to
capture the rising service and office industries. New Haven has not been one of
these. Since the fifties, its employment base has contracted sharply in the old sectors
without sufficiently offsetting growth in the new. As in social conditions, the city
economy has gone the typical route.

The changing economy of the city may be described in terms of trends within
the main industry sectors. The manufacturing sector grew from the beginning of

TABLE 2.3
Employment within New Haven for Selected
Industries and Local Government, 1954–1977

	1954	1972	1977
	000s (%)	000s (%)	000s (%)
Manufacturing	33.0 (58)	13.7 (36)	13.8 (38)
Retail trade	11.1 (20)	9.4 (25)	7.9 (22)
Wholesale trade	5.4 (10)	3.5 (9)	3.0 (8)
Selected services	4.0 (7)	7.2 (19)	7.2 (20)
Local government[a]	3.2[b](6)	4.1 (11)	4.1 (11)
Total Employment[c]	56.7 (101)[d]	37.9 (100)	36.0 (99)[d]

SOURCE: International City Management Association, *The Municipal Yearbook*, 1981; U.S. Bureau of the
Census, *County and City Data Book*, 1977, 1956; *Census of Wholesale Trade, Geographic Area Series: Connecticut*, 1977; *Census of Governments, Government in Connecticut*, 1957; Connecticut Department of Labor,
Bureau of Research and Information, *Non-agricultural Employment*, 1972, 1977.
[a] Includes school-system employees.
[b] Government employment in 1957.
[c] Totals are for these industries only and are less than employment for all industries within New Haven.
Additional data available for 1972 and 1977 include employment in finance, insurance, real estate,
transportation, communications, utilities, and nonlocal government. Including these industries brings
total employment up to about 62,500 in both 1972 and 1977, but private-sector employment decreased
by about 3,000 during that period.
[d] Figures deviate from 100 percent due to rounding.

the century and remained strong through the Korean War. After that it contracted more or less steadily, so that almost two-thirds of 33,000 manufacturing jobs in 1954 had disappeared by 1977 (Tables 2.3 and 2.4). This decline was not, however, balanced by growth in other industries. The service sector did expand by 80 percent, but its very small base meant that only about 3,000 new jobs were created in the face of 20,000 lost jobs in manufacturing. Moreover, service employment grew faster elsewhere: by almost 200 percent in Connecticut as a whole during the third quarter of the century, with even higher figures for many nearby towns and cities.

Throughout the first half of the century New Haven was the primary retail center for its region. But changing residential patterns, highway construction, and suburban shopping centers combined to undermine the comparative advantages of centrality and density, and thereby devastate the city's central business district. When inflation is taken into account, we see a collapse in New Haven retailing comparable to that in manufacturing (Table 2.5). In recent years, the city has fared especially poorly in relation to its suburbs: while New Haven retailing grew by 23 percent between 1967 and 1977, the competition (West Haven, Hamden, East Haven, and Milford) expanded by more than 80 percent (International City Management Association, 1981; U.S. Bureau of the Census, 1977). The precipitous decline of retailing, reinforced by the similar performance of the manufacturing sector and

TABLE 2.4
Trends in Manufacturing and Service Industries, 1954–1977

	1954	1958	1963	1967	1972	1977	Cumulative Change 1954–1977 (%)
Manufacturing Employment							
New Haven (000s)	33.0[a]	26.0	29.7	22.2	13.7	13.8	
Percentage change from previous period							
New Haven		−21	+14	−25	−38	+ 1	− 58
Connecticut		− 6	+ 6	+14	−17	+ 3	− 3
Service Employment							
New Haven (000s)	4.0	4.6	5.0	7.0	7.2	7.2	
Percentage change from previous period							
New Haven		+14	+10	+40	+ 3	0	+ 80
Connecticut		+26	+16	+25	+19	+37	+198

SOURCE: U.S. Bureau of the Census, *Statistical Abstract of the United States, 1980,* Table 792; *County and City Data Book,* 1977, 1972, 1967, 1956; International City Management Association, *The Municipal Yearbook,* 1981.
[a] Figure for 1947 is 33.5.

TABLE 2.5
Trends in New Haven Retail Sales, 1954–1977

	1954	1958	1963	1967	1972	1977	Cumulative Change 1954–1977 (%)
Volume in Current Dollars (millions)	248	247	232	289	324	357	
Percentage change from previous period		0	− 6	+24	+12	+10	**+44**
Volume in Constant Dollars (millions)[a]	754	699	619	708	635	482	
Percentage change from previous period		−7	−11	+14	−10	−24	**−36**

SOURCE: U.S. Bureau of the Census, *Statistical Abstract of the United States, 1980,* Table 792; *County and City Data Book,* 1977, 1972, 1967, 1956; International City Management Association, *The Municipal Yearbook,* 1981.
[a] Based on consumer price index normalized for 1980 current dollar = $1.00 constant.

the slow growth of services, left the New Haven economy seriously weakened by the 1980s.

Contraction of the city's economic base and the changes in its social composition outlined earlier have had their effect on property values. While the gross assessed value of city real property increased by 50 percent from 1956 to 1978 (Table 2.6), in constant dollars it dropped precipitously, from $1,014 million in 1954 to $629 million in 1978. Surveys of the actual sales prices of residential and commercial buildings (Table 2.6, note b) indicate, moreover, that the decline in assessed value was not an artifact of assessment practices, but rather was a reflection of a commensurate decay in market values. Thus the estimated value of the entire taxable real estate base of New Haven declined in constant dollars from $2,414 million in 1956 to $1,906 million in 1978, a contraction of 21 percent.

In sum, then, all of these data about New Haven's residents and economy show that the city started out in 1950 in a position similar to that of other small northern manufacturing cities, and ended up in 1980 in the same place as they did. But this is not the whole story, for, in between, government officials and citizens actively engaged in major programs of physical and social revitalization. The rest of this chapter tells the story of the politics and programs which bridge the gap between the city of 1950 and the city of 1980.

CHANGE AND CONTINUITY IN THE POLITICS OF DEVELOPMENT

There have been three distinct periods in the history of development politics in New Haven. When Robert Dahl published *Who Governs?* in 1961, he argued that

TABLE 2.6
Changes in New Haven Real Property Base, 1956–1978

	1956	*1971*	*1976*	*1978*
Gross Assessed Value, Locally Assessed Real Property ($ millions)				
Current dollars	337	457	509	503
Constant (1980) dollars[a]	1,014	923	733	629
Assessed Value as Fraction of Sales Price (median ratio)	.42[b]	.40[b]	.33[b]	.33[c]
Estimated Value of Locally Assessed Real Property ($ millions)				
Current dollars	802	1,143	1,542	1,524
Constant (1980) dollars[a]	2,414	2,308	2,221	1,906

SOURCE: U.S. Bureau of the Census, *Statistical Abstract of the United States, 1980,* Table 792; *State and Local Government Special Studies Number 92: Property Values Subject to Local General Property Taxation in the United States: 1978; Census of Governments, Taxable Property Values and Assessment/Sales Price Ratios,* Vol. 2, 1977, 1972; *Census of Governments, Taxable Property Values in the United States,* Vol. 5, 1957; authors' computations.

[a] Based on consumer price index normalized for 1980 current dollar = $1.00 constant.

[b] Based on sample during six months of 1956 of sales for nonfarm, single-family houses; figure is median value. For 1971 and 1976 survey data were also available for transactions involving all types of property, not just single-family houses. Median ratios were .41 in 1971 and .37 in 1976. Because these figures differ little from the ratios for only single-family houses, we decided to base our computations on the latter. In this way we could establish a time series extending back to 1956.

[c] This ratio was not empirically derived, but is presumed to be the same as two years previously.

Mayor Richard Lee had established an "executive-centered coalition" built upon a daring urban renewal program and the Redevelopment Agency (RA) which grew with it. The executive-centered coalition brought together business and government in a collective effort. It was the product of a strong, entrepreneurial mayor, who learned to use federal resources and technical expertise not only to transform large parts of the city, but to strengthen his own office. The executive-centered coalition, however, had already broken down before the Mayor completed his record eighth (two-year) term in 1969.

The basis for Lee's triumphs eroded in the mid-sixties with the rise of black power. The dream of making New Haven a "model city" began to fade as local government disintegrated under intense fire from a multiplicity of conflicting interests. Douglas Yates (1976: 244), for obvious reasons, called the ensuing period "street-fighting pluralism," and we have followed suit. Street-fighting lasted only a few years before giving way to a more subdued politics and a reintegrated local government. In 1975, New Haven implemented the Community Development Block Grant program (CDBG). CDBG was designed to strengthen the administrative and political control of local regimes, to end street-fighting pluralism, and to distribute federal funds more evenly across the country. Where the city had been spending huge sums under urban renewal, it was now faced with the certain future of disappearing federal money. The impact of the CDBG program, the final dismantling of the War on Poverty by Ford and Carter, and, as we saw previously, the contraction of the entire New Haven economy, converged simultaneously. The objective of government became forestalling municipal collapse, and the mood among developers and community organizations alike was to protect their own share of a shrinking program pie—hence our designation of "conserving clientelism" to describe the period from 1975 through the end of our study in 1980.

Throughout these three periods city administrators have contended with a fragmented and cumbersome set of government institutions. The mayor as chief executive has little direct authority. The administration is divided among more than nineteen separate agencies, each with its own independent citizen board. Although the mayor appoints most board members, terms are staggered and require approval of the city council, known in New Haven as the Board of Aldermen. The mayor cannot directly appoint a police chief, fire chief, or director of the Redevelopment Agency. Furthermore, power over the budget is divided between the mayor and a semi-autonomous board of finance. Adding to the mayor's difficulty in imposing central control over this system is the necessity of running for election biannually. On the legislative side, the Board of Aldermen further checks executive authority. Its thirty or so unpaid members (the number has varied between 27 and 33) are elected biannually by ward. The Board, too, has limited authority. It must approve the budgets of most, though not all, city agencies. It can cut the overall city budget and raise taxes, but not the reverse. The Board rarely meets more than once monthly. A ceremonial Board of Selectmen further complicates the governmental structure.

The electoral system has been inherited from the nineteenth century intact. Elections are partisan. While the capacities of political parties have steadily declined in New Haven as throughout the nation, there is still an elaborated party organization on the Democratic side. The Democratic Party is overwhelmingly dominant. No Republican has sat in the mayor's office since 1953, and Democratic majorities among the aldermen have ranged between 70 and 95 percent. The traditional political culture emphasizes ethnic and neighborhood symbolism combined with the divisible, material goods government can dispense. Thus for thirty years mayors have been careful to appoint ethnically (and eventually racially) balanced commissions and boards, to speak to the interests of every ward, but to glue their regimes together with jobs, contracts, and personal favors. Mayor Lee knew how to do this better than anyone.

THE EXECUTIVE-CENTERED COALITION: 1954–67

Richard Lee came into office intent on being an active mayor who would overcome the institutional weakness of the city's government. He promised in his campaign that, unlike his opponent who ran an undertaker's business while mayor, he would make the city job his only pursuit. From his inauguration on January 1, 1954, he established the character of his regime. The next day he institutionalized his link with the Democratic Party organization by appointing its leader, Arthur Barbieri, as Public Works Director, traditionally the central allocator of patronage. In his first week, Lee challenged the autonomy of the Police Board, the Fire Commissioners, and the Board of Finance, winning in each case his right to control senior appointments (Talbot, 1967: 243). At the same time as he moved to gain control over extant centers of power, the Mayor began to develop new ones. He brought Edward Logue on as a staff assistant with the promise that he would create for him the position of Development Administrator, which he succeeded in doing the following year by executive fiat. All the while the Mayor conducted a campaign to mobilize public opinion behind the idea that New Haven was a dying city which only his urban renewal program could save. Around it he organized a supporting coalition of Yale professors, businessmen, politicians, and government administrators. Within a very few years the coalition became self-sustaining on the tens of millions of federal dollars the RA procured. But in the beginning it was a risky business which depended on Lee's nerve and political skill.

From afar the Lee coalition seemed to have the order, body, and unity of a symphony. But in many ways it was a one-man act with Lee assuming the combined role of composer, arranger, conductor, and performer. (Talbot, 1967: 99)

And urban renewal was the dominant theme of the performance.

Urban Renewal and Political Power

Much of the script for redevelopment in New Haven was written elsewhere or before Lee took office. The master plan which Logue implemented was designed by a Yale professor, Maurice Rotival, adopted by the nascent City Planning Commission in 1942, and revised in 1953. The Redevelopment Agency was established by the Board of Aldermen in 1950 under the initiative of Republican mayor Celentano. The next year the Celentano administration entered into prolonged negotiations with the State Highway Department over three new roads planned to cross the city. Local officials persuaded the state to help finance industrial development along the harbor route of the Connecticut Turnpike, to relocate a proposed freeway connection to Hartford (later designated I-91) so that it avoided the core residential area of Wooster Square, and to build a downtown link with the Turnpike—the Oak Street Connector—which would raze the city's worst slum. Each of these highways later determined the location of an urban renewal project. The plans for Oak Street were virtually complete before Celentano left office; so, too, was a new building code and enforcement program recently mandated by the federal government as a requirement for urban renewal grants. Finally, the U.S. Housing Act of 1954 effectively broke the original link between urban renewal and public housing, thereby unencumbering the federal resources to finance redevelopment in New Haven.

But these resources had to be won. It was the entrepreneurial ability of Logue and the professional competence of the staff he assembled in the RA which permitted the implementation of urban renewal. With Celentano much was on paper, but there was no force to produce results. Logue initiated the search for intergovernmental funds. He and his professional colleagues devised ingenious ways to minimize local contributions. And he began to negotiate with the private developers who would invest in the cleared sites. Lee, for his part, handled the politics of the coalition and played a critical role in the Washington connection, especially after 1960 when his close ally, John Kennedy, won the presidency. Together, Lee and Logue created the institutional base for the reconstruction of New Haven.

In effect, New Haven developed a new government, overlaid upon the cumbersome old structure, more firmly (but by no means entirely) under Lee's control (Miller, 1966: 148). The redevelopment establishment—comprising the RA, office of the Development Administrator (essentially the deputy mayor), the Department of City Planning, and numerous ancillary agencies—responded only to the narrow constituencies with which it chose to interact: Yale, business leaders, developers, state and federal officials. Until well into the sixties the politics of redevelopment was conducted by professional elites free from virtually any citizen participation, much less resistance (Dahl, 1961: 125, Table 10–3).

The magnitude and political importance of this second government was impressive. The RA at its peak employed approximately 700 people (Singerman, 1980: 113), about 20 percent of all government employment in New Haven. While Lee refused to make patronage appointments to the top positions in the RA, he did not hesitate to use lower-level jobs as political resources (Singerman, 1980: 190). The RA had a huge budget. In 1967, for example, the city operating budget (not including the RA and other independent agencies) was about $39 million (Singerman, 1980: 103), whereas the RA alone was expending close to $18 million in federal funds. By 1969, New Haven had received $87 million for urban renewal, amounting to about 30 percent of the aggregate local tax levy for the period 1954–68. All of this money was free, in the sense that it was not extracted from local taxpayers or scrutinized closely by the Aldermen. It created the basis for a redevelopment clientele of property owners, lawyers, contractors, appraisers, developers, rehabilitation organizations, and housing sponsors.

Government and the Private Power Structure. Government was the leading force in the redevelopment of New Haven. The city's business community was divided among many firms and sectors with no dominant corporations or leaders. The most important business organization, the Chamber of Commerce, was inactive: "it neither led nor dragged; it was just there" (Talbot, 1967: 63). While the Chamber favored doing something about the city's decline, it itself did nothing. Lee for many months had a difficult time persuading business elites actively to support redevelopment. Finally, in the summer of 1954, President Griswold of Yale agreed to be vice chair of the Citizens Action Commission (CAC), and others joined quickly thereafter. The CAC became a useful propaganda vehicle for the urban renewal program. It gave "the business community the appearance of unity and power" (Talbot, 1967: 63), but rather than being an instrumentality of the business class, the CAC was dominated by the Mayor (Wolfinger, 1974: 247ff). To the extent there was a "progrowth coalition" (Mollenkopf, 1981) in New Haven, it was organized by Lee himself;

and even the Mayor was never entirely successful in getting the backing of the conservative local newspapers, or of businesses that believed they would be adversely affected by particular projects.

If redevelopment was not initiated outside of government, it nonetheless depended upon private-sector networks and was confined by business interests. It was the Yale connection that brought together Lee (Director of Public Relations for the university) and Logue (son-in-law of the Dean of Yale College). It was from Yale that the Rotival master plan emerged. It was Yale President Griswold who got the CAC off the ground. William Domhoff (1978: 48ff) was almost certainly correct in claiming that without Yale the city would have received a much smaller urban renewal allocation. Yale provided the critical linkages between New Haven and the cosmopolitan world of national political leaders and corporations. Beyond this, opposition from either Yale or the major downtown businesses (especially the influential banks and utilities) undoubtedly would have killed most of the redevelopment program at an early stage. But why should there have been such opposition? Lee, Logue, and other leaders of the regime attempted to anticipate and further the interests of the business class and Yale.

The Plan for New Haven.   The strategy which emerged from the Rotival plan and the urban renewal projects of the fifties was the reconstruction of New Haven in all of its parts. Rotival saw the city as a transportation junction, but with highways replacing railroads and shipping (see Talbot, 1967; Wolfinger, 1974; Domhoff, 1978). New expressways would, moreover, screen residential neighborhoods from industrial areas. The downtown was to be rebuilt with an expanded retail capacity, the elimination of manufacturing uses, and their replacement by offices. The biggest stores would get new homes. Adding to the attraction of this core would be a sports arena and convention center. The CBD would be opened up through the replacement of the Oak Street slum by a modern highway which would provide a *cordon sanitaire*. New space would be made available for the expansion of the University medical complex through the removal of lower-income populations around the Yale–New Haven hospital. The city's three high schools adjoining the Yale campus would be rebuilt elsewhere, and Yale would be able to erect a new college. In the first set of plans and projects there was something for everyone—except for those who lost their homes through highway and urban renewal projects. The reason, therefore, that the executive-centered coalition was able to implement redevelopment so successfully lay in the character of its redevelopment scheme, which was radical in the physical changes it would produce, but conservative in the interests it served (Dahl, 1961: 139). The city would be rebuilt for its current leading occupants.

Urban Renewal and Housing Programs[4]

In order to accomplish this vision, some groups would have to relinquish their control of central locations. Each of the first three projects in the core of the city (Oak Street, Church Street, and Wooster Square) involved substantial demolition and displacement. Slum clearance, however, was viewed as a positive benefit to low-income slum dwellers, who would be liberated from their fetid tenements into decent housing. Mayor Lee established this definition of the situation with the city's first big redevelopment venture in Oak Street. He recalled to Robert Dahl (1961: 120) how his commitment to urban renewal originated in a 1951 campaign visit to the neighborhood:

I went into the homes on Oak Street and they set up neighborhood meetings for me. . . . And I came out from one of those homes on Oak Street, and I sat on the curb and I was just as sick as a puppy. Why, the smell of this building. . . . Right then was when I began to tie in all these ideas we'd been practicing in city planning for years in terms of the human benefits that a program like this could reap for a city.

The Mayor and the Redevelopment Administrator cultivated the popular perception that urban renewal would "get rid of slums and provide good housing" (as reported by a 1957 Harris survey [Wolfinger, 1974: 285]). This theme, combined with "the rebirth of business" and "retaining the middle class," was sounded continually by the Lee Administration for more than a decade after the first wreckers hit Oak Street in 1956.

Oak Street.   The administration, through active lobbying in Hartford, convinced the state to expend $15 million for a major access road linking the Connecticut Turnpike, then under construction, with Route 34, the Derby Turnpike. Along the right-of-way the city implemented an urban renewal project aimed at encouraging business and "quality" residential construction. The Oak Street Connector was viewed as a major coup, for not only did it eliminate an increasingly black tenement area abutting downtown and the Yale medical complex, it also solved a major problem of the central business district, inadequate access roads and insufficient parking for suburban shoppers. Well after the last dust had settled, the RA relocation officer waxed:

It runs right through the middle of the Oak Street project area. Known as the Oak Street Connector, it promised to bring inner-city traffic directly to the heart of the proposed new shopping center in New Haven and to allow for more imaginatively planning the entire area, assuring that the *entire* Oak Street slum would be wiped out. (Mermin, 1970: 19; emphasis in original)

Looking back in its last report under the federal urban renewal program, the Redevelopment Agency, too, saw the Connector as the key to its CBD strategy:

The Oak Street Interstate Highway Connector . . . plus the availability of 4,750 parking spaces in new, structured facilities, has gone a long way toward redirecting attention to the central City. Latest traffic reports show that 45,400 cars flow into New Haven daily via the connector. This traffic, carrying potential business for the City, might otherwise have been lost to us or deflected to other, more congested, inner-city streets. Creation of the Connector in 1958 was the initial public improvement that contributed most significantly to redeveloping and revitalizing downtown. (New Haven Redevelopment Agency, 1974: 15H)

Whatever its contribution to "revitalizing downtown," the Oak Street project had serious costs for local residents and businesses (see Table 2.7). All structures within its boundaries were demolished. Almost 900 households were officially recorded as displaced, 40 percent of whom were minority. Most of these families moved to Wooster Square and Dixwell, low-income areas which would soon themselves be renewed. The project also eliminated economic "blight" in the form of at least 250 businesses, mostly small commercial and manufacturing operations, many of which probably disappeared entirely. Yet another consequence resulted from the planned extension of the Connector west through the solid if not prosperous Dwight residential neighborhood. The mapped route established a corridor of disinvestment and flight. By 1959 the city said Dwight was an area requiring clearance (primarily along the proposed Connector route) and rehabilitation (Hallman, 1959).

Church Street. Two logics came together to define the most central and important of all the urban renewal projects. The first was the Oak Street Connector, which cleared part of the project area. The second was a complex series of business deals and negotiation centering on the three square blocks extending from the expressway to the central Green. The maneuvering began with the 1953 closing of Gamble-Desmond, a big department store located on the city's most expensive land. The actors included several real estate investors, a bank, the mayor, and Roger Stevens, a developer and 1952 chairman of the Democratic National Committee. When Stevens, even with Lee's help, was unable to implement a private redevelopment scheme for the core blocks, Lee and Logue extended the boundaries of the Church Street "blighted area" to the center of town. All of this was accomplished very quietly; the Board of Aldermen had little idea of its boldness when it approved the Church Street plan in 1957. There was no planning participation from the numerous residents and small businesses who would be displaced. Opposition from individual firms was ignored or handled by giving them special benefits. In general, the Mayor dominated the political situation (Wolfinger, 1974: Chapter 10).

Implementation did not prove to be so easy. While the hurdle of convincing the federal Urban Renewal Agency that the best blocks in town were blighted was quickly overcome (Wolfinger, 1974: 309), lining up a developer took years. The downtown blocks were eventually completed in the middle sixties with the opening of two large department stores, an indoor mall, and a new hotel. But from 1958 to 1962 a big piece of the CBD consisted of parking lots and holes in the ground. Not surprisingly, the city economy absorbed a $15-million loss in retail sales which could never be recouped (see Table 2.5). And the property tax payoffs of the project were partially offset by the inducements required to attract reluctant investors.

The rest of the area was finished in the early seventies, more than a dozen years after destruction of the old neighborhood. Investment here was mainly in public or nonassessable private construction; the most notable projects were a well-planned development of mixed-income housing in the south of the project area, the commanding tower of the Knights of Columbus national headquarters, and the much-heralded New Haven Veterans Memorial Coliseum. Its 11,000-seat arena provided a new home to the city's minor-league hockey team, and its floor areas

TABLE 2.7
Urban Renewal Activity in New Haven, 1955–74[a]

	Housing Units Before Renewal	Units Demolished	Households Relocated[b]	Businesses Relocated[c]	UR Expenditures (Federal)[d]	Direct Public Construction[e]	Nonpublic Construction[e]
Core Area Projects							
Oak St. (1955)[f]	884	521	886	250	8.7 (4.4)	19.9	40.8
Church St. (1957)[f]	746	675	707	785	66.0 (31.0)	37.5	64.1
Long Wharf (1958)					10.6 (0)	6.2	26.7
Temple-George (1966)					2.8 (1.8)		12.0
State St. (1968)			270	385	54.0 (29.3)	57.7	27.8
Wooster Sq. (1958)[f]	3,069	2,155	2,710	450	42.5 (30.1)	6.9	16.3
Ring Area Projects							
Dixwell (1960)[f]	3,201	889	1,127	193	28.7 (19.6)	10.5	16.4
Hill H.S. (1963)					0.9 (0.6)		
Dwight (1963)			485	54	21.7 (14.1)	4.5	20.6
Newhallville (1968)			363	10	20.6 (12.5)	3.9	1.8
Fair Haven (1969)			107	8	4.0 (4.0)[g]	3.9	3.3
Hill (1973)			1,049	81	12.1 (12.1)[g]	9.6	2.3
Unallocated			146[h]				
Totals			7,850[i]	2,216	272.6[j] (159.5)	160.6	232.1
(minority households:)			(3,815[k])				

SOURCE: New Haven Redevelopment Agency, *Annual Report, Financial and Statistical Information*, 1972; *Annual Report*, 1967; Janet Rothenberg Pack, "Household Relocation: The New Haven Experience," 1973, mimeo, from files of the Family Relocation Office, New Haven Redevelopment Agency; Alvin Mermin, *Relocating Families* (Washington, D.C.: National Association of Housing and Redevelopment Officials, 1970).

[a] This table reflects budgeted expenditures as of January 1973 for urban renewal and code enforcement programs. We account for about $160 million of the

$180 million spent in New Haven by the federal government over the life of urban renewal. Most of the remaining $20 million was allocated for property acquisition in the Hill and Fair Haven project areas.

Evidence on relocation should be viewed as a rough estimate and, probably, an understatement. Pack (1973), in a study for the Redevelopment Agency, finds inconsistencies in several projects between counts of units demolished and households relocated. She also suggests that State Highway Department records may have lost cases of households displaced by road construction, particularly in the rights of way for Oak Street and I-91. Even more important may be the exclusion from official records of households who moved prior to eviction in anticipation of renewal or in response to landlord disinvestment and communal disintegration exacerbated by urban renewal. Also uncounted are households within project areas (which are very large in New Haven) but not in target sites. Depending on which of these additional categories of households are defined as "displaced" by urban renewal, the final figure for *displacement* may easily be 50 to 100 percent greater than that for *relocation*.

Unless otherwise indicated, all data are derived from New Haven Redevelopment Agency (1972).

[b] Includes relocation due to urban renewal and code enforcement for families and unrelated individuals.

[c] Derived from New Haven Redevelopment Agency (1967). Figures for Church Street, State Street, and Wooster Square are estimated from a graphical presentation in New Haven Redevelopment Agency (1972).

[d] Millions of dollars. About $79 million of public construction expenditures constituted the bulk of the city's contribution to urban renewal (i.e., the one-third, local share).

[e] Millions of dollars. *Direct public construction* includes infrastructure, public buildings, and public housing. *Nonpublic construction* includes a major share of publicly assisted housing (e.g., 221(d)3, Sec. 236, etc.). Both categories include all construction within project boundaries and not solely on cleared sites. Estimates for construction expenditures are as of early 1973.

[f] Relocation data are from Pack, 1973.

[g] Includes only federal planning grants and loans for early property acquisition.

[h] Calculated as follows: Subtract 7,704 from the sum of (1) RA figures by project and (2) RA estimate of relocation due to State highway construction (1,856 households).

[i] Pack's total of households displaced from all causes through June 1971 is 7,871. Although our figure represents actual plus expected displacement, it is *lower* than Pack's. We can be quite certain, therefore, that actual displacement through 1974 must have exceeded 7,850 households. Since Mermin (1970: 85), who directed relocation for the RA, estimated *persons* relocated through 1967 at 22,000, the actual number of persons relocated through 1974 must have exceeded 22,000, perhaps by a large number.

[j] The largest expenditure categories were $109.5 million for property acquisition and $96.5 million for capital improvements in project areas.

[k] Computed from Pack, Tables 3–5 and 1–2.

were suited to convention activities. The potential economic payoff was seen as greatly outweighing the $23-million public debt incurred for construction:

In the development of downtown New Haven the completion of the Veterans Memorial Coliseum is a keystone. It will add to the tax base, supply a source of jobs and provide big name entertainment and sports functions to the New Haven taxpayer. It will also be a prime attraction when the city begins its efforts to sell New Haven as a convention Mecca. (New Haven Redevelopment Agency, 1972a: 3)

Direct city expenditures for Church Street were minimal in comparison to social and economic costs more difficult to calculate or to agree upon. New Haven's cash contribution was less than $500,000 (New Haven Redevelopment Agency, 1972b). But clearance for the project razed at least 700 housing units, most of which were occupied by elderly men living in inexpensive hotels (Table 2.7). While government reports suggested that relocated households usually got better accommodations than before, poor record keeping and self-serving definitions of displacement left grave doubts as to the damage done to original residents.

The effect of renewal on local businesses was just as severe. The Redevelopment Agency documented 785 firms displaced by redevelopment, of which 40 percent were acknowledged to have left town or disappeared (Wolfinger, 1974: 336). Yet officials perceived business displacement as necessary and probably desirable:

It was felt that many of the Church Street concerns were marginal enterprises that could not survive a move and the likelihood of higher rent, and that some of them were in businesses unsuited for a central downtown location. One of the causes of the CBD's uncompetitive position was the unappealing character of many of its stores; neither the city nor Stevens [the developer] thought that the project would be a success if it merely offered the same old shops in new surroundings. (Wolfinger, 1974: 319)

Regardless of the short-term economic costs of reconstructing downtown, officials believed that with the opening of the Macy's and Malley's department stores, the CBD had turned the corner.

From the perspective of the eighties the picture looks a good deal bleaker. Retail sales did pick up with the unveiling of the rebuilt downtown and with the rapid economic growth that characterized the mid-sixties in the whole country (Table 2.5). But after 1967 the figures became illusory, blown up by inflation. In real terms New Haven sales figures declined 10 percent from 1967 to 1972 and another 24 percent in the next five years. By 1981, the downtown was again in big trouble. Malley's was closed by the bankrupt United Department Stores, which had previously acquired the local firm, and its 260,000-sq.-ft. store stood vacant. The Chapel Mall was occupied largely by cheap shops catering to the trade of lunch-hour office workers and was a hangout for idle teenagers. The Coliseum did not transform New Haven into a "convention Mecca." Barely a decade after its opening, Mayor DiLieto called it " 'a colossal white elephant' on which the city will pay $1.4 million in debt service a year until 2012" (Freedman, 1982: 6E).[5]

Wooster Square and Long Wharf.   Like Oak Street and Church Street, the initiative and planning for these two core projects resulted directly from state and federal highway programs, which local officials actively encouraged as a boon to the city's economy and redevelopment. Wooster Square was primarily an Italian working-class district adjacent to the city's major industrial concentration along the harbor, Mill River, and New Haven Railroad yards. At the time of its redevelopment in the early sixties, it also housed perhaps 2,000 black people, many of whom had been previously displaced from Oak and Church streets. These individuals lived in the most rundown part of the district, just where the city rerouted I-91 in order to save the stately Victorian homes around the square which gave the neighborhood its name. Unlike the previous projects, the city implemented what was at that time a nationally innovative plan for Wooster Square, one which combined neighborhood preservation and housing rehabilitation with clearance and new construction. Nonetheless, there was more displacement in this project than anywhere else, and nearly all of it outpaced construction of publicly subsidized housing. More than two-thirds of the area's 3,069 housing units were demolished; hundreds more were vacated for gut rehabilitation, rarely to be reoccupied by their original inhabitants. Many homeowners in the areas spared by the highway benefited from redevelopment, and there was minor gentrification on a few streets with especially good architecture. But most of Wooster Square's residents lost their homes; in the process a growing black neighborhood was surgically removed from the downtown area. There was virtually no popular opposition to any of this; blacks were politically inactive in the city, and Italian-American homeowners saw distinct advantages from renewal.

The city again eliminated a sizable chunk of its economic infrastructure. At least 450 businesses were displaced. This time, however, effort was made to facilitate rehabilitation and new construction for small firms spared by the highway, and to relocate viable enterprises that were in its path. The direct and indirect economic death toll of urban renewal and highway construction in Wooster Square was not calculated, but the city could point to more than sixty small firms which invested in the project area. The contracted economic and residential base stabilized in the seventies. In many ways, city officials saw Wooster Square as their most successful project.

Long Wharf differed from almost every other redevelopment effort by the city government in requiring no demolition or displacement. The project encompassed previously vacant land bordering the harbor and bisected by the Connecticut Turnpike. Intergovernmental revenues came entirely from the state. Long Wharf had as its objective the preservation of New Haven's manufacturing base. It provided developed land for industry to build modern plants yet remain in New Haven. Several large firms did just that; in addition, Armstrong Rubber Company erected its national headquarters in the project, and Gant Shirtmakers entered the city for the first time with a $3.5-million plant. Various shipping firms, markets, a motel, the city's newspapers, and a well-known regional theater also erected facilities. Long Wharf was too expensive for most of the marginal businesses that had been displaced by urban renewal, and it was unable to live up to its promise of reestablishing the city's base of big manufacturers. By 1980 Gant had closed, and other firms were threatening to do likewise. Nonetheless, the project must be viewed as an economic success. For a cash outlay of $3.7 million, the city generated almost $27 million in private investment, virtually all of which was taxable property. Without Long Wharf, several major employers would undoubtedly have closed down in New Haven, and others would never have come. The balance sheet here had few negatives.

State Street. This last core-area project of the Lee administration was intended to upgrade the eastern flank of the CBD. By the time implementation began in earnest in 1968, the project had languished on the drawing boards for a decade. Again, the RA and Melvin Adams, the second Development Administrator after Logue's departure in 1960, had to convince the federal Urban Renewal Administration that the area was blighted. Lee, along with area Congressman Robert Giaimo, spent much time lobbying Washington. The Mayor also supported one of the few successful community uprisings against neighborhood destruction, as affluent East Rock Park residents forced the state to circumvent their neighborhood with Interstate 91. The big problem, however, was flagging investor interest in downtown New Haven. State Street became viable only after the federal General Services Administration agreed in 1963 to move several thousand government employees to the city and construct an office building. The RA began clearance during the late sixties. At least 385 allegedly marginal businesses were displaced. Several hundred households lost their homes. In their place arose a government center consisting of a federal building, state courthouse, and new city hall. Nearby were a center for the performing arts and two major private office buildings. Of a total $86 million in new construction, $58 million was publicly funded. The federal urban renewal expenditure alone was almost $2 million greater than total private investment.[6]

Ring Area Projects. Urban renewal in the area outside the central core did not begin until after 1960, with the last plan approved in 1973. On the whole the approach to these outlying neighborhoods reflected a multifaceted strategy involving reduced clearance, and expanded rehabilitation and new-housing components. The city turned its attention from exorcising the worst slums to preserving the "middle ground" neighborhoods (where it had, of course, already sent many minority and low-income households displaced by earlier projects):

While New Haven wages all-out war on its slums, blight is spreading through the city's middle-aged neighborhoods. If no preventive action is taken soon, these neighborhoods, too, will require substantial slum clearance programs to make them fit to live in. . . . New Haven has the opportunity to achieve its goal of being America's first slumless city, but it cannot rely solely on clearance activities. (Hallman, 1959: 1)

Preservation required spot clearance, but also infusions of public investment, efforts at getting landlords to fix up their property, and assistance to community organizations constructing new housing. The city pursued all these avenues with zeal.
    While the Redevelopment Agency began to dissociate itself from the heavy-handed approach typified by Oak Street, it never abandoned clearing land. Its Dixwell and Dwight projects involved substantial clearance in the parts of these neighborhoods abutting Yale or the CBD. More than 25 percent of housing units in Dixwell

were in fact demolished during the early sixties (Table 2.7). Most of these units were in the southeastern part of the project area, a territory uneasily divided between lower-class ghetto and upper-class university. Between 1963 and 1965, about 75 percent of relocated households were black (Pack, 1973). After clearance, Yale spent more than $7 million in constructing Morse and Stiles Colleges, and a couple of million more went to university-related facilities. New mixed-income housing provided a buffer against the remaining Dixwell ghetto, which expanded northward into "middle ground" Newhallville. Yale erected a $4-million art and architecture building, two downtown motels opened, and Saint Raphael's Hospital expanded its plant on cleared land in Dwight immediately proximate to the university. The Redevelopment Agency razed additional strategic sites in both Dwight and Dixwell despite the lack of immediate development prospects. Even in its very last projects (Newhallville, Fair Haven, and the Hill), the RA continued with a spot-clearance strategy, although by then it was obvious that there would be little private investment (see Table 2.7).

Construction of public facilities was used by the city to fulfill the federal requirement of a local financial contribution. New Haven thus built three high schools to replace the ones situated in the middle of the Yale campus and rebuilt nine elementary schools. The city also provided Dixwell with a large community center—which would later stand mostly vacant for want of operating funds—constructed a police headquarters, and erected several fire houses. Total city infrastructural investment amounted to somewhat more than $80 million (calculated from New Haven Redevelopment Agency, 1972b).

Housing and Neighborhood Development. By the late fifties, every renewal venture promised new housing construction for low- and moderate-income households. The city continually requested more federal housing funds than were granted. It was a pioneer in facilitating local sponsorship (often by churches) of publicly assisted construction of rental and cooperatively owned housing. Many of these units were constructed in the Dixwell project area, as well as in Church Street South and along the Oak Street Connector. Annual reports of the Redevelopment Agency trumpeted the fact that New Haven was building housing for its residents.

But in fact housing construction was grossly inadequate. About half of all new construction was designated for elderly households, who probably constituted only about a quarter of those displaced by public activity. The timing of construction meant that people uprooted by the early renewal projects were only accidentally beneficiaries of new lower-income housing. In the core-area renewal site, low-income housing was replaced either by luxury buildings or by housing only for the elderly. But the most telling figures were those which compared total demolition with new construction. At least 7,850 housing units were demolished in the period 1956–72 (Table 2.7). During these same years, 2,214 new units were opened, resulting in a net loss of 5,636 units for low- and moderate-income households. *In fact, total new housing construction through 1980 fell more than a thousand units short of demolition through 1972* (Table 2.8). By the seventies it could not be said that there had been any real improvement in the quality of housing of New Haven's lower classes.

TABLE 2.8
Public and Publicly Assisted Housing Units Made Available for Occupancy in New Haven, 1956–80, and Units Eliminated, 1956–72

Public, low-income family	344
Public, low-income elderly	1,226
Publicly assisted, low and moderate income: 221(d)3, 236	1,380
Publicly assisted, low- and moderate-income elderly: 236, 202H	1,893
Section 8	1,848[a]
Total (1956–80)	**6,691[b]**
Units opened 1956–72	2,214
Units eliminated as a result of urban renewal and highway construction, 1956–72	7,850
Net Loss through 1972 in housing available to low- and moderate-income households	5,636

SOURCE: New Haven City Planning Department, "Government Assisted Housing in New Haven," April 1980, processed file copy, Table 2.7.
[a] Of which, new construction constituted about 500.
[b] About 50 percent of which were occupied by elderly households.

The city did also seek to preserve and upgrade existing housing and to stabilize neighborhoods. To this end it launched a number of campaigns to prosecute slumlords for housing code violations, to get owner-occupants to fix up their properties, and to encourage neighborhood pride and self-help. The Redevelopment Agency implemented major programs of rehabilitation loans and grants in every project area; by 1972, 10,531 units had been rehabilitated, with another 3,747 underway (New Haven Redevelopment Agency, 1972a, b). Investment in these properties amounted to more than $32 million. New Haven not only created prototypes of neighborhood stabilization programs, its officials influenced the development of national legislation and efforts in other cities.

The effect of such programs was not, however, necessarily positive. The flow of minority and low-income people into the city quickened during the sixties, so neighborhood residents often got poorer as some of the housing looked a little better. By the end of the decade massive disinvestment could be seen everywhere. Rehabilitated structures stood next to empty lots previously cleared for nonexistent investors by the RA. In the Hill, Dixwell, Dwight, and Newhallville—black and increasingly Hispanic areas—abandonment and arson became commonplace. The most important effect of first the core-area projects and then those in the next ring was to produce a continuous flow of displaced persons; *as much as one-fifth of the entire population of the city was uprooted between 1956 and 1974* (see notes to Table 2.7). Community social networks were in part destroyed by the very officials who sought to stop physical decay and make New Haven slumless.

The federal bulldozer changed the face of New Haven with little community opposition in its path. Not until 1964 did some Yale professors begin to question publicly the sense of the programs in New Haven. Citizen mobilization against projects, when it did occur, came first from businesses and well-off residents in Church and State streets. Mass opposition and demands for participation did not develop until the onset of Model Cities in 1966. In this respect New Haven was not especially unusual. Widespread resistance to highway and renewal projects did not appear in the United States until the mid-sixties. Because New Haven got such a quick head start, it could implement most of its clearance activity earlier than other cities.

Beyond the matter of timing, several other factors contributed to the weakness of opposition. The administration kept its planning relatively secret and then moved very quickly to implementation. The aldermen rarely defied the Mayor, in part because none of them represented the interests of groups and communities most hurt by redevelopment. Singerman (1981) was probably correct in suggesting that the forced mobility of lower-income and minority households allowed aldermen in "receiving neighborhoods" to ignore their new constituencies until well into the sixties. On top of this, blacks in New Haven were weak politically and excluded for most of the Lee years from the political party organization and the Board of Aldermen.[7] The administration, for its part, appeared to be generous in its provision of social services to displaced households and to be committed to rebuilding lower-income neighborhoods. Indeed, paternalism was the primary vehicle for citizen participation during the period of the executive-centered coalition.

Financial Impacts. Urban renewal proved to be of no great financial benefit. Even by the Redevelopment Agency's figures, increases in property assessments for renewal areas were small. Assessed values did increase by $26.4 million or 62 percent within project areas, producing a net tax increment of $4.3 million (Table 2.9). These figures, however, were hardly impressive. During these years assessed values *outside* renewal areas also increased—by 34 percent. The $4.3-million tax increment amounted to only 10 percent of locally raised taxes and was considerably less than the $10 million or so *cash* contribution the city had already made to urban renewal, not to mention its in-kind expenditures of $80 million, more than half of which went directly into site preparations necessitated by land clearance rather than into new public facilities.[8] The federal expenditure of $160 million would have generated the tax increment attributed to redevelopment had it been invested with a return of only 2.5 percent. Overall, then, a rough assessment of renewal not only suggests that the costs of the city's activities were borne disproportionately by lower-income and minority communities, but that their net impact on the condition of the city

TABLE 2.9
Changes in Assessed Value and in
Tax Returns for Urban Renewal
Project Areas, New Haven, 1956–71

	1956	1971	Change 1956/71
Assessed Value			
Current dollars (millions)	42.6	69.0	26.4
Constant (1980) dollars (millions)[a]	128.9	140.0	11.0
Tax Return			
Current dollars (millions)	1.5	5.8	4.3

SOURCE: New Haven Redevelopment Agency, *Annual Report, Financial and Statistical Information*, 1972.
[a] Calculated by authors; see Table 2.5.

was probably negative. Even if we were willing to posit a unitary economic interest for the city, we could not agree with the assessment that "there is little doubt . . . urban renewal enhanced the economic productivity of New Haven" (Peterson, 1981: 144).

Human Renewal

The War on Poverty began early in New Haven. In April 1962, Mayor Lee announced the creation of an independent agency, Community Progress, Incorporated (CPI), which would attempt to break the cycle of poverty in lower-income and minority neighborhoods, coordinate social-service delivery, and improve the capabilities of other government bureaus, especially the Board of Education. CPI began as one of six Gray Area Projects sponsored by the Ford Foundation. Besides an initial grant of $2.5 million from Ford, it received substantial support from President Kennedy's Committee on Juvenile Delinquency, and the Department of Labor (Marris and Rein, 1973: 23). CPI was a model for federally sponsored community action programs and was designated as the city's community action agency in 1965. Over its first four years the agency expended $16.3 million (Murphy, 1971: 143), roughly 20 percent of New Haven's locally financed budget at this time. Thousands of visitors from other U.S. cities streamed through New Haven to learn from CPI's example. Along with the Redevelopment Agency, CPI became part of the "second government" of New Haven, as it channeled outside resources into city neighborhoods and into the Lee Administration.

CPI was rooted in the city's urban renewal program. Its originators were leaders of the redevelopment coalition (Murphy, 1971: 4). The main program architect was Howard Hallman, RA Director of Neighborhood Improvement, who became second in command of the anti-poverty agency. Edward Logue established the connection with the Ford Foundation through his old college classmate, Paul Ylvisaker. While

Richard Lee's identification with CPI was less direct than with redevelopment, he provided critical connections with Washington, facilitated support for the endeavor in New Haven, and defined its institutional form (Murphy, 1971: 50).

The organizational model for CPI was the RA. The agency had a strong top-down, professionalized structure; its elite was comprised of people from outside the city with no personal bases of power who were beholden to the CPI executive director, Mitchell Sviridoff. Sviridoff, whom the Mayor had first used to reform the school system as President of the Board of Education, provided the connection to the executive coalition. Like the RA, CPI in its early years was an extraordinary entrepreneur in the federal system; less than 10 percent of its funds came from city taxpayers (Murphy, 1971: 143). The Mayor employed CPI, just as he did the RA, to dominate and reform the decentralized and independent city bureaucracy, and he maintained the nonpartisan image of CPI by keeping direct patronage appointments to a minimum. In due course, however, CPI itself developed a large array of individuals and organizations dependent on its largesse and, thereby, on the perpetuation of the Lee Administration.

Human renewal was a logical outgrowth of urban renewal. The household relocation activities of the RA made it aware of the broad dimensions of poverty. In response, the Agency implemented a program of unified social services during the late fifties, but found itself severely limited by the hardware orientation of the federal urban renewal program. Several times it sought outside funds to fight poverty before succeeding in 1962. Displacement also gave the agency political concerns: "Unless the slum dwellers could be convinced that clearance would no longer cause them hardship, all the redevelopment plans might founder in the face of popular outcry" (Marris and Rein, 1973: 174). Finally, it became apparent to RA officials that moving lower-income people around the city could only contribute to further neighborhood deterioration unless their poverty itself were ameliorated. The theory of trickle-down was inadequate to produce neighborhood renewal without the codicil of social improvement.

CPI implemented dozens of programs in the pragmatic style which had come to characterize redevelopment. Nonetheless, the agency was guided by a strategy against poverty, one which emphasized educating and training poor people, especially minority youth. During its first four years it spent more than 70 percent of its funds on manpower programs and improved services within the public school system (Murphy, 1971: 56). CPI studiously avoided direct action, community mobilization, and even, for several years, citizen participation. In its copious publicity it stressed the traditional American goals of individualism and opportunity, of helping the poor to overcome their personal handicaps. Thus, like urban renewal, the city's war on poverty constituted a governmental initiative defined to be palatable to middle-class sensibilities and business interests.

Demise of the Executive-Centered Coalition

By the time CPI reached its apogee of prestige and funding around 1966, community action was turning into a much more open game than the politics of redevelopment. Political forces beyond local control were redefining the situation in New Haven, and even an agency with conservative intentions could not assure conservative outcomes. As early as 1963 some CPI staffers tried—and failed—to get the agency to adopt a group-advocacy role in legal services (Marris and Rein, 1973: 171–75). The agency became subject to criticism for its middle-class orientation (Cahn and Cahn, 1964). In a move unprecedented for New Haven, a black community organization lodged a complaint with the federal Office of Economic Opportunity (OEO), forcing CPI to include seven elected representatives of the poor in its governing board of city notables (Murphy, 1971: 51–53). At the same time as minority communities were beginning to stir, white ethnics in New Haven mobilized in opposition to school integration and efforts by the city to build scattered-site public housing. If the Redevelopment Agency was long successful in avoiding minority demands and racial-group crossfire, CPI, the Board of Education, the Mayor, and his new Model Cities Agency were not. CPI, claiming to represent the interests of the poor, helped raise the expectations of its clients, not only for improvements in material well-being, but for participation in governing programs of which they were ostensible beneficiaries (Murphy, 1971: 148). The executive-centered coalition was becoming severely strained.

STREET-FIGHTING PLURALISM: 1967–74

City governments were in flux by the late sixties, beset with racial conflict, demands for community control and social reform. Douglas Yates' definition of street-fighting pluralism came close to the mark in characterizing New Haven. He said cities had become "ungovernable" (1976: 236) and their politics defined by "a pattern of unstructured, multilateral conflict in which the many different combatants [fight] with one another in an almost infinite number of permutations and combinations" (1976: 244). The period following Lee's executive-centered coalition was defined by two dimensions: (1) racial mobilization and pacification, and (2) enfranchisement of lower-income people through bureaucratic and political mechanisms.

Racial Mobilization and Pacification

The black demand for equality, participation, and governmental resources was expressed in many different ways, ranging from street violence to middle-class reform organization. For five days in 1967 perhaps 1,800 of the city's black people participated in civil insurrection; 353 were arrested and property damage in the Hill, Dixwell, and Newhallville was in the millions (National Advisory Commission on Civil Disorders, 1968: 393; Fogelson and Hill, 1968: 231). Conflict with the police was endemic. While police performance during the riot was apparently relatively controlled, this was not the case in numerous incidents during the same period involving teenagers, journalists, and radical groups (Powledge, 1970: 128ff). In 1977, Police Chief DiLieto (who became mayor two years later) was forced to resign when it was disclosed that the department had conducted a program of wiretapping and *agents provocateurs* for almost a decade, as it waged covert war against blacks and the political left. There were repeated demonstrations for tenant rights in public housing, better treatment of welfare clients, minority hiring in downtown businesses, and community control of social services, schools, and police. For the first time urban renewal was actively opposed, as several organizations (including the Congress of Racial Equality [CORE] and the American Independence Movement) mobilized Hill and Dwight residents against the Route 34 extension of the Oak Street Connector. Perhaps the most extreme moment of racial tension was reached during the 1970 murder trial of Bobby Seale, national leader of the Black Panther Party, when thousands of supporters rallied on the New Haven Green (Freed, 1973).

Black organization in the city was divided between radical and moderate leaders. On the left was Fred Harris, president of the Hill Parents Association. Harris repeatedly mobilized demonstrations as he pressed for community control of CPI, the Model Cities program, and the public schools. Harris was under continual attack from the police and was eventually implicated in a conspiracy to blow up police headquarters and several banks (Powledge, 1970: 175). On the right was the Black Coalition, an umbrella organization for many neighborhood groups and service agencies. It pressed for decentralization of social services and black professional direction of their provision. Henry Parker, its leader, ran unsuccessfully for mayor several times and became Connecticut state treasurer during the late seventies.

Private and public agencies responded to the pressure from below through a series of initiatives made more or less begrudgingly. Yale, which was pulled into the maelstrom in 1967 when Fred Harris demanded it house families burned out by the riot, established a Council on Community Affairs. It gave the Black Coalition $100,000, provided summer jobs to local youth, opened its athletic fields to the community, and established various black- and urban-oriented academic programs, including an institute for training minority public officials that was headed by Frank Logue, who would become Mayor in 1976. Business, too, suddenly recognized its social responsibility. Local firms established the Urban Alliance of Greater New Haven, as well as a related development organization. The biggest utility speeded up minority hiring programs, and banks set up mortgage pools. Minority youth were provided summer jobs (Powledge, 1970: 226–37). The city government put more minority professionals in high positions (including director of CPI) and increased minority presence in the police department. It also established new vehicles for service delivery and political representation. The result of all these reform efforts—combined with counterattack and an unknown level of police violence—was the pacification of minority communities. Many leaders found jobs with the city; advocacy organizations got contracts to provide social services; and the intransigent few were driven out of town, jailed, or killed.

Enfranchisement

Minority communities were granted power to implement service programs of their own and participation in the governance of administrative agencies with social reform missions. They were the beneficiaries of bureaucratic enfranchisement,[9] as they managed to capture some power and resources in local agencies which were funded primarily by Washington. Bureaucratic enfranchisement was extended by the three

agencies most centrally involved in social and physical development: CPI, Model
Cities, and the RA.

CPI was under attack from all sides, and by 1968 had slipped out of mayoral
control. Congressman Robert Giaimo attacked the agency for its fat salaries and
insensitivity to community needs (U.S. Congress, 1968). Arthur Barbieri, the Democratic Town Chairman who wanted CPI patronage, got the Board of Aldermen to
declare itself the city's community action agency, but Lee managed to uphold his
veto with OEO support (Murphy, 1971: 133). The Ford Foundation declared in a
secret 1967 report which was reprinted after the riot on the front page of the *New
Haven Register:*

The "executive coalition" strategy has resulted in limited, elitist resident participation at
the neighborhood level as at the city-wide level. Needed is machinery for large-scale participation. . . . Within a developing national climate of open urban democracy, no city can successfully keep to a control strategy in social development programming. (Report to John R. Coleman from Consultant Review Team, Ford Foundation, August 1967, as quoted in Powledge,
1970: 141)

In 1968, CPI announced its plans to decentralize. After endless administrative
and legal problems, it finally established eight neighborhood corporations in 1971
(one of which was in fact citywide, the Hispanic Junta for Progressive Action).
They provided jobs to minority residents and gave them multiple channels for citizen
participation. The corporations served as community mobilizing vehicles and were
relatively skillful at using protest as a political resource. Yet they also channeled
and institutionalized conflict and, as the seventies wore on, became ever more ob-
sessed with organizational maintenance:

The open conflict that once existed between city agencies and neighborhood protest groups
has been institutionalized through the corporations. Instead of protest and confrontation,
protracted discussion and negotiation are characteristic of the relationship between city hall
and the neighborhoods. (Yates, 1973: 53)

Fred Harris' street fighting became the conserving clientelism of the community
corporations.

From the start, the Model Cities program in New Haven was designed to be a
vehicle for bureaucratic enfranchisement. The City Demonstration Agency (CDA)
was established in 1968 outside of mayoral control. Under strong pressure from
target-area residents, the Board of Aldermen gave the Hill Neighborhood Corporation
(HNC) control of CDA. One interpretation was that the city washed its hands of
Model Cities to buy off the Hill (Powledge, 1970: 292). In any event, the federal
Department of Housing and Urban Development overturned the New Haven arrangement in 1970, saying that city hall had to have direct authority over the program.
This reversal was followed by several years of sometimes vicious conflict between
the Hill and CDA, much of which concerned the more than 200 jobs created under
the program. These, in effect, were divided between two major clienteles, the Italian
machine of the Guida administration (1970–75) and the minority clientele of HNC
and its ancillary organizations such as the Hill Health Corporation. But even this
picture was a simplification of the cleavages and shifting centers of combat associated

with dividing up the spoils. By all accounts, enfranchisement in Model Cities was expressed through salary lines more than policy victories. At its termination in 1974, more than one-third of program funds had been committed to administrative overhead alone (Yates, 1973: 50). The only legacies of the program were the Hill Health Center and Neighborhood Corporation.

The Redevelopment Agency, too, came under attack and sponsored new structures for citizen participation. But the pressure community groups were able to exert against the Agency was relatively weak, and its efforts at bureaucratic enfranchisement were correspondingly modest. The RA was pressed most in the Hill, one of its last urban renewal project areas. Community groups, in alliance with a white liberal organization—the Coalition of Concerned Citizens—asked for more construction and less clearance, for the RA to attack slumlords, and for citizen participation in planning (Singerman, 1980: 264–65; Powledge, 1970: 193). The RA responded by establishing community organizations called project area committees which advised it on clearance and rehabilitation targets. The most successful (from the agency viewpoint) were the committees in Newhallville and Fair Haven which were controlled by homeowners. The RA left the Hill alone until political calm was restored in the late seventies.

With passage of the federal Housing and Community Development Act (HCDA) of 1974, New Haven politics entered a new stage. Racial demobilization, new institutional mechanisms for political representation, and the frugal federalism of block grants combined to reshape development programs and interactions. The inertial forces of past programs continued through the period, yet the dominant objectives of local government shifted. Under the executive-centered coalition the aim was to make New Haven a new city, both physically and socially. During street-fighting pluralism it was to maintain political legitimacy and social control over the insurgent lower classes. After 1975 the objective was to establish a climate and set of programs conducive to the business class and to private capital accumulation.

CONSERVING CLIENTELISM: THE POLITICS OF URBAN DEVELOPMENT, 1975–80[10]

The Community Development Block Grant (CDBG) program became the main source of funds for a set of divergent objectives lumped together under the rubric of community development. CDBG replaced not only programs with a "hardware" orientation, but also Model Cities with its social service emphasis. It elevated economic development into a distinct goal. In ambiguous and constantly shifting regulations, however, it required that cities direct resources primarily to low- and moderate-income neighborhoods. CDBG thus became the centerpiece of a development game which pushed virtually all possible local claimants against one another. The fact that resources under the program were inadequate to meet expectations in 1975, and rapidly declined thereafter, added to the sense of urgency and gloom felt by the city's lower-income neighborhoods.

Although the focus of administration policy moved toward the right in comparison with the previous period, lower-income beneficiaries of earlier programs continued to press their demands. CDBG itself enhanced the power of both the mayor and the Board of Aldermen, with the result that each established new clienteles of its own. Our designation of the period as conserving clientelism is intended to capture these elements: (1) the conserving of past relationships with government agencies, especially the RA; (2) the conservative objectives of successive administrations trying to preserve the city's economic base; and (3) the clientelistic politics of material exchange, unstable alliances, and segmentation, which left only a small share of public resources for the city's poor.

In this section we examine more closely the character of politics within the housing and development arena during the period of conserving clientelism. Our evidence was obtained mainly during 1979 and 1980. We and a team of researchers interviewed more than sixty community, business, and government leaders, observed many community meetings, and traced governmental decision-making. The analysis is presented in two parts. The first looks closely at the allocational decisions associated with the CDBG program. The second cuts into the politics of development by discussing the roles of major actors—such as the Redevelopment Agency and business groups—their objectives and activities.

CDBG and the Distribution of Benefits

Federal policy, beginning with the Nixon election in 1968 and continuing through the seventies, aimed at reestablishing city hall control of intergovernmental revenue and reducing the political resources available to poor and minority communities. Community Action met its demise after Nixon's "conservative mandate" in the 1972 election. His "new federalism" diminished the power of both Washington and the urban lower classes. By the mid-seventies, major categorical programs for social services, urban renewal, manpower, and neighborhood development had been transformed into block grants. Requirements for citizen participation were severely weakened by Republican administrations and were not much changed by President Carter. The language of Washington shifted its emphasis from rebuilding cities and ending poverty to promoting fiscal retrenchment and economic development.

Political events in New Haven paralleled and were strongly influenced by the national situation. Community Progress, Inc., after years of contraction, was effectively displaced by Mayor Frank Logue in the mid seventies. Two of its major sources of funds, the Comprehensive Employment and Training Act (CETA) and CDBG, were channeled through city hall already. It was only a logical step for the mayor to establish a Human Resources Agency (HRA) over which he had greater control than CPI. The Redevelopment Agency held out longer. Its federal entitlements were guaranteed for some time, and it had a much more powerful clientele than the poverty agency.

Shifting federal programs were accompanied by sharp cutbacks in funding levels. New Haven was hard-hit because it had done so well in Washington during the sixties and had plans which required continued high levels of federal funding in the seventies. This was especially the case for construction of new housing on sites cleared by the Redevelopment Agency. By the late seventies it had become obvious that the Nixon housing moratorium of 1973 was just the beginning of federal with-drawal. The opening statement of the city's 1978 Housing Assistance Plan (HAP), which accompanied its CDBG application, reflected anger and frustration:

Although the City is required, under the HAP, to assess its housing needs . . . HUD, not the City, determines how many units of specific kinds of housing . . . will be allocated to the New Haven area. Unfortunately, these allocations have proven to have little to do with the level of need. . . . The City's previous and present Housing Assistance Plans indicate that over 10,000 City households are eligible for assistance under the Section 8 Program, [yet] the only substantial amount of new construction the City has received is for elderly (473 units). . . . There is a far more critical need for family housing. Funding is so limited, however, that only 72 units of the first 3 CD years' allocations have gone for family hous-ing. . . . The HAP itself can be considered a useful document only as it defines . . . goals and priorities for future housing actions in the event Federal housing policies and programs become more responsive to the needs of the nation's cities. (New Haven, 1978: 1–2)

The consequences of federal defunding were equally devastating for urban re-newal, Model Cities, code enforcement, and several other programs incorporated into CDBG. Here there was a grace period, however, as the HCDA included a "hold-harmless" provision which maintained funding at the same level received under the categoricals until 1978. When the axe finally fell on New Haven, it cut deep. CDBG funding averaged about $18 million for entitlement years I–III; by year VI (1980–81), the amount was down to $6 million (Table 2.11). When inflation was taken into account, the contraction in federal resources for urban redevelopment was extreme: the real 1980–81 grant was under 25 percent of the amount five years earlier.

The city responded by doing less with less. It eliminated activities for which there were no longer federal funds, most significantly, the construction of lower-income family housing. It contracted the CDBG budget more or less across the board (Table 2.11). In doing so it maintained the *relative* shares allocated on the one hand to urban renewal, and on the other to social services (renamed "public services"). Entitlements established by the clienteles of the old categorical programs and the semi-autonomous agencies which administered them were thus maintained. In this way the political balance among the government's constituencies was pre-served in spite of curtailed funding.

Lost federal dollars were not replaced by locally raised revenues. This was in keeping with the mode by which the city's government expanded in the first place. As we saw, federal programs were additions to a traditional government structure. The core government always remained fiscally conservative. Thus a business-oriented study of urban fiscal stress applauded New Haven for living within the means of an old, industrial city with little private investment (Touche Ross and First National Bank, 1979). New Haven managed to keep its own capital expenditures down while spending a great deal of federal money. Long-term city indebtedness was lower in 1978 relative to operating revenue than twenty years earlier (Table 2.10). Moreover, in constant dollars locally raised revenue was no greater in 1978 than it had been in 1962. In the absence of external resources, the city would not maintain the govern-

TABLE 2.10
Fiscal Trends, New Haven City Government, 1957–79

	1957	1962	1966/67	1976/77	1978/79
Locally Raised Revenue					
Current dollars (millions)	18	26	30	62	62
Constant (1980) dollars (millions)	51	69	72	83	69
Long-Term Debt Outstanding					
Current dollars (millions)	21	36	58	81	80
As percentage of total revenue from all sources	95	103	132	65	75

SOURCE: U.S. Bureau of the Census, *City Government Finances in 1978–79*, Table 5; *Census of Governments, Finances of Municipalities and Township Governments*, 1957, 1962, 1967, 1977.

mental activity which was established by Lee's executive-centered coalition and became such a matter of contention during the days of street-fighting pluralism.

New Haven's Community Development (CD) program can be summarized under three broad categories of activities: elimination of slums and blight, economic development, and public services. We relate each of these activities, or programs outputs, to an associated set of outcomes in terms of distribution to income groups. We also examine geographical allocations among neighborhoods, but argue that program mix and levels of funding are more important than territory in determining benefits.

Elimination of Slums and Blight.   The inertial force of the Redevelopment Agency strongly influenced CDBG expenditures. Table 2.11 breaks down the functional allocations of CD funds according to six classifications for the programs' first five years. The category "land acquisition . . . relocation" encompasses the set of activities formerly included in the urban renewal program. This category consistently comprised New Haven's largest use of CD funds, and in the fourth and fifth program years greatly increased in relative magnitude to reach a peak of 46 percent, compared with a national average of about 25 percent. The typical U.S. city spent a larger proportion of its funds on rehabilitation grants and loans than did New Haven (USDHUD, 1979: Chapter 2; Dommel et al., 1980: 121–22). The stress on neighborhood preservation incorporated in the 1974 HCDA, as well as the "back to the city" movement (Laska and Spain, 1980), encouraged this change of emphasis from demolition to rehabilitation. New Haven did mount a major preservationist effort in the Wooster Square historical district. In addition, it budgeted $6 million for two years (1978 and 1979) of its own bond money to finance a citywide rehabilitation loan and grant program, with a 1978 income eligibility ceiling of $17,000 for a family of four. But overall it persevered in defining its principal neighborhood strategy as clearance to eliminate slums and blight.

TABLE 2.11
CDBG Allocations, New Haven, by Activity, Years I–V and Total Grant, Years I–VI (thousands of dollars)

	1975/76 $	1975/76 %	1976/77 $	1976/77 %	1977/78 $	1977/78 %	1978/79 $	1978/79 %	1979/80 $	1979/80 %	1980/81 $
Public services	2,301	13	3,206	17	3,955	23	2,906	22	1,927	21	
Rehabilitation	625	3	3,178	17	2,283	13	—	—	840	9	
Land acquisition, demolition, disposition, relocation	6,652	36	5,278	28	4,320	25	5,539	42	4,228	46	
Public works, facilities, site improvements	4,376	24	1,846	10	1,735	10	760	6	1,080	12	
Administration and planning	2,087	11	3,090	16	3,789	22	2,922	22	912	10	
Other (including code enforcement, contingencies, etc.)	2,221	12	2,145	13	1,422	8	1,016	8	150	2	
Total[a]	18,262	99%	18,743	101%	17,504	101%	13,143	100%	9,137	100%	6,024
Total in Constant (1980) Dollars	27,796		26,966		23,638		16,493		10,302		6,024

SOURCE: Derived from New Haven, *Community Development Plan, Years I–V*, submitted to U.S. Department of Housing and Urban Development, 1975, 1976, 1977, 1978, 1979, and New Haven, "Proposed Community Development Budget," March 10, 1980.

[a] May not add to 100% due to rounding.

New Haven possessed an unusual, perhaps unique, example of a neighborhood-based clearance program in the Fair Haven area. Here the Redevelopment Agency bought scattered properties on small sites, razed existing structures, relocated the occupants, wrote down the land, and resold it to the Fair Haven Project Area Committee (FHPAC): "The PAC recognized early on that one of the primary causes of decay was an abundance of large, unmanageable, decaying tenements" (FHPAC, n.d.). FHPAC acted as sponsor, developer, and general contractor, constructing two-family homes which it then sold to local residents. It planned in the future to switch to single-family dwellings. The program resulted in new, moderate-income housing and the destruction of existing, substandard low-income units. But, while increasing moderate-income homeownership, it diminished the available low-income rental stock.

The Fair Haven operation was directly related to new housing construction. However, a greater proportion of urban renewal programming was intended simply to remove deteriorated property. Public and private construction and demolition in 1978 reduced New Haven's total housing stock by 179 units in the face of a low overall vacancy rate of 3.7 percent (New Haven, 1979). The 1979 Housing Assistance Plan (HAP) listed 395 units of federally subsidized low-income (Section 8) housing underway, of which 323 units were reserved for the elderly, but much of this new construction was matched with further demolition in 1979.

Many people interviewed commented that CDBG in New Haven was just urban renewal under another name, an observation largely corroborated by the program data. They welcomed the recent federal stress on preservation and argued that the New Haven Redevelopment Agency's persistence in completing old urban renewal plans was ill-founded. They contended that there was too much demolition and displacement, too much emphasis on downtown economic development, and not enough redevelopment in poor neighborhoods, either residential or commercial.

The director of a neighborhood development corporation characterized the city's program in his district as follows:

Right now we essentially just direct the Redevelopment Agency's purchasing and demolition activities in the neighborhood. They cooperate readily on the demolition of the buildings that we want torn down, but we have real battles with the Agency whenever we want a building saved. The Agency still operates under the old redevelopment plan for the neighborhood, which essentially involved flattening *all* of the neighborhood and constructing new middle class housing near the hospital.

The only respondents among the citizen participants who commented favorably on the Redevelopment Agency's acquisition and demolition policies were connected with the Fair Haven Project Area Committee.

One official cited the demolition of a factory in Newhallville as an example of harmful program effects. The Redevelopment Agency tore down the building as a "blighting influence" on a residential neighborhood, thereby destroying the jobs of 100 minority workers. Despite the Agency's promise of low-income housing, the land remained vacant; since it lay within a black "racially impacted" area, HUD would not permit Section 8 construction on it.

A high official appointed more recently than most of the redevelopment staff sharply dissented from the viewpoint, typically favored by city administrators, that the principal faults of the CD program arose from its broad distribution of limited funds and weak planning control.[11] Instead, he contended that urban renewal, as categorical program and in its CDBG continuation, resulted in "disaster":

The problem in New Haven was that the Redevelopment Agency was so strong that it never died even with the end of urban renewal. It has continued in the old way, like a dinosaur, with outdated renewal plans and processes. New Haven is one of the very few cities where CDBG was used to continue urban renewal plans. . . . Therefore, CDBG has been a disaster and has been used only to buy off community groups while the Redevelopment Agency has continued to implement the old renewal plans without any attempt to reevaluate them and change them. . . . Under urban renewal the city could make things happen even over the opposition of a neighborhood and all sorts of other forces in the city. Therefore, it tended to discourage and destroy private investment, and could thereby devastate a neighborhood. To the extent that CDBG has continued the urban renewal policy and program, CDBG has had the same effect in New Haven.

Determining whether the Redevelopment Agency's clearance strategy improved neighborhood conditions and was ultimately beneficial to lower-income people or not depended on a judgment of what might have taken place in its stead. Rehabilitation strategies produced gentrification and the displacement of low-income households in some cities (e.g., Denver and San Francisco). The typical restriction of rehabilitation assistance to owner-occupants discriminated against renters, who tend to be poorer than owners, and constituted 70 percent of the city's population. Rehabilitation often resulted in lower densities and a consequent reduction of available units (DeGiovanni, 1982). One of our informants, however, convincingly argued that such would not have been the case in New Haven:

Given the economic situation of the country in general and the Hill neighborhood in particular, gentrification is *good* for this community. Any kind of investment in the neighborhood is good. Without it the neighborhood would become a wasteland in which nobody wins, we all lose. . . . The real challenge is not the inflow of higher-income residents, but to find a way to enable the lower-income residents to stay in the neighborhood. . . . As a center of blight, this area isn't conducive to the growth of anyone or anything.

In other words, outmigration and abandonment in New Haven were so extensive that rehabilitation would not necessarily have reduced the housing supply available to low-income people. Clearance of deteriorated but still occupied structures, on the other hand, produced vacant lots and no new investment.

Economic Development. New Haven continued to use federal funding to subsidize business during the 1970s. Economic development activities were exemplified by a 1979 expenditure of $1.9 million to retain the G & O Manufacturing Company (see Table 2.12). The city spent $1.2 million of CD and $200,000 of state funds to relocate the firm and purchase its old site, "disposition of the remaining land and building [to be] initiated under an active sales program within a year" (New Haven, 1979: Project Summaries A–4, C–1). An additional $705,000 of CD money, as well

TABLE 2.12
Largest Planned CDBG Expenditures, New Haven, 1979–80, by Individual Project

G & O Manufacturing		$1,855,000
Purchases and disposition of old factory site		
Fair Haven portion	$580,000	
Dixwell portion	570,000	
Site improvements, new location	705,000	
Hill-Redfield—acquisition and clearance		645,000
Costs related to acquisition and clearance—nonsite specific		575,000
Rehabilitation loans and grants		503,000
Special Purchases in NSAs		500,000
Hill-Thorn—acquisition and clearance		442,510
Hill—public services[a]		373,760
Costs related to rehabilitation—nonsite specific		340,000
Relocation in NSAs		290,000
Fair Haven—public services[a]		283,150
Dwight—public services[a]		199,210
Legal Assistance Association		150,000
Dixwell—public services[a]		130,200
Newhallville—public services[a]		127,090
Fair Haven—acquisition and clearance		125,800
Elderly Housing Security		125,000
Total		$6,664,720

SOURCE: Derived from New Haven, *Community Development Plan, Year V.*

[a] General category includes senior citizens, after-school, daycare, youth recreation and training, health, homemaker, Hispanic cultural, and crime prevention services located in neighborhood strategy areas (NSAs).

as $4.7 million of city funds, was apportioned for street, sewer, and other site improvements at the Middletown Avenue industrial park, to which the factory moved (New Haven, 1979: Project Summary E). The purchase of the original plant, which would not otherwise have found a buyer, was, according to an official involved, part of the scheme to "keep them from moving south."

In January 1979 the city established an Office of Economic Development to use $1 million of CD funds formerly set aside, but unspent, for assisting small businesses. The new office's primary activities were funding a local development corporation, loans for neighborhood commercial revitalization, and technical assistance to small businesses. This new thrust represented a switch from the Redevelopment Agency's preoccupation with large-scale projects and the attraction of new businesses. A senior administrator commented:

One major problem with urban renewal was that it didn't deal with existing businesses. New Haven, and the Northeast in general, have learned that much of business growth comes from the expansion of existing business, rather than from the establishment of new business. . . . When you get this shift [in the employment base] from industrial to service, you have to think seriously about the commercial strips in a city; urban renewal didn't deal with commercial strips.

Nevertheless, the city continued to program its CD funds to complete previously planned, large-scale projects. The 1980 (Year VI) proposed CD budget allocated $1.2 million of the $6 million block grant (one-third, if associated administrative costs were included) to the State Street downtown renewal project (New Haven, 1980). The ostensible purpose of this, and previous big development projects, was to provide jobs. In fact, there was little evidence to show that New Haven's development program had not destroyed more jobs than it created; the Newhallville factory example was a case in point. Even where, as in the G & O case, manufacturing jobs were saved, the owner received a large public subsidy which he appropriated privately, a classic example of the mechanism described by O'Connor (1973). The city contended that, had it not been for urban renewal, its job loss would have been even greater:

By investing millions of dollars of urban renewal and Community Development funds in commercial and industrial redevelopment the City has been able to retain some of its largest manufacturing and retail employers, and continues to attract some light industrial and commercial business to the City. (New Haven, 1979)

Whether more or fewer jobs would have been retained under a different redevelopment strategy cannot be proved here. We can, however, conclude that business interests were a principal beneficiary of New Haven's redevelopment program.

Public Services. Public (social) services constituted the second largest expenditure category in all but the first year of CDBG (see Table 2.11). These mainly comprised old Model Cities and War on Poverty activities, such as afterschool programs, daycare, and services for the elderly. They were typically run by target area organizations which were previously federally funded and which now acted as third-party grantees. New Haven spent much more on such programs than the typical U.S. city, which allocated only 7 percent of its CD expenditures to public services (USDHUD, 1979: Chart II–5). CDBG in New Haven thus represented a continuation of Model Cities as well as urban renewal, and a further example of this city's effort to keep on serving the clienteles of previous programs.

Many respondents asserted that public services funds were misused to satisfy vocal constituencies rather than allocated according to need. As a result, cost effectiveness was seriously diminished, and fragmentation of resources resulted in the dissipation of the grant with little measurable result. Respondents complained that evaluation processes were weak, and it was difficult to determine the program's impact. Even supporters of the income-targeted nature of these expenditures doubted their efficacy. In the words of one alderman:

A lot of CD money was used to appease the neighborhood residents, to keep the natives happy and quiet. . . . Many third-party contracts and social service groups are a waste of money. There are problems with the coordination of these programs and funds in New Haven. And now with huge cuts in the city budget we can't address these problems very well. Poorly conceived and executed CDBG programs are often all that the target areas get; other funds are poured into the downtown area.

Administrators with the Redevelopment Agency, who recalled the days of urban renewal as a golden age, regarded CD as providing "something for everyone," in contrast to the rational, "nonpolitical" effort of the past:

CDBG lacks focus, objectives, standards, and it dissipates money away from a plan of attack on problems. . . . It is more difficult to convince private investors that we have the capacity to meet future needs in an area. CD lays it all open to political machinations of the body politic. . . . It is politicized to a far greater degree than any categorical grants ever were.

Officials traced inadequate benefits for low-income people to the limited overall amount of federal funds available, rather than to the city's priorities for block grant uses. While some felt that HUD restrictions, particularly as they affected housing in minority ("impacted") areas, prevented the city from employing appropriate means for low-income assistance, several argued that public expectations were simply unrealistically high.

Citizen participants and administrators were unanimous in identifying public service funds as rewards to particular client organizations. But while public services constituted the principal means by which CDBG was used to satisfy neighborhood groups, they amounted to only 21 percent of the grant. Two aldermen, who witnessed the annual hearings where organizations pressed their claims, reacted similarly to the contest for these funds:

You see neighborhoods competing with each other for very small funds. It is a demeaning process in some ways.

It is depressing to see the poor fighting each other for crumbs.

The arena, therefore, in which bureaucratic enfranchisement was principally established, represented but a small proportion of New Haven's total redevelopment effort.

Outcomes: Function and Territory. The CDBG application form during the Carter administration required cities to specify the extent to which expenditures benefited low- and moderate-income persons. New Haven classified 100 percent of its expenditures as such, reasoning that any action taken under the program constituted a benefit. According to this criterion, acquisition of substandard housing or site improvements for an employer comprised benefits to lower-income people if they occurred within a poor neighborhood, regardless of their actual effects on poor people. HUD, in its evaluation of CD applications, accepted the cities' claim that money spent in targeted areas automatically benefited low-income people, even though such was often not the case (see Rosenfeld, 1980: 226–31).

Further analysis of the distribution of program benefits reveals that the assumption of low-income benefits was misleading, as it did not distinguish between positive and negative benefits, nor did it differentiate among neighborhood residents. Geographical distributions mainly indicated which particular neighborhoods managed to be "treated." It was the kind and level of "benefits" which provided a better indication of responsiveness to need. If we assume that direct benefits to low-income people resulted from spending on social services, housing improvement, and public construction in their areas, then eleven of the sixteen large project expenditures listed in Table 2.12 principally benefited low- and moderate-income persons. In dollar terms, however, these added up to only $2.7 million, or about 40 percent of the amount spent on major projects. The program data (see Table 2.13) also showed an uneven distribution of funds to areas.[12] To an extent the geographic dispersion of CD funds reflected relative neediness of areas. The clearance strategy, however,

TABLE 2.13
Distribution of Planned Expenditures,[a] New Haven, 1979–80, by Neighborhood

All NSAs[b]	$2,439,300
Middletown Ave. Industrial Park[c]	1,855,000
Hill	1,625,310
Fair Haven[d]	647,650
Dwight	199,210
Dixwell[d]	130,200
Newhallville	127,090
Wooster Square	99,240
West Hills	96,000
East Rock	20,000

SOURCE: Derived from New Haven, *Community Development Plan, Year V.*

[a] Table only includes those expenditures explicitly attributed to neighborhoods in the plan.

[b] Primarily rehab, public works, and public services not attributed to specific NSAs.

[c] Includes all expenditures connected with the move of G & O Manufacturing Co.

[d] Excludes expenditures connected with move of G & O Manufacturing Co. to Middletown Avenue attributed in the CD plan to these neighborhoods.

implied that the best way to make poor neighborhoods less blighted was to expel the poorest residents; thus neighborhood improvement in poor or transitional areas could not be equated with assistance to those in most need. Neighborhood allocations also responded to the argument that investment should be directed to prevent the deterioration of still stable neighborhoods (the "triage" or as Downs [1979: 469] calls it, "opportunity-oriented" strategy).

To sum up: our exploration of the CDBG Program suggests that the vision supported by the Redevelopment Agency of a New Haven cleared by demolition of slums and blight remained the predominant program emphasis. In addition, there were subsidies to business and specific benefits to neighborhood groups, mainly for social services, but also, in the case of the Fair Haven PAC, for clearance. We now turn to the process of participation in order to discover how some bureaucratic and neighborhood organizations managed to achieve at least some of their ends, while others were excluded.

Participation, Segmentation, and Representation

Distinct spheres of influence and bilateral relations gave the CD program its particular flavor of competition and clientelism. The absence of any unifying force either within or outside government meant that the program did not incorporate a coherent set of priorities. Even the Redevelopment Agency's clearance efforts operated sporadically and in discrete projects, implementing the remains of twelve urban renewal plans, not one overall strategy. From the neighborhood point of view, the lack of coherence could be partly attributed to the absence of a citywide advisory board such as the ones in San Francisco and Denver. Since organizations were unable to form a coalition without an institutional framework to support it, they acted independently to gain funding. The splits went down to the community level; for example, in Fair Haven the Project Area Committee competed with the Neighborhood Planning Team, Neighborhood Housing Inc., and the Neighborhood Corporation. Each organization had its own local constituency. The success of FHPAC's construction program resulted from its close ties with the Redevelopment Agency and possibly from its predominantly Italian ethnicity.

Vehicles established for bureaucratic enfranchisement during the period of street-fighting pluralism lingered on through the decade and became incorporated into laocöon mechanisms for citizen participation under CDBG. Added to the community corporations and project area committees were a host of third-party grantees, generally small, not-for-profit corporations delivering social services and governed in part by local residents. When the city first implemented CDBG in 1975, Mayor Guida established a citywide advisory board, but the opposition of the aldermen (who themselves represented very small districts) and of incoming mayor Frank Logue, killed the board. Instead, Logue created yet another set of organizations. Like the RA's committees, his neighborhood preservation teams were open to all residents of lower-income areas. Their main function was to advise the Office of Community Development on microtargeting of rehabilitation and infrastructural expenditures—which blocks were to be treated. These layers of participatory structures created the organizations active in the housing and community development arena at the end of the decade. Most had their roots in prior federal programs (Table 2.14). Each had its own clientele which it linked through jobs and services with various city agencies, factions of the Board of Aldermen, and sometimes the mayor. A fragmented system of bureaucratic enfranchisement was thus superimposed upon the city's normally fragmented political structure.

In spite of bureaucratic enfranchisement, minority groups were never able to achieve electoral representation proportionate to their share of the population. During most of Lee's years there was virtually no black presence in electoral politics. But even during the seventies, when blacks and Hispanics had come to comprise more than 40 percent of the population, there was only modest improvement in their electoral power. Black mayoral candidate Henry Parker lost in the 1969 and 1971 Democratic primaries. Blacks then moved into an alliance with white liberals to elect Frank Logue mayor in 1975 and 1977, only to make another thrust for the mayor's office themselves in 1979. The result was devastating. The perennial, moderate black candidate, Henry Parker, managed to win only about 15 percent of the Democratic primary ballots, just enough to let former police chief DiLieto defeat the incumbent Logue (*New York Times*, 1979). Minority representation on the Board of Aldermen was often divided and ineffectual, though stronger than it had been. In 1979 there were seven blacks and no Hispanics on the 27-member Board, a decrease of one minority representative from the previous election.

As a result of their relative electoral weakness, minority groups had little influence over the major programmatic decisions in housing and community development, such as the policy of the RA or the share of funds it received under CDBG. Equally important, they were cut off from the large number of patronage positions dispensed through the Democratic party machine. Thus a study of how Mayor Guida dispensed CETA jobs in 1974 showed that he strongly favored Italian neighborhoods, in spite of the much greater need of black and Hispanic areas (Johnston, 1979: 393). Its author concluded: "The importance of ethnic particularism in the New Haven case . . . suggests that if a machine is to benefit blacks . . . it had better be a black-led machine" (397). The inability to control the mayor's office was especially important given actions taken by the federal government which transferred power from communities to city hall, and then reduced the flow of program funds into cities.

Because New Haven did not establish a structure of institutions at either the neighborhood or city levels to give permanent representation to community groups, participation was limited in scope and sporadic. Allocation of public service money constituted the principal battleground; for minority residents public services were the only place where their participation mattered. Organizations defined themselves according to the federal program from which they emanated or the agency with which they worked. Their main involvement with the CD planning process was at the point when the mayor presented his proposed budget to the Board of Aldermen. At that time they devoted great energy to bringing their supporters to the public hearings so as to plead for their particular request. The majority of organizational leaders felt that lobbying the aldermen was their sole input. Funding was uncertain

TABLE 2.14

Sample of Organizations and Groups Active in Housing and Community Development Arena, New Haven, 1980

Name	Area or Social Group Represented	Program Origin/Decade Founded	Sources of Funds			Activities			
			Private	Non-CDBG Government	CDBG	Hardware and Housing Assistance	Public Services	Planning	Community Mobilization and/or Advocacy
Home Maintenance Corp.	Hill	UR/CDBG 1970s		o	o	o			
People Acting for Change	Hill	1970s	o	o	o		o		o
Hill Health Center	Hill	CAP 1960s	o	o	o		o		
Project More	Hill	CAP 1960s	o	o			o		
Christian Community Action	Hill	1960s	o		o		o		o
Hill Cooper Youth Services Preservation	Hill	CAP 1960s	o	o	o		o		
Hill Neighborhood Planning Team	Hill	CDBG 1970s			o			o	
Upper Hill Project Area Community	Hill	UR/CDBG 1970s		o	o	o		o	
Latino Youth Development	Hispanic Hill/ Fair Haven	1970s		o	o		o		
Junta for Progressive Action	Hispanic Hill/Fair Haven/Dwight	1960s	o	o	o		o		
Spanish Cultural Association	Citywide Hispanic	1960s		o	o		o		
New Homes, Inc. (Div. of Urban League)	Black/low income Hill/ Newhallville	UR/CAP 1960s	o	o		o			o

TABLE 2.14 (continued)

Name	Area or Social Group Represented	Program Origin/ Decade Founded	Source of Funds			Activities			
			Private	Non-CDBG Government	CDBG	Hardware and Housing Assistance	Public Services	Planning	Community Mobilization and/or Advocacy
Newhallville Neighborhood Corp.	Newhallville	UR/CAP 1960s		o	o		o		o
Dixwell Community House[a]	Dixwell	UR/CAP 1950s	o	o	o		o		
Dixwell Neighborhood Corp.	Dixwell	UR/CAP 1960s	o	o			o		
Dwight Neighborhood Preservation Planning Team	Dwight	CDBG 1970s			o			o	
Neighborhood Housing, Inc.	Fair Haven	1970s	o	o	o	o			
Fair Haven Project Area Community	Fair Haven	UR 1960s	o	o		o		o	
Farnam Neighborhood House	Fair Haven	1960s	o	o	o		o		
Fair Haven Neighborhood Corp.	Fair Haven	CAP 1960s		o			o		
Fair Haven Neighborhood Preservation Team	Fair Haven	CDBG 1970s			o			o	
Wooster Square Neighborhood Preservation Team	Wooster Sq.	CDBG 1970s			o			o	
Regional Rehab. Institute	New Haven SMSA	HUD 1970s	o	o	o			o	
New Haven Legal Assistance	Citywide Lower income	CAP 1960s	o	o	o		o		o

SOURCE: Field research by authors.

[a] Dixwell Community House originated in the 1920s, but took on an expanded mission in the 1950s.

from one year to the next. Citizen activity in implementation was primarily limited to the software programs; participation in evaluation was nonexistent.

Community leaders, even when they profited from it, portrayed the process in unflattering terms. The executive director of a service agency described the relationship between participation and benefits as follows:

The strongest groups survive. It is internal structure and political assertiveness that leads to survival. Home Maintenance Corporation is a good example of this and the power of lobbying. A media campaign and connections enabled Legal Assistance to avoid CD reductions and cutting back neighborhood offices. Project More is very politically connected, especially with the state. The Project for Battered Women had HMC support and battered women are in the climate of opinion. Junta and Latino Youth Development are in because they needed Hispanics.

One of the few community supporters of urban renewal observed:

The whole CD process is a political football. Urban renewal was straightforward, you followed the plan. Now you have to fight the Hill, Dixwell. It's pitting neighborhood against neighborhood.

An alderman declared:

Some groups get funded which shouldn't get it because of political expediency, and others may support it just to get their own proposals through. There is no question that CD third-party grantee organizations provide political constituencies for aldermen, even direct help to candidates. . . . Those who really need are not organized, never get the money.

Another alderman commented:

The mayor [Logue], of course, also has connections with community groups. However, these connections seem to me to be looser than those of some of the members of the Board of Aldermen. . . . His appeal seems to be more as a hardheaded manager of the city's fiscal affairs. Nonetheless, he does have groups which he supports and groups that he opposes. His action is more in the way of a veto. If a group comes out in opposition to his candidacy, they are very likely to be hurt in the CD allocation process, to the extent that he can overcome the initiative of members of the Board of Aldermen.

The president of a neighborhood corporation board said: "If you don't know the right ones, you just don't get." The staff head of one of the organizations most successful in gaining additional funding from the aldermen noted: "The really poor are embarrassed by their issues and are not organized."

Board of Aldermen.   As the preceding discussion reveals, New Haven's Board of Aldermen played a leading part in the CD planning process. An insider described it this way:

The Board of Aldermen has taken on a much greater role in recent years. I do not think this has had very much to do with federal programs, but there has been a major change in local politics in New Haven, such that inner city neighborhoods are now becoming increasingly represented through the Board of Aldermen. As a result, in contrast to the first couple of years of the CD program, more CD resources are now being directed to poor areas. Aldermen have begun to take much more initiative in relation to the professionals and bureaucrats.

The unreformed nature of New Haven's government led the aldermen to become unusually involved in customarily administrative matters. In contrast to many other cities, the CD application was by no means a finished product when it reached the council. The aldermen moved large sums among budget categories. Since they were susceptible to pressures from neighborhood constituencies, they acted as the principal channel for bureaucratic enfranchisement. Thus *New Haven evidenced a somewhat unusual consolidation of the bureaucratic and electoral circuits of representation through the legislative body.* A mayoral staffer saw this anomaly as wholly counterproductive:

People come in to those [aldermanic] hearings and literally beg and cry. I feel this procedure is dead wrong and doesn't work. This sort of nastiness will occur in any program that has to be approved by a political body of elected officials with constituencies, through a public-hearing process. The whole problem is that this procedure is wrong in terms of our theories of government. These are properly executive branch decisions being made by the legislative branch. For example, imagine the Congress holding public hearings on the federal defense budget. Yet here the legislature has the authority to approve a budget on a line-item basis. So it's a constant battle between the executive and legislative branches over who has what powers.

Indeed, there were disadvantages to citizen groups in this mode of participation, as opposed to one where they participated on a year-round basis through administrative mechanisms. By the time the program reached the Board of Aldermen, the planning process was in its final stage. While funds could be shifted in response to pressures from vocal groups, it was too late to reformulate the overall priorities of the plan. Moreover, the absence of staff controlled by the aldermen made it impossible for them to evaluate past performance or develop an overarching strategy that might better reflect constituency interests. Therefore, while the aldermen did provide a vehicle for enfranchisement, the results took on the piecemeal form that frequently characterizes legislative policymaking.

Redevelopment Agency. The Redevelopment Agency, despite the demise of the program which created it and the loss of its independence as the direct recipient of federal funds, retained considerable influence over the CD program until its termination in 1981. It shrank from its former stature of 700 staff to a mere 70, but it continued to formulate the CD plan, thus providing the agenda to which all other parties had to react. It managed to retain its hold on power through the acumen of its director; its protected status as a result of having its own board; the momentum of old programs, commitments, and favors; the maintenance of its own neighborhood constituencies in the project area committees; and its control of information and technical expertise. It was protected, too, by the program segmentation incorporated in CDBG, with its separation of social and physical programs. HUD regulations prevented social services from cutting deeply into the allocations for physical development. Since most community demands centered on this portion of the budget, decisions on the larger physical part proceeded relatively unchallenged, rationalized as they were by prior commitments under the old urban renewal program.

The key role of the Redevelopment Agency, however, was not simply the consequence of bureaucratic domination. The Agency's programs embodied two sets of

interests, which did not need to assert themselves in order for the Agency to act
on their behalf. One was business, which profited from the Agency's support of
capital accumulation. Especially downtown business benefited from urban renewal
plans still being implemented by the Agency—first, from the subsidies to development; and second, from the clearing of a buffer area around downtown so that
lower class people did not encroach on the central shopping and office core. Middle-
class residents comprised the second interest which gained advantages from Agency
activities. These citizens benefited from a more attractive downtown, the removal
of lower-income people from their proximity, and improvement in property values.

Mayor.   The demands of neighborhood groups, the increased authority of the Board
of Aldermen, and the prominence of the Redevelopment Agency were all at the
expense of the authority of the mayor. With the demise of Richard Lee's executive-
centered coalition, the glue that bound together administrative and elected, public
and private entities disappeared. As a competing force among the multitude of rival
actors, the mayor's office offered an additional vehicle for access to those community
groups closely associated with his electoral coalition; the nature of these groups
shifted according to the particular person who was in power. The mayor's two-
year term, the virtual demise of an integrative party machine, and the narrow mandates and personal characters of the mayors since Lee all contributed to the decline
in mayoral power.

   Mayoral control was further diminished by the variety of administrative agencies
involved with development policy, only some of which were under his direct control.
These included the Development Administrator, the Development Commission, the
Office of Economic Development, the City Planning Commission, the Redevelopment
Agency, the Human Resources Agency, the Housing Task Force, and a plethora of
housing agencies. This functionally divided administrative hodgepodge interacted
with neighborhood groups, including the quasi-official neighborhood corporations
and planning teams, the district-based Board of Aldermen, and private organizations
with overlapping concerns (e.g., the New Haven Foundation, the United Way—
headed in this period by Richard Lee—Yale University, the Downtown Council,
the Chamber of Commerce, etc.). The result conformed to an amalgam of the two
governing models presented by Dahl (1961: 184) as characterizing New Haven before
Lee's regime: "rival sovereignties fighting it out" and "independent sovereignties
with spheres of influence." Before Lee, however, the sphere of government and
expectations for it were much smaller than after his reign. In the 1950s political
decision-making extended only over the electoral process, routine service delivery,
and a traditionally narrow group of capital expenses. Post-Lee, community social
services and private physical development came to depend heavily on government
financing and supervision. Thus the stakes for political participants were much
higher.

Elite Institutions: Business and Yale.   Major business firms and Yale University
played the same role around 1980 as twenty years earlier. Yale, large retailers, banks,
utilities, and manufacturing corporations were regional or national institutions, which

could realize their interests without influencing local political events (see Domhoff, 1978). Only a small minority of their executives were residents of the city. Nonetheless, they did involve themselves in urban development issues concerning the central business district, major industrial tracts, the environs of Yale and its large medical complex, and economic growth. They backed efforts to devise a collective strategy and organizational vehicle to express their viewpoint. During the period of conserving clientelism, business interests promoted the formation of a development commission, a major study and plan for the CBD—the "Halcyon Report" (1978), a planning organization—Goals for New Haven, and a business-oriented foundation—Downtown New Haven. The Rouse Company, a national real estate development firm with widely publicized urban projects, waged a campaign for the creation of a climate favorable to economic growth (DeVito, 1979). Henry Chauncey, a high Yale official and officer of Goals for New Haven, worked to make New Haven a corporate headquarters city like Greenwich or Stamford:

The top officers of 150 major companies received a letter in April from Henry "Sam" Chauncey Jr., secretary of Yale University. "If your company is thinking of moving," Chauncey wrote, "I hope you will look into . . . Gateway Landing," a $40 million office-hotel-retail complex planned for a site overlooking New Haven Harbor. Then he reminded these Yale alumni, all of whom are now in powerful decisionmaking positions: "The health of Yale is intimately tied to the health of New Haven." (*Business Week*, 1979)

The Halcyon Report concluded with five recommendations for the CBD: (1) more office space, (2) upper-income housing and cultural amenities, (3) hotel space and a convention center, (4) a major retail shopping mall, and (5) establishment of a downtown council representing Yale and business interests. The effectiveness of these efforts remained unclear as of this writing (except for the successful creation of the downtown council). Capital was not rushing to invest in New Haven. The very proliferation of objectives for New Haven suggested lack of agreement on a *specific* strategy, even if there was an implicit consensus that what New Haven did *not* need was more lower-income and working-class people.

After Richard Lee left office in 1969, the "progrowth coalition" which he forged in support of urban redevelopment became disaggregated. But business and related interests did not necessarily need to be unified in order to be served by New Haven's government and programs. First, businessmen and officials of Yale routinely dominated commissions concerned with matters of planning and economic development, and had disproportionate representation on other commissions, task forces, and advisory bodies. Second, certain programs were presumed to be within the business sphere. These provided benefits to private business and Yale in order to accomplish such public goals as commercial revitalization and employment. Thus the city supported an Urban Development Action Grant (UDAG) proposal for a $10 million project to turn a "deteriorating area" into an entertainment district (Belmont, 1979). It floated $20 million in revenue bonds to construct a garage in conjunction with expansion of Yale–New Haven Hospital (New Haven, 1979). Such expenditures dwarfed the allocations aimed primarily at lower-income people.

Third, owners of capital bargained with the city one at a time, using their control over jobs and tax resources—their systemic power (Stone, 1979)—to force special treatment and concessions. They threatened to close or move unless they were provided land for expansion, tax "relief," or some other form of public subsidy. In spite of opposition from members of the Board of Aldermen, the city "reluctantly" met the demands of three major corporations—G & O Manufacturing, Olin, and the New Haven *Register* (see Venoit, 1979). On its own the Redevelopment Agency arranged various land deals for a downtown furrier and other smaller firms. Such decisions were made incrementally in New Haven. They added up to a de facto public program of subsidy to capital, a program which resulted from the controlling position of business and the dependent position of local government (cf. Judd, 1979: chapter 12).

Fourth, business in New Haven and elsewhere enjoyed a systemic power which was realized not only by individual firms, but by capital as a whole through the content of public programs formulated at the national level. CDBG provided a remarkable example. For here was a program ostensibly intended to make lower-income groups prime beneficiaries. Yet because CDBG incorporated urban renewal, and permitted the city to use funds for economic development and for the elimination of slums and blight, the program provided business interests with a segment to which they felt entitled. While the overt politics of CDBG in New Haven centered about the allocation of the "lower income" portion of the pie, the underlying cleavage of economic interests was between expenditures aimed at capital accumulation (CBD and economic development) and those aimed at social consumption (housing and public services). The program was segmented (see Friedland, Piven, and Alford, 1978) in New Haven by the mayor and administrative agencies. Segmentation was not, of course, presented as a public decision, and high officials did not define one piece in terms of capital accumulation. Rather, they saw the choice as between, on the one hand, the particular interests of some residential areas and organizations which served the poor, and on the other hand, the *public interest* of all New Haveners in a city liberated of slums and blight with a large middle class, clean industry, a revitalized downtown, and, most important, a greatly expanded tax base that could only be provided by business and upper-income residents. The systemic power of business thereby routinely gave it benefits without requiring direct political representation, much less a fully organized business class.

Representation of Lower-Income People: An Overview.   Compared with their position under the executive-centered coalition, lower-income groups became much better represented in New Haven's government and programs. The interaction of federal mandates and resources with local political movements and disorder during the late 1960s resulted in new modes of bureaucratic enfranchisement. These were maintained and expanded in the 1970s. The outmigration of upper-income whites facilitated better, if inadequate, minority-group electoral representation on the Board of Aldermen. Lower-income groups had influence over certain programs and resources within the housing and community development arena. But they were not capable of creating a strategy for city government which might serve their collective interests. They could not use routine politics to overcome the segmentation of city programs, or the equation of business interests with the collective good. And they were too deeply divided among white ethnics, blacks, and Hispanics to create an electoral majority to capture the mayoralty. Increased bureaucratic enfranchisement in the sixties was the product of a crisis of social control brought about by mobilization of minority groups. The crisis of the seventies were created by capital, and the response was fiscal constraint, local commitment to economic development and business, and national withdrawal of resources for lower-income groups in places like New Haven. As a consequence, the payoffs for better representation in local government programs were severely reduced.

Suppose that over the years the relatively powerless in New Haven—racial minorities, the poor, small businesses—had been much more effectively represented in successive governmental regimes. Could there have been a redevelopment strategy which would have served their interests better than the approaches actually pursued? There was only one example among U.S. cities in similar states of economic decline where planners tried something different. That was in Cleveland during the years 1969–79 when Norman Krumholz directed the Cleveland Planning Commission (see Krumholz, et al., 1975; Krumholz, 1982). Cleveland planners developed government policies with the explicit intention of targeting benefits toward lower-income people at the expense of the business class and the progrowth coalition. To varying degrees they were able to gain the support of successive mayors. By 1980, however, the radical departure in Cleveland had ended with its results uncertain. We cannot determine what the outcomes of such a policy would have been in New Haven. It is clear, however, that a radical strategy could never have attracted sufficient local political backing to be implemented. Moreover, the relatively vast federal resources which the city obtained depended precisely upon New Haven being a model city for the imposition of extant federal programs, few of which were redistributive. The question which remains imponderable is whether the benefits of these funds actually outweighed the hardships experienced by thousands of New Haven residents and the destabilizing effects of redevelopment on the city's communities and economy.

NOTES

1. New Haven Board of Education and Community Progress, Inc., "Opening Opportunities: New Haven's Comprehensive Program for Community Progress," 1962, as quoted in Powledge, 1970: 51.
2. Calculation is the authors' and assumes that national per capita expenditures by the federal government over the history of the urban renewal program were equal to federal per capita expenditures in New Haven. For the purposes of this calculation the New Haven population is assumed to be 140,000 and the U.S. 200 million.
3. Data are for families and unrelated individuals. This is a better indicator of interjurisdictional inequality than is median income for families, since comparisons using the latter "control out" the concentration of low-income unrelated individuals in central cities.
4. In addition to the sources cited, information on urban renewal projects was drawn from the annual reports of the New Haven Redevelopment Agency—especially those of 1967,

1969, 1972 and 1974—from Singerman (1980), and from field work by the authors in the period 1978–81.

5. The article also reported that the Army Corps of Engineers had just approved the construction in suburban North Haven of a 1.1-million-square-foot shopping mall, which would equal the total occupied retail space in New Haven.

6. State Street was a product of the redevelopment machine created by Lee and the federal commitment to New Haven under the Kennedy and Johnson administrations. The reorientation of HUD with Nixon's election in 1968, combined with loss of corporate interest, brought the era of core-area redevelopment to an end well before this last project ever reached fruition. Much of the project area still comprised parking lots in 1980.

7. According to a senior official on the New Haven Human Rights Commission, minority representation was as follows: 1950–61, one black alderman; 1962–65, three blacks; 1966–69, four blacks. Maximum minority representation was reached in 1980, with nine blacks and two Hispanics, but decreased to six blacks and one Hispanic in 1982.

8. It is, of course, true that the cash contribution was a one-time outlay while the tax increment presumably would be realized over many years. But a counterfactor here is the debt service on the city's $40 million or so in-kind outlay. We did not consider the latter in our fiscal accounting.

9. By *bureaucratic enfranchisement* we mean political representation on the "output" side of government, usually through client- or neighborhood-based boards which oversee agency operations and program implementation. Various citizen-participation mechanisms are one means to increased bureaucratic enfranchisement. In contrast, *electoral enfranchisement* defines political representation on the "input" side of government, through election of mayor and city council who set policy for the city government. (See the introductory chapter of this volume.)

10. Most of the field research for the following discussion of the CDBG program was conducted in New Haven during 1978–80 under the auspices of the Community Development Strategies Evaluation. This research project was sponsored by the U.S. Department of Housing and Urban Development (HUD) and conducted through a cooperative agreement with the University of Pennsylvania School of Urban and Public Policy. The authors of this chapter were members of the project staff over the period 1978–80. However, findings and conclusions reported here are not official products of the research supported by HUD, nor do the views of the authors necessarily reflect those of the University of Pennsylvania or of the U.S. government.

11. This group of administrators tended to see the problem not in clearance, but in not *enough* clearance or in insufficient resources to finish the job started in earlier, better-funded years. A member of Mayor Logue's staff described the planning process and the difficulties presented by reduced HUD funding as follows: "When working out our proposal, we use as a base point previously planned, uncompleted urban renewal projects. We estimate it would take $100 million to complete all these projects. We prioritize these projects; these planned urban renewal projects are all obligations, commitments that have all gone through the long local approval process, plans which we've promised are going to eventually be completed. Unfortunately HUD doesn't realize or acknowledge the fact that these are obligations and commitments which we have already made."

12. With regard to geographical distribution of benefits (Table 2.13), if we exclude the sums apportioned generally to unspecified areas and the G & O relocation, the Hill received by far the greatest amount of program benefits. While it was one of the worst-off sections of New Haven as measured by housing quality, poverty, and ghettoization, it continued to have some predominantly white census tracts and a number of handsomely rehabilitated

Victorian homes. Relatively little urban renewal money was spent in the area, but it was a Model Cities site. The large public services expenditures here (see Table 2.12) were directed to agencies spawned under the earlier program. Fair Haven, the next largest recipient, was a racially and ethnically mixed area with a large population of Italian descent. It had a substantial stock of one- and two-family frame houses as well as a number of units of public housing. Dwight, third in rank, resembled Fair Haven in its mixed racial and ethnic composition, but its white population was more ethnically heterogeneous and its original housing stock of a higher quality. Dixwell was the home of approximately 50 percent of New Haven's black population. Reminders of earlier urban renewal activities existed in Dixwell's vacant $2 million shopping plaza, the little-used community center, the deteriorated federally assisted (Section 236) housing units, and the vacant tracts of undeveloped land, now cleared of slums and blight. Newhallville was also predominantly black and represented a continuation of Dixwell. It was the recipient area for many blacks who were displaced from the central business district during the first stages of urban renewal. Wooster Square was a centrally located, economically and ethnically mixed neighborhood with an influx of young professionals and an historical district designation. West Hills and East Rock were relatively affluent sections of the city.

REFERENCES

Belmont, J. 1979. "City officials support Schiavone's proposals." *New Haven Register,* March 7: 52.

Business Week. 1979. June 18: 42.

Cahn, Edgar, and Jean Cahn. 1964. "The War on Poverty: a civilian perspective." *Yale Law Journal* 73: 1317–52.

Dahl, Robert. 1961. *Who Governs?* New Haven: Yale University Press.

DeGiovanni, Frank. 1982. "An examination of selected consequences of revitalization in six U.S. cities." Paper presented at Symposium on the Changing Face of Urban America, University of Cincinnati, April 29.

DeVito, M. 1979. "New urban renaissance has to be a cooperative venture." *New Haven Register,* December 12: 19.

Domhoff, William. 1978. *Who Really Rules?* Santa Monica, CA: Goodyear.

Dommel, Paul, et al. 1980. *Targeting Community Development.* Third Report on the Brookings Institution Monitoring Study of the Community Development Block Grant Program. Washington, D.C.: U.S. Department of Housing and Urban Development.

Downs, Anthony. 1979. "Key relationships between urban development and neighborhood change." *Journal of the American Planning Association* 45 (October): 462–72.

Fair Haven Project Area Committee. n.d. *Action Not Words, Housing Program.* New Haven.

Fogelson, Robert M., and Robert Hill. 1968. "Who riots? A study of participation in the 1967 riots." Pp. 217–44 in *Supplemental Studies for the National Advisory Commission on Civil Disorders.* New York: Praeger.

Freed, Donald. 1973. *Agony in New Haven.* New York: Simon and Schuster.

Freedman, Samuel. 1982. "Will North Haven's big mall be New Haven's death knell?" *The New York Times,* February 21.

Friedland, Roger, Robert Alford, and Frances Fox Piven. 1978. "Political conflict, urban structure, and the fiscal crisis." Pp. 197–225 in Douglas Ashford, ed., *Comparing Public Policies.* Beverly Hills, CA: Sage.

Halycon Ltd. 1978. *An Analysis of Market Potentials, New Haven Central Business District.* Hartford, CT.

Hallman, Howard. 1959. *The Middle Ground: A Program for New Haven's Middle-Aged Neighborhoods.* New Haven Redevelopment Agency.

Herbers, J. 1979. "Activist groups are becoming a new political force." *New York Times,* June 18.

International City Management Association. 1981. *The Municipal Yearbook.*

Johnston, Michael. 1979. "Patrons and clients, jobs and machines: a case study of the uses of patronage." *American Political Science Review* 73 (June): 385–97.

Judd, Dennis. 1979. *The Politics of American Cities: Private Power and Public Policy.* Boston: Little, Brown.

Krumholz, Norman. 1982. "A retrospective view of equity planning." *Journal of the American Planning Association* 48 (2): 163–74.

Krumholz, Norman, et al. 1975. "The Cleveland policy planning report." *Journal of the American Institute of Planners* 41 (5): 298–304.

Laska, Shirley, and Daphne Spain, eds. 1980. *Back to the City.* New York: Pergamon.

Marris, Peter, and Martin Rein. 1973. *Dilemmas of Social Reform,* revised edition. Chicago: Aldine.

Mermin, Alvin. 1970. *Relocating Families.* Washington, D.C.: National Association of Housing and Redevelopment Officials.

Miller, William Lee. 1966. *The Fifteenth Ward and the Great Society.* Boston: Houghton Mifflin.

Mollenkopf, John. 1981. "Neighborhood political development and the politics of urban growth: Boston and San Francisco, 1958–78." *International Journal of Urban and Regional Research* 5 (1): 15–39.

Murphy, Russel. 1971. *Political Entrepreneurs and Urban Poverty.* Lexington, MA: Lexington Books.

National Advisory Commission on Civil Disorders. 1968. *Report to the President.* Washington, D.C.: U.S. Government Printing Office.

New Haven, City of. 1980. "6th year Community Development." Draft plan submitted to Board of Aldermen. February 21.

———. 1979. "5th, 6th, 7th years Community Development." New Haven: Office of the Mayor.

———. 1978. "4th, 5th, 6th years Community Development." New Haven: Office of the Mayor.

New Haven Journal Courier. 1979. March 7.

New Haven Redevelopment Agency. 1974. *Annual Report.*

———. 1972a. *Annual Report.*

———. 1972b. *Annual Report, Financial and Statistical Information.*

———. 1969. *Annual Report.*

———. 1967. *Annual Report.*

New York Times. 1979. September 12.

O'Connor, James. 1973. *The Fiscal Crisis of the State.* New York: St. Martin's.

Pack, Janet Rothenberg. 1973. "Household relocation: the New Haven experience." Files of Family Relocation Office, New Haven Redevelopment Agency.

Peterson, Paul. 1981. *City Limits.* Chicago: University of Chicago Press.

Polsby, Nelson. 1963. *Community Power and Political Theory.* New Haven: Yale University Press.

Powledge, Fred. 1970. *Model City.* New York: Simon and Schuster.

Rosenfeld, Raymond. 1980. "The uses of Community Development Block Grants." Pp. 211–36 in Donald Rosenthal, ed., *Urban Revitalization.* Beverly Hills, CA: Sage.

Salisbury, Robert H. 1964. "Urban politics: the new convergence of power." *Journal of Politics* 26 (November).

Singerman, Phillip Allan. 1980. "Politics, bureaucracy, and public policy: the case of urban renewal in New Haven." Ph.D. dissertation, Yale University.

Stone, Clarence. 1979. "Systemic power in community decision making." Paper presented at the annual meeting of the American Political Science Association, Washington, D.C.

Talbot, Allan R. 1967. *The Mayor's Game.* New York: Harper & Row.

Touche Ross & Co. and The First National Bank of Boston. 1979. *Urban Fiscal Stress.* New York: Touche Ross & Co.

U.S. Bureau of the Census. 1980. *Statistical Abstract of the United States.* Washington, D.C.: U.S. Government Printing Office.

———. 1977. *County and City Data Book.* Washington, D.C.: U.S. Government Printing Office.

———. 1972. *County and City Data Book.* Washington, D.C.: U.S. Government Printing Office.

U.S. Congress. 1968. *Congressional Record.* Washington, D.C.: U.S. Government Printing Office, January 18.

U.S. Department of Housing and Urban Development (USDHUD). 1980. *The President's National Urban Policy Report.* Washington, D.C.: U.S. Government Printing Office.

———. 1979. *Fourth Annual Community Development Block Grant Report.* Washington, DC: USDHUD.

———. 1975. *Urban Renewal Project Directory.* Washington, D.C.: U.S. Government Printing Office.

Venoit, S. 1979. "*Register* and hospital get expansion approval." *New Haven Register,* February 27: 1.

Wald, M. 1979. "Primary in New Haven defies the melting pot." *New York Times,* September 16.

Wolfinger, Raymond. 1974. *The Politics of Progress.* Englewood Cliffs, NJ: Prentice-Hall.

Yates, Douglas. 1977. *The Ungovernable City.* Cambridge, MA: MIT Press.

———. 1976. "Urban government as a policy-making system." Pp. 235–64 in Louis Masotti and Robert Lineberry, eds., *The New Urban Politics.* Cambridge, MA: Ballinger.

———. 1973. *Neighborhood Democracy.* Lexington, MA: Lexington Books.

3

Crisis in the Motor City: The Politics of Economic Development in Detroit

Richard Child Hill

The nation's sixth largest city, Detroit has a population numbering nearly 1.2 million encompassed by a sprawling metropolis of some 3 million additional residents residing in over 70 suburban communities. But the significance of the Motor City transcends its demographic dimensions. For most of this century Detroit has graphically reflected the dynamic and contradictory forces informing the advanced phase of U.S. industrial capitalism. Locus for the growth and development of the auto industry, terrain where the class relations between "Big Capital" and "Big Labor" were first institutionalized, national staging point for urban black political struggle, exemplifying the syndrome of problems referred to as the "urban crisis," highly touted model of the "new urban renaissance," and today at the center of debate over the meaning of the global reorganization of capitalism for social life in our industrial cities, Detroit is symbol and substance of the central economic, political, and urban issues facing our society. "The birthplace of good times and bad," the forces shaping postwar Detroit shaped the nation.

The automobile industry spurred Detroit's growth and molded its spatial development, while setting the rhythm of the nation's postwar cycles of economic expansion and contraction. At the close of the 1970s, one in six U.S. workers—14 million—worked for the 800,000 businesses directly or indirectly dependent upon the automobile industry: steel, rubber, oil, glass, service stations and garages, motel and hotel chains, parking lots, and highway construction. The interstate highway system, 45,000 miles of asphalt and concrete, amounted to a $72 billion public investment. Some 26,000 dealers sold as many as 14 million new and 20 million used cars each year to the 85 percent of families owning one or more of the 140 million motor vehicles registered in the U.S. Auto related expenses, consuming 13 percent of the average citizen's salary, captured one out of every four retail dollars in the U.S. (Cray, 1980: 7–10).

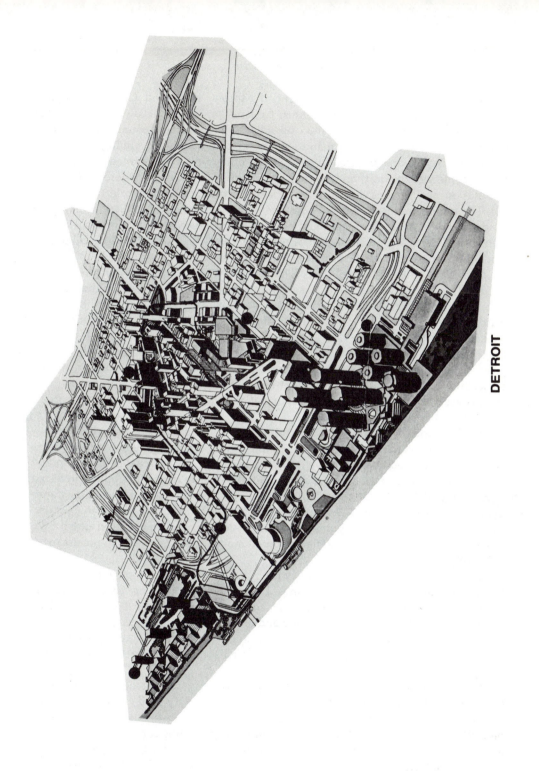

DETROIT

The Motor City's Big Three—General Motors, Ford, and Chrysler—number among the world's largest corporations. General Motors alone owns 121 factories in 77 U.S. cities and an additional 35 subsidiaries in 26 foreign countries. Producing one out of every four autos manufactured in the world, consuming $30 billion annually in goods and services from 40,000 suppliers on five continents, employing more people worldwide than live in Washington, D.C., General Motors, if treated as a nation, would constitute the 24th richest economy in the world (Sklar, 1980: 10). The public ramifications of the private decisions made and ratified in the world headquarters of GM, Ford, and Chrysler have structured the institutional life of Detroit and directly and indirectly affected the lives of tens of millions of people throughout the U.S. and the rest of the world.

The roots of the industrial labor movement were also planted in the Detroit region. The city serves as home base for the leadership of several of the nation's largest labor unions, including, most prominently, the 1.3-million-strong United Auto Workers (UAW). It was in Detroit that the early postwar confrontations between the Big Three and the UAW ushered in a new era of institutionalized collective bargaining and set labor-relations standards for other industries and unions to the present day. Productivity bargaining, cost-of-living adjustments, group insurance plans, and supplemental unemployment benefits have afforded this blue-collar city the highest working-class standard of living of any major North American metropolis (Ticknor, 1978: 268).

To the world of the late 1960s, Detroit also was identified with the urban crisis—the 1967 violent black uprising and the unemployment, poverty, deteriorating neighborhoods, misguided urban renewal, flight to the suburbs, and chaotic urban sprawl which stoked the flames of that rebellion. More recently, with $3.6 billion invested in and around the downtown district (including construction of the Renaissance Center), and with the scheduled construction of thousands of new and rehabilitated inner-city housing units, a subway and people-mover, and an enclosed downtown shopping mall, Detroit became a highly touted model of the "new urban renaissance" (Hill, 1978).

The nation's largest black-majority city, "Motown" is also a preeminent center of black culture and political leadership. Detroit's current mayor, Coleman Young, is considered by many political analysts to be the nation's most powerful black political official. Today, Coleman Young and his administration are leading advocates of a black urban economic development strategy—a political strategy designed to put to the test the meaning of the "urban renaissance" for black America (Hill, 1980).

Finally, the current crisis in the automobile industry, the threatened bankruptcy of Chrysler, the global reorganization of the auto industry, and the corresponding fate of Detroit, whose past growth trajectory has been set by the rhythm of auto production, have put the Motor City at the heart of the contemporary political debate over alternative reindustrialization and urban revitalization strategies in the United States (Hill, 1983). Today, Detroit is at a crossroads. What happens in the Motor City foreshadows the future of our nation's industrial cities.

DETROIT'S SPACE ECONOMY

Auto Capital U.S.A.

The economic vitality of a metropolis hinges upon its *export* industries—those industries oriented toward regional, national, and international markets. Export industries are connected to *complementary* industries which produce goods for use by the export industries. Export and complementary industries are in turn connected to local service industries which supply residents with "food, clothing, shelter, medical care, education, recreation . . . and the like" (Fusfeld, 1973: 32). Viewed in this way, Detroit's metal-bending economy is distinguished by its dependence upon one export industry: motor-vehicle production.

Detroit became a manufacturing center in the 1840s with the production of steel, metal castings, and the processing of food. Industrial production and population expanded in the city during the Civil War and by 1900 the framework for rapid industrial growth was in place. A pool of skilled workers gravitated to Detroit to work for industries producing ships, freight cars, pharmaceuticals, paints, farm tools, and stoves. But it was the city's carriage industry, the second largest in the country, which was to serve as the nucleus for the development of the automobile (Mutlu, 1979: chapter 3). And Detroit's location on the Great Lakes facilitated importing raw materials and exporting manufactured goods along the major waterways threading the midwest manufacturing region (City of Detroit, 1978: 11).

Spurred by the development of the automobile and mass production techniques, Detroit's central city population grew from 250,000 in 1900 to 1.6 million in 1930 and peaked at 1.85 million in 1953. By gathering vast quantities of raw materials and semi-finished products and converting them into finished, heavy, durable goods to be distributed throughout the world, Detroit had now become the hub of one of the world's greatest manufacturing regions and the heart of an urban industrial system. Connected to Detroit through transportation and communication networks were "the rubber plants of Akron, Ohio, and Kitchener, Ontario; the metal foundries of Chicago and Cleveland; the machine-tool shops of Cincinnati, Ohio, and Windsor, Ontario; the steel industries of Gary, Indiana, and Buffalo, New York; and the electronics and hydraulic research laboratories of Columbus and Dayton, Ohio" (Sinclair, 1972: 28). Detroit had become "the largest factory town in the world" and the auto capital of the U.S. (City of Detroit, 1978: 12).

With the exception of Pittsburgh, Detroit's specialization in one branch of manufacturing is greater than the nation's other major metropolitan areas. In 1958, over 41 percent of the labor force in the Detroit region was employed in manufacturing, with 38 percent employed in motor-vehicle production. By 1978, these figures were 33 percent and 41 percent respectively. Today, direct auto industry employment still accounts for 42 percent of the central city's manufacturing workforce, while auto-related work employs an additional 37 percent of the industrial labor force (City of Detroit, 1978: C–263). So Detroit continues to stand out as the U.S metropolis with the greatest share of employment in manufacturing and in motor-vehicle production.

TABLE 3.1
Total Population, City of Detroit
and Detroit Metropolitan Area,
1900–80 (in thousands)

Year	Detroit Metropolitan Area[a]	City of Detroit	City as % of Metropolitan Area
1980	4044	1203	30
1970	4200	1511	36
1960	3762	1670	44
1950	3016	1850	61
1940	2377	1623	68
1930	2177	1569	72
1920	1306	994	76
1910	614	466	76
1900	427	286	67

SOURCE: City of Detroit, 1981.
[a] Wayne, Oakland, and Macomb Counties.

Apart from auto-parts suppliers, three complementary industries play a special role in Detroit's economy. In order of size of local employment, these include nonelectrical machinery, fabricated metals, and primary metals. A large share of the machine tools, machinery, foundry products, metal stampings, and sheet steel produced by these complementary industries eventually flow into automobile plants and thus

TABLE 3.2
Employment, Selected Industries,
Detroit Metropolitan Area (in thousands)

Industry	1958	1968	1978
Total Employment	1,138.8	1,491.9	1,740.9
Total Manufacturing Employment	473.9	596.9	579.9
As a percentage of Total Employment	41.6%	40.0%	33.3%
Vehicles and Equipment Industry Employment (SIC 371)	183.3	232.8	236.8
As a percentage of Total Employment	16.1%	15.6%	13.6%
As a percentage of Manufacturing Employment	38.7%	39.0%	40.8%
Auto Related Manufacturing Employment			
Primary Metal Products	42.2	54.8	47.3
Fabricated Metal Products	51.4	79.6	83.1
Machinery Except Electrical	73.8	98.9	78.9
As a percentage of Total Employment	14.7%	15.6%	12.0%
As a percentage of Manufacturing Employment	35.3%	39.1%	36.1%

SOURCE: Potkin and Friedman, 1981.

tie their prosperity directly to that of the automobile producers (Sinclair, 1972: 18–19).

The Metropolitan Hierarchy

Experimentation among many small companies characterized the early years of the auto industry. But the second decade of the century ushered in mass production techniques and the emergence of a fast growing middle market for the automobile. During the 1920s and the 1930s small firms were gradually eliminated, remaining companies were absorbed into a handful of larger, integrated units, and these corporate giants concentrated their administrative operations in the southeastern Michigan metropolis, Detroit.

Concentration and centralization of corporate control over capital, technology, and organization, and the decentralization of production gave birth to a metropolitan hierarchy of auto cities characterized by four great spatial rings radiating from the heart of Detroit through the Midwest manufacturing belt to the rest of the nation and abroad. Corporate headquarters are located in the inner circle: General Motors in downtown Detroit, Chrysler in Highland Park (an incorporated city within the boundaries of the city of Detroit), and Ford Motor Company in Dearborn (an adjacent suburb to the southwest of the central city). The inner circle is bounded by a second ring consisting of suburban Detroit and the metropolitan areas of Flint, Lansing, Windsor, and adjacent towns. Here the administration, research, engineering, and much of the manufacturing and assembly operations are concentrated. The third ring is the integrated complex of parts, fabricating, and assembly operations distributed throughout the Midwestern region of Ohio, Indiana, northern Illinois, southern Wisconsin, southern Michigan, and southern Ontario. And the outer circle is the band of assembly plants dispersed in localities throughout the continent and abroad at strategically located distributing points (Sinclair, 1972: 36; Ticknor, 1978: chapter 3).

City vs. Suburb

The physical and social contours of the Detroit region thus emerged in concert with spatial growth in the auto industry. According to Detroit geographer Robert Sinclair (1972: 36), the auto companies expanded through a leapfrog locational logic. A new automobile factory was built alongside a major railroad line, in open terrain at the perimeter of the expanding metropolis, yet within sufficient proximity to the urban core to ensure an adequate labor supply. A new factory attracted complementary metal and machinery industries, and then residential subdivisions followed. Further expansion repeated the process farther out.

The first workshops in the auto industry located in neighborhoods throughout the city of Detroit. But as small shops were consolidated into large plants, new mass production facilities located along the principal railway lines converging on the east side of the city. These plants were the center of industrial and residential

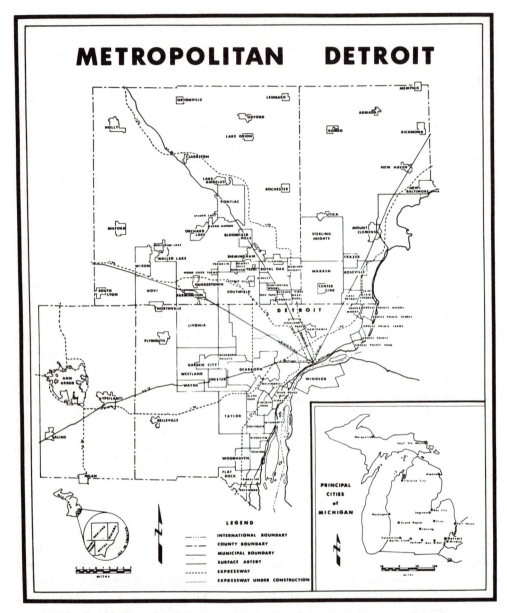

FIGURE 3.1   Metropolitan Detroit. (*Sinclair, 1972: 8*)

life in turn of the century Detroit. When Henry Ford built the renowned Highland
Park plant in 1913, the communities of Highland Park and Hamtramck became
locational centers of the industry, and northwest industrial and residential development followed. Ford next built the Rouge plant to the southwest of the central
city. And "The Rouge" became the dynamic center of one of the world's largest

FIGURE 3.2   Industrial Corridors of Metropolitan Detroit. (*Sinclair, 1972: 39*)

manufacturing complexes and the stimulus to Ford sponsored suburban development in Dearborn (Sinclair, 1972: 38).

So, prior to World War II, the auto industry developed within an urban core bounded by the central city of Detroit, the inner suburbs of Highland Park and

Hamtramck, Dearborn to the southwest, and Windsor across the Detroit river as the locale for the Canadian subsidiaries of the Ford and Chrysler Corporations. A few auto facilities also were located outside the core in Flint, Pontiac, and Lansing—southeastern Michigan locations for once independent companies now absorbed as internal divisions within the General Motors Corporation.

World War II gave birth to another wave of factory construction and spatial growth but now in the suburban and exurban fringe of the region. Past location considerations—major railroads, undeveloped land, and proximity to a sufficient labor supply—were now supplemented by a national defense policy urging dispersal of war production to satellite cities as a protection against attack. War-generated production facilities were constructed in Warren Township, Ypsilanti, and the Pontiac area. Turned over to private production after the war, these plants set the locational growth pattern for the early postwar boom in auto construction. Between 1947 and 1955, the Big Three constructed some 20 new plants in the suburbs of the Detroit region (Jacobs, 1981). As in the past, complementary metal and machinery industries clustered around the new factories, and residential growth and services followed industrial expansion.

By the early 1950s, massive suburban emigration had begun. Continued decentralization of the automobile industry turned part of the central city into a blue-collar dormitory for workers commuting to suburban plants. Automobile sales boomed after the war, freeing families and businesses to spread outward to green spaces on the city's periphery. Suburban expansion was facilitated by federal financing for an enormous freeway network. City officials argued that highways would bring commercial and industrial growth to Detroit. But in combination with Federal Housing Administration practices, which insured loans for new suburban homes while redlining older areas in Detroit, the freeway system further stimulated the suburban exodus of businesses and the more advantaged segments of the working population (Serrin, 1971).

Distinct sectors mapped the spatial contours of the Detroit region. Industrial corridors following the major railroad lines alternated with suburban residential corridors bounding the main highway arteries. Working-class suburbs emerged in the industrial corridors, often in chaotic fashion, often without central service facilities. Wealthier suburbs, housing the administrative and professional groups connected to the auto industry, developed along the radial freeway arteries, usually in a less haphazard fashion, usually with central services (Sinclair, 1972: 38; Jacobs, 1981).

Manufacturing plants moved outward along suburban industrial corridors. Commercial establishments flocked to suburban shopping malls. Warehouse facilities left loft structures at points of central city railway convergence for single story structures located on suburban interstate freeways. And the suburban office complexes drew professional service activities. So by 1970, the six-county Detroit metropolitan area was a thriving economy, stimulated by high levels of capital investment. It contained nearly 50 percent of Michigan's population. Residents of this Detroit were primarily white, lived in single-family houses located in suburban areas, and earned an income above the state average (Taylor and Willits, 1971: 18). But within the metropolitan area lay the central city of Detroit. During the decades following World War II this Detroit had increasingly become a segregated bastion of unemployment, underemployment, poverty, and near poverty amidst one of the wealthiest metropolitan regions in the world (Taylor and Peppard, 1976: 15–18).

Cities within the City

Land use and the social complexion of neighborhoods within Detroit follow the classic concentric ring pattern characterizing older industrial cities located within larger metropolitan regions. Class composition and physical quality of residential areas tends to be related to distance from the city center. The oldest, poorest, and most congested areas, occupied by the lowest income groups, are found in the inner zones of the city. As one traverses outward from the city center, the quality of housing improves, population densities decline, and the income level of neighborhoods rises.

The City Planning Commission groups subcommunities in Detroit into three zones—"cities within the city"—classified according to land use, age of physical structures, and degree of residential blight. They are: (a) The Inner City, within Grand Boulevard; (b) the Middle City, a three-mile-wide belt encircling Grand Boulevard; and (c) the Outer City, in the northwest, north, and northeast of Detroit (City of Detroit, 1978: 20).

The Inner City contains the riverfront, the Central Business District, Eastern Market, the Medical Center, Wayne State University, and Detroit's library and museums. But the Inner City also contains the oldest housing stock—much of which is classified as unsound.

The Middle City developed between 1910 and 1930. It is a densely populated belt of residential communities where 75 percent of the housing units are constructed for single families on small lots. The Middle City is a "zone of transition" in which housing abandonment and neighborhood deterioration have become substantial problems—more than half of the housing in this zone is considered unsound.

The Outer City developed in the late 1930s with the benefit of zoning regulations. Here 95 percent of the housing is designed for single families and nearly all is classified as sound. Residential communities in the Outer City cluster around well-planned parks and schools.

These "cities within the city" are the physical expression of unequal social relations in Detroit. Social groups bearing the burden of uneven development are segregated in the inner city and transition zones. The working poor and the unemployed live in neighborhoods bordering upon industrial corridors with obsolete and abandoned manufacturing facilities. In these areas population decline and commercial competition with suburban shopping malls left blighted retail strips, housing deterioration, and the decline of entire neighborhoods. Rates of infant mortality and diseases like tuberculosis show a similar concentration in the inner subcommunities and a decline toward the outer rim; so do crime rates (Sinclair, 1972: 41).

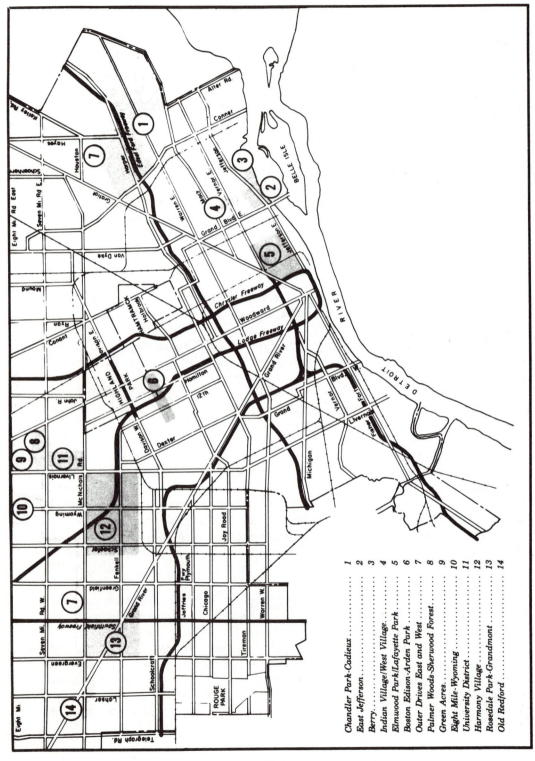

FIGURE 3.3 City of Detroit and Selected Neighborhoods. (*City of Detroit, 1978: 20*)

Chandler Park-Cadieux............ 1
East Jefferson..................... 2
Berry............................. 3
Indian Village/West Village....... 4
Elmwood Park/Lafayette Park....... 5
Boston Edison-Arden Park.......... 6
Outer Drives East and West........ 7
Palmer Woods-Sherwood Forest..... 8
Green Acres....................... 9
Eight Mile-Wyoming................ 10
University District............... 11
Harmony Village................... 12
Rosedale Park-Grandmont........... 13
Old Redford....................... 14

UNEVEN DEVELOPMENT:
POPULAR REBELLION AND ELITE RESPONSE

Detroit's black population carried the brunt of the social costs of urban industrial growth during the postwar era. The boom years of World War II lured Southern migrants to job openings in Northern industrial centers. Then, during the 1950s, the mechanization of Southern agriculture pushed millions of agrarian workers off the land. Primarily black, poor, unskilled, and unfamiliar with the urban scene, this wave of migrants poured into the inner core of Detroit and other northern industrial metropolises in search of work. What they encountered was confinement to lower-paying jobs, and prohibitions against entering most suburbs and many central-city neighborhoods by open racial policies, unwritten covenants, and the high cost of housing (Fusfeld, 1973: chapter 1).

The White Noose

The growing black population found residential space within the central city by expanding outward "from two core areas, one the original 'black belt' on the lower east side, and one on the near northwest side, into a generally concentric area within five or six miles of the Central Business District" (Sinclair, 1972: 48). White residents in Detroit identified "neighborhood succession" with "ghetto expansion" and all its ugly concomitants: rumor spreading, panic selling, and real estate blockbusting. The turmoil unleashed by this "succession" process undermined neighborhood efforts to conserve inner-city communities and blight spread rapidly through Detroit's central core. Detroit's landscape was now demarcated by a predominantly black central area, a surrounding belt of mixed neighborhoods, and predominantly white communities to the northwest, northeast, and southwest perimeters of the city—a pattern corresponding to the inner-outer distribution of social ills among the three "cities within the city" of Detroit (City of Detroit, 1981).

Postwar uneven development within the Detroit region also coincided with the concentration of blacks in the central city and whites in the suburban ring. Between 1930 and 1970, Detroit's black population more than quadrupled while the city's white population decreased by 56 percent. In 1940, 91 percent of the population of the central city was white. By 1970, Detroit was 44 percent black. Of the 757,000 blacks residing in the Detroit metropolitan area in 1970, 660,000 were residents of the city of Detroit, and 23,000 more lived in Hamtramck and Highland Park—two incorporated industrial enclaves within the boundaries of the central city. So while 87 percent of the region's black population lived in Detroit, only 36 percent of the region's total population resided in the central city (City of Detroit, 1978: 23). By the early 1970s Detroit had become a black-majority city encircled by a white suburban ring.

The small number of suburban blacks were concentrated in 5 of the 72 suburban municipalities in the metropolitan area: Pontiac, River Rouge, Ecorse, Inkster, and Mount Clemens. Pontiac, River Rouge, and Ecorse are old, large, industrial satellite cities. Inkster and Mount Clemens, on the other hand, are low-income residential

TABLE 3.3
Black Population as a Percentage
of Total Population, City of Detroit
and Detroit Metropolitan Area, 1900–80

Year	Detroit Metropolitan Area[a]	City of Detroit
1980	21.9	63.1
1970	18.0	43.7
1960	14.9	28.9
1950	11.9	16.2
1940	7.2	9.2
1930	6.3	7.7
1920	3.5	4.1
1910	1.0	1.2
1900	1.1	1.4

SOURCE: City of Detroit, 1981.
[a] Wayne, Oakland, and Macomb Counties.

suburbs with rundown housing stock. In 1970, the rest of suburban Detroit was typified by its three largest suburbs—Warren, Livonia, and Dearborn—which together had a black population of 186 out of a total population of 393,568 (Schnore, et al., 1976: 89–90).

Postwar uneven development within the Detroit region, coinciding with the concentration of blacks in the central city and whites in the suburban ring, enmeshed inner city residents in an oppressive pattern of social relations in the region's industries, housing markets, and political institutions.

A Dual Labor Market

Although a vocal advocate of equal rights and integration, the United Auto Workers never systematically opposed discriminatory corporate hiring, transfer, and upgrading policies. As blacks entered the plants in production jobs during and after World War II, the company and the union reacted with dual seniority lists, dual assignment of jobs, and other castelike divisions of the labor force (Denby, 1968; Hill, 1969).

As blacks moved into Detroit during the postwar period, residential segregation increased. Black neighborhoods surrounded inner-city auto plants. White workers sought employment in new suburban plants while inner-city auto operations became progressively black. By the middle sixties, some downtown Chrysler plants had a majority of black hourly employees. On the second shift at Chrysler the ratio was as high as 85 percent (Northrup, 1968: 45–46; Jacobs, 1970: 4).

Chrysler's older, inner-city plants dated from an earlier era and lacked many of the technological features of the newer suburban facilities. Company efforts to cut costs and generate higher productivity at the older plants were accomplished less by the introduction of advanced technology and automated assembly procedures than by the classic method of speed-up, now synchronized to the pace set by more automated plants in the suburbs. Speed-up in the aging plants was termed "niggermation" by many black workers, denoting their view that one black worker was being hired to do the job previously done by more than one white worker, that work was becoming more hazardous, that if black workers resisted the speed-up they faced harassment by white supervisors, dismissal before the end of the 90 day probationary period, and easy replacement by a new black worker from the large, surrounding pool of unemployed (Watson, 1969: 14; Hamlin, 1970: 36; Georgakas and Surkin, 1975: 106ff; Fujita, 1977).

Seniority provisions allowed many black workers to gain access to the proliferating suburban plants, but housing discrimination forced them to commute long distances, deeply embittered white and black relations in the workplace, and prevented active black participation in the union affairs of suburban plants. This pattern of "reverse commuting" reflected a spatial transformation in the region's postwar political economy.

In 1960 most metropolitan commuters traveled from a suburban residence to a central city workplace: 16 percent of employed Detroit residents commuted to the suburbs, and 33 percent of employed suburban residents commuted into the city of Detroit. By 1970, the balance had reversed. Now, 30 percent of the employed city residents commuted to the suburbs, while 17 percent of suburban workers commuted into the city (Michigan Employment Security Commission, 1975: Table 10).

Warren, Southfield, Dearborn, and Livonia offered the most suburban employment opportunities for central-city residents in 1970. Each is a large suburb adjacent to the Detroit city limits. Warren, Livonia, and Dearborn house large automobile plants, while Southfield is a financial and commercial center often referred to as Detroit's "second downtown." Over 23,000 black workers, 12 percent of the resident black labor force of Detroit, worked in these four suburbs in 1970. Yet only 177 black workers—0.07 percent of the total metropolitan black labor force—resided in Warren, Southfield, Livonia, or Dearborn (U.S. Bureau of the Census, 1971: 532–64).

Detroit workers who commuted to Warren, Dearborn, and Livonia were predominantly male and mostly employed in blue-collar manufacturing jobs (particularly as operatives) in auto plants and complementary industries. Southfield firms, on the other hand, drew upon Detroit for female clerical and sales workers. Blacks composed over three-quarters of inner-city suburban workers and were overwhelmingly concentrated in blue-collar and service jobs (McKay, 1973: 44–45). At the same time, median household incomes in these suburbs ranged from $3,500 to $8,300 higher than in Detroit. And Detroit's poverty level was two to six times that of Warren, Southfield, Dearborn, or Livonia (Markusen, 1974: Table 1).

Neoclassical economic theory implies higher suburban wages for comparable central-city jobs as compensation for the inconvenience and cost of commuting. A shortage of workers in the suburbs should compel firms to offer incentives sufficient to induce commuting from the urban core, or so the theory goes. But, in fact, inner-city commuters made essentially the same wages as inner-city resident workers employed in comparable jobs (Danziger and Weinstein, 1976). Inner-city workers were forced to commute to the suburbs without full compensation for travel costs due to the absence of employment opportunities in the central city. And suburban employers could draw upon a central-city surplus labor pool without having to increase their wage bill.

In sum, constrained to reside in deteriorating neighborhoods through high housing costs and exclusionary suburban policies, central-city workers increasingly constituted a low-wage labor pool for suburban firms. Forced to absorb the costs of commuting to jobs located in suburban jurisdictions in times of economic expansion, Detroit workers were politically isolated in central-city neighborhoods during downturns in the economy. And given postwar trends in the social composition of Detroit, the burden of this institutional arrangement fell ever more heavily upon Detroit's black working class.

Renewal and Rebellion

By the close of World War II, blight afflicted one-third of Detroit's central business district and industrial landscape. The city administration responded with the "Detroit Plan"—a scheme for subsidized redevelopment. The city designated redevelopment areas, condemned land, acquired lots from individual owners, demolished slums, and offered the cleared land for sale to developers at one-quarter to one-fifth of the acquisition cost.[1] The first two redevelopment sites bordered the Central Business District: "Gratiot" to the east and "Corktown" to the west. Both areas were occupied by poor people living in deteriorated housing. Gratiot was primarily black; Corktown was a blend of Southern European, Maltese, and Mexican immigrants.

Blacks in the Gratiot area were poorly organized and moved out with little visible protest—half those displaced "simply disappeared" from the Housing Commission Register. But the residents of Corktown, dismayed by the example of Gratiot, organized to prevent the demolition of their community. With churches and voluntary associations as rallying points, Corktown residents prepared a study challenging the city's designation of their area as a slum, and charged that urban renewal was a land grab to provide big business with subsidized property on which to build. Between 1952 and 1957 renewal was delayed as Corktown grievances bounced back and forth between the regional office of the federal Urban Renewal Administration and the City Planning Commission. But in the end Corktown went the way of Gratiot (Conot, 1975: 537–38).

Many uprooted residents moved into the Twelfth Street area on the northwest border of the Central Business District as their former neighborhoods became checkerboarded with high rises and town houses. But city subsidies were insufficient to lure developers to redirect much investment from the suburbs to the inner city. So once an area was designated for urban renewal, deterioration and slum formation grew even amidst the building of new skyscrapers.

In the early 1960s, the Kennedy administration sought to link urban renewal to its new antipoverty programs. Concerned with the hit-and-miss implementation of urban renewal throughout the country, "community renewal" was now to be implemented through a federal-city partnership. In 1962, Detroit had the largest Community Renewal Program in the nation. Detroit's mayor, Jerome Cavanagh, had strong connections to the Kennedy administration and saw the Community Renewal Program as an opportunity to establish central control and coordination over a myriad of overlapping city agencies. The "new technocrats" in the Cavanagh administration established a computerized "social data bank" to monitor housing data block by block for "danger signals" (Conot, 1975: 643).

In 1966, Model Cities was enacted in yet another attempt to coordinate fragmented urban renewal programs. A nine-square-mile section of Detroit's inner city, containing all the urban renewal projects and a population of 134,000, was designated the Detroit Model Cities Area. As with previous attempts at bureaucratic reorganization, opposition to the Detroit Model Cities Program was immediate, widespread, and intense. People employed in the federal antipoverty effort saw Model Cities as a rival to their programs and power. Since Model Cities extended the concept of citizen participation to all residents of the area, local organizations feared elite cooptation of the program. Activist community organizations with a record of struggle against neighborhood displacement (e.g., the "Alinskyist" West Central Organization and the militant Congress of Grass Roots Organizations) saw Model Cities as simply urban renewal by another name (Conot, 1975: 648).

By 1967 the jurisdiction of the Detroit's Housing Commission included public housing, urban renewal, neighborhood development, service and conservation programs, model cities, and numerous rent-supplement and low-income housing programs. Yet inner-city deterioration continued to outpace the resources of all programs combined. More to the point, urban renewal programs had actually aggravated blight and the lack of low-income housing in postwar Detroit. Freeway construction demolished over 20,000 homes within the metropolitan area. Lands containing over 10,000 housing units were taken for urban renewal projects. Those projects designed for residential purposes were meant to attract middle- and upper-income inhabitants. Since virtually no low-cost public housing was constructed in Detroit between 1957 and 1970, many of the poor were forced to "double up in already substandard dwellings, live in poor rooming houses, and/or become dependent upon landlords of 'slum tenements,' who quite often charged rents out of proportion to the meager facilities which they offered" (Sinclair, 1972: 48).

Higher rents, escalating insurance rates, loss due to theft, inadequate city services, and local "monopolies" led neighborhood merchants and national chain stores operating in the urban core to charge higher prices for lower quality goods. Inner-city residents were the least mobile of the metropolitan population and least able to take advantage of shopping alternatives. So the highest prices were paid by those least able to afford them (Bunge, 1971: 169).

The spatial distribution of political power and administrative control bypassed Detroit's inner-city population. At-large elections turned over decision-making to people living in outlying, wealthier districts. Police officers lived in areas removed from the inner city. School teachers commuted into central areas from outlying neighborhoods. Downtown merchants took their profits home to the suburbs. Many black residents of central Detroit saw themselves as employed, policed, serviced, and governed by an occupying army of foreigners who left the city at night and returned during the day to pick its bones clean (Aberbach and Walker, 1970; Hahn, 1969, 1970).

In July 1967, a police raid on an after-hours tavern in the inner city ignited festering black resentment into an explosion of arson, looting, and pitched battles with the police. The July 1967 black uprising left forty-two people dead and marked one of the most intense outbreaks of civil rebellion in the history of urban America. The "Great Rebellion" confronted the region's leadership with a fundamental challenge: Could they reach an accomodation with the black community of such a nature as to restore political stability? The stakes were high, for no less than a struggle for control over the city of Detroit had been set in motion.

An Urban Coalition

The Detroit region had long been dominated by the auto companies and a handful of complementary industrial and commercial interests (Ewen, 1978). Having made a postwar commitment to enhancing worker prosperity through supporting business expansion, the UAW leadership became the leading force in Michigan's Democratic Party and joined Detroit's postwar governing coalition as a junior partner (Greenstone, 1961, 1969; Stieber, 1970). Business and union leadership worked together in the Metropolitan Fund, Inc.—the central policy planning and consensus seeking organization in the Detroit region. A nonprofit regional affairs foundation, Metropolitan Fund's officers and board of trustees read like a "Who's Who" in the corporate world. Private business contributions and periodic foundation grants allowed the Fund to "identify and seek the best possible public and private alternatives" for solving the problems of southeastern Michigan. Through its research arm, the Citizens Research Council of Michigan, the Fund identified metropolitan needs and suggested alternative policies and programs; it disseminated its research findings and policy proposals to civic organizations, businesses, and local governments throughout the region; and it "assembled leadership support to implement action programs to attain regional answers" (Mathewson, 1974).

The mass violence in July 1967 shocked the civic and business elite into a determination to do something about the deterioration of the inner city. Detroit's mayor and the state governor invited representatives from business, labor, government, and the city's neighborhoods to a meeting at the City County Building. This meeting established the New Detroit Committee, the nation's first "urban coalition."[2] The New Detroit Committee was to represent all elements of the Detroit community. But its staff came on loan from various corporations. Joseph L. Hudson, Jr., president of Hudson's (the "world's largest privately owned department store"), was selected to chair New Detroit. Under Hudson's leadership, coalition members organized to pressure for federal and state urban programs and the channeling of private resources toward reconstruction of the central city.[3]

During its first two years, New Detroit allocated $10 million in grants to social research projects, summer reading programs in the schools, activities in the arts, and to campaigns for welfare, health, and police reform (New Detroit Committee,

1968). But its principal target was ameliorating the economic plight of the inner-city black population. With this aim in mind, the New Detroit Committee established the Economic Development Corporation of Greater Detroit (EDC). An effort to put white capitalism to work to promote black capitalism, EDC was designed to demonstrate that "the private business and financial communities are best equipped to lead the way in opening the benefits of the free enterprise system to minorities" and that "minority business development is one of the key solutions to our nation's problems" (New Detroit Committee, 1973a).[4]

With a few million dollars in seed capital provided through New Detroit, EDC gave financial and technical assistance to a variety of minority businesses and offered grants to the Inner City Business Improvement Forum (ICBIF). ICBIF helped establish black businesses like Global Gourmet (a meat-processing firm) and Renmuth, Inc. (a metal-stamping plant). Ford Motor Company made purchasing commitments to Renmuth, Inc., at a cost well above what the corporation would have incurred had it made the parts itself (New Detroit, 1973b; Conot, 1975: 785).

Yet black capitalism could do little to improve the economic plight of Detroit's inner-city black population. Self-employment and small business were declining institutions in Detroit as in the rest of the country. And small minority enterprises faced special difficulties. Their markets were largely poor and circumscribed. When their markets did expand, so did competition from large, white-run companies. The limitations of black capitalism were apparent in the city of Detroit. In 1966, 65 percent of the inner-city population was black, but only 38 percent of the businesses were black owned. Of these—mostly small retail and service companies—60 percent had an annual net income of less than $8,000. And urban renewal programs had devastated black business ventures in Detroit. Fifty-seven percent of black-owned businesses had failed to survive urban renewal as compared to 35 percent of white firms (Brimmer and Terrell, 1969). The $3 million in New Detroit projects made hardly a dent in the economic life of the black community when compared, for example, to the $14 million received by black workers from each wage increase of 10 cents an hour won by the UAW (Widick, 1972: 195–96).

By 1970 many of Detroit's major corporate heads were losing interest in the whole effort. One auto executive, referring to the calm that had come over Detroit, remarked in a *Fortune* magazine interview, "you lose interest if people aren't creating any trouble for you. There always has to be some tension in the air if anything is going to be accomplished " (Scott, 1970). Many corporations responded to the black quest for independence with the argument that addressing inner-city ills directly would only be construed as unseemly intervention in black affairs. By 1970, Chrysler had put one Detroit dealership in black hands but had done little else. General Motors had been even slower to respond to EDC pressure. This was the kiss of death in a city where smaller firms follow the pattern laid down by the auto companies—particularly the direction taken by General Motors. And GM adopted the position that anything it could do alone would be insignificant (Scott, 1970).

Run aground by infighting among various factions, and functioning like a small foundation, the New Detroit Committee was hardly equipped to promote the economic transformation of Detroit. So in the fall of 1970, "the top leaders of the top corporations in the Detroit area pledged to commit their personal talents and some of their corporate clout to effect a physical and economic revitalization of the city of Detroit" through yet another organization, Detroit Renaissance (Conot, 1975: 786). Detroit Renaissance was to specialize in the economic renewal, while New Detroit, Inc., was to focus on racial and social problems. Cochaired by Max Fisher, Henry Ford II, Robert Surdam (chair of the board of the National Bank of Detroit), the aim of Detroit Renaissance was to stimulate the rebuilding of the central core of the metropolitan area.

CRISIS IN THE MOTOR CITY

Suburbanization, institutional racism, and uneven urban growth defined the politics of development in Detroit during the 1960s. But in the early 1970s another impediment to the revitalization of the central city began to dominate political discourse: capital flight to other regions and abroad. Older industrial cities in the North, whose economies were dependent upon mature and declining industries (e.g., autos, steel, tires), were being critically affected by regional and international shifts in investment and employment growth (Mazza and Hogan, 1981).

Capital Flight

In 1972, New Detroit commissioned a study of the "exodus of nonautomotive manufacturers" from the Detroit area (Mandell, 1975). At that time 60 percent of the region's labor force worked for the Big Three auto companies. Nonautomotive employment was scarce and dwindling further as companies shut down Detroit facilities and moved elsewhere. The study was designed to afford comparison with Michigan industrial location studies conducted in 1950 and 1961.[5] This investigation helped clarify the sources and the magnitude of disinvestment likely to confront Detroit during the 1970s. Significant findings numbered among the following:

- Many employers wished to leave Detroit. Twenty-eight percent thought a move was either very probable or probable within the next five years. This compared to 15 percent in 1950 and 18 percent in 1961.
- Employers wishing to move most favored relocation to the South. Nineteen percent favored a move to a Southern state in 1972, as compared with only 3 percent in 1961.
- Detroit employers ordered the advantages of relocation as follows: (1) lower labor costs, (2) lower taxes or compensation plans, and (3) other "favorable" labor-force characteristics, including productivity, skills, and labor supply.
- Detroit employers viewed the "legal climate"—legislative acts, court interpretations, workmen's compensation, environmental regulation, local taxes, and local ordinances—as "far more oppressive" in Michigan than in other states. Three out of four employers said the Michigan legal climate was worse than in other states, none said it was better.

- Seventy percent of Detroit employers had no plans for plant expansion; 42 percent said they employed fewer workers than a decade ago; and 61 percent did not expect to increase employment.

Baldly stated, the study's conclusion was simply this: With dated production facilities, a public infrastructure in poor condition, and a highly unionized and aggressive labor force, Detroit would be hard pressed to retain business activity, let alone attract new capital investment.

Economic Crisis

Because Detroit's economy relies so heavily upon a "postponable" durable good, the city has been particularly sensitive to cycles in the national economy—an "economic barometer," so to speak, for the nation. During the first two decades of the postwar period, Detroit's economy bounced back with each upswing of the business cycle. In the 1970s, however, recession levels of unemployment failed to respond to national economic expansion. Having grown tough and resilient weathering the hazards of cyclical ups and downs during much of this century, the Motor City was now faced with a persistent, structurally rooted economic crisis. A few trends tell the tale.

Population Decline. The population of Detroit peaked in 1953 at some 1,850,000 inhabitants. By 1978, Detroit's population stood at 1.26 million—a 17 percent drop since 1970, and one-third less than during the pinnacle of its growth period (City of Detroit, 1980a: III–1).[6]

Employment Decline. Between 1968 and 1977, Detroit employment fell from 630,000 to 421,800—a decline of 208,200 jobs or 33 percent of the total employment generated in the city (City of Detroit, 1978: 27).[7] Detroit's sharpest employment losses came in manufacturing and retail trade industries. Between 1958 and 1972, the number of central city manufacturing firms declined from 3,363 to 2,378 (City of Detroit, 1978: 33). Between 1970 and 1975, Detroit lost 19 percent of its manufacturing establishments to the suburbs (Mattila and Kurre, 1977). Business transitions during the 1980 fiscal year alone produced a net loss of 8,400 jobs, including the permanent shutdown of Chrysler's Hamtramck Assembly Plant (3,200 jobs) and Eight Mile and Outer Drive Stamping Plant (1,000 jobs), Uniroyal Tire's Detroit plant (1,700 jobs), and Parke-Davis's Joseph Campau facility (1,700 jobs) (City of Detroit, 1980a: III–4).

Declining purchasing power due to reduction in manufacturing employment, and the shift of commercial establishments to suburban shopping malls sharply reduced the volume of retail trade conducted in Detroit. Between 1972 and 1977, Detroit lost 4,000 jobs in the general merchandising category alone. This included the bankruptcy of the Federal Department Store, the closing of both Sears' and Crowley's stores downtown, and the job reducing consolidation of Hudson's department store (City of Detroit, 1980a: III–5).

Composition of Employment.   In spite of the sharp overall decline in the number of manufacturing jobs in Detroit, the *percentage* of the city's labor force working for the auto industry has actually increased in recent years. However, automation and the performance of "headquarters functions" have restructured the distribution of jobs within motor-vehicle production. The percentage of workers employed in engineering, computer programming, clerical work, finance, and management has risen, while the availability of blue-collar, production jobs has dropped (City of Detroit, 1980: III–6).

Permanent Unemployment.   Detroit has been burdened with a much higher unemployment rate than the nation, the state of Michigan, or the metropolitan area as a whole. While the population of Detroit has declined 13 percent since 1970, the employed labor force has declined 20 percent (City of Detroit, 1978: 23). Outmigrants tend to be employed persons. A growing percentage of those left behind have been elderly, disabled, and permanently unemployed

In March 1972, for example, officially defined unemployment stood at 11.1 percent for the central city and 7.7 percent for the region. Yet a more careful investigation revealed that the city's unemployment rate approximated 18 percent, while 35 percent of workers residing in inner-city neighborhoods were without jobs. "Structural unemployment" is a catch-all phrase referring to a "mismatch between jobs and available labor supply." But there was essentially no "structural unemployment" in the Motor City in 1972. For 115,510 unemployed persons, the total number of available jobs (i.e., those listed in the newspapers, with the Chamber of Commerce, and with the Michigan Employment Security Commission) was less than 10,000. Unemployment in the central city of Detroit, this business-initiated investigation concluded, was more the result of inadequate demand for employees of any kind than a lack of skills or training among the unemployed (New Detroit, 1974: i–iv).

For Detroit, the 1974–75 national recession was an economic depression rivaling unemployment conditions in the Great Depression. An investigation of unemployment then revealed that "in February 1975, when the national rate of unemployment was 8.2 percent, the state had an unemployment rate of 15.8 percent, the Detroit SMSA had a rate of 16.1 percent, and the city's rate was 23.2 percent. But some city neighborhoods had unemployment rates more than six times . . . the national average, more than three times . . . the state average, and more than double the city's average" (Taylor and Peppard, 1976: 15).[8]

Surplus Population.   Detroit's bleak employment picture coincided with a rapid rise in welfare case loads. The increase in welfare recipients began in the latter part of the 1960s. Between 1969 and 1974; the number of central-city recipients of Aid to Families with Dependent Children (AFDC) and General Assistance (GA) increased from 80,000 to 256,000 persons—a total rise of 167,000 or 209 percent (Michigan Task Force, n.d.).[9] By 1975, 31 percent of Detroit households had no earned income, 16 percent survived on welfare payments, and 29 percent received some form of Social Security (City of Detroit, 1978: Table III–9).

TABLE 3.4
Occupation and Industry Distribution,
City of Detroit

	1960	1970	1976
Total Labor Force (thousands)	680.2	605.0	481.0
Occupation			
Professional	11%	11%	13%
Managers	6	5	7
Sales	8	5	4
Clerical	18	20	17
Craftsmen	14	12	11
Operatives	24	25	24
Laborers	5	5	4
Service workers	14	16	21
Total Employed	100%	100%	100%
Industry			
Agriculture, forestry, fishing, mining	—	1%	—
Construction	3%	4	3%
Transportation equipment manufacturing	19	18	22
Other manufacturing	21	18	12
Transportation, communication, utilities	6	6	6
Wholesale trade	3	4	2
Retail trade	16	15	14
Finance, insurance, real estate	4	5	5
Business, repair, personal, entertainment, recreation services	12	17	10
Professional service	10	9	20
Public administration	5	5	7
	100%	100%	100%
Class of Workers			
Private	84%	83%	78%
Government	10	14	17
Self-employed	6	3	5
	100%	100%	100%

SOURCE: City of Detroit, 1980a: VI–14.

Fiscal Collapse.   Capital flight, job loss, and the concentration of unemployment and poverty in the central city brought intensifying fiscal problems. Between 1968 and 1974, for example, personal income grew 122 percent in the state of Michigan but only 33 percent in Detroit, reflecting the rising percentage of families on low and fixed incomes in the central city (City of Detroit, n.d., b). Ranked by median family income, Detroit was 22nd among 39 municipalities in the SMSA in 1950; 41st among 58 municipalities in 1960; and 66th among 72 area municipalities in 1970 (Radtke, 1975: Tables 1–3).

Detroit's assessed property value rose 15 percent between 1966 and 1976 as compared to a 76 percent rise in the consumer price index (City of Detroit, 1977: 139). Increased service needs, rising prices, and stagnant property values eroded the property tax base—Detroit's primary source of local revenue. The city responded with increased income and utility taxes, and Detroit residents ended up paying four times the tax rate of the average city in Michigan. Even so, tax revenues fell far short of expenditure demands, the municipal work force was steadily reduced, and city services cut back (City of Detroit, 1976).

THE CORPORATE-CENTER STRATEGY

In the face of economic crisis and central city decay, Detroit's urban coalition renewed its pressure for federal and state programs—now directed toward augmenting the city's development capacities and creating public incentives to compensate for its competitive disadvantages with growth centers in the sunbelt. The political effort mounted in Detroit, and multiplied by similar efforts in numerous Northern urban centers, produced results. State governments in the frostbelt created grant, loan, and tax-incentive programs to encourage private investment—programs often targeted to distressed urban areas (Vaughn, 1979). New state legislation also enabled central-city governments, like Detroit's, to expand their local development capacity. State legislation authorized the formation of economic development corporations, expanded the city's capital-financing capacity by establishing tax-increment financing procedures, and broadened the city's control over its land by redefining eminent-domain authority to include development projects which prevent or alleviate unemployment through the retention or expansion of industry.[10]

The role of state government in funding local development projects has been small in comparison to federal programs. Important federal programs created or amended during the 1970s to facilitate economic development in distressed cities include Urban Development Action Grants, Community Development Block Grants, the HUD Section 108 loan program, and grants and loans by the Economic Development Administration (U.S. House of Representatives, 1980). These programs use public resources to stimulate private investment, and they help channel federal funds to distressed cities.[11]

Urban economic development in the 1970s thus came to be characterized by (1) the creation of local development corporations which intertwine public and private interests, (2) the growth of a "dual investment process" as the involvement of public funds in what previously would have been considered private development increased dramatically, and (3) a redefinition of the public interest to encompass private development projects which retain or expand jobs and investment.

The Corporate City

Working closely with the city's major corporations, and within the framework of state and federal enabling legislation and programs, Detroit's public officials created a structure and a strategy for economic development in Detroit. An Overall Economic Development Program provides a comprehensive blueprint and rationale for the city's economic revitalization efforts. And Detroit's development efforts are organized through a structure which knits together private development organizations and public development agencies.

Detroit's capacity to organize development centers upon a cluster of Economic Development Corporations (EDCs)—organizations now constitutionally authorized to wield expanded development powers and designed to coordinate public and private development efforts through a membership roster heavily weighted toward Detroit's business and civic elite. Detroit's principal EDCs—the Economic Growth Corporation, the Economic Development Corporation, the Downtown Development Authority, and the Development Corporation—are connected one to the other and to local private development organizations, city and state development agencies, and county and regional authorities, through a system of overlapping memberships modeled upon the interlocking corporate directorate system in the business world. The activities of these Economic Development Corporations are in turn overseen by an "Overall Economic Development Program Committee" composed of representatives from the EDCs, chaired by the mayor, and staffed by the city's Planning, and Community and Economic Development Departments (City of Detroit, 1978: Appendix H).

In the past, city government has been able to acquire land through urban renewal funds, and to provide public improvements through its routine capital expenditures. Today, state enabling legislation authorizes Economic Development Corporations to utilize public funds to acquire, hold, develop, and dispose of land. So now transfers from private to public ownership can be accomplished with greater ease.[12]

Economic Development Corporations are also authorized to wield expanded financial powers. They can issue industrial revenue, tax increment, and job development authority bonds, and they can establish industrial revenue districts. They can receive and administer grants and loans from higher levels of government. And they can offer further public incentives for such private developments as land banking and tax abatement schemes. This development structure has afforded city officials added capacity to leverage scarce funds provided by federal and state programs and has helped the city's capital improvement budget to attract private investment and to initiate private development projects in Detroit.

Detroit's current development strategy is detailed in its *Overall Economic Development Program*.[13] This development plan is organized around four general objectives: (1) to retain and modernize existing commercial and industrial activities; (2) to attract new commercial and industrial activities which have the potential to expand employment, sales, and tax revenue; (3) to improve Detroit's overall capacity for economic development; and (4) to increase the role of minority entrepreneurs in the economic development process. These development objectives are applied to seven geographical sectors which play individually unique yet interrelated economic functions in Detroit's space economy: (1) the Riverfront, (2) the Central Business District, (3) the Central Functions Area, (4) Industrial Corridors, (5) the Port of Detroit, (6) Housing and Neighborhoods, and (7) Transit Corridors.

The linchpin for *Riverfront* development is the Renaissance Center—Henry Ford II's skyscraping office, hotel, commercial, and residential complex. The Renaissance Center's location, design, and functions are meant to symbolize the rebirth of Detroit and the city's image of its own future. The Cobo Hall convention center and the Joe Louis sports arena further flesh out the city's intent to develop the Riverfront into an upper-income residential, commercial, and recreational area supplemented by selected redevelopment of industry compatible with riverfront uses.

Detroit's Central Business District (CBD) is the financial and administration center of the regional economy. New development plans include retail and office facilities, a high-rise downtown neighborhood, and locating the CBD at the hub of a new rapid transit system. The centerpiece of CBD redevelopment is the projected construction of the Cadillac Center—a commercial complex containing three major department stores, an enclosed shopping mall with 100 retail firms, a 3,000 space parking garage, and a rapid transit station.

The *Central Functions Area,* Detroit's "second downtown," is the region's center for cultural and medical services. Wayne State University, the city's public library, art and science museums, the Detroit medical complex, and the headquarters of General Motors and Burroughs are located here. Redevelopment plans include housing and commercial complexes designed for use by the managers and professionals who work in the area, and a "Growth Technology Research Park" mean to connect research and development activities at Wayne State to those of the area's major private employers.

Detroit's *Industrial Corridors* provide existing economic infrastructure, economies of agglomeration, proximity to suppliers and markets, and easy access to a surrounding labor pool. Here city planning efforts include redevelopment of sites to retain and attract large industrial plants and smaller industries based on the kind of new growth technology that will move the city toward greater diversification. A site for a major manufacturing facility is now under preparation (the Connor Industrial Project), and Airport West is being renovated for expanded industrial use.

The *Port of Detroit* has locational advantages over other Great Lakes ports and comparative advantages relative to increasingly expensive surface transportation. Port development objectives include land acquisition to provide space for containerized freight facilities, efforts to facilitate financing for modern loading and unloading equipment, and creation of an international free-trade zone.

The rising cost of suburban housing, fed by high interest rates and energy costs, makes the wide variety of sound housing available in Detroit *neighborhoods* an asset to the city. But population loss and redlining have led to blighted commercial strips and neighborhood deterioration in many parts of the city. Overall planning objectives include neighborhood rehabilitation, demolition of unsound structures, and promotion of neighborhood vitality throughout the city. But the primary focus today is on the creation of new neighborhoods along the Riverfront, Downtown, and in the Central Functions Area.

Transit Corridor plans center upon construction of a Woodward Avenue rapid transit line connecting the "first downtown" to the "second downtown," and both to outlying neighborhoods and suburbs. Also in the works is the development of a People-Mover System to facilitate quick access to activity points spread throughout the central area.

Detroit's geoeconomic development objectives can thus be summarized as follows: a riverfront teeming with the tourist and convention crowds, a strong "first downtown" serving as the financial pillar to the region's economy, a "second downtown" thriving on "culture and silicon," a surrounding expanse of neighborhoods whose population stability and economic well-being are assured by the retention and attraction of modern industries to renovated industrial corridors and port facilities—all interconnected by an efficient public transit system. This is the best of all possible worlds: the full flowering of the Detroit Renaissance.

But in this world of scarce resources, access to development funds is shaped by the size and use provisions of state and federal programs and by the profit calculus of private investors.[14] "Leverage"—the matching of scarce public incentives to restricted private interests—is the name of the game. Development priorities must follow.

The necessity to establish investment priorities raises a series of questions: (1) Should retention of existing industry or attraction of new industry be given priority? (2) In what directions should diversification of the economy be pursued? (3) Should new investment concentrate on commercial or industrial activities? (4) Should investment be targeted to a few, large, big-business-oriented projects or toward a larger number of projects on a smaller scale? Clearly these are not mutually exclusive alternatives. Rather, the basic issue is what underlying logic and corresponding mix of investment is most likely to maximize the city's development across all geoeconomic sectors.[15]

In Detroit, as in all large U.S. cities today, the logic shaping investment priorities and the practical application of development plans is the corporate-center strategy.[16] Overall investment priorities are to transform this aging industrial city into the modern corporate image: a financial, administrative, and professional services center for auto and related industries; a research and development site for new growth industries (e.g., robotics, new auto materials and components technology, leisure-related activities); an emphasis upon recommercialization rather than reindustrialization; and an orientation toward luxury consumption that is appealing to young corporate managers, educated professionals, convention goers, and the tourist trade. Detroit's public redevelopment blueprint has been worked out in close cooperation with a private coalition of corporate executives, bankers, downtown merchants, real estate developers, and service professionals who provide management, finance, real estate, scientific, technical, and luxury consumption services for corporate operations located in the Detroit metropolis.

In areal terms, the corporate-center strategy affords priority to the creation of a "Golden Arch" radiating from the Riverfront through the Central Business District to the Central Functions Area, the creation of upper-income neighborhoods within this arch, and the construction of a transportation system knitting activities in this arch into a unified whole.

A New Governing Coalition

Yet, as the 1967 rebellion made clear, any strategy for the rebirth of Detroit would count for little if it remained poorly connected to Detroit's black community. In the fall of 1973, Coleman Young was elected the city's first black mayor. Raised in the "black bottom" neighborhood on Detroit's east side, Coleman Young climbed the ladder from the bottom rung. First a left-wing labor organizer during the early days of the UAW, and then an activist in Michigan's Democratic Party, Young later became a state representative from Detroit. He resigned his state seat after his election as mayor of Detroit. Since then Young has assumed a pivotal role in forging a new governing coalition in the Motor City.

Coleman Young's biography expresses the contradictory relationship between big business, big labor, and the black community in Detroit. In his youth, Young was twice fired from the Ford Motor Company, first for hitting a race-baiting white foreman over the head with a steel pipe, then for helping to organize a labor union. Even so, the UAW blacklisted Young from jobs in retaliation for his radical activity within the labor movement. And the UAW opposed Young's bid for mayor in the 1973 primary campaign (Tyson, 1975: 237–40).

Coleman Young's self-described ambition was to become the "Mayor Daley of Detroit." And Young put together an electoral coalition designed to realize that aim. Studies of the November 1973 election revealed that Young won on the basis of the combined voting strength of blacks, unionists, and white liberals (Tyson, 1974). Population shifts over the ensuing years have helped Young cement this coalition into a smoothly functioning political machine.

But an electoral coalition is not a governing coalition. It is indicative of Young's political sophistication that his approach to business and labor in Detroit has been structured less by his past trajectory than by his current political agenda. Having fought the interests of big business for much of his life, Young now courted the corporate establishment. "I don't give a goddamn about them making money," Young explained in an interview, "so long as it's not excessive, and so long as they have the city's interest at heart." Shortly after his election, Young established a close working relationship with Henry Ford II. "I'm impressed by Henry Ford as a man," Young explained. "He's big, rich, and he doesn't stand on ceremony. I can reach him easier than I can reach Tom Turner (the black president of Detroit's AFL-CIO Council). I have to go through three secretaries to get Tom. I call up Ford's private number and he comes on the line: 'Hello, Henry' and 'Hello, Coleman' " (Tyson, 1975: 238).

Young also shunted aside his past conflicts with the UAW leadership. "That was a power struggle. . . . I let bygones be bygones." Early into his first term in office, Young persuaded Douglas Fraser, then UAW vice president and a key leader in Michigan Democratic politics, to chair a new police commission designed to counter conservative Republican monopoly over anticrime campaigns in the city. Young also turned to black labor leaders to help him avoid strikes by municipal workers. For example, a threatened strike by city garbage workers, whose contract expired in his first year as mayor, would have upset the city's white voters. Cornelius Hudson, the assertive black leader of the garbage workers, had joined other labor representatives in backing white City Council president Mel Ravitz for mayor in the 1973 Democratic primary. But Young had helped organize the garbage workers in the late '40s, and no black labor leader in Detroit, least of all Cornelius Hudson, dared call a crippling strike against a black mayor during his first year in office. A settlement was quickly reached. Shortly afterward, the Detroit Public Works Department hired Hudson as a foreman. "I have been in the labor movement a long time," Young later observed; "I've seen management buy off the union guy. I'm not above that tactic" (Tyson, 1975: 238–39).

Upon his election to office, Young's immediate concern was to gain control of the city's bureaucracies, particularly the police department. Young had won the election by defeating the former Police Commissioner on a promise to rid Detroit of "blackjack rule by police." The depth of the breach between Detroit's black community and its majority white police department was expressed in Young's publicly stated fear "that some hate-eyed white sharpshooter from within his own Police Department might try to assassinate him" (Tyson, 1975: 237). Drawing upon powers instituted in a new city charter, the Mayor appointed more city officials than any previous incumbent, replaced most department heads and deputies with his own candidates, and accomplished the most extensive bureaucratic reorganization in Detroit's postwar political history (Mitchell, 1974).

Having established a measure of control over the city's bureaucracies, Young began reaching out to neighborhood leaders. Young initiated a series of "reports to the people" at neighborhood city halls; his press secretary undertook a campaign to make the Mayor more visible in the subcommunities, and Young increased his public appearances before local constituents (Mitchell, 1974). Young had stressed during his campaign that Detroiters would have to "pull themselves up by their bootstraps" and rebuild the city "block by block." But neighborhood efforts would hardly suffice in the absence of massive state and federal aid to the depressed city. A positive connection to the federal government was therefore imperative (Warbelow, 1975a, 1975b).

Young was the first influential black politician in the North to support Jimmy Carter's drive for the presidency. The mayor campaigned hard for Carter in Detroit, and his political aides assisted Carter's electoral campaign in a number of Northern and Southern states. Once victorious, Carter appointed Michael Blumenthal head of the U.S. Treasury Department. Blumenthal, president of Bendix Corporation, was an active member of Metropolitan Fund and New Detroit, and a major investor in the Renaissance Center. William Beckham, Young's top aide, took a key urban policy position under Blumenthal in the Treasury Department (Mitchell, 1977). Young's aides also moved into positions in HUD and other agencies allocating grants to cities. And federal money began flowing into Detroit: grants for a people-mover system, commercial renovation downtown, initial backing for a new mass-transit system, and a partial subsidy for a new riverfront area (Ostman and Tyson, 1977; Stroud, 1977).

Genuine accomplishments notwithstanding, Young's political future remained inextricably tied to the investment agenda set by the corporate business community. As Remer Tyson, who has sketched Young's political activities in the pages of the *Detroit Free Press,* put it, "Mayor Young and Henry Ford II . . . struck up a deal that neither could refuse. The Mayor needs Ford's influence with moneymen . . . to develop the riverfront. Ford needs the Mayor to help protect his and his fellow businessmen's investments on the riverfront and in the suburbs by keeping down revolt in the nation's largest black dominated city" (Tyson, 1975: 237). It is apparent to Coleman Young, as to most informed observers of Motor City politics, that Detroit's future hinges upon one question: Can current economic and political institutions respond effectively to the needs of Detroit's black population? Coleman Young's response has been advocacy of what amounts to a new postrebellion black economic development strategy.

Black mayors are wielding today's methods of city governance to serve the interests of their black constituencies in a fashion that parallels the political machines of old. Strict enforcement of affirmative-action standards, racial criteria in the use of mayoral appointment powers, and enforcement of residency requirements for municipal workers are the principal methods used by black mayors and their administrations to widen black access to public and private economic resources (Eisinger, 1979: 3–4).

Since taking office, Coleman Young has appointed blacks to 51 percent of positions heading city departments and agencies and to 41 percent of the top posts on municipal boards and commissions. The Mayor has thereby enhanced black influence over agency personnel practices. City personnel departments actively recruit black college students by offering senior-year internships as a prelude to placement in city government after graduation. Twelve percent of the city's administrators and 23 percent of the city's professionals hired in 1973 were black; by 1977 these figures had increased to 24 percent and 41 percent. Between 1967 and 1978, the black percentage of the city's police force increased sixfold: from 5 to 30 percent. And it has recently been estimated that municipal employment directly supports 7 percent of Detroit's black population (Eisinger, 1979: 17).

The Young administration also expanded black business access to municipal purchases and contracts. The percent of city contracting and purchasing accruing to minority owned enterprises increased from 3 percent in 1973 to 20 percent in 1977.[17] The Detroit purchasing department advises black firms on the range of products and services the city purchases, and invites black entrepreneurs for site visits to review city purchasing requirements. A Detroit preference system gives city bid advantages to small businesses owned by "socially or economically disadvantaged persons," and local firms are given preference over those based outside Detroit. The city places deposits in black-owned banks. And firms who bid on city contracts, who wish city tax abatements, and who participate in city economic development plans must meet strict affirmative-action employment criteria (City of Detroit, 1979b: 22–25).

This municipal-based strategy for the development of a black professional and managerial class, expanding black employment in city services, and fostering a government-connected black entrepreneurial group, is founded upon an alliance between the Young administration and Detroit's white corporate elite. Why Young has entered this alliance is simple enough to explain. All one need do is juxtapose a list of Detroit's largest employers with a list of the city's largest taxpayers. In 1977, for example, the city's largest employer was Chrysler (52,000) followed by GM (40,200). Taken together, these two firms employed more than double the workers of the next 15 largest private employers combined. However, Detroit's third and fourth largest employers were not private companies at all, but rather the City of Detroit (23,600) and the Detroit Board of Education (20,000). This indicates the importance of municipal jobs in the city's economy. Yet when one turns to the city's largest taxpayers, the major auto firms and related companies reappear while the city and school board are, of course, absent from the list (City of Detroit, 1978: Tables III–17, III–18). The lesson is straightforward: A strategy for generating jobs and capital in the black community via municipal employment and purchases tied to affirmative action enforcement is, in a capitalist economy, completely dependent upon tax revenue tied to private economic investment.

So the Young administration, in concert with state and federal enabling legislation, has created a number of interconnected public and private development corporations to channel municipal, state, and federal expenditures into the kind of infrastructure, tax abatements, labor education and training programs, and technical assistance demanded by today's modern corporations as a prerequisite to investing in the city. The city's redevelopment blueprint, worked out in close cooperation with the corporate business community, is responsive to the profit demands of Detroit's corporations and stimulates the growth of a black urban political-professional-entrepreneurial class. But an issue remains: How responsive is this strategy to problems faced by the rest of Detroit's population?

THE POLITICS OF AUSTERITY

The corporate-center strategy imposes a redistribution of public resources between classes within the Detroit political economy. Elected officials offer tax breaks and social investment subsidies to business to succor investment, while reducing social consumption services to residents in Detroit's neighborhoods.

A careful study of trends in the Detroit budget between 1966 and 1979 (Russell, 1981) drew the following conclusions. First, industrial and commercial disinvestment severely eroded the Detroit tax base. Second, disinvestment and inflation forced dramatic increases in the level of taxation and a more regressive tax structure indicated by rising millage rates, flat rate income tax levies, and the imposition of a utility excise tax. Third, changes in the tax structure,[18] and the decreasing weight of industrial and commercial property in the Detroit tax base due to corporate disinvestment, steadily shifted the tax burden from business to individuals. Finally, the percentage of Detroit's budget devoted to various social consumption services (e.g., mass transportation, health, sanitation) remained stationary or declined, while outlays to maintain social stability rose sharply.[19]

Social Investment: Public Aid for Private Profit

In the midst of the 1974–75 national recession (a "depression" in Michigan), the Michigan State Legislature passed three bills—Public Acts, 198, 255, and 438—enabling corporations to apply to city councils for tax abatements.[20] Public Act 198 was passed to insure that Chrysler carried through with a planned addition to its Mack Avenue stamping plant in Detroit. Chrysler had threatened to move the plant out of Detroit if it did not get a tax break. Chrysler withdrew its threat after the City Council approved its application for a 50 percent tax abatement under the new bill (Danton, 1980).

The Economic Growth Corporation is the organizational core of Detroit's development strategy.[21] The Economic Growth Corporation directs the Economic Development Corporation and the Downtown Development Authority. The Downtown Development Authority administers a separate tax district created by state legislation in 1975. In this scheme, all new tax revenues produced in the Downtown Development Area are given back to the Downtown Development Authority to *reinvest in that area alone*. The Downtown Development Area covers the Golden Arch and includes Renaissance Center Phases II and III financed by a group headed by David Rockefeller. The 50 percent tax abatement for Renaissance Center II alone adds up to $7 million over 12 years (Danton, 1980).

The Downtown Development Area also is to house the Millender Center—a projected hotel, apartment, and commercial complex to be constructed across from the Renaissance Center. Millender Center developers have applied for a 12-year tax abatement worth $7 million, a HUD mortgage guarantee saving $11 million in lower interest charges, a tax grant of $8 million from the Downtown Development Authority, and an Urban Development Action Grant (UDAG) worth $12 million—all for a combined total of $38 million. Apartments in the Millender Center will rent for an estimated $500 a month for a one-bedroom with a skywalk across Jefferson Avenue to the Renaissance Center. Developers of Riverfront West, a highrise apartment complex on the Riverfront, are also seeking HUD mortgage insurance, a UDAG grant for $14 million, and a 12 year/100 percent tax abatement. This project will contain 2,500 units with rents between $500 and $1,000 a month for living accommodations which include covered walkways, a downtown people-mover connection, tennis courts, and a seawall (which will block public access to the Riverfront).[22] All told, some $260 million in tax abatements, subsidies, and federal grants have thus far been allocated to reconstruct downtown Detroit (Danton, 1980).

The Central Industrial Park Project, slated to house a new General Motors Cadillac Assembly plant valued at $500 million, further illuminates the magnitude of social investment subsidies offered to corporations willing to invest in Detroit (City of Detroit, 1980; Moberg, 1981; Serrin, 1981). The new Cadillac facility will occupy the site of the old Dodge Main Plant in Hamtramck and the adjacent Detroit neighborhood known as "Poletown." It is one of five new assembly plants GM is building to replace older facilities; in this case, the assembly operations at the Clark Avenue Cadillac factory and the Fleetwood Fisher Body plant in Detroit.[23]

The new factory, a one-story assembly plant designed for "cornfields" but built within the city of Detroit, has led to the destruction of 1,021 homes and apartment buildings, 155 businesses, churches, and a hospital, displaced 3,500 people, and all but obliterated a more or less stably integrated community embodying a century of Polish cultural life. Land acquisition, demolition of buildings, relocation of individuals and businesses, building a new road, sewer, and other service connections, will eventually reach $200 million in city, state, and federal funds. And General Motors will receive as much as $170 million in additional tax abatements over the next twelve years.

Direct benefits to Detroit, city officials have estimated, include 6,000 jobs (although the UAW sets it at 5,200); but 3,800 are merely transfers from the Clark Avenue and Fleetwood plants, and automation is likely to reduce the total during the next decade.[24] Fifteen hundred to 2,000 jobs have been eliminated in the Poletown neighborhood, although city officials hope eventually to pare this down to 500 as businesses are encouraged to relocate elsewhere in the city.

Social Consumption: The "Self-Service City"

As massive social investment subsidies flow to downtown developers and transnational auto corporations, the city administration has sharply reduced social consumption services to Detroit residents. Between 1979 and 1980, for example, the city laid off 1,500 employees in recreation, public works, police and fire departments.

In his April 1980 "State of the City" address Mayor Young declared that Detroit was facing a $59 million deficit—the largest in the city's postwar history, and he predicted the debt would reach $100 million by October 1980. Young then told the story of "Pingree's potato patches." In the panic of 1893, 600 bank closings led to bankruptcy in the railroad industry. At that time Detroit specialized in producing locomotives and other railroad equipment. The Detroit economy was ruined, the city's budget collapsed, and thousands were thrown out of work. Detroit Mayor Hazen Pingree, a Progressive Republican, let the unemployed grow potato patches on city land and on donated private property.

Evoking the tradition of Pingree, Mayor Young then suggested one response to the threatened collapse of Detroit's budget: "do-it-yourself" government whereby disappearing municipal revenues are replaced by voluntary contributions of income and labor from local residents. Dimensions of the "Self-Service City," Detroit style, now number among the following (Cheyfitz, 1980):

A city *gift catalogue*. Contributions are solicited from residents at every income level. Items in the 1980 catalogue ranged from the gift of time (e.g., the Recreation Department needed volunteers to staff recreation centers, teach classes, and coach neighborhood teams), to gifts of trees and shrubs (ranging from $15 honeysuckles to $60 evergreens), to gifts for city parks (including such items as picnic tables, benches, and swing sets). Six of seven skating rinks were to be closed unless the twelve-week, $6,000 operating cost was met. The ultimate gift: $3.5 million for the Belle Isle Regional Arts Center—a combined cultural and senior citizens complex.

An *Adopt a Park* program. Neighborhood groups assume responsibility for maintaining a public park—cutting grass, retrieving litter, planting flowers, painting equipment. Thirty neighborhood organizations joined this program in 1978; by 1980, 90 were involved.

A *Police Reserves* program. After 80 hours of firing-range and classroom training, Detroit residents between the ages of 18 and 50 can now serve without pay as a supplement to the police force. They carry weapons, wear city-supplied uniforms, ride in scout cars, and aid in crowd and traffic control at special events. As of 1980, 1,350 individuals were donating 100,000 hours a year. Mayor Young seeks to increase the police reserve to 2,000.

A *Fire Department Auxiliary.* Volunteers are prepared to serve the city in case of "riot, natural disaster, or enemy attack."

Vacant Lot Brigades. Neighborhood recruits cut weeds and clear Detroit's vacant lots. Why? Because the city now has 23 municipal workers to clean 25,000 vacant lots. In 1974, the Detroit Public Works Department employed 1,900 workers to collect garbage. By 1980, the city employed 800 to accomplish this task.

Neighborhood groups also staff untended school yards, run special summer programs, and seek grants and gifts to develop school facilities.

There is much that is laudable about voluntary civic enterprise: social responsibility, community pride, collective solidarity. But since enormous tax subsidies are going to private corporations, voluntary civic enterprise also amounts to the exploitation of collective concern for private advantage. In effect, Detroit residents are compensating for public resources flowing to private corporations with their voluntary labor time.

DARE to Win

Detroit's new governing coalition and its "Renaissance" image of the city's future have not gone unchallenged. One of the most articulate and outspoken opponents of the Young administration's plans for the city is Ken Cockrel, a radical black attorney who was elected to the Detroit City Council in 1977. Cockrel, in association with a group of city political activists experienced in the labor movement, black worker struggles, and the new-left politics of the 1960s, founded the Detroit Alliance for a Rational Economy (DARE). DARE was a "city-wide, multiracial, community-based organization with socialist leadership," composed of some 200 members, and with a capacity to attract several hundred additional community organizers and political activists to its conferences (Judis, 1979).

DARE combined electoral politics with community organizing, political education, and direct-action strategies. DARE sponsored candidates for elected offices; organized conferences on city issues which brought together local activists to coordinate strategies for urban change; created an alternative city bus tour and "City Tour Guide" focusing upon who benefits and who loses from the corporate Renaissance plan; published newsletters, a newspaper, and a journal; and founded a policy research institute devoted to community education and alternative policy development and planning (Lafoon, 1979; DARE, 1980).

DARE members vocally opposed tax abatements to corporations, the use of government social investment funds to benefit private developers rather than low- and moderate-income workers, the dislocation of inner-city families through the city's revitalization schemes, the inequitable distribution of the city's tax burden, deterioration in city services and the layoff of city workers, and the kind of job creation implied in the Renaissance redevelopment blueprint. More concretely, DARE led a successful campaign to defeat regressive tax proposals in the 1978 general election, mounted a partially successful effort to obtain relocation funds for residents displaced by General Motors-sponsored redevelopment in the Central Functions area, led a petition campaign opposing the 12 year/100 percent tax abatement application by Riverfront West developers, pressured for city financing for low- and moderate-cost housing, and marshalled support for Detroit General Hospital against proposed city cutbacks. As the DARE leadership saw it, urban-based issues like these were to provide the foundation for a broadly based socialist politics in U.S. cities during the 1980s (Cockrel, 1979).

By all accounts, DARE seemed to be a political organization with considerable potential. With DARE members Ken Cockrel on the City Council and Justin Ravitz on the Recorders Court bench, the organization had political legitimacy. And with an array of community organizations and issue coalitions as natural allies, DARE had established a network of contacts for rapid mobilization on specific issues. But DARE foundered, then disbanded on the divisive and demoralizing shoals of economic crisis, forced fiscal austerity, and in the face of the enormous prestige and allegiance that Mayor Coleman Young continued to wield with Detroit's black electorate. DARE activists recognized that the difficult path ahead lay less with defensive opposition to fiscal austerity measures than with the construction of a comprehensive alternative to the Renaissance image of Detroit's future and the coalition that stood behind that vision. The use of local government as a tool for urban development that benefits the majority of city residents required a break with the profit logic. But it was precisely this logic which was reshaping Detroit's landscape to fit the organizational imperatives of the global corporation.

CAR WARS: THE GLOBAL REORGANIZATION OF THE AUTO INDUSTRY

In 1980, the U.S. auto industry experienced its worst economic downturn since the Great Depression. The auto giants lost a combined $3.5 billion, 250,000 workers were indefinitely laid off, and an additional 450,000 lost their jobs in the industries which supplied the Big Three (Skaiken, 1980: 345). The deep slump in the auto industry issued from a combination of factors: economic recession, rising energy prices, a saturated U.S. market for fuel-guzzling cars, intensified foreign competition—all translating into a falling profit rate. Given the geographical organization of auto production in the United States, the severe hardship centered in Detroit and among the industrial cities of the automotive realm and manufacturing belt.

The present crisis is immediate, close at hand, painfully visible. Less apparent, but more significant, is the corporate revitalization strategy developed in response to the crisis, for it entails the reorganization of the auto industry on a world scale—a transformation in depth and scope unprecedented in the industry. This reorganization includes: (1) changes in product design, (2) global concentration and centralization of capital in fewer firms, (3) redesign of the labor process in relation to new technologies, (4) a transformation in the international division of labor in the industry.

Today's competition among transnational auto corporations focuses upon a common objective: the development of the world car. The world car, "suitable for American highways, European city streets, and African trails," is a small, energy efficient, downsized vehicle with standardized, interchangeable components, designed to be manufactured and marketed throughout the world. The development of the world car is a vast cost-cutting strategy to lower the expenses of design and engineering, realize economies of scale, and enhance manufacturing flexibility by allowing the car giants to multiply their production locations for major components (Hainer and Koslofsky, 1979). The success of the world car is meant to counter foreign competition at home and abroad and thus renew the vitality of the U.S. automobile and supplier industries.

Yet today's car wars point to a further increase in the international concentration and centralization of capital in the auto industry. The capital investment requirements to build the world car and enter expanding markets are very high.[25] Enormous investment requirements are forcing capital-short firms into mergers with more powerful competitors—a repeat of the historical trajectory of the U.S. auto firms but now on a global plane. Most forecasts suggest the world's 30 independent auto companies will be reduced to between 7 and 12 over the next two decades (*Le Monde*, 1980).

International competition also brings the introduction of new labor-saving technology in the form of robots and computerized numerical-control procedures. The microprocessor revolution—the ability to attach the core of a computer to a silicon chip the size of a fingernail—is leading to pervasive automation in the auto industry. Auto components can now be produced by computer-controlled machine tools and assembled into the final car by robots. And the weight of automation is being felt in "design studios, engine plants, warehouses, foundrys, and tool shops" along with the traditionally more mechanized assembly lines (Shaiken, 1980: 345).[26]

The development of the world car also means global sourcing: auto transnationals maximize global profits by minimizing production costs through locating different segments of the production process in low-wage areas that offer favorable government subsidies.[27] As components produced in a range of individual countries are going into cars assembled by American auto companies and their foreign competitors, imports of components by U.S. firms are rising dramatically.[28]

This corporate revitalization strategy suggests that the employment crisis afflicting Detroit and the industrial heartland of the United States will be less than fully ameliorated by the return to vitality of the U.S. auto industry. First, downsizing of automobiles means less machining, cast iron and steel production, and foundry work. Second, intense competition today is likely to lead to overproduction tomorrow in an attempt to maximize efficiencies from economies of scale. So Detroit will continue to confront the possibility of failure of its auto producers and suppliers. Third, more pervasive automation suggests that production will outstrip employment growth at a more rapid rate. Fourth, the global sourcing strategy threatens Detroit with further disinvestment and reduced employment.[29] Finally, the flexibility afforded by the corporate revitalization strategy—the increased centralization of capital in a few global firms, the new international division of labor, and the standardization of the production process on a global scale—undercuts the collective bargaining and strike power of auto workers and threatens further losses in wages, benefits, and working conditions.[30]

Regional shifts in capital investment and the global reorganization of the auto industry are now striking the manufacturing facilities which gave birth to the industrial suburbs of Detroit. With suburban disinvestment has come redlining, housing deterioration, and the flight of commercial enterprises—a repeat of the cycle afflicting the central city (Jacobs, 1981). Suburban Macomb County, to the northeast of the central city, provides a striking illustration. Macomb County is highly industrialized. More than 38 percent of the Macomb population is employed in manufacturing. Over half of this manufacturing labor force is employed in major auto plants; the remainder work in chemical, glass, machine, metal fabrication, and other hardware manufacturing which complement auto production.

In March 1981, the unemployment rate in Macomb County was 15.3 percent—more than double the rate of the metropolitan area as a whole. According to the Director of the Michigan Employment Security Commission (MESC), this represented a shift in unemployment from urban to suburban areas. In March 1981, some 21,000 Macomb County residents were drawing regular unemployment insurance and an additional 6,300 residents were drawing extended unemployment benefits. During 1980, over 21,000 workers living in the Macomb suburbs of Mt. Clemens and Sterling Heights exhausted all unemployment benefits. For many, welfare was the only alternative: the number of Macomb welfare recipients increased 26 percent, while total welfare spending rose 44 percent. Most unemployed Macomb County workers are between the ages of twenty and thirty-four. The vast majority worked in the machine trades and in structural occupations—the jobs most severely affected by the current crisis and reorganization of the auto industry. The employment prospects for these workers, MESC analysts have concluded, are "extremely poor" (Jazowski, 1981).

As for the central city of Detroit, in June 1981, carrying the burden of an auto industry in crisis, the Motor City once again moved toward bankruptcy. Sixty percent of the city's 1.2 million residents were receiving some form of government assistance. Local income tax revenues had fallen by $30 million in 1980–81. The city ended its fiscal year on June 30 with a $120 million deficit, and it projected an additional $150 million deficit for fiscal 1982 (*Business Week*, 1981). The city administration responded with a complex three-part rescue plan prescribed by Felix Rohatyn, senior partner in the New York investment firm of Lazard Frères and Company, and chief architect of New York City's financial rescue. This plan entailed (1) $77 million in

further wage concessions by the city's 20,000 workers, (2) $94 million through an-
other increase in the payroll tax, and (3) a $100 million bond issue to start paying
off the deficits (Peirce, 1981).

URBAN CRISIS OR URBAN RENAISSANCE?

Yesterday, Detroit was the largest factory town in the world. Today, the Motor
City's factories—Detroit's raison d'être—are being abandoned. The auto industry
is reorganizing and decentralizing on a global scale. Industrial and commercial capital
flows to suburbs, the sunbelt, and foreign locations. In the brief span of three decades,
Detroit has seen 27 percent of its population, 50 percent of its industrial firms, 70
percent of its jobs in manufacturing disappear (Luria and Russell, 1981: 5). Unemployment is permanent and crippling. The city's financial resources have plunged so
low as to recall the Great Depression of the 1930s. These are stark, palpable signs
that the economic premises upon which the Motor City developed—cheap energy,
a hegemonic position in national and international auto markets, and expanding
employment opportunities in industries linked to car production—have become a
subject for study by economic historians.

Detroit's fate has been wed to an economic base controlled by a small number
of multinational corporations. Corporate stability and growth are premised upon
the capacity to respond to changing national and international costs and conditions.
The profit logic that once brought investment and growth to Detroit now brings
disinvestment, decline, and decay. And there is no reason to believe that an invisible
hand will transform today's disinvestment into the conditions conducive to the
scale and kind of reinvestment necessary to rebuild Detroit tomorrow. No, the issue
is plainly political: What is to be done to save Detroit?

Bluntly put, Detroit's plight is that of a city which is no longer competitive
within the institutional rules of the game. Private corporations accumulate and reinvest capital, Detroit does not. Capital is mobile, Detroit is not. In the absence of
national and regional development planning and coordination, Detroit's own strategy
has been shaped through bitter rivalry with other governments for corporate smoke-
stacks and skyscrapers. Mobilizing public incentives to leverage private resources,
city officials now call themselves "entrepreneurs in the public interest." But in the
nature of the case this version of the public interest boils down to the needs of
private investors.

Will the corporate-center strategy revitalize Detroit? It seems doubtful. The
Renaissance of the urban core in Detroit is fragile. The central-place activities performed by the Riverfront, CBD, and Central Functions areas are tied to the economic
well-being of the region as a whole. And the economic vitality of the region remains
tied to manufacturing. Continued industrial disinvestment threatens to undermine
the whole Renaissance effort.

Detroit, unlike many urban competitors for corporate-center status, is a city
that "spread" to maturity during the epoch of the automobile. The assumption
that thousands will settle in gentrified neighborhoods in the Golden Arch is shaky

in a metropolis that contains a large supply of attractive and reasonably priced housing in outlying neighborhoods and suburban areas.

But more to the point, in a blue collar, union town, a development strategy which emphasizes headquarters functions, recommercialization, leisure activities, and high-technology industries seems unlikely to produce the number of jobs at the level of remuneration required to reconstruct Detroit. New technology-based industry starts small, produces few jobs in the short term, and flirts with failure. Recommercialization and the transition toward a leisure economy are targeted toward the better-paid professional, technical, and managerial groups. But for Detroit's less-advantaged workers, the Renaissance means trading a former possibility for blue-collar jobs at decent wages for the future probability of scarce, low-paying, dead-end, service work—all at a high public cost per job.

In short, the corporate-center strategy—the Detroit Renaissance—will not end the traumas induced by industrial disinvestment. At best the Detroit Renaissance will reverse the historical correlation between privileged residence and distance from the inner city by creating a Golden Arch surrounded by deteriorating and impoverished workers' neighborhoods. At worst the Detroit Renaissance will itself collapse under the weight of continued industrial disinvestment and fiscal decline.[31]

Detroit must stem the tide of industrial disinvestment, draw upon its manufacturing past to reconstruct an industrial future, and do so on a scale that will replace the number and kinds of jobs that have left town. If the city is to survive and thrive, there must be a well conceptualized and coordinated national commitment to reindustrialization, targeted to revitalize cities like Detroit, and backed by a massive investment of financial resources. The problem is clear. But the means for achieving a solution founder against firmly entrenched obstacles.

U.S. federal urban policy lacks coordinated planning and agreement on what ought to be done. There is little coordination between urban programs and general economic policies. Federal, state, and local urban programs are fragmented, program requirements are often in flux, and financing is unpredictable. And the commitment of federal revenues for urban redevelopment falls woefully short of what is required (U.S. House of Representatives, 1980).

The reign of the market, the fragmentation of government, and the lack of federal planning, coordination, and control mean that urban economic development strategies are formulated within the context of bitter local, regional, and national competition for investment funds. Governments attempt to outdo one another in marshalling public incentives to court private favor. The upshot is programs too often distinguished by their negative tone and focus—not "What would constitute a rational strategy toward economic development?" but "What will happen if we don't offer those incentives?"

Public incentive programs, rather than working to attract private investment where it would otherwise not go, actually appear to be wasteful of scarce public revenues. So many governments have proliferated so many incentives that these enticements may have lost their selective power of attraction (Vaughn, 1979). More to the point, there is little evidence that public incentives strongly influence corporate location decisions. Public tax incentives are usually less important corporate lures

than wage, land, transportation, and energy costs, and the presence of a network
of suppliers. And these are factors often beyond the control of local governments
(Mazza and Hogan, 1981).

The terms currently defining the "public/private partnership" development strategy also raise serious issues of accountability. Private influence over the development
process was traditionally based upon technical expertise and the ability to relocate
capital. Today, Economic Development Corporations have become an instrument
through which the private sector more or less directly allocates public revenues
and wields public powers in such a fashion as to redistribute public resources from
neighborhood residents to private investors. And, as the definition of the public
purpose with respect to eminent domain and other government powers is enlarged
to encompass unemployment reduction through retention, expansion, and attraction
of private economic activity, it becomes less possible to recognize a potential conflict
of interest or, indeed, even to distinguish between public and private interests. Since
private corporations provide jobs and investment, the city's public purpose becomes
indistinguishable from the corporation's private interest.

The administration in Washington is likely to continue to promote the current
public/private partnership, some targeting to distressed areas, and the leveraging
of private investment through public incentives. All of these principles are embodied
in the hotly debated Kemp-Garcia urban-enterprise-zone proposal incorporated in
the 1980 Republican platform. Kemp-Garcia designates areas of high unemployment
and poverty in cities as "enterprise job zones." State and local governments reduce
property taxes and the federal government reduces Social Security, capital gains,
and business taxes for enterprises which locate in and draw a majority of their
employees from these targeted areas.

But the Reagan administration is also scaling down HUD programs, plans to
scuttle the Economic Development Administration, and is incorporating various urban programs into broader but more weakly funded block grants to localities. This
means a drop in federal revenue available for economic development projects, even
less federal policy review and coordination over urban development programs, and
intensified city competition for scarce resources.

Current federal policies are likely further to aggravate uneven regional development. Supply-side tax cuts suggest increased movement of manufacturing firms
from North to South. Increased defense spending disproportionately benefits the
sunbelt at the expense of the frostbelt. Federal welfare cuts will hurt the North
more than the South. And the decontrol of oil and gas prices signals a massive
transfer of capital to energy-producing sunbelt regions and higher energy costs to
consumers in the frostbelt. The implications seem clear: further job and capital
flight, unemployment, and fiscal deterioration in Northern industrial cities like Detroit.

The outlines of an alternative urban redevelopment strategy have emerged from
groups, like DARE, grappling with the issues of capital flight, uneven regional development, worker and community dislocation in the United States. This redevelopment
strategy focuses upon the planned conversion of idle and underutilized infrastructure,
plant, and equipment, to the production of alternative goods for which there is a

clear social need and a potential economic demand (Alperovitz and Faux, 1980). The calculus governing what is to be produced encompasses social benefits beyond private profits—indirect benefits derived from employment retention—including lower unemployment insurance, welfare, health, and crime-control costs which are borne today by the public sector rather than by the private investor. Here the role of government in the economy encompasses the current range of public incentive tools and a proposed national development bank, but also extends to the creation of joint public/private or full public enterprises capable of producing a reinvestible surplus. And the meaning of development planning is extended to include workplace governance, employee-ownership plans, and combined business, worker, neighborhood, and city representation at the enterprise and redevelopment area planning levels.

Dan Luria and Jack Russell (1981) have recently forwarded a development plan, embodying these tenets, for the "rational reindustrialization" of Detroit. Their plan suggests replacing declining auto assembly, parts and machining industries in Detroit with new activities that take maximum advantage of idle labor skills, infrastructure, plant, equipment, and industry linkages. Through an elaborate feasibility analysis, the authors propose that investment in Detroit can be targeted to the conversion of abandoned or underutilized industrial capacity to the production of energy hardware products.[32]

This conversion strategy recognizes that the modernization of global enterprises is unlikely to revitalize distressed industrial cities like Detroit. This strategy also addresses the issue of public accountability by seeking to establish new institutional arrangements for joint public/private participation in the development process. However, it also runs up against stiff obstacles posed by the rules governing urban economic development in the United States. Michigan law sharply restricts the range of revenue-generating enterprises a city can create.[33] And there are a number of legislative hurdles to be surmounted before public and private employee pension funds can be drawn upon for investment capital. Ultimately, a comprehensive democratic-socialist alternative will require a national alliance among urban activists engaged in mobilizing popular support behind the struggle for a more just and humane city.

NOTES

1. Many of the provisions of the Detroit Plan were incorporated into the Federal Housing Act of 1949.
2. The New Detroit Committee was the forerunner of the National Urban Coalition.
3. Hudson also happened to be chief executive officer of Metropolitan Fund, Inc. Sitting beside Hudson were some of the world's most powerful corporate chieftains: James M. Roche, chairman of the board of General Motors; Henry Ford II, chairman of the board of Ford Motor Company; Lynn A. Townsend, chairman of the board of Chrysler; Walker Cisler, chairman of the board of Detroit Edison; William Day, president of the Michigan Bell Telephone Company; Max Fisher, leading investor in the Marathon Oil Company and one of Richard Nixon's chief fund-raisers; Ralph McElvenny, chairman of the board

of the Michigan Consolidated Gas Company; and Stanley Winkelman, president of Winkelman Stores (Widick, 1972: 187–88).

4. EDC's board of directors included Henry Ford II and other business members of the New Detroit Committee. It also included the heads of Great Lakes Steel, American Motors, Bendix Corporation, Parke-Davis, S. S. Kresge Company, the Burroughs Corporation, Kelsey-Hayes, Rockwell Standard, the Budd Company, Wyandotte Chemical, and most of the leading banks in the city.

5. Mandell's study (1975) was based upon a sample of manufacturing plants and interviews with "chief company decision-makers"—ostensibly those persons making the final location decisions. Interviews were conducted with 106 Detroit employers. The response rate was 79 percent.

6. The balance of the region, on the other hand, gained some 1,163,000 new residents during the same period. This adds up to an enormous drop in Detroit's share of the total metropolitan population: from 61 percent in 1950 to 33 percent in 1974 (Holli, 1976: 269).

7. During the same period, employment in the suburban balance of the metropolitan region increased by 14 percent (227,100 jobs).

8. With the exception of 1973, Detroit's officially defined unemployment rate did not drop below 8.1 percent during the 1970s.

9. The share of the metropolitan AFDC and GA population residing in the city of Detroit increased from 59 percent in 1969 to nearly 70 percent in 1974.

10. State funding in grants and loans is usually a small share of the public costs of local development projects. More significant has been the role of state governments in granting new powers to cities to facilitate development efforts (Jones, Bachelor, and Wang, 1981).

11. Trends in direct federal aid as a percentage of Detroit's "own source" general revenue indicate the extent to which the Motor City became dependent upon federal support during the 1970s: 1957, 1.3%; 1967, 13.1%; 1976, 50.2%; 1978, 76.8%.

12. EDCs are authorized to buy land through options, planned purchases, and "opportunity" purchases. Public Act 87, passed by the Michigan legislature in 1980, and popularly known as the "quick-take law," also established procedures by which a municipality can obtain title to a property acquired through its eminent-domain powers before reaching a settlement with property owners for just compensation. This reduces the time required to assemble land for development projects while raising serious issues of due process of law.

13. This annual document synthesizes and updates previous city development plans, including the Detroit Master Plan, the Moving Detroit Forward Plans of 1975 and 1977, the 1978 Comprehensive Economic Development Strategy, and material from the city's Capital Agenda, Public Works Program, and Community Development Block Grant Program.

14. Needless to say, there are severe obstacles to the full realization of Detroit's current economic development plan. Obstacles to development of the Riverfront include high land costs, poor retaining walls, and abandoned and obsolete plants and warehouses. Obstacles to development of the CBD include the high cost of land preparation and development, the spatial distance separating centers of activity downtown, and an excess of surface parking lots. Development hurdles in the Central Functions Area include blighted residential areas and poor transportation links between activity points. Barriers facing redevelopment of Industrial Corridors include aging and obsolete production facilities, and sites landlocked by residences or other industries. Financing problems have also inhibited port expansion and improvement, as well as land acquisition and development for downtown neighborhoods.

15. The city sets development project priorities according to the following criteria: (1) number

of jobs created or retained and cost per job; (2) the long-range impact with respect to diversification, spin-off, and growth potential; (3) probability of attracting private sector interest; and (4) total leverage generated in public and private resources (City of Detroit, 1980a: 4).

16. Robert Fitch (1977) labels this approach to urban development the "national-center strategy" and traces its origins to plans created in New York City during the second decade of this century. This urban development strategy corresponds to changes in the spatial organization of national and multinational corporations: the centralization and concentration of conception, coordination, and control activities ("headquarters functions") and the regional, national, and international decentralization of production activities. Therefore it seems best characterized as a corporate-center strategy for urban development.

17. In 1977 this amounted to a $22 million flow of city funds to black entrepreneurs (City of Detroit, 1979b: 23).

18. With the advent of a single business tax in 1976, inventory became exempt from local property taxation in Michigan.

19. For example, expenditures on police tripled in Detroit between 1947 and 1979 (Russell, 1981).

20. Tax abatements allow a specified percentage of a firm's property tax to be waived for a specified number of years, usually twelve, in return for investment in the city.

21. The Economic Growth Corporation's $1 million budget is paid by the city of Detroit and the state of Michigan out of state CETA (Comprehensive Employment Training Act) funds and out of city revenues from a Community Development Entitlement Grant.

22. The list also includes the Cadillac Shopping Center with $100 million in projected UDAG and other federal dollars, the Woodward and Washington Mall with $2.7 million in block grant funds, and the Joe Louis Sports Arena and Cobo Hall run by a "sweetheart" deal between the city of Detroit and the Olympia Corporation which includes a property tax ceiling of $250,000 for the two facilities plus a low cost-payment schedule to the city for operating rights (Danton, 1980).

23. GM is constructing these new facilities to avoid the costs of meeting pollution requirements for older plants and in response to the pressure of international competition to downsize cars and introduce new automated equipment. It located the plant in Detroit partly in response to political pressure to arrest disinvestment in the city that houses its headquarters.

24. General Motors actually committed itself to only 3,000 jobs "if economic conditions permit." And, as it turns out, GM has delayed the project for at least a year due to the current slump in the auto industry.

25. It takes an estimated $1 billion to enter the new market for the world car. By 1980, Ford had already laid out $3 billion on the Escort, and the Big Three will spend an estimated $80 billion on world-car development by 1985 (Shaiken, 1980: 345).

26. Industrial robots, now widely used for welding operations, are rapidly being introduced into other facets of the labor process in the auto industry. Because they merely require new programming, industrial robots cut expenses on model changeovers by reducing the high cost associated with retooling. A $40,000 unimate robot can now do two 8-hour shifts at an average cost of $4.80 per hour. This compares to $15 in total hourly costs for a human auto assembler (Shaiken, 1980: 347).

27. Global sourcing is also a corporate response to the national requirements of those less-developed countries which have imposed local-content laws (requiring a certain percentage of locally produced components) on their domestically assembled cars.

28. The U.S. imports of auto parts amounted to $6.8 billion in 1979 (McDowell, 1980).

29. Detroit will import an estimated 10 percent of its parts by 1985, and 15 percent by 1990 (McDowell, 1980). This is a fundamental departure from just a short time ago when almost all of the equipment in a car assembled in the Motor City was manufactured in the automotive realm.
30. For example, it is estimated that wages at Ford installations in the Philippines and Brazil are roughly 10 percent of those in the U.S. In Mexico, wages run about 40 to 50 percent of the U.S. rate (Woutat, 1980).
31. For example, the Renaissance Center—the $600 million riverfront hotel-office complex masterminded by Henry Ford II—was meant to symbolize the rebirth of Detroit, signal to the investment community that Ford and his financial partners were committed to the city's future, and provide a linchpin for redevelopment of central Detroit in the modern corporate image. Yet the Renaissance Center is now in severe financial difficulty. Having lost $103 million since opening in 1977, the Renaissance partnership has been in default on its first mortgage for over a year and has been attempting to sell some of its assets (Luke and McNaughton, 1981).
32. Specifically: (1) deep natural gas and heavy oil production and upgrading equipment; (2) residential and industrial steam/electric cogeneration units; (3) large coal and diesel fuel-fired industrial process engines; and (4) mine-mouth coal gasifiers.
33. For example, a city in Michigan cannot own stock in a private enterprise and a city- or state-owned bank is unconstitutional.

REFERENCES

Aberbach, J. D., and J. L. Walker. 1970. "The meaning of black power: a comparison of white and black interpretations of a political slogan." *American Political Science Review* 64 (June): 367–88.

Alperovitz, Gar, and Jeff Faux. 1980. "Beyond bailouts: notes for next-time." *Working Papers for a New Society* (November/December): 14–18.

Brimmer, Andrew F., and Henry S. Terrell. 1969. "The economic potential of black capitalism." Paper presented at the Annual Meetings of the American Economics Association.

Bunge, William. 1971. *Fitzgerald: Geography of a Revolution.* Cambridge, MA: Schenkman.

Business Week. 1981. "Behind the fiscal bind that plagues Detroit." June 29.

Cheyfitz, Kirk. 1980. "The self-serve city." *Monthly Detroit* (November): 79–82.

City of Detroit. 1981. "Population, population change, and percent black by subcommunity: 1970, 1980." Detroit: Planning Department, Data Coordination Division.

———. 1980a. *Annual Overall Economic Development Program Report and Program Projection.* Detroit.

———. 1980b. *Central Industrial Park—Final Environmental Impact Statement.* Detroit.

———. 1979a. *Downtown Detroit Development.* Detroit: City Planning Department.

———. 1979b. *Overall Economic Development Program (annual) Report and Program Projection.* Detroit.

———. 1978. *The Overall Economic Development Program.* Detroit.

———. 1977. *Moving Detroit Forward: A Plan for Urban Economic Revitalization.* Detroit.

———. 1976. *Report of the Mayor's Task Force on City Finances.* Detroit.

———. 1975. *Detroit: Needs vs. Resources, 1976–1981.* Detroit.

———. n.d., a. "Detroit fact sheet." Detroit.

———. n.d., b. "Economic indicators: city of Detroit." Detroit.

Cockrel, Ken. 1979. "Left city politics must focus on working and poor peoples interests." *In These Times,* September 26–October 2.

Conot, Robert. 1975. *American Odyssey.* New York: Bantam.

Cray, Ed. 1980. *Chrome Colossus: General Motors and Its Times*. New York: McGraw-Hill.

Danton, Marilyn. 1980. "Renaissance for wealth." *Changes* (March): 8–20.

Danziger, Sheldon, and Michael Weinstein. 1976. "Employment location and wage rates of poverty area residents." *Journal of Urban Economics* 3 (April): 127–45.

Denby, Charles. 1968. "Black caucuses and the unions." *New Politics* (Summer): 10–17.

Detroit Alliance for a Rational Economy. 1980. "City life in the '80s tour guide book." Detroit.

———. n. d. "What is D.A.R.E.?" Detroit.

Eisinger, Peter K. 1979. "Black mayors and the politics of racial economic advancement." *Discussion Paper*. Institute for Research on Poverty, University of Wisconsin, Madison.

Ewen, Lynda Ann. 1978. *Corporate Power and Urban Crisis in Detroit*. Princeton, NJ: Princeton University Press.

Fitch, Robert. 1977. "Planning New York." Pp. 246–84 in Robert E. Alcaly and David Mermelstein, eds., *The Fiscal Crisis of American Cities*. New York: Vintage.

Friedman, Sheldon, and Loen Potok. 1981. "Detroit and the auto industry: an historical overview." Paper presented at an International Conference on "Economic Crisis and Political Response in the Auto City," sponsored by the Harvard Center for European Studies, Detroit.

Fujita, Kuniko. 1977. "Black workers struggles in Detroit's auto industry, 1935–1975." Masters thesis, Michigan State University, East Lansing.

Fusfeld, Daniel. 1973. *The Basic Economics of the Urban Racial Crisis*. New York: Holt, Rhinehart & Winston.

Georgakas, Dan, and Marvin Surkin. 1975. *Detroit: I Do Mind Dying*. New York: St. Martin's.

Greenstone, David. 1969. *Labor in American Politics*. New York: Knopf.

———. 1961. *Report on the Politics of Detroit*. Cambridge, MA: Harvard–MIT Joint Center for Urban Studies.

Hahn, Harlan. 1970. "Black separatists: attitudes and objectives in a riot torn ghetto." *Journal of Black Studies* 1 (September): 35–43.

———. 1969. "Ghetto sentiments on violence." *Science and Society* 33 (Spring): 197–208.

Hainer, Marg, and Joanne Koslofsky. 1979. "The world car: shifting into overdrive." *NACLA Report on the Americas* (July–August): 3–9.

Hamlin, Mike. 1970. "Our thing is drum!" *Leviathan* (June): 35–40.

Hill, Herbert. 1969. "Black protest and the struggle for union democracy." *Issues in Industrial Democracy* (Fall): 19–29.

Hill, Richard Child. 1983. "Transnational capitalism and urban crisis: the case of the auto industry and Detroit." In Ray Pahl and Ivan Szelenyi, eds., *Cities in Recession: Public Policies*. Beverly Hills: Sage.

———. 1980. "Race, class and the state: the metropolitan enclave system in the United States." *The Insurgent Sociologist* 10 (Fall): 45–59.

———. 1978. "At the cross-roads: the postwar political economy of Detroit." *Urbanism Past and Present* 6 (Summer): 1–21.

Holli, Melvin G., ed. 1976. *Detroit*. New York: New Viewpoints.

Jacobs, Jim. 1981. "Suburbs and disinvestment." Unpublished manuscript, Macomb Community College, Detroit.

———. 1970. "Our thing is drum!" *Leviathan* (June): 1–4.

Jazowski, A. R. 1981. "Statement before the Michigan congressional budget impact hearing." Lansing, May 22.

Jones, Bryan D., Lynn W. Bachelor, and Richard Wang. 1981. "Rebuilding the urban tax base: local policy discretion and the corporate surplus." Paper presented at the Midwest Political Science Association, Cincinnati, OH.

Judis, John. 1979. "Cockrel's DARE challenges Detroit renaissance." *In These Times,* October 10–16.

Lafoon, Polk. 1979. "Fighting city hall is a serious business for activist group." *Detroit Free Press,* October 14.

Le Monde. 1980. "A Detroit, l'omelette se prepare en cassant des oeufs." March 4.

Luke, Bob, and David McNaughton. 1981. "RenCen loses $33.5 million; behind on debt." *Detroit News,* October 25.

Luria, Dan, and Jack Russell. 1981. *Rational Reindustrialization: An Economic Development Agenda for Detroit.* Detroit: Widgetripper.

McDowell, Edwin. 1980. "Made in USA—with foreign parts." *New York Times,* November 9.

McKay, Roberta V. 1973. "Commuting patterns of inner city residents." *Monthly Labor Review* (November): 44–45.

Mandell, Lewis. 1975. *Industrial Location Decisions: Detroit Compared with Atlanta and Chicago.* New York: Praeger.

Markusen, Ann Roell. 1974. "The economics of social class and metropolitan local government." Ph.D. dissertation, Michigan State University, East Lansing.

Mathewson, Kent, ed. 1974. *The Regionalist Papers.* Detroit: Metropolitan Fund, Inc..

Mattila, John M., and James A. Kurre. 1977. *Detroit Intrametropolitan Location Study.* Detroit: Wayne State University.

Mazza, Jacqueline, and Bill Hogan. 1981. *The State of the Region 1981: Economic Trends in the Northeast and Midwest.* Washington, D.C.: Northeast–Midwest Institute.

Michigan Employment Security Commission. 1975. *Annual Manpower Planning Report.* Detroit: State of Michigan.

Michigan Task Force. n. d. "City of Detroit vs. rest of 3-county SMSA: ADC and GA recipients as percent of total city population, 1969–1974." Lansing.

Mitchell, William J. 1977. "Deputy mayor ready for key federal job." *Detroit Free Press,* February 7.

———. 1974. "Shake-up sets stage for Young to act." *Detroit Free Press,* March 4.

Moberg, David. 1981. "Detroit—I do mind moving." *In These Times,* February 4–10.

Mutlu, Servet. 1979. "Interregional and international mobility of industrial capital: the case of the American automobile and electronics companies." Ph.D. dissertation, University of California, Berkeley.

New Detroit Committee. 1974. *Action Program Against Unemployment.* Detroit.

———. 1973a. "NOW." Detroit, April.

———. 1973b. "NOW." Detroit, August.

———. 1968. *Progress Report.* Detroit.

Northrup, Herbert. 1968. *The Negro in the Automobile Industry.* Philadelphia: University of Pennsylvania Press.

Ostman, Robert, Jr., and Remer Tyson. 1977. "Young kicks off re-election bid." *Detroit Free Press,* February 1.

Peirce, Neal. 1981. "Detroit recovery plan a model." *Lansing State Journal,* July 18.

Radtke, Allen Edward. 1975. "Political fragmentation and inequality among municipalities in Detroit." Masters Thesis, Michigan State University, East Lansing.

Russell, Jack. 1981. "Disinvestment and the fiscal/social stress of Detroit." Unpublished manuscript, Detroit.

Schnore, Leo F., et al. 1976. "Black suburbanization, 1930–1970." Pp. 70–95 in Barry Schwartz, ed., *The Changing Face of the Suburbs.* Chicago: University of Chicago Press.

Scott, Ann. 1970. "Report from Detroit." *Fortune* (February): 80–85.

Serrin, William. 1981. "Huge new GM plant, like many, to get subsidies." *New York Times,* February 25.

———. 1971. "Detroit grows lean while suburbia fattens." *Detroit Free Press,* November 1.

Shaiken, Harley. 1980. "Detroit downsizes U.S. jobs." *The Nation* (October 11): 345–48.

Sinclair, Robert. 1972. *The Face of Detroit: A Spatial Synthesis.* Detroit: Wayne State University, Department of Geography.

Sklar, Holly. 1980. *Trilateralism: The Trilateral Commission and Elite Planning for World Management.* Boston: South End Press.

Stieber, Carolyn. 1970. *The Politics of Change in Michigan.* East Lansing: Michigan State University Press.

Stroud, Joe. 1977. "Uneasy alliance turning Detroit around." *Detroit Free Press,* February 2.

Taylor, Milton, and Donald Peppard. 1976. *Jobs for the Jobless: Detroit's Unresolved Dilemma.* East Lansing, MI: Institute for Community Development.

Taylor, Milton, and Richard Willits. 1971. *Detroit: Agenda for Fiscal Survival.* East Lansing, MI: Institute for Community Development.

Ticknor, Thomas. 1978. "Motor city: the impact of the automobile industry upon Detroit." Ph.D. dissertation, University of Michigan, Ann Arbor.

Tyson, Remer. 1977. "Young has good reason for high hopes for city." *Detroit Free Press,* February 1.

———. 1975. "Mayor Young a year later." *The Nation,* March 1.

———. 1974. "New coalition could give Young Daley-style clout." *Detroit Free Press,* January 2.

U.S. Bureau of the Census. 1971. *Journey to Work.* Washington, D.C.: U.S. Government Printing Office.

U.S. House of Representatives, Committee on Banking, Finance, and Urban Affairs, Subcommittee on the City. 1980. *Hearings on Urban Revitalization and Economic Policy.* Washington, D.C.: U.S. Government Printing Office.

Vaughn, Robert J. 1979. *State Taxation and Economic Development.* Washington, D.C.: Council of State Planning Agencies.

Warbelow, Kathy. 1975a. "Detroit's plight demands city, state, federal plan." *Detroit Free Press,* March 11.

———. 1975b. "Young asks president for billions." *Detroit Free Press,* May 22.

Watson, John. 1969. "To the point of production." *The Movement* (July): 12–16.

Widick, B. J. 1972. *Detroit, City of Race and Class Violence.* Chicago: Quadrangle.

Woutat, Donald. 1980. "Auto money moves south of the border." *Detroit Free Press,* March 2.

4

"Managed Growth" and the Politics of Uneven Development in New Orleans

Michael Peter Smith
Marlene Keller

From its beginning, New Orleans has been an anomaly in the South—a French and Catholic-influenced "exotic" metropolis in an Anglo and Protestant-dominated rural region. It made its connection to the outside world through its port. Thus, to a large extent, it could turn its back on hinterland and region. People flocked to New Orleans. It did not have to engage in serious civic boosterism to induce them to do so. Moreover, its cultivated style of gaudy decadence drew wealth and stimulated the local economy.

Yet, even in the nineteenth century, there were social and individual costs to being a travelers' delight. Crime and corruption became commonplace in the port city, while an emphasis on commercial services with little manufacturing gave bustling commerce an air of genteel decay. Because port activities and tourism prospered, manufacturing played an insignificant role in New Orleans' economic life. Both commerce and tourism required attracting capital investment and people; if either or both faltered, the city's fiscal health would be jeopardized (see Green, 1957; Lewis, 1976; Brownell, 1977).

Today this remains precisely the contradictory situation facing New Orleans. It is often described as "the city that care forgot." It attracts many tourists, drawn to its fine architectural heritage, traditional jazz, good food, and carefree spirit. Yet New Orleans is also the city that industrial investors in the sunbelt forgot. Despite the rapid growth of tourism, an abundant energy supply, the third largest port in the world, and the use of state and local incentives to attract business and industry, a recent study has described New Orleans as an "economic backwater" that has largely missed out on the sunbelt boom (Breckenfeld, 1977: 239).

Although a business-government coalition has sought to foster capital accumulation through a strategy of "managed growth," its rhetoric is rooted in the myth of New Orleans' cultural uniqueness, oblivious to the contradictions revealed in

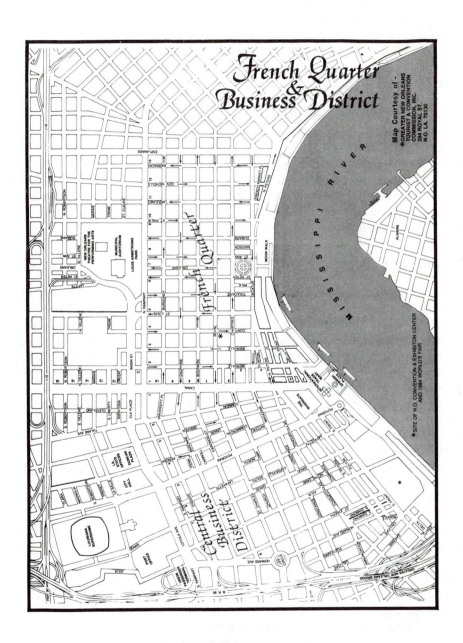

NEW ORLEANS

the city's pattern of uneven urban development. Placed in the larger context of the changing American political economy, New Orleans appears to be an anomaly: a fiscally and socially distressed city in a largely prosperous, growing region.

In a number of related ways, New Orleans resembles the declining industrial cities of the Northeast and Midwest more closely than its sunbelt brethren. Confronting an anomalous situation—a rapidly expanding tourist sector, a downtown office and hotel construction boom, and a national reputation as a livable American city, on the one hand; declining industrial jobs, a revenue crisis, persistent poverty, rising fears of street crime, and growing racial polarization, on the other—New Orleans Mayor Morial has vigorously devoted himself to a thus far unsuccessful attempt to diversify the city's economy. Although his efforts have been considerable, larger systemic factors stand in the way. These include the structural transformation of the overall American economic system throughout the 1970s from a manufacturing to a service base; the dual structure of the local labor market; the institutionalizing of the lower strata, particularly low-income blacks, in inferior public schools; and a woefully inadequate local tax base restrained by state law, local ideology, and a heretofore nearly exclusive reliance on federal urban aid.

UNEVEN REGIONAL AND INTRAMETROPOLITAN DEVELOPMENT

Although Houston is seen by many native New Orleanians as a symbol of the sprawling vulgar modernism that their city has averted, Houston is also envied as a principal sunbelt competitor that has achieved striking growth and diverse economic expansion. While Houston adds population and expands its tax base through annexation, New Orleans has continued to lose population and is prohibited by state law from annexing its rapidly growing suburbs. Houston gained over 600,000 residents, a population increase of 69.9 percent between 1960 and 1980 (Hirsch, 1981: 7). In contrast, New Orleans lost 16 percent of its white population to suburban growth between 1960 and 1970, while its black population increased by an identical percentage (Glassman, 1978: 10). Orleans Parish, which is coterminous with New Orleans, experienced a −8.2 percent outmigration from 1970 to 1975. In contrast, its surrounding suburban parishes, Jefferson, St. Bernard, and St. Tammany, expanded rapidly, owing largely to the expansion of oil-related industries. As 1980 census reports are tabulated, the data reveal that New Orleans has declined even more in the second half of the 1970s, in relation to growth in surrounding parishes and the state as a whole. While Louisiana grew by 15.3 percent, and New Orleans' three surrounding parishes grew by percentages ranging from 25.2 to 73.9 percent, the city lost 6.1 percent of its population (U.S. Bureau of the Census, 1981: 1–11). As Table 4.1 indicates, when outmigration alone is considered as an indicator of "white flight," the population change for the city is even greater. Thus by 1980 New Orleans had become a predominantly black central city.

Just as New Orleans' demographic patterns ran counter to sunbelt and southern Louisiana trends, it also lost out in terms of employment growth. Statewide economic growth in Louisiana during the 1970s was extremely uneven: nonservice, nonextractive, and minority workers sustained the greatest income and employment losses.

TABLE 4.1
City and Suburban Population Change, 1970–78

	Percent Change	Net Migration Change	
		Number	Percent
New Orleans	− 5.8	−64,800	−10.9
Inner suburbs			
Jefferson Parish	+26.3	+50,900	+15.0
Outer suburbs			
St. Bernard Parish	+21.6	+ 6,100	+12.0
St. Tammany Parish	+45.6	+23,400	+ 36.8
Louisiana			
average	+ 8.8	+23,000	+ 0.6

SOURCE: U.S. Bureau of the Census, *Estimates of Population of Counties and Metropolitan Areas,* 1977 and 1978.

Although statewide economic and social indicators such as real per capita income, median income, and persons below the national poverty line improved between 1960 and 1980, these figures serve to mask the persistence of black urban poverty in New Orleans. Much of Louisiana's economic improvement resulted from expansion of the petrochemical industry, accruing either to white-collar professionals who lived in the suburbs or blue-collar primary workers employed in skilled jobs located upriver from New Orleans, stretching toward Baton Rouge and Lafayette (U.S. Bureau of the Census, 1980a).

Just as an employment boom in one sector of a regional economy can mask continuing distress in another sector, statewide employment figures can also mislead, disguising the uneven character of economic growth. Thus while unemployment in Louisiana declined as a labor force percentage from 7.4 percent to 6.7 percent between 1975 and 1979, reflecting oil-related expansion, in absolute numbers statewide unemployment actually increased by about 6,000 persons during the same period. Furthermore, unemployment in the New Orleans SMSA (Orleans Parish) grew markedly from 20,000 to 32,000 between 1970 and 1976. This increased joblessness, occurring at the height of downtown New Orleans' "revitalization," represented about twice the state unemployment rate and about one-third of the state's total joblessness. Thus despite statewide expansion of oil-related jobs and citywide expansion of the tourist sector, the unemployment rate for Orleans Parish remained high, estimated at between 11 and 17 percent. Furthermore, the racial distribution of unemployment in New Orleans has been highly skewed against blacks (see Table 4.2).

During the main period of sunbelt and Louisiana economic growth, New Orleans experienced relative economic decline, particularly in manufacturing. The manufacturing sector in New Orleans, except for shipbuilding, had never been a growth

TABLE 4.2
New Orleans Employment and
Unemployment, by Race, 1980

	Percent Black	Percent White
Total persons 6 to 65 years old	53	45
Total labor force	52	47
Employed	50	49
Unemployed	80	19

SOURCE: Derived from City of New Orleans, Office of Analysis and Planning, Data Analysis Unit, *Citizen Attitude Survey*, 1980.

sector. Much of it was in the apparel, food, tobacco, wood, and paper-products fields, which employed relatively few, albeit also relatively unskilled, workers. Yet even this limited industrial base had been stagnant during the 1950s and 1960s. Since 1967 manufacturing jobs in New Orleans declined in every year but one. By 1977 only 11 percent of the labor force was employed in manufacturing. This placed the city among the lowest in industrial employment in the nation. Growth of the petrochemical industry north of New Orleans has been capital intensive and highly automated. Thus it has provided few jobs for city residents to offset the general decline in manufacturing.

A comparison of central city with suburban per capita income in the New Orleans metropolitan area and the rest of the South in 1976 provides a further indicator of New Orleans' relative distress. Whereas per capita income in other central cities in the South was $4,771 in 1976, New Orleans per capita income was $4,398. Moreover, per capita income in other Southern cities actually averaged 6 percent higher than in their suburban rings, but New Orleans per capita income was over 9 percent lower (Advisory Commission on Intergovernmental Relations, 1977). The principal reason for this income disparity is the high level of unemployment combined with the fact that the jobs which tourism has brought to the city are low-paying, unskilled service jobs that depress wage rates generally and compound the problem of New Orleans' dual labor market.

Income differences are exacerbated by racial ones. White New Orleanians have left the city in sufficient numbers in the last ten years to reverse the racial balance from 55 percent white and 45 percent black, to nearly 45 percent white and 55 percent black. Lacking the legal power of annexation, the city has not been able to avoid a loss in property tax revenues as a consequence of this shift. Faced with continued white flight, New Orleans has attempted to retain its remaining white middle class by keeping its property taxes among the lowest in the nation. Its tax base to finance schools, public services, and improvements in the urban infrastructure has thus been quite limited.

The city's lack of investment in public education has produced a largely unskilled black underclass. The problem of declining industrial jobs is thus compounded by the fact that many potential workers have had insufficient education or training for entry into the primary labor force. This has resulted in a high proportion of unemployed, subemployed, and "discouraged workers" who have dropped out of the labor force because they have lost hope. This latter group has been so sizable that the proportion of the New Orleans population considered a part of the labor force also has been among the lowest in the nation. In 1970 the figure was 55.5 percent, as compared to 65.7 percent in Dallas and 67.8 percent in Houston (Breckenfeld, 1977: 233–39).

These facts explain the finding of a Brookings Institution study that rated New Orleans the third-worst-off central city in the country, after Newark and Saint Louis (Nathan and Adams, 1976). The index of social hardship upon which this study was based included level of poverty, unemployment rate, dependency, education, and crowded housing. Taken together these indicators paint a rather dismal picture of New Orleans, linking it to snowbelt cities in economic distress like Cleveland, Detroit, Buffalo, Newark, and St. Louis, rather than to such sunbelt leaders as Houston or Dallas.

Recent literature on urban America stresses responsive growth as an index of urban and regional vitality. Watkins and Perry (1977), for instance, argue that sunbelt cities, unburdened by "outmoded infrastructure and habits characteristic of past eras," could respond more easily to in-migration of population and technological changes. Their rise was shaped by federal highway and housing monies, tax codes which encouraged new enterprises and business relocation, and federal allocation decisions which put the aerospace industry and military bases in the South. This responsiveness rested on the ability to attract and retain dynamic sectors of the economy: oil and natural gas production, high technology, tourism, agribusiness, and real estate and construction. With a low-paid, mostly nonunionized work force, few taxes, limited intrusion of state and local government, and abundant natural resources, sunbelt cities were said to appeal to leading-edge capital and industry (see, for example, Sale, 1975; Smith, 1979: chapter 6).

Sunbelt cities such as San Jose, Dallas, and Denver clearly fit this growth pattern—as do many other cities in the South, Southwest, and Far West. But there are also urban areas in the sunbelt which have done less well and which can be likened to northern industrial cities displaying signs of distress. Abravanel and Mancini (1980: 28) enumerate the characteristics of these areas: decline in central city population, loss of higher-income and employed persons, decreasing tax revenues, declining capital stock, disinvestment of firms, and increasing public safety and welfare costs.

In numerous ways New Orleans has been a clear loser in the uneven national pattern of urban vitality and urban distress. It has a concentrated and expanding underclass, extreme dependence on a shrinking pool of federal aid, a declining white middle class, an aging infrastructure, and indigenous cultural patterns and structural factors that reinforce a secondary labor market and exert a negative influence on future capital investment. Furthermore, neither port revenues nor tourist dollars alone can sustain New Orleans' economy in the face of nearby aggressive competitors with more diversified economies like Houston or Dallas.

The remainder of this chapter is divided into three parts. The first examines the political economy of downtown development. It reveals the social roots of conflicts between pro- and antigrowth forces and underlines the historical basis for contemporary land-use struggles. The second part explores the second face of urban development in New Orleans. It analyzes the inadequacy of downtown "revitalization" as a strategy to transform a segmented labor market or resolve a crisis of urban public service delivery embedded in the fiscal crisis of the state (O'Connor, 1973). The chapter concludes by examining the social costs of uneven development in New Orleans and their political implications.

MANAGED GROWTH AND DOWNTOWN BOOM

In many parts of the South, ideological opposition to an expanded state role has historically limited the use of eminent domain to disrupt existing commercial uses of downtown areas. Where enthusiasm for downtown redevelopment did occur, it was generally on behalf of civic ventures to provide "a center of public activity in the downtown core without creating competitive office or retail space" (Sanders, 1980: 119). In New Orleans in the 1950s the only development activity by the local state was the bulldozing of a low-income gray area adjacent to the central business district (CBD) to put up a civic center.

Sanders (1980) suggests that interventionist urban redevelopment in a city's CBD, while threatening to existing business users, may nevertheless occur because of potential short-term financial gains to land investors and long-term revenue benefits to public authorities. But this infusion of venture capital to alter urban geography generally requires a mobilized effort by influential business elites, as in San Francisco, or elected officials, as in New Haven, or both (Denver), to produce major urban redevelopment. In New Orleans, local preservationists blocked efforts by progrowth interests to construct an expressway over the French Quarter in the late 1960s. Only in the next decade did finance capital become sufficiently venturesome to promote downtown redevelopment.

Prior to 1970, redevelopment of downtown New Orleans had been limited by both technology and traditionalism. Given the available technology, the cost of extensive high-rise construction on poorly drained land was prohibitive. Furthermore, conservative public policies at the state level both restricted the local revenue that New Orleans could generate and prevented participation in federally sponsored urban renewal until 1970. Third, dominant local business and professional elites were tied to a traditional ethos and social structure which directed their energies away from entrepreneurial economic activities. From their perspective, rapid economic growth through infusion of national or international capital might disrupt their economic and political power base and perhaps dislodge them socially.

This local social elite maintained a dominant position in a traditional social structure through their control over access to prestigeous Mardi Gras organizations ("krewes") and downtown social clubs. Leadership in both types of organizations was restricted to a relatively small circle of native families who had maintained a prominent position in society, local business, and the law since Reconstruction. For new members to gain access to these organizations it was necessary to seek favor with the traditional leadership. According to one commentator, currying favor "often takes the form of business and professional concessions in order to gain approval" (Byrne, 1972). Significantly, the traditional practice of excluding national corporate business elites from positions of prominence in the Mardi Gras structure has been cited by the New Orleans Economic Development Council as a major deterrent to attracting new corporate investment in New Orleans (Glassman, 1978).

One member of the social elite described his cohorts as prone to a "schizophrenic tendency."[1] They acknowledged their behavior and the traditional social structure as obstacles to "progress" (i.e., to economic growth and greater capital accumulation as a whole), yet they were unwilling to attempt to change the traditional system, which clearly benefited their individual business interests. Another commented: "These social kings simply want stagnation" (Chai, 1972).

Since the late 1960s, however, structural economic and demographic changes in the metropolitan region have engendered new economic and social forces, hastened the sociospatial transformation of downtown New Orleans, and brought new political conflicts to the surface. In the process, the political cohesiveness of the traditional social elites has been shaken, some members siding with progrowth forces in order to capture some of the returns of development, others joining with preservationist forces to resist growth.

Improved technologies for landfill and engineering developments geared to high-rise construction both accelerated suburban growth and facilitated the emergence of a progrowth business faction in New Orleans. Suburban parishes (counties) grew by nearly 177,000 between 1970 and 1980—largely a white influx in response to the industrial decentralization that had been spurred by the completion of new transportation arteries in the previous decade. Out-migration from New Orleans was initially reflected in slumping retail sales, a crime-ridden downtown shopping area, and general CBD decay. As is typical in the sunbelt, many shoppers from the city began to commute to outlying malls, often in adjacent Jefferson Parish, to do one-stop convenience purchasing. Traffic and parking remained problems of the city center.

As CBD land values declined with increased suburbanization and continuing neglect, investment capital began to be drawn to the city center by the increasing possibility of large speculative profits. In 1970 the geographic and cultural heart of the metropolitan region was still the French Quarter (Vieux Carré). By the end of the decade, the district which gave a unique flavor to life in New Orleans was under threat at its borders. Publicly financed and privately developed projects, particularly high-rise hotels and office-shopping complexes, surrounded the Vieux Carré historic treasures (Hirsch, 1981: 17). More were planned or underway. During the mayoral administrations of Moon Landrieu (1970–78) and Ernest Morial (1978–), both of whom had been elected by coalitions of black voters and white liberals, a downtown construction boom began. It added 3.5 million square feet of office space, several high-rise office buildings, luxury hotels, publicly financed theme parks, and the Superdome.

Two urban battles in the mid 1960s and early 1970s significantly shaped New Orleans' development history. The first was the successful attempt to build the Superdome. The second was the defeat of efforts to construct a Riverfront Expressway and a Napoleon Avenue Bridge. The Superdome acted as a lure to the arrival of a number of chain hotels, increased out-of-state tourism, and aided political efforts to justify rejuvenation of the CBD. Yet the Dome also came to be viewed as a symbol of crass urban architecture and of the delays and unanticipated cost overruns of most publicly subsidized, large-scale construction projects. Defeat of the expressway and bridge plans prevented the Vieux Carré and uptown New Orleans from being swamped by "congestive blight." The absence of the highway projects, however, left open the possibility for commercial and residential riverfront development, "gentrification" of surrounding neighborhoods, and, ultimately, location of a 1984 World's Fair. The pivotal nature of these developments and the political insights they reveal warrant their consideration in some detail.

The Superdome Controversy

Development of the Superdome set the stage for a tourist-based growth strategy for the future development of downtown New Orleans. The politics of that development nicely illustrates both the unique convergence of interests leading to its construction and the more typical distribution pattern of its costs and benefits. The Dome was built because of the interactive effect of national finance and property development capital, a state and local political structure rooted in the politics of jobs and contracts, and an opposition limited mainly to reluctant local financial capitalists and fiscally conservative "good government" forces.

Because the state of Louisiana had not yet authorized local governments to participate in federal urban renewal projects in 1965, when the Superdome project was originally conceived, the Superdome development involved neither federal financial support nor federal policy constraints. Additionally, although it was a megastructure involving massive site development, it entailed little if any displacement. It was built on land that had been occupied mainly by railroad yards. Yet the project might never have been deemed economically or politically feasible if a nearby low-income gray area had not been bulldozed fifteen years earlier to construct the city Civic Center.

James Jones, the national banking executive who assembled the out-of-state financial backing for the Dome, established the connection between this earlier action and the Superdome in a statement that also reveals the underlying logic of urban development in societies where the revenue needs of the local state are dependent on private property development. According to Jones, the low-income neighborhood torn down to build the Civic Center

was a downtown gray area where a late and visionary postwar mayor—deLesseps (Chep) Morrison—successfully exorcised a wretched, festering slum and replaced it with a civic center complex, thereby raising the value and the attractiveness of adjacent land. The subsequent addition of office buildings, apartment, and hotel structures confirmed the wisdom of municipal regeneration. . . . [With the addition of the Dome] Poydras, once a drab and forgotten street, may now become one of the great thoroughfares of America. . . . The *protection* this will give the central business district, the effect it will have on the bulldozed blocks in between us is, naturally, beyond measure. (Byrne, 1972: 22, emphasis added)

James Jones' involvement in developing the Superdome also indicates the leading role that national finance capital has played in the postwar urban development of New Orleans. A native of Dallas, Jones became president of the National Bank of Commerce in New Orleans in the early 1960s. Faced with fiscally conservative local banking competitors and a traditional social structure, Jones brought much new outside capital to the city and began to lend aggressively to real estate developers. When New Orleans' largest bank, the Whitney, refused to purchase Superdome bonds, he turned to the Citizens and Southern National Bank of Atlanta for the needed financial support (Glassman, 1978: 10ff). Jones eventually left New Orleans to head the Bank of California, after failing to persuade the Louisiana legislature to "liberalize" an antibranch banking law, originally enacted during the Huey Long era to protect small in-state banks from competition by outside capital.

In selling the Dome to Governor McKeithen and to his successor Edwin Edwards, Jones was aided by a state political structure and ethos that had thrived since the Long era on the exchange of contracts for large-scale, state-financed development projects in return for political support. The national political ambitions of both governors also gave them an interest in taking credit for promoting a megastructure certain to gain the city and state considerable national publicity.

In selling the Superdome to the public, progrowth forces argued that the project would pay for itself within a few years, causing no drain on the state or local economy. The Dome would be a benefit to the "community as a whole," displacing no one and providing such spinoff effects as more tourist money, greater tax revenues generated by tourism, and a boost to the regional economy that would create many new service jobs. In this context of costless growth, the project was approved by state voters 3 to 1 in 1966.

Widespread public support for the project began to wane, however, as Superdome construction was beset by large cost overruns and charges of political cronyism. In the 1966 election campaign to secure bond approval for the Dome, voters had been told that the total cost would be about $35 million, the cost of Houston's Astrodome. Instead, the total actual cost was about $165 million, and the Superdome has had a large deficit for each year of operation. Delays in construction as well as legal suits by fiscally conservative taxpayers and good government forces combined with inflation to produce the large overruns. The 1977 operating loss was $5.5 million, on top of yearly debt service of about $10 million.

Rising costs prompted a series of unsuccessful legal suits objecting to the lease-financing arrangement by which the state of Louisiana absorbs all of the above costs. Lease-financing is a common practice used to build public projects in Louisiana. Its use in financing the Dome made it unnecessary for officials to go back to the voters for approval of additional bonded debt when the Dome experienced its large cost overruns. The arrangement obliges the state, as technical "tenant" of the Super-dome, to pay a "rent" equal to the difference between the stadium's revenues and its expenses, including bond payments (see Byrne, 1972: 25). Through this provision, the general taxpayers of the state have been required to absorb the cost and all of the risk of a deficit-ridden project that may never become self-financing.

Who are the main beneficiaries of this large public subsidy? Substantial profits have been realized by the interests that developed an office-hotel-shopping complex on land adjacent to the Superdome and by the Hyatt Corporation that built the hotel. The Illinois Central Railroad also was a clear winner. It owned the land near the Dome on which the Hyatt complex eventually was built. It sold the land to a group of real estate investors for less than half its estimated value, but, through a subsidiary, Lasalle Properties, it retained a 49 percent interest in the property. Further, the railroad retained ownership of adjoining property, the value of which was sub-stantially enhanced by the Hyatt development. James Jones's bank was another winner. It received a $100,000 fee for acting as "trustee" for the construction accounts, the accounts themselves, and a $1 million return on the two-coupon pricing of the bond issue (Byrne, 1972).

Architects, contractors, insurers, lawyers, and service companies connected to this constellation of interests all reaped sizable tangible benefits. The panel chosen to advise the Superdome Commission on the granting of insurance contracts consisted of five insurance company executives. Several of the insurers were tied either by family relationship or by political alliances to prominent state legislators or to then governor Edwin Edwards. Among the recipients of legal fees from the Commission was Pascal Calogero, now a state Supreme Court judge, who was then a law partner of Moon Landrieu. Another particularly well-connected lawyer, who defended the Dome in all of its court challenges, negotiated a rental fee with the Dome on behalf of the New Orleans Saints. He also was counsel to the Illinois Central, an attorney for Jones's bank, and provided legal advice to the bond company that provided the underwriting advice on stadium financing. In turn, a land investment group indirectly connected with the bond company purchased the Hyatt parcel from the railroad (see Byrne, 1972: 22–25).

Through similar political relations some tangible benefits did trickle down to low-income blacks. Following complaints that black interests were being excluded from the returns on Dome development, a multimillion-dollar contract for servicing public events at the stadium was awarded to Sherman Coplin, a former antipoverty activist during the 1960s who had become a political ally of Mayor Moon Landrieu. Coplin created a profit-making corporation, Superdome Services Incorporated, to fulfill the service contract. Superdome Services was used to award low-skilled service jobs (e.g., ticket takers) to supporters of Coplin's black political organization, SOUL, which came to resemble a traditional urban political machine in form and function.

In the final analysis, a state and local political system that thrived on jobs and contracts comprised a fertile milieu for the forging of a curious alliance of "liberal" politicians, national property developers, local land speculators, suppliers of skilled services, and black political-interest groups arrayed against a traditional social elite, conservative local bankers, and "good government" interests upset by the normal political practices of patronage politics. The former coalition emerged victorious, setting the stage for further development of a tourist-based economy. A growth strategy premised on expanded tourism was rendered increasingly feasible by the defeat of progrowth forces on another front—their effort to expand the interstate highway system to create better access in and out of downtown New Orleans.

The Riverfront Expressway and Bridge Controversies

The Riverfront Expressway was a proposal first advanced by New York City planner Robert Moses in 1946 to build a 40-foot-high, 108-foot-wide, six-lane interstate highway along the Mississippi riverfront of the Vieux Carré, dwarfing the French Quarter's Saint Louis Cathedral and many of the area's historic buildings. The expressway would have been linked to the North-South Dixie Freeway, permitting easier travel between New Orleans, other parishes, and Texas, Mississippi, and Florida. The proposal was a source of continuing controversy from its inception until its ultimate defeat in 1969.

The plan had the support of the Greater New Orleans Chamber of Commerce, a group of downtown financial and business interests organized into an umbrella coalition known as the Central Area Committee, and some leading civic elites. It also was backed politically by New Orleans congressman Hale Boggs and, initially, by the press and then city councilman Moon Landrieu. Arrayed against the project was an intensely committed coalition of historic preservationists, affected neighborhood groups, members of other civic elites, including the owner of one of the city's television stations, and the Catholic archbishop of New Orleans, Philip Hannan, who feared the highway would structurally damage historic Saint Louis Cathedral.

The 1960s was a decade of ceaseless struggle between these interests. In *The Second Battle of New Orleans* (1980) Bombach and Borah categorize the conflict surrounding the expressway development as a "bitter" and "wasteful" struggle that diverted attention from other pressing urban social problems, such as poverty and rising crime rates. Although the core of the antigrowth coalition was primarily parochial, protecting the participants' interests in existing land use patterns, it was able to use ideological commitment to "historic preservation" to build a useful and effective centralized operation. The "obstructionists," as they came to be called by progrowth forces, conducted a nationwide, articulate opposition, calling on federal environmental bureaucrats and historic preservationist organizations to join in the battle to halt the highway. Through their efforts to broaden the scope of the conflict (see Schattschneider, 1960), the Riverfront Expressway was effectively killed in 1969, when United States Secretary of Transportation John Volpe cut off all federal financial support for the project. Volpe cited the damage the highway might do to the historic character of the French Quarter as grounds for his decision, thereby placating national pressure directed at his agency and the new Nixon administration.

Subsequently, part of the planned highway development was revived in the form of a proposed bridge across the Mississippi River at Napoleon Avenue. The bridge would have placed access ramps in an affluent neighborhood in uptown New

Orleans. This plan, too, provoked considerable controversy. The bridge was intended to link New Orleans more directly to its southern suburbs, in the hope that this would draw shoppers, stimulate commuting, and encourage more investment in the CBD. In this instance, progrowth interests faced a well-organized opposition, spurred on by the lessons of the Riverfront Expressway controversy concerning successful resistance. Neighborhood residents in the affected area were mobilized into an effective political force by a sympathetic city councilman, Eddie Sapir.

Determined to avoid prolonged resistance by a coalition of upper-middle-class homeowners, whose class interest in residential property was threatened by the bridge, proponents shifted their political strategy. They proposed to move the bridge site to a black neighborhood on General Taylor Street. But this strategy of relying on the expected passivity of lower social strata backfired because of the particular historical context in which the maneuver was attempted. Having integrated the public schools in the 1960s, black civil rights activists were still highly mobilized. A particularly skillful community organizer, Orthea Haley, successfully mobilized vocal opposition to the bridge's probable displacement effects in the black community. The maneuver also cost progrowth forces the support of Moon Landrieu, who dramatically converted from proponent to opponent of the bridge when the plans were shifted from a white to a black neighborhood. This change of heart served to legitimate the Landrieu administration in the black community and shored up black political support for his two-term mayoralty. In 1973, in the context of intense politicization and declining political support, both bridge plans were defeated (Bombach and Borah, 1980; Katz, 1981b: 35).

The expressway and the bridge proposals stood to benefit progrowth interests by encouraging increased real estate development in both the downtown and the metropolitan ring. Business investors and real estate developers reasoned that shoppers and commuters, even those from nearby states, would likely follow the new transportation arteries which directed the location of new development. They argued that metropolitan-wide expansion was a prerequisite to economic growth, and that New Orleans, unlike Houston, was hemmed in by water. The city, thus, would need to build across it, or fill it in, in order to grow.

The defeat of the progrowth forces in these controversies illustrates the limits of economic power without political support. When growth cannot be sold as a costless process that benefits everyone, or when elites are divided on the question, political struggle can prevail over the logic of growth. In the case of the expressway, unity and cohesion among French Quarter aesthetes, property owners, and the Catholic church to protect their stake in the preservation of existing land uses was aided by the unique historical character of the Vieux Carré, enabling local interests to build a wider coalition with national political forces motivated by an ideology of "preservationism." These forces were sufficient to outweigh the influence of progrowth oriented economic and political elites. Successful resistance to displacement by civil rights activists and community organizers opposing the General Taylor Bridge was a historically specific by-product of the high degree of politicization among blacks in New Orleans during the late 1960s and early 1970s. Their growing voting strength and heightened consciousness made their political support indispensable to the careers of emergent local politicians, including normally progrowth activists like Moon Landrieu.

Ironically, the very failure of the expressway and bridge plans to spur development of the CBD by a strategy of highway construction created the preconditions for a more successful tourist-based "managed growth" strategy throughout the 1970s. As one local commentator, sympathetic to the expansion of tourism and its implications for further development, said: "Had the riverfront expressway been built as proposed, the character of the Vieux Carré would have been destroyed and there would be no plans today for a riverfront 1984 New Orleans World's Fair, nor for condominiums and hotel rooms atop the Poydras Street wharf" (Katz, 1981b: 35).

"Managed Growth" and the Downtown "Renaissance"

With the defeat of a concerted urban development strategy, the progrowth coalition shifted to an incremental, "managed growth" approach. This approach had the appearance of rational planning and shrewd fiscal policy; it partially deflected further en masse preservationist resistance. A key feature of "managed growth" was to focus development in areas where high-intensity land use already existed, rather than allowing it to take place on scattered sites that could provoke resistance. Ostensibly the concern was to concentrate profits under the aegis of rational land management. Thus in April 1974, the New Orleans City Council first imposed a "moratorium" on "wholesale" destruction of older property in the central business district, thereby placating preservationist sentiment (New Orleans *States-Item*, 1976).

A key preliminary step in pursuit of this strategy for downtown "revitalization" was establishment of control over revenue generation and the planning process. For two years, from 1973 to 1975, the Landrieu administration joined with the Chamber of Commerce to draw up a growth management program for the CBD. The completed program called for the creation of a special CBD tax district, the enactment of new zoning provisions to regulate the location of development projects within the district, the encouragement of CBD residential construction as well as new office and hotel buildings, "high quality pedestrian amenities," and a shoppers mall, all connected to improved transportation out of the CBD. The newly created local urban-renewal arm, the Community Improvement Agency, was to oversee the entire development process, under the watchful eye of CBD tax district commissioners and the City Council. To further placate preservationists, as well as to garner bicentennial funding, the plan called for the designation of two new historic districts in the CBD, one along Canal Street, the other in the vicinity of Lafayette Square (New Orleans *Times-Picayune*, 1975c; *Preservation Press*, 1975a, 1975b).

Although the tax district was created by an act of the state legislature that authorized the core area development district (CADD), the plan ran aground on a number of other issues which threatened profits from CBD land. Among these were a controversial zoning recommendation that the floor area ratio (the ratio of total built floor area to the site area) be reduced. As in post-1970 downtown development of San Francisco, this proposed qualification on site expansion in favor of environmental and aesthetic considerations was bitterly opposed by progrowth developers.

New Orleans investors and lot owners similarly resisted efforts at downtown land-scaping, preferring unimproved parking lots and vacant land (New Orleans *Times-Picayune,* 1975a, b).

The expressed aim of "managed growth" was a CBD functioning as a central city "magnet" to well-planned, quality growth and gradual urban reinvestment. Increasingly, however, decisions about CBD land use, aesthetics, and public cost were made on a building or block basis, often in an ad hoc fashion. The typical results have been single-building construction, scaled-down plans as interest rates have climbed and financing has become scarce, frequent grants of "spot" zoning and zoning variances, and continuing problems with downtown traffic congestion. Despite a general moratorium on building demolition, older CBD buildings have been removed piecemeal to make room for high-rent, high-rise offices and luxury hotels. Owners and speculators invariably urged denser development to capture more profits. The French Quarter per se, with strong, proven defenders and clear value to tourist-based CBD investment, was left fairly intact, its preservation resting on the strict regulations of the Vieux Carré Commission. Yet by the end of the decade, variances and exemptions granted to adjacent development threatened to wall in the historic district.

Despite the absence of any real public management of urban growth, the symbol-ism of "managed growth" has usefully masked the speculative, uneven nature of CBD development. The "Growth Management Program" has been used as a symbolic resource by the Downtown Development District when possible alternative land uses threatened proposed large-scale commercial uses of space in the CBD. For example, when the Louisiana State Health Educational Authority (HEAL) proposed in 1980 that land on Poydras Street be used for its heat and air-conditioning generat-ing station, development district officials agreed with the Real Estate Board of New Orleans that this would not be the best use of the land. The district took the posi-tion that the proposal violated the sound planning and tax-revenue-raising prin-ciples annunciated in the growth management program. (New Orleans *Times-Picayune,* 1980b: 7).

In opposing the health project the president of the Real Estate Board vividly captured the social opportunity costs embedded in the very logic of intermetropolitan competition for business location. He argued that such an "unwise," purely public development in the CBD would "permanently erase" the Poydras Street development corridor's "potential for assisting the city in efforts to meet its financial obligations in a manner that harms nobody and is fair to all" (New Orleans *Times-Picayune,* 1980b: 7). Once again economic growth was sold as a process that inevitably lifts all boats and has no losers. In the process, alternative uses of space that might be of general public benefit are automatically discounted as no more than a drain on the city's revenue base. All forms of private development, in contrast, are welcomed as a boon to the city and its taxpayers. A closer examination of the actual development of high-rise hotels, office buildings, and residential property in New Orleans' down-town core from the mid 1970s until the early 1980s, reveals the real pattern of benefits and costs entailed by this model of urban development.

Canal Place.   Downtown property owners, real-estate developers, and firms serving these interests have gained the most from downtown revitalization. The development of Canal Place illustrates the politics and outcomes of "managed growth." Using a favorable provision of the city charter, a major New Orleans developer, Joseph Canizaro, arranged a land swap by which his development company, Canizaro Interests, obtained a large plot of riverfront land previously owned by the city, in exchange for a smaller plot elsewhere. The city, in turn, used federal funds to erect the Plaza d'Italia, a neo-Baroque public square on the smaller property. The plaza was intended to provide an additional tourist attraction as well as to shore up political support among Italian-American voters, by supplying a visible symbol of their political ties to city hall.

To Canizaro, the Canal Place plan represented urban "physical evolution," extending CBD development riverward. To preservationists, French Quarter residents, and small businessmen, it symbolized unrestrained growth. Preservationists once again were mobilized to resist the project's adverse impacts on urban scale, historic-district regulations, open space, public access to the river, and excess demand on existing transportation. Small property capital interests joined these forces, objecting to the "threat of unequal regulation of small Quarter businesses and homes as opposed to the large developer" (*Preservation Press, 1978*).

In the struggle to win support from authorities in the face of vocal opposition, Canizaro Interests enjoyed a structurally privileged position. First, the systemic position (see Stone, 1980) of private capital investors in the American political economy is such that the elites who manage the local state are dependent upon them to provide the basic outputs of the local political economy—employment, alterations in the built environment, and revenues to finance public services. The local state thus is structurally required to facilitate the private accumulation process in order to be able to act on behalf of any other interests in society. Secondly, in the case of New Orleans, it was becoming increasingly clear to local political elites that despite massive infusions of federal aid, the city was in a fiscal crisis. Canizaro represented a major source of venture capital to local authorities needing downtown development to shore up an inadequate tax base which exempted most households from paying property taxes.

In addition to this privileged position, Canizaro used resources instrumentally to gain political support. Thus, for example, he now heads CADD. After Moon Landrieu stepped down as mayor, he went to work for Canizaro Interests in an advisory capacity. More recently, Canizaro has allied himself with Mayor Morial's efforts to attract foreign capital to New Orleans. In this political milieu of close public and private interdependence, a scaled-down version of Canal Place, modified into three stages, won official approval, political support, and financial subsidy (New Orleans *Times-Picayune*, 1978).

Nevertheless, the second and third phases of the project still required review by the President's Advisory Council on Historic Preservation. In June 1981, the Council informed the U.S. Department of Housing and Urban Development (HUD) regional office that its funds could not be released to support Canal Place because no environmental impact assessment had been made of the third phase of the project, even though the approved second phase was a prelude to the third. The city argued that because no federal funds were involved in phase three, no such evaluation was necessary. Faced with outraged preservationists and the Advisory Council ultimatum, the city was forced to develop support for its position that the new phases would have no adverse impacts on the French Quarter (New Orleans *Times-Picayune/ States-Item*, 1981b: 14). Once again an organized ideological opposition had slowed the pace, but not altered the form, of downtown development by enlisting support from one federal agency to oppose the actions of another. The basic logic of the local situation, combined with the spate of new high-rise buildings that have arisen elsewhere in the CBD in the late 1970s, however, suggests that ultimately the vacant land on which Canal Place Two and Three are to be built will see a continuation of the high-density development pattern that has characterized "managed growth."

The Big Oil Office Boom.   Under Moon Landrieu's administration large hotel chains were the most prominent feature of downtown development. Under Ernest Morial, petro-dollars began to make their mark. Eight high-rise office buildings were either started or completed during the last six months of 1980. Much of the new spurt of high-rise office construction was stimulated by a heavy demand by major oil companies for office space for themselves, combined with demand resulting from ancilliary services. During 1980, 35 oil firms rented nearly 30 percent of CBD office space. The oil companies themselves have sought managerial proximity to their many Louisiana and offshore oil operations. Thus Shell has its own building and is seeking more space; Amoco, Chevron, Exxon, and Gulf are building (New Orleans *Times-Picayune/States-Item*, 1981: 8, 2). The oil company expansion also has brought in spinoff skilled service jobs: it has attracted hundreds of smaller oil-related firms, geological and engineering consultants, and increased demand for certain professionals such as lawyers and accountants.

The rapidity of this influx raises the possibility that the oil boom might cause overbuilding through excessive speculation in office development, as was true of Atlanta in the early 1970s. The first stages of office location and some of the early oil company locational choices were prompted by bargain-basement rents and landlords willing to make concessions to attract tenants. As CBD development proceeded, CBD real estate values skyrocketed, a shortage of office space developed, rents rose, and oil companies decided to become their own landlords. By 1981 some long-time tenants in downtown offices were being forced out by rising rents and nonrenewal of earlier, more favorable leases. In cases where oil companies were landlords, when their space needs increased, they took over more square feet of their own buildings. Tenants losing leases were forced to relocate, sometimes to nearby suburbs (New Orleans *Times-Picayune/States Item*, 1980a). While the impact of these job relocations is not yet clear, the long-run probability is the concentration of more oil-related jobs spatially, hence a reduction in diversified downtown employment.

Whose class interests have been served by what has been termed the downtown "renaissance"? The billion-dollar-a-year tourist sector has benefited, as have the tourists who get subsidized crime prevention from CADD, a relatively well-manicured French Quarter, and a rare look at an American city where historic preservation has become an asset to the tourist industry. So too have affluent urban and suburban shoppers drawn to expensive retail outlets like Brooks Brothers and Saks that located in the core area in the late 1970s to attract the trade of the white-collar professionals working in the new high-rise office buildings (Katz, 1981a: 39). Plans to locate a condominium tower on top of the Poydras Street wharf once the 1984 World's Fair is completed indicate that a new class of luxury-apartment dwellers may well emerge to take advantage of the sociospatial transformation of downtown New Orleans.

The core area boom has not trickled down to the second New Orleans—a deteriorating, predominantly poor, black residential city facing a structurally rooted crisis of joblessness and chronic neglect. Before turning to that second face of New Orleans, we will consider a final aspect of the downtown boom, the planning of the 1984 New Orleans World's Fair.

The 1984 World's Fair.   Efforts to advertise New Orleans to the world as a tourist mecca by the city's sponsorship of the 1984 World's Fair reflect once again the extent to which those who benefit most directly by growth resort to the misleading metaphor that growth is a rising tide that lifts all boats. The corporate and financial sponsors of the fair have much to gain from the ongoing sociospatial transformation of downtown New Orleans into a tourist, office, and luxury housing zone. A leading force behind the Fair is Lester Kabacoff, a partner in developing the Hilton Hotel complex which is located near the Fair site. The Fair will transform 84 acres of warehouses and docks located along the riverfront into a short-term tourist attraction that holds forth the promise of long-term commercial and residential development. Corporate and financial sponsors of the fair include other likely direct beneficiaries, including tourist-related industries, utility companies, and financial institutions (Hager, 1981: 3; Hager and Anderson, 1981: 19).

The Fair's sponsors have been insured against risk by the state government under Republican Governor David Treen. The state is providing $30 million for construction of a riverfront exhibition hall and convention center, which is to be the centerpiece of the Fair, and has agreed to pay $14 million to the New Orleans Dock Board to relocate two docks. To attract additional private investors, Treen also agreed to absorb the first $5 million of any Fair deficit. Thus insured of minimal risk, the corporate sponsors have stressed the long-term benefits to the city as a whole in new jobs, economic activity, and tax revenues once the fair is over and the district is permanently transformed into a commercial and residential addition to the CBD (Katz, 1981: 33).

The Fair's professional organizer and general manager claimed that in addition to creating 14,000 short-term and 39,000 total jobs, the Fair would have a $2 billion ripple effect on the New Orleans regional economy. He even claimed that the Fair would "harness" the city's energies to "do something" about crime, blight, and street disrepair. In his words: "There is a lot of Alice in Wonderland here. . . . Everybody gets a prize" (quoted in Anderson, 1981: 20).

Mayor Morial's support for the Fair, while less hyperbolic, is equally enthusiastic.

Using a $14 million Urban Development Action Grant (UDAG), the city is joining forces with the state and adding $40 million in hotel-motel tax revenues to construct the New Orleans Convention and Exhibition Center. Thus tax revenue which might otherwise alleviate the crisis in public service delivery in the rest of the city will not "trickle down." Instead it will be recycled to benefit directly the very interests who paid it, and whose arrival was hailed as a major step toward fiscal solvency. Nevertheless, city officials justify the expenditure as a form of investment, predicting that the facility will be "capable of attracting more than 1,000 conventions and trade shows annually." The additional construction and service jobs stimulated by the facility are used by city officials to justify the public cost. The dubious conclusion is reached that "the opportunity is present to include all citizens in this economic prize."

Despite this benign image of costless growth, Fair advocates have ignored various short-term and some possible long-term costs. For instance, the initial environmental impact assessment report underlined the extensive new demands that the project will make on local public services, including police, fire, health, sewer, water, drainage, and sanitation (*Gambit,* 1980: 5) Additionally, the Fair's sponsors have yet to obtain rerouting agreements with railroad companies that regularly haul dangerous cargo on tracks near the Fair site.

Over the long run the New Orleans Dock Board has indicated that it wants its two wharves put back into their original, pre-Fair condition so that they can once again be used to accommodate river commerce. This signals a possible future controversy between a faction of capital that seeks maximum use of scarce riverfront land for international trade, and real estate and finance capitalist interests, who project this area as a key building block of residential and commercial development of the central business district (see New Orleans *Times-Picayune,* 1981a: 14). Should the former be successful, a small number of primary labor market industrial jobs along the waterfront will be a likely result; should the latter faction prevail, a larger number of construction and service-related secondary labor market jobs will result. In neither case will the structural defects of the New Orleans economy be addressed, let alone resolved. It is to these defects that we now turn.

STRUCTURAL ECONOMIC CHANGE AND POLITICAL RESPONSE

In a statement before a 1979 Congressional committee, New Orleans Mayor Ernest Morial declared that one-half of New Orleans' residents were still "poor or impoverished." What economic development had occurred in the 1970s, failed to provide "adequate employment opportunities" for the bulk of the city's residents. The 1970 Census revealed that New Orleans' low-income areas contained 90 percent of the city's black labor force and 82 percent of the New Orleans SMSA unemployment. Poverty had become even more widespread among New Orleans' black residents, who also were more geographically concentrated, and hence spatially segregated, within the central-city core than had been true at the start of the decade.

But unemployment rates were, by themselves, misleading and insufficient indicators. Some New Orleanians were not in the labor force at all and could be characterized by grave poverty, little education, and lack of training. "Subemployment" was the city's "critical and intractable problem." A labor force unable to participate in whatever high-income, skilled jobs accompanied sunbelt growth became a drag on productivity and the local economy. New Orleans had become (or reverted to) "two economies and two societies." This time the demarcation was not free or slave, but primary or secondary labor market. The "human, social, and physical blight" which uneven urban and national development fostered, made a distressed city like New Orleans less responsive to solely private-sector economic expansion. Private capital invested in the city only reluctantly, and in too small and uncoordinated a way to affect the most needy residents. New Orleans' problems required "clear, decisive" local and federal policy. In Morial's view it also required substantial federal aid (New Orleans Office of Policy Planning, 1979: iii–vi).

The Mayor's 1979 report on economic development also acknowledged the urgency of the city's subemployment problem. The report indicated that the Mayor sought to use public incentives to promote all forms of economic growth, in the hope that this would generate enough jobs to absorb secondary workers. He has described economic growth as "urban salvation."

Planning Economic Development

Starting from the common but dubious premise that growth per se can eliminate subemployment, Morial created an Economic Development Planning Unit at city hall. His initial economic development plans were shaped by his growing dependence on programs and funds emanating from the Carter administration's urban policies. An examination of one such program reveals the inadequacies of the policies as a strategy for dealing with subemployment.

Using the combined resources of the federal Economic Development Administration (EDA), HUD, and the Small Business Administration (SBA), Morial set up a "local development company" (LDC) termed the New Orleans Citywide Development Corporation (NOCDC). Its purpose was to attract private sector jobs and investment back to declining central cities. Morial sought to coordinate this effort locally by naming prominent local business, academic, and banking leaders to sit on the board of directors of the quasi-public corporation. The board's job was to assist businesses in obtaining credit through arranging joint ventures between the Small Business Administration, private lenders, and the NOCDC.

This complex policy structure was needed because the institutionalized practices of commercial banks and insurance companies make it very difficult for small and even medium-sized businesses to secure long-term loans privately on affordable terms. Savings and loan associations, the other possible source of private investment capital, are legally prohibited from making sizable loans for commercial purposes.

What has been the impact of this policy in New Orleans? Several small and medium-sized businesses, primarily already existing firms with strong credit ratings, have been given public subsidies to expand or relocate through lowered down-payment requirements, SBA loan guarantees, interest-rate subsidies, and stretched-out payback terms. Private lenders have had a veto power over all loans issued even though their risk is entirely underwritten by the taxpayer. Yet, because of this veto power, a "strong credit history" is a required condition for obtaining a loan. Thus newer kinds of employment structures like community development corporations, neighborhood-based producers' cooperatives, or even new private businesses in low-income neighborhoods are effectively screened out of the process. Because existing firms are already part of the dual labor market structure, there is little likelihood that the policy will even address, let alone resolve, the structural problem of subemployment. Its chief benefit is the limited one of keeping somewhat more capital in circulation in the local economy, by slowing the rate of small-business failure.

A more fundamental problem with this approach to the problem of subemployment is that it altogether ignores the structurally stratified character of a dual labor market (Gordon, 1972; Piore, 1976). The "subemployed" include part-time workers who are seeking full-time employment, those already employed full time but at wages below the official poverty level (i.e., the "working poor"), and "discouraged" workers, who have dropped out of the labor force because they have given up hope. These subemployed workers comprise a separate segment of the labor force. The very nature of the types of employment available in the secondary market— its unskilled, transient, deadend, and low-paying character—is the issue that gets deflected by calls for growth-stimulating public policies. Even if a growth strategy were to generate significant numbers of new jobs in an urban area, cities plagued by a dual labor market structure face the following contradiction: If the new employment is in the primary labor market, entailing skilled, relatively permanent career lines, the limited mobility that currently exists between the segmented primary and secondary sectors would prevent a significant reduction of subemployment. Yet if the jobs created by new growth match up more closely with the limited skills, erratic work histories, and minimal career lines that are functional for firms employing secondary workers, expansion of the size of the secondary labor market compounds the subemployment problem.

Local consciousness of this contradiction is minimal. The image of New Orleans' recent downtown boom depicted in the press supports Mayor Morial's image of economic growth as "urban salvation." Thus press headlines term New Orleans the "Number 1 U.S. Port"; declare an employment boom in aerospace technology; hail the city's "Giant Plan" for developing eastern New Orleans; and assert that "Boom isn't coming to N.O.—it's here."

The realities behind these images are quite different from the headlines' incessantly upbeat tone. Consider the following discrepancies: Despite the large volume of cargo passing through New Orleans, the economic value of that cargo still ranks third nationally. More important, little of the trade passing through the port is locally based. Thus it has had only a limited multiplier effect on the circulation of capital in the local economy. Additionally, because of technological changes in labor processes, primarily the containerization of ship cargo into preloaded vans, longshore work has become much less labor intensive, thereby limiting the effect of increased shipping on local employment opportunities.

Other structural changes in the American economy have widened the distance between the subemployed and the jobs being created in the growth sectors of manufacturing. Thus, for instance, the people employed by the Martin Marietta Aerospace Center in eastern New Orleans to build fuel tanks for the space shuttle consist of 2,300 highly skilled workers, most of whom commute from nearby white suburbs. Meanwhile, as noted above, the 1970s witnessed a steady decline in manufacturing jobs in New Orleans requiring fewer skills. Food manufacturing alone, once a major employer of blue-collar industrial workers, fell from 12,700 to 8,700 in the decade, thereby offsetting the growth in aerospace production (New Orleans *Times-Picayune*, 1980a: 41).

Because of New Orleans' favorable location as a port city, there are objective possibilities for expanding wholesale employment. Yet, here too, contradictory pressures are present. Land that might be upgraded along the Mississippi River to improve the city's warehousing facilities is being competed for by factions of capital that would expand tourism and luxury housing outward from downtown along the riverfront. Great hope also has been placed in deepening the port of New Orleans to accommodate the exporting of coal. Congress has authorized a cost-benefit analysis of such a project along with similar studies for Mobile, Alabama, and Hampton Roads, Virginia. In addition to this competition, New Orleans confronts an effort by proponents of further development of the port of New York to persuade Congress that New York harbor can be deepened nearly two-thirds more cheaply than can New Orleans (see, for example, O'Brien, 1981: 27). In sum, both the logic of intracity competition for scarce urban land and the logic of intercity competition for employment stand as barriers to the expansion of this sector of New Orleans' economy.

The "giant plan" for the development of 4,000 acres in eastern New Orleans also is unlikely to rectify the dual labor market. The plan is a proposed large-scale residential, office, light industrial, and warehouse development project financed by Clinton Murchinson, a Texas oil millionaire, and planned by an Australian town planner and land developer, Barton Higgs. Higgs defends his proposed plan, while acknowledging New Orleans' particular subemployment problem. He argues that there is enough undeveloped land in eastern New Orleans to permit development of a postindustrial economy based on computers, microelectronics, and new means of production. How will this affect secondary workers? In Higgs' words, New Orleans

somehow managed to avoid most of the effects of the Industrial Revolution. While that had some good aspects, the resulting lack of employment opportunities also resulted in the creation of about 30,000 permanent unemployed and 60,000 underemployed in an urban population of less than 600,000. . . . While the new technology won't overnight create jobs for the underclass, it will create wealth and ancillary opportunities for entry-level jobs that don't currently exist. . . . Our project is a chance to create new homes for the middle class and new schools, but also to attract new industries and open job opportunities that have never before existed.[2] (Quoted in Katz, 1981a: 39)

To generate more industrial jobs for New Orleans, Mayor Morial's Office of Economic Development sent two alternative industrial development plans to the state legislature in 1980. The city requested $2 million in state support for drainage, sewer, and road improvements for a massive industrial park in eastern New Orleans known as the Almonaster Industrial District. The city estimated that the park would generate 50,000 new industrial jobs when completed. The spatial advantages of the area, particularly its proximity to port, rail, and highway routes, were highly touted by officials. Left unspecified was any detailed strategy for actually attracting firm commitments for industrial location to the city.

The Mayor has also joined with private interests seeking to attract foreign manufacturers to New Orleans. A public-private coalition has recommended that the city's small, duty-free, and tax-subsidized foreign trade zone be expanded and moved to Almonaster. Trade zone proponents, encouraged by other foreign assembly plants springing up throughout the United States, hope to attract labor-intensive assembly manufacturing to eastern New Orleans. The zone would be a duty-free area where imported parts are assembled into finished products by local workers. Such zones were originally used to lure international industrial capital to undercapitalized third-world countries with large pools of cheap labor. The fact that the zone is being planned for New Orleans is another measure of its chronic inability to absorb a large unskilled labor pool. Proponents of the zone have argued that, compared to third-world countries in Latin America, New Orleans offers the political stability that would make it attractive as a manufacturing site (Bookhardt, 1981: 1ff).

The validity of these assumptions is open to question. A reserve army of cheap labor does not automatically attract advanced industrial capitalist investment. There may be situations, as Castells (1975) contends, where 21st century capital seeks 19th century labor to maintain its position of dominance or exploitation. But, as another commentator has noted, "the promise of 'cheap labor' implies the lack of a highly skilled labor force and may repel the kind of sophisticated enterprise that can achieve the highest rate of growth" (Adams, 1981: 8). In the case of New Orleans, the current difficulty Mayor Morial and his allies are experiencing in attracting industrial investment to the city corroborates the latter view. The situation supports Breckenfeld's (1977: 239) general finding that industrial investment in the South "has tended to build new factories where it can find surplus white labor and has avoided places with a high ratio of poor and unskilled blacks."

Even if this assessment is overdrawn, and the Mayor's efforts to lure industrial capital prove successful in the long run, structural barriers to absorption of a largely preindustrial urban underclass cause the new employment possibilities to remain problematic. In this instance, the newly created jobs would more likely attract new migrants from other areas of the United States, such as displaced Michigan automobile workers, drawn south by the prospect of job opportunities that match their skills. An examination of the critical condition of the New Orleans public schools further indicates the problem of subemployment and underlines the inadequacy of the growth-stimulating political responses that have been relied upon to remedy the situation.

The Educational Crisis

Following mandatory desegregation of the New Orleans public schools in the 1960s, white enrollment continued a decade-long decline. There was not a sudden white flight. Yet the politics of desegregation did influence public attitudes, reinforcing a perception already well established among whites that the public schools could not provide quality education. Such attitudes, along with the preexisting movement to the suburbs and increasing reliance on private and parochial school alternatives, gradually resegregated the schools. The new form of racial segregation was far more class-based than the old. By 1981, in a city where 55 percent of residents were black, 84 percent of public school students were black, almost all of these from low-income families.

As a result of these demographic changes, the public schools of New Orleans had become isolated institutions for processing, controlling, and reproducing an urban underclass. Given their narrow base, they faced the same low level of public financial support that other racially and class segregated institutions, like public housing projects, have experienced in urban America. Currently, they are described by school officials as among the most dilapidated in the nation. Local budgets contain negligible amounts for maintenance and repair. Upkeep has been so limited that on occasion the New Orleans School Board has been forced to build a new school to replace one that would actually cost more to repair than to replace (Moore, 1981). Yet the cycle of deterioration is repeated when no local operating funds are appropriated to pay for maintenance of the new buildings. During the 1970s, for instance, the New Orleans School Board put only $90,479 into its capital outlay budget. In 1979, the minuscule amount allocated to the capital budget was diverted to pay for teaching programs. Following a teachers' strike the year before, these funds were used to supplement teacher pay raises following the strike settlement.

The crisis of school facilities is repeated in other aspects of schooling. Because of state contributions to local teachers' salaries, the city-suburban salary gap is narrower in New Orleans than in many other central cities. Nevertheless, the schools experience difficulty maintaining a quality staff. Those teaching basic skills are denied funds to update textbooks or refurbish antiquated laboratory facilities. One remedial reading teacher complained in 1981 that she was forced to spend several hundred dollars of her own money to buy books (Moore, 1981: 10). Although fewer than one in four children attending the New Orleans public schools will attend college, the system offers only minimal vocational training. Forced to work in dilapidated buildings, given very few resources, confronting an increasingly ill-served and alienated student population, teachers become, by default, little more than guardians of discipline and agencies of social control.

The problem of New Orleans' inadequate schools can be traced, in part, to a long history of neglect by state government. Additionally, because of its large Catholic population, Louisiana has had a more extensive private school system than any other southern state. State public-school expenditures for the period 1975–79 reflect traditional patterns of low funding and private system dependence. Compared to the other Southern states Louisiana spent slightly below the mean; on a per capita basis its yearly expenditures were 85 percent of the national mean (Louisiana, 1977: Tables 222, 247, 265; Bureau of the Census, 1980a: Table 265).

What are the results of this long history of neglect by state and local government? In 1980, New Orleans ranked last of 67 parish-wide school districts in Louisiana in minimal competency examinations. Students in grades four through twelve ranked in the bottom third of children nationally in standardized reading tests. In one predominantly black high school only 13 of 154 freshmen passed the fourth-grade reading test. Dropout rates are high and social promotion is widespread. Even students who successfully gain admission to college are handicapped by their experience. Fifty percent of the entering freshmen at the University of New Orleans coming from the city's public schools are found to have basic math and reading deficiencies, in contrast to one in three graduates of New Orleans' private schools, and 15 percent of its Catholic-school graduates (Moore, 1981).

In sum, New Orleans public school students are at an educational disadvantage initially, which worsens as they proceed through school. Many parents of both races have removed their children from the system. The dim long-term prospects for improvement are compounded by the city's woefully deficient local tax structure, which had brought it to the point of fiscal crisis even before the impacts of President Reagan's cutbacks in federal programs were felt.

The Fiscal Crisis of the City

Unlike many other large Southern cities, New Orleans lacks the power to annex its rapidly growing suburbs. Hence, while the revenue base of cities like Houston has benefited from expansion on the periphery, New Orleans confronts suburban growth, like most snowbelt cities, as a major threat to its already limited and overburdened tax base. To stave off further white flight, it has done little to resist state-imposed barriers on the expansion of its local property tax base. It has, instead, relied largely on sales taxes as the main source of local tax revenue. This revenue bind further solidifies the city's support for the growth of tourism, since the sales-tax revenues generated by tourism have become an indispensable source of funds to meet rising operating costs.

Expanding tourist dollars from local sales taxes has become all the more crucial because the very structure of the state taxing system has placed major limitations on the capacity of local governments in Louisiana to provide public services. Revisions of the state constitution enacted in 1974 impose three major legal limitations on the ability of local governments to raise revenue: (a) a prohibition against local income taxes, (b) a requirement that two-thirds of both houses of the state legislature must approve any increase in an existing local tax, and, most importantly, (c) an expanded exemption on home-owners' property taxes which excludes the first $50,000 of assessed valuation from taxes. This homestead exemption was increased to $75,000 for 1982 by a subsequent action of the state legislature.

This latter constraint, in particular, has been a spur to local politicians' unified effort to attract ever-expanding commercial investment in the CBD. In 1981, only 16 percent of owner-occupied homes in New Orleans paid any property taxes. This generated only 6 percent of the city's anticipated revenues for 1981 (Amoss, 1981: 5) and inexorably shifted the local property tax burden to owners of commercial property. The attraction of commercial development has become an essential priority of local government, but the structure of the tax system may discourage new commercial investment, creating a further contradiction.

To illustrate concretely: in 1979, New Orleans' City Planning Commission director, Albert Saputo, warned that the lack of any substantial local capital budget for the past three years, stemming largely from low property tax rates on taxable property, had caused New Orleans to fall behind other Southern competitors in its effort to attract diversified economic growth. Saputo outlined $600 million in needed, but historically deferred, maintenance for city streets, public buildings, police and fire stations, sanitation facilities, and public parks and recreation (Massa, 1979a: 49). Despite his plea, minimal local revenues were forthcoming. City administrators and local politicians were caught in a bind: without adequate public investment in infrastructure they could not rely on sustained economic growth as a long-term strategy to absorb the surplus population and resolve the fiscal crisis. Yet if taxes on commercial property were raised, or the tax structure itself were changed to place a heavier burden on local home-owners, the pace of new commercial development would slow, or the pace of white flight could well accelerate. Either eventuality would compound the city's immediate revenue problems even further.

New Orleans has faced an additional obstacle to drawing more extensively on property tax revenues as a mainstay of its tax base—its system of popularly elected local tax assessors, which is strongly supported by fiscally conservative local voters. The 1974 Louisiana constitutional convention, which limited local revenue options, also mandated adoption of "fair and uniform" property taxes. Yet how fair or uniform such assessments can be has depended elsewhere on the virtual depoliticization of the assessment process. In New Orleans, the present elected-assessor system, with its nearly sacrosanct homestead exemption, first enacted in the Huey Long era, represents vestiges of past Louisiana political machines; it now serves the interests of those who have the biggest stake in owner-occupied property. This system is unlikely to change without a protracted political fight. The structural bind they are in prevents local politicians from waging such a struggle.

The sales tax, the largest single source of locally raised revenue, is highly regressive, since it is levied on some food, as well as clothing and drug items. It grosses over $600 million a year in revenue. Even this source (3 percent state and 4 percent local) is checked by the need to avoid taxing tourist purchases too heavily. Accordingly, the preponderant reliance on the regressive sales tax forces the city's working class and poor to shoulder a disproportionate burden of local taxes.

What has been done in the area of local taxing and spending in the face of this contradictory situation? General revenue sources for New Orleans reveal a pattern of fiscal imbalance, with skewed results in the pattern of spending for public services. For 1978, the city received 34.7 percent of its monies from state and local resources. The federal government provided 65.3 per cent. The largest share of its local revenues (63.2 percent) came from sales and gross receipts. To provide a point of contrast, in the same year Atlanta had a more balanced pattern of revenue collection: 42.8 percent from state and local sources, 33.4 percent from the federal government. The different revenue packages have accounted for different patterns of spending for public services in the two cities. Comparing the same types of services as a percentage of the city budget for 1978, the data presented in Table 4.3 reveal the following differences. Public safety expenses were proportionately similar for

TABLE 4.3
New Orleans and Atlanta
Expenditures Compared, 1978

| | Percent of Budget, 1978 | |
Type of Service	New Orleans	Atlanta
Police protection	31.2	27.7
Fire protection	14.8	14.0
Highways	21.9	14.2
Housing and urban renewal	19.5	0.6
Health and hospitals	8.0	0.2
Education	1.1	4.7
Other	3.5	38.6
Total	100.0	100.0

SOURCE: Adapted from U.S. Bureau of the Census, 1978: Table 515.

the two cities. Differences in housing/urban renewal, health, and education are striking, suggesting the extent to which federal money, particularly Urban Development Action Grants (UDAG) and Community Development Block Grants (CDBG), combined with local interest, directed priorities toward urban redevelopment at the expense of services. Finally, Atlanta's more diversified revenue base allowed it to offer a greater variety of public services, transcending the scope of federal social welfare and urban development priorities.

Thus a limited local property tax structure, combined with a generally low-tax ideology, even in the face of objectively very limited state and local taxation, and a politically biased property tax assessment process have together produced a public expenditure pattern of very low investment in human and social capital, particularly education. These factors also limit local resources for maintenance of basic physical infrastructure, though money has been expended on more visible, federally subsidized urban development projects. In the 1960s a consulting study of New Orleans' city finances by the Bureau of Government Research (1966) predicted that the city would face clear economic "disaster" by the mid 1970s without changes in municipal finance. That the fiscal crisis was avoided until the early 1980s is largely due to sizable federal funds flowing to New Orleans during the 1970s that produced a condition of extreme dependence on federal dollars and policy priorities.

New Orleans' present fiscal and social crisis reflects the irony of a city located in an oil-rich state that is a virtual federal ward. From 1970 to 1980 the magnitude of federal dollars to New Orleans has been enormous and on a par with needy snowbelt cities. Measures of the city's dependence on direct federal aid per capita and per dollar of local revenues show that the city has increasingly relied on Washington to provide fiscal relief. Five programs are primarily responsible for the dramatic increase in urban aid: (1) General Revenue Sharing (GRS), (2) Community Development Block Grants (CDBG), (3) Comprehensive Employment and Training Act

TABLE 4.4
Federal Contribution to New Orleans
Capital Budget, 1970–80

Year	Total in capital budget	Federal percent of total local capital budget
1970	$ 1,245,674	7.09
1971	$ 5,471,658	15.02
1972	$ 7,927,010	19.35
1973	$ 6,867,180	12.76
1974	$21,627,891	58.56
1975	$15,915,283	36.77
1976	$14,376,993	43.11
1977	$19,469,442	22.68
1978	$27,038,941	56.94
1979	$27,567,803	58.12
1980	$61,329,493	84.54

SOURCE: New Orleans, "The Dynamics of Growth," 1980.

(CETA), Titles II (Skill Training) and VI (Public Services Employment), (4) Anti-Recession Fiscal Assistance (ARFA), and (5) the Local Public Works Program (LPW). These primarily formula-based programs targeted dollars to places with large populations, high unemployment rates, and high proportions of older housing stock—all common indicators of urban distress, and usually provided formula weights that favor older industrially crippled and largely Northern cities. By 1980 the city's capital outlays were nearly entirely determined by federal policy priorities (see Table 4.4).

Table 4.5 indicates the magnitude of federal grant money supplied to New Orleans and its relative infrequency for the sunbelt. In per capita aid to the 48 largest cities in 1978, New Orleans, at an estimated $232, far outdistanced Atlanta ($189) and Birmingham ($122)—both distressed sunbelt cities—and came closest to the aid provided Detroit ($237). That New Orleans received so much federal aid partly reflects aggressive federal grantsmanship by city officials during the Landrieu and Morial administrations. It also points to the city's distinctively disadvantageous position in the growing, prosperous sunbelt. Indeed, when poverty alone is considered as part of the CDBG entitlement formula, New Orleans ranked as the most needy large American city, tied with San Antonio, and slightly poorer than Newark (Bunce, 1979: 450).

The fiscal impact of major federal support is ambiguous. If a city does not substitute federal dollars for its own revenue, then no local money is freed for other expenditure. But even "capped" block grants with matching provisions can produce fiscal dependency, skewed resource allocations, local budget uncertainty, and state neglect. Much depends on local government's ability and propensity to

TABLE 4.5
Per Capita Federal Aid, 1960–78 (in dollars)

City	1960	1970	1975	1978[a]
Sunbelt				
Houston	0.44	3.28	34.57	59.78
Jacksonville	0.32	2.97	57.23	76.83
Birmingham	1.69	3.82	64.64	122.92
Atlanta	0.67	8.15	88.40	189.20
Norfolk	33.59	26.47	103.50	207.32
New Orleans	3.39	4.83	81.59	232.35
Frostbelt				
New York	4.13	19.99	82.03	171.39
Philadelphia	5.29	15.77	72.05	185.85
Boston	0.01	26.09	104.85	196.85
Cincinnati	4.39	50.06	148.31	201.44
Baltimore	2.58	33.92	127.65	212.55
Detroit	2.04	29.40	124.47	237.34
Rank of New Orleans[b]		32	14	4

SOURCE: U.S. Bureau of the Census, *City Finances*, adapted from data in John P. Ross, "The Impacts of Urban Aid," in Donald Rosenthal, ed., *Urban Revitalization* (Sage: Beverly Hills, 1980), p. 129.

[a] Population estimates, 1976.

[b] Rank order of federal dependency among 48 largest U.S. cities.

spend and generate taxes (see Ross, 1980: 128 ff). Fiscal dependency, whether for individuals or cities, produces particular stresses and conditions, one of which is the expectation that the aid will continue and the countervailing fear that it will not. In New Orleans' case massive injections of federal funds produced highly adept grantsmanship but also great overconfidence. The 1979 Mayor's Office of Economic Development (OED) strategy report detailed its short- and long-range CBD development plans. It listed almost no state aid sought or committed, but over $100 million in UDAGs, EDA, Department of Transportation, General Services Administration, and SBA grants or loans (New Orleans, 1979: 56–62).

The potential for political conflict inherent in the basic inadequacy of New Orleans' local revenue base surfaced as the Morial administration was preparing its 1980 budget. An analysis of the politics of the budgetary process reveals the class character of the distributional effects of fiscal crisis.

The Politics of Service Cutbacks

Confronting an inadequate tax base, compelling legal and political constraints on revenue raising, and spiraling inflation, Mayor Morial balanced his 1980 budget by laying off 700 city workers and severely cutting back virtually all public services. In instituting across-the-board cuts, the mayor openly sought to politicize the situation. He instituted the cuts without first consulting with the City Council on priorities. He feared that, if consulted, some members of the Council would prefer to use traditional budgetary gimmicks to mask the scope and scale of the problem. As he described the strategy:

We've reached a point where we have to move collectively to convince the public of the need for revenue reform so that we can move toward a fair and equitable tax structure. (Quoted in Massa, 1979)

Some Council members perceived this to be an impossible task. They believed instead that what fiscally conservative voters wanted was precisely a stop-gap approach that would allow local government to survive without expanding either services or taxes. In a swift reaction to the Mayor's budget, the seven Council members unanimously passed a resolution criticizing its provisions and proposing instead increased transit fares, user charges, state assistance, and new accounting procedures (New Orleans *States-Item,* 1979: 1). The Council especially wished to avoid major layoffs in fire and police services.

After considerable contention between mayor and Council, the 1980 budget was balanced by a combination of increased user charges, new accounting techniques, the substitution of voluntary for paid labor, and personnel cutbacks and attrition. The upshot was to delay the crisis for another year, while local politicians continued to hope that growth was the ultimate answer to their political quandary. The annual report on the state of the city, entitled "The Dynamics of Growth," reveals the extent to which the gospel of growth underlay the city's plans and the ways in which the uneven character of budgetary cutbacks can be masked by the rhetoric of "sound fiscal management."

The City Council's portion of the report pointed with pride to its cooperation with the mayor in efforts to improve the local economy by "the development of the New Orleans Exhibition Hall, the 1984 World's Fair, the development of several large new office buildings and hotels, and several programs aimed at neighborhoods" (New Orleans, 1980a). The Mayor's statement depicted New Orleans as a city on the move, its government forcefully managing "the dynamics of change to shape our future progress." Praising a "surge" in economic development during 1980, Morial hailed the increase in high-rise construction and described the growth of tourism as an economic boon that "continued to draw record numbers of visitors to New Orleans, filling our hotels, restaurants, and stores."

Morial converted the public service cutbacks necessitated by the fiscal crisis, which ultimately reduced the city's work force by 1,500, into a triumph of sound management. Gradually, over the past three years, he stated:

We have reduced the workforce of the city by nearly 14 percent due to the ever widening gap between municipal revenues and expenditures. This has required better management and increased efficiency to continue providing the services and public facilities that our city requires. (New Orleans, 1980a)

In park maintenance, new equipment had displaced labor, thus "enabling smaller crews to do more work in a shorter period of time." Citizen participation in crime prevention was substituting for decreased police patrols. Free labor was being given voluntarily by citizen task forces in various other areas. In the short run, taxpayers were getting more for less. In the longer run, economic growth would solve the city's persistent fiscal and social problems.

Reports from various departments further developed this theme. In 1980 the city began charging user fees for the police department's medical services unit. It also initiated a productivity study to insure that the street department would maintain "existing levels of output" in the face of sharp staff reductions, despite citizen surveys revealing a high level of neighborhood dissatisfaction with the existing level of street repair (New Orleans, 1980b). The city's bureau of food stamps, one of the largest in the nation, sharply cut its client transaction time, while noting, without irony, that food stamps generate $1.7 million annually in sales taxes (New Orleans, 1980a: 5). Fire prevention services were cut back by the closing of three fire stations. Neighborhood police anticrime councils, neighborhood watches, taxis on patrol, and a reserve police officers voluntary patrol program were introduced, thereby diverting attention from cuts in manpower and police patrols that prompted this extensive reliance on voluntarism. Likewise, in sanitation the city initiated an "adopt an area" project, using citizen volunteers to keep 150 public grounds litter free, thereby masking cuts in sanitation services (New Orleans, 1980a: 11).

While city political elites waited for the anticipated prosperity from the downtown boom, city budget estimates through 1985 projected revenue shortfalls of over $205 million, before any of Ronald Reagan's 1981 budget cuts had even passed in Congress (see Ridenhour, 1981). Federal monies had staved off fiscal crisis during the Landrieu administration, but proved insufficient, in the absence of state or local support, to prevent a fiscal crisis under Morial, even when greatly expanded by Carter's urban and countercyclical fiscal policies. The Reagan cutbacks thus further complicated New Orleans' fiscal crisis and forced the issue back on the political agenda, where it still remains.

Political Fallout: Channeling Discontent

Several historically specific conditions converged during the early 1970s in New Orleans to absorb the political energies that had been unleashed by the civil rights revolution of the 1960s, channeling discontent into the conventional routines of electoral politics, patronage, and neighborhood services. (On this process of depoliticization generally see Katznelson, 1981.) First, the experience of government-imposed massive clearance, displacement, and relocation was largely missing from New Orleans, due to legal and ideological barriers to urban renewal in the 1960s. Displacement that had taken place earlier had occurred prior to the civil rights awakening, without resistance. Thus the more subtle and incremental displacement that took place during the 1970s because of private gentrification in neighborhoods close to the newly emerging downtown produced only localized resistance and did not become a major citywide issue. A highly visible target for such broader coalitions, like renewal displacement, was not present as a background against which to mobilize wider discontent.

Furthermore, many of New Orleans' neighborhoods adversely affected by gentrification or the poor level and quality of city services had been organized into neighborhood associations that formed the base and institutional structure of both Landrieu's and Morial's political support. The rise of federal program dollars made these political relations possible. The political exchange took the form of social service and neighborhood improvement projects allocated to politically supportive neighborhoods.

The resources needed to cement the political ties were by-products of the political-economic realities of the time—two aggressive mayors, adept at federal grantsmanship, and an unevenly developing economy with a large secondary labor market and high levels of black poverty that appreciably increased New Orleans' share of formula-based federal grants. To illustrate concretely, sizable portions of New Orleans' $21 million CDBG program for 1980 were allocated to provide neighborhood health clinics and daycare centers in Central City, Desire/Florida, and the Lower Ninth Ward, three of New Orleans' poorest black neighborhoods. Multiservice centers, recreation facilities, playgrounds, trash cleanup and related services have all been distributed to such neighborhoods with CDBG funds. Over the course of the operation of the CDBG program in New Orleans, politically supportive low- and moderate-income neighborhood groups have been able to obtain substantial direct funding in exchange for their support. Over 30 community-based organizations have received approximately $40 million to operate a variety of social service and employment related projects through CDBG funds (New Orleans, 1980a: 11).

For these reasons, when organized activity by discontented social forces did occur, it was localized, issue-specific, and short-lived. For the most part, the large influx of federal funds and programs under Landrieu, and, initially, under Morial, provided a cushion which held off the impending fiscal crisis and its adverse consequences for public-service delivery. As long as these funds kept expanding, the city could have it both ways—taxing home-owners far less than citizens of other major cities, while still maintaining basic public services, and providing patronage and federally designed services to the city's neighborhoods. Initially it could use neighborhood-oriented community development funds to compensate for the class character and uneven impact of the ongoing urban economic development pattern.

With the arrival of the Reagan budget cuts, however, the contradictory roots of the crisis could no longer so easily be submerged. By 1981, the city's Office of Federal Programs had documented approximately $130 million in immediate federal support that the city had counted on to keep its fiscal crisis within manageable bounds, but that Reagan's fiscal policies would eliminate (Ridenhour, 1981: 6). In June 1981, the Morial administration was forced to cut the staff of the CETA program by 57 percent and to terminate CETA training services to 1,000 underemployed residents (New Orleans *Times-Picayune/States-Item*, 1981a: 23). Proposed federal cutbacks in aid to education would reduce the already inadequate school budget by 25 percent. Hardest hit would be programs directly beneficial to low-income families such as Title I funds for supplementary math and reading programs for students from low-income families who were performing below their current grade levels.

The new dimension of the crisis forced some new actions by local political elites. Mayor Morial's revenue revision task force recommended lobbying the state legislature to broaden the city's home-rule powers to remove state constitutional constraints on property, sales, and income taxes. In addition, the city sought an increase in bonded indebtedness to meet immediate capital maintenance needs. In the main, however, the Morial administration staked its reputation and political fortunes on its links to the private sector. The city offered tax advantages, technical assistance, and public support to tempt firms to build and hire in New Orleans. The Almonaster Industrial District, eligible for industrial revenue bond money, was touted as both an example of "positive government" and "privatism" in cooperation, and as a magnet to further capital investment that could resolve the fiscal crisis (Ridenhour, 1981; New Orleans *Times-Picayune*, 1981d).

Overall, the Morial approach to the crisis amounted to a plea for future action without having to take immediate steps that would impose costs on affluent white voters, such as altering the inequitable tax-assessment process. Low-income residents were placated by promises of eventual increases in private-sector jobs, assurances of fair and efficient management of the remaining federal programs and any future cuts. Fearful that other local political alternatives would be worse, they had little choice except to go along with Morial's program.

How well did this political strategy work? In February 1982 Morial became the first incumbent mayor of the 20th century in New Orleans to face a runoff reelection. With 46.9 percent of the vote, Morial only narrowly exceeded State Representative Ron Faucheux, a conservative, law-and-order candidate, who successfully stressed the fiscal crisis and played on rising fears of street crime among middle- and upper-income whites. Morial was particularly vulnerable on social-control issues since, faced with the mounting revenue crisis, he had broken a police strike called during the 1979 Mardi Gras. In 1980 several incidents heightened tensions. A number of tourists were killed in robbery attempts. A policeman patrolling a low-income neighborhood was also murdered. In the aftermath of these events, five black people were shot and killed by policemen in three different incidents, each time allegedly for resisting arrest. As a result, cracks began to show in Morial's political base. In June 1981 a group of black activists formed a police-brutality committee and mounted protest activities against the police department, including a dramatic seizure of the mayor's office.

These events were the culmination of a long-standing climate of hostility between members of the predominantly white New Orleans police department and low-income blacks. The United States Justice Department, for example, receives more police-brutality complaints against New Orleans than for any other American city. Between January and June 1981 the city paid over $1 million of its scarce resources to settle police-brutality suits. The New Orleans police department also is under a court order to increase the number of black sergeants and officers from their currently negligible levels to reflect more accurately the fact that New Orleans is now a predominantly black city (see Harris, 1981: A2).

By breaking the police strike, Morial won the enmity of the fledgling policemen's union. Because of his handling of the police shootings of blacks—condemning lawlessness, whatever its source—some black voters supported another black candidate as a symbolic protest. Morial also earned unfavorable publicity over the forced resignation of his police chief, in part because of the latter's mismanagement of the shootings, and over the suit against his police department for racial discrimination (Stuart, 1982a). Most importantly, by cutting back sharply on personnel, including police, during a period of rising fear of crime, Morial set the stage for Faucheux's conservative effort further to polarize sentiment around the issue of social control.

Despite these difficulties, and the loss of support from leading political figures like former Mayor and HUD Secretary Moon Landrieu, Morial won the runoff on March 19, 1982, beating back Faucheux's challenge 53.2 to 46.8 percent. Black voters returned to the fold, as did some liberal whites. Voters in low-income black precincts, fearful that Faucheux's election might usher in a new round of repression, turned out in atypically high numbers, approaching 60 percent in some precincts. Overall, Morial received 98 percent support from black voters, but only 15.9 percent of the white vote. He won because the overall turnout of black voters of 75 percent represented a substantial increase in turnout over the first ballot. Although Faucheux ran strongest in upper-income white precincts, the fact that he obtained over 84 percent of the white vote suggests that social-control issues and racial polarization will continue to pose problems for the political authorities.

In policy terms Morial did not seem inclined to use his victory to pursue a redistributive agenda which might exacerbate racial tensions and provoke further white flight. Instead he called for a reorganization of city government and for more of his brand of industrial development to generate new jobs. In short, he hoped to resolve the fiscal crisis by managerial improvements and economic growth, without undertaking the restructuring of the inequitable local property tax structure or its political supports. In the third part of this study we examine the long-term social costs that have resulted from precisely this limited approach to a structurally rooted problematic.

THE SOCIAL COSTS OF UNEVEN DEVELOPMENT

As a consequence of New Orleans' uneven spatial, sectoral, and sociocultural development, a high level of poverty continues to plague the lower social strata. The physical and investment structure of tourist development is in place and is difficult to reverse or even supplement by diversification. Greater investment in human resources through education and job training requires changes in ideology and political support. However, the unequal and uneven access to social development reflects vital needs of dominant structural interests: a cheap labor market for the tourist industry and for housing renovation entrepreneurs in smaller ventures in gentrifying neighborhoods; the status needs of traditional elites; a downward pressure on wages in all service-related employment; and low taxes for middle- and upper-class whites, enabling them to afford an exclusive, class-segregated system of private schools.

Arrayed against these factors are contradictory pressures: outside economic competition from other sunbelt cities experiencing more extensive and more diversified growth; the presence of some new large corporations, requiring more skilled and better educated labor power; high crime rates and fears of crime, possibly forcing reassessment of the distributional effects of existing patterns of development, if for no other reason than the possibly adverse impact on tourist industry growth; and the repoliticization of public-school performance issues, as Reagan's budget cuts sharply curtail federal education and manpower training subsidies.

A significant question is whether the uneven pattern of New Orleans' economic development in the 1970s and early 1980s simply bypassed or actually had harmful effects on the city's poor, subemployed, and ill-educated population. On occasion, the rush for tourist dollars could actually engender beneficial social changes in a traditional, racially dual, social order. For example, following his first election in 1970, to attract national conventions with black delegates in attendance, newly elected Mayor Landrieu, along with downtown business interests and the *Times-Picayune,* campaigned successfully for a municipal ordinance banning discrimination in places of "public consumption." The ordinance was touted, in a city with histori-cally rooted racial antagonisms, as broader than the federal requirement (New Orleans *Times-Picayune,* 1969; see also New York *Times,* 1963).

Even though legal barriers to integrated public accommodations could fall rela-tively easily when growth-oriented interests perceived them as impediments to downtown development, other impacts of the rise of tourism on low-income residents have been neither benign nor even neutral. An implicit growth model (see Judd and Collins, 1979; Smith and Judd, 1982) underlies public and private support for urban development within American capitalism. According to this model, increased private investment and accumulation will necessarily produce increased city taxes and jobs. With this comes an increase in per capita income that appears as rising local spending. The original catalyst is a favorable business climate, particularly city expenditure in the form of tax breaks, industrial development bonds, loans, and technical assistance. Business interests, in this model, equate with the public interests of the "city as a whole."[3]

In fact, "managed growth," premised on this model, has altered the economic base of the city in such a way as to make life harder for low-income residents. Manufacturing jobs continue to decline, as they do in many snowbelt cities. The tourist-related service sector has expanded greatly, but typically jobs here are lower-paying, part-time, and often deadend. Furthermore, the solace that these jobs are better than none at all may be jeopardized by Hispanic migrants who could displace native workers, as they have done in Miami and San Francisco.

In addition to its employment effects, reliance on tourism produces an assortment of neighborhood and central-city costs. There is, first of all, a "saturation level" for tourism in any locality. Local businesses may expand based on tourist dollars, but this source of stimulus and revenue is particularly vulnerable to inflation. If fuel costs or rising airplane prices decrease travel, cities have to hope for foreign tourists or risk business and job losses. There are signs that this has already become problematic for New Orleans. In 1980 the number of people boarding planes at New Orleans International Airport declined by 5 percent, compared to 1979. The decline was due to a drop in domestic vacation travel because of the sagging national economy and because of rising costs of air travel since deregulation of the airline industry (New Orleans *Times-Picayune,* 1981c: 8, 4). It is doubtful if foreign tourism can be expected to offset domestic decline while tight money policies in the United States continue adversely to affect the European and global economy.

Various physical capital and public safety costs to the city occur as a result of increased tourism (e.g., police, fire, airports, sewers, added congestion), but these have not been calculated or factored into cost-benefit equations. Nor have the "opportunity costs" emanating from the fact that as land devoted to tourism increases and more public funds are taken up to attract it, less land and public revenue is available for alternative uses like housing, schools, or social welfare. In choices entailing land development for revenue production versus service demand, the very logic of their fiscal dependency on private capital inevitably tilts local political elites toward the former. Apparently, even though tourism mixes service demands with revenue production, it is still seen as less purely service demanding, and hence less fiscally handicapping to officials than are social welfare choices. This was well illustrated in the case of New Orleans by the resistance of progrowth forces and officials to expanded hospital facilities in the CBD.

As an unintended effect of this logic, the loss of residents and firms displaced by a boom in downtown tourist and office facilities may hinder diversified economic development, because of escalating rents. Examples include the departure of numerous small businesses located near the French Quarter when the tourist-based "managed growth" strategy prompted city officials to support a publicly financed restoration of the historic French Market, which dramatically drove up rents. The net result was a decrease in commercial facilities catering to neighborhood and city residents and their replacement by tourist-oriented shops featuring luxury goods and tourist paraphernalia.

The costs of intercity competition for location of new firms also often run quite high. For example, other cities may expend equal revenues to attract tourists through services and tax advantages to tourist-related development. In this context, as Judd and Collins (1979: 185–93) have noted, a "bidding war" is a likely result. The winning tourist "islands of affluence" may need more costly police protection and other public services. The losers may become a new form of urban blight representing such a large sunk capital investment that private backers may seek and obtain "bail out" money to keep their profits intact.

Another by-product of uneven development, the high rate of violent street crime and the political reaction to it, also poses special problems for an economy that is primarily tourist-based. Both objective indicators of increased street crime (Louisiana, 1977: Tables V–6, V–7, I–30) and subjective fears of it, especially among white residents (see New Orleans, 1980a; New Orleans *Times-Picayune/States-Item,* 1981c), may induce still further out-migration of whites and/or may intensify security in downtown traffic corridors and gentrified neighborhoods. This, in turn, may encourage more scarce city funds to be spent on public safety rather than education or social services. There are emerging signs of just such policy outcomes. For instance, the downtown development district created to stimulate new capital investment in the CBD has been spending the lion's share of its annual operating budget to subsidize special policing of the area. Influential downtown business elites have pressured the district to underwrite additional police and sanitation services since 1977. The long-term implications of these developments may be a slowing of the downtown boom and a further politicization of social-control issues.

Finally, and most important, changes taking place in the larger political economy severely constrain New Orleans' effort to develop a broadly diversified economy. Viewed sectorally, New Orleans' economy is highly dependent on tourism, retailing, and personal services. Its mining, manufacturing, wholesaling, and "government-technical" sectors are underdeveloped. In the extractive sector, the vast majority of primary labor market blue-collar employment in Louisiana's oil and natural gas industries is located outside New Orleans, in refineries stretching upriver to Baton Rouge. The majority of the new "white collar" jobs created by the boom in office building spurred by the oil companies actually have been relatively low-paying clerical jobs. Higher-paying managerial employment has largely benefited a social strata residing outside Orleans Parish (see Ridenhour, 1981: 7).

Therefore, if the landlocked political jurisdiction of New Orleans were to diversify its economic base, the growth of new jobs would have to come in wholesale, "government-technical," or manufacturing employment. We have already seen that wholesaling is constrained from significant expansion by local competition for scarce urban land and national competition from other port cities. After decades of expansion, state sector, or "government-technical," employment can be expected to experience decline for the foreseeable future in the United States, given the implications of Reaganomics, the reliance of both national political parties on a strategy of stimulating economic growth through various forms of corporate tax reduction and individual tax cuts that reduce the revenue base of the state sector, and the continuing efforts of the various fractions of capital to extract ever more tax concessions from all levels of government (the so-called "recapitalization of capital" [Tomaskovic-Devey and Miller, 1982]).

In the final analysis, larger structural changes that have taken place throughout the 1970s and early 1980s have sharply slowed the overall surge in manufacturing employment on which New Orleans political elites are placing their hopes of economic recovery and political stability. The rate of growth in manufacturing employment, which was quite high in many parts of the South in the 1960s and 1970s, has slowed considerably in the current period, long before many parts of the South, including New Orleans, had reaped any benefits of such growth (see Stuart, 1982b: 1, 32). Former competitive advantages of the South, such as cheaper freight rates and lower living costs, which depress wage demands, have begun to even out nationally. Additionally, federal support for manpower training and water and sewer improvements to newly developing areas, which socialized key costs of industrial development, face cutbacks under Reagan's "new federalism." Northern states experiencing plant closings and relocations have begun to offer locational incentives such as industrial revenue bonds. Moreover, the high cost of credit, stemming from current national monetary and tax policies, is stalling industrial construction, location, and relocation plans generally, and contributing to the increasingly frequent recessions that further undercut new economic growth. High interest rates in the United

States have also contributed to a decline in manufacturing investment by foreign corporations in both 1980 and 1981.

Accordingly, at the very time that global and national political-economic conditions are least favorable, New Orleans' local political elites have embarked upon a course which is unlikely to yield significant economic results—greater economic diversification through local incentives to spur industrialization in an overall economy undergoing chronic recession, a continuing flight of capital from domestic manufacturing to cheaper points of production, and a mounting fiscal crisis of the national state. More importantly, even if the above obstacles to diversified economic growth were somehow overcome, there is still no guarantee of general affluence. As Smith and Judd (1982) have shown, widespread poverty and subemployment still persist in even the most prosperous sunbelt cities, thus illustrating that growth and the distribution of the benefits of growth are separate processes (see also Herbers, 1980: 14). As long as the segmented nature of the labor market, the critically uneven development of human and social capital, and the unevenly distributed costs of economic growth remain as the central unaddressed issues of urban and national politics, growth is more likely to create new categories of marginalized workers than to spread prosperity evenly. The overlapping boom and bust that have characterized the development of the New Orleans economy are an inevitable by-product of a structure of thought and practice in a political economy whose key elites accept economic growth as the best response to the social crisis of inequality. Given the structural predicament faced by officials, and the currently limited possibilities for transformation of the systematic biases we have observed, it is unclear whether even more enlightened elites could overcome the crisis.

NOTES

1. Göran Therborn (1980) defines the ideology of human subjects as a simultaneous process of subjugation and qualification. This may explain the ambivalent nature of this comment.
2. In this formulation, exactly how 21st century capital can possibly absorb 19th-century labor is left entirely to the imagination. Despite this unanswered question, initial support from Mayor Morial and state politicians has been enthusiastic. This is so despite the fact that (a) it will be up to the public planners to lure the industries that would comprise the employment component of the project, and (b) the project would use up more than 70 percent of the city's undeveloped residential land (Hardy, 1981: 14).
3. This is precisely the erroneous assumption underlying Paul Peterson's (1981) "unitary" model of urban development, which greatly weakens an otherwise perceptive analysis. For an extensive theoretical critique of the logic of the "city as a whole," see the argument developed in Smith (1979: Chapter 5).

REFERENCES

Abravanel, Martin D., and Paul K. Mancini. 1980. "Attitudinal and demographic constraints." Pp. 27–47 in Donald B. Rosenthal, ed., *Urban Revitalization*. Beverly Hills, CA: Sage.
Adams, James. 1981. "The sunbelt." Paper presented at Symposium on the South, Tulane University, New Orleans, February 6–7.

Advisory Commission on Intergovernmental Relations. 1977. *Central City-Suburban Fiscal Disparity.* Washington, D.C.: A.C.I.R.

Amoss, Jim. 1981. "City in the hole." New Orleans *Times-Picayune,* January 11: 1; New Orleans *Times-Picayune/States-Item,* January 12–16: 1ff.

Anderson, Ed. 1981. "Federal officials will decide fate of 1984 world's fair." New Orleans *Times-Picayune/States-Item,* February 12: 20.

Bombach, Richard O., and William E. Borah. 1980. *The Second Battle of New Orleans.* University, AL: University of Alabama Press.

Bookhardt, D. Eric. 1981. "New Orleans needs foreign trade zone." *Citibusiness* 1 (9) (February): 1, 32–35.

Breckenfeld, Gurney. 1977. "Refilling the metropolitan doughnut." Pp. 231–258 in David C. Perry and Alfred J. Watkins, eds., *The Rise of the Sunbelt Cities.* Beverly Hills, CA: Sage.

Brownell, Blain. 1977. "The urban South comes of age, 1900–1940." Pp. 123–58 in Blain Brownell and David Goldfield, eds., *The City in Southern History.* Port Washington, NY: Kennikat.

Bunce, Harold L. 1979. "The Community Development Block Grant formula." *Urban Affairs Quarterly* 14 (4) (June): 443–64.

Byrne, James S. 1972. "Superdome: high stakes in New Orleans." *American Banker,* June 26–July 6; American Banker Reprint No. 138.

Castells, Manuel. 1975. "Immigrant workers and class struggles in advanced capitalism: the Western European experience." *Politics & Society* 5 (1): 33–66.

Chai, Charles. 1971. "Who rules New Orleans? A study of community power structure." *Louisiana Business Survey,* October: 2–11.

Gambit. 1980. December 8: 5.

Glassman, James K. 1978. "New Orleans: I have seen the future, and it's Houston." *Atlantic Monthly,* Summer: 10–18.

Gordon, David M. 1972. *Theories of Poverty and Underemployment.* Lexington, MA: Heath.

Green, Constance M. 1957. *American Cities in the Growth of the Nation.* New York: DeGraff.

Hager, George. 1981. "Six companies made pledges for 1984 fair." New Orleans *Times-Picayune/States-Item,* April 24: 13.

————, and Ed Anderson. 1981. "List of pledges for fair withheld." New Orleans *Times-Picayune/States-Item,* May 9: 19.

Hardy, Jeannette. 1981. "Development plan for eastern New Orleans hailed by officials." New Orleans *Times-Picayune/States-Item,* March 30.

Harris, Art. 1981. "In carefree mardi gras city many blacks are terrified of police." *Washington Post,* June 11: A2.

Hays, Charlotte. 1974. "Joe Canizaro and the erector set." *New Orleans Magazine,* December.

Herbers, John. 1980. "The poor in thriving Southwest cities face woes as tax revolt widens." *New York Times,* December 21: 14.

Hirsch, Arnold R. 1981. "Sunbelt in the swamp: New Orleans and the rising south, 1945–1980." Unpublished manuscript, Departments of History and Urban and Regional Studies, University of New Orleans.

Judd, Dennis R., and Margaret Collins. 1979. "The case of tourism: political coalitions and redevelopment in central cities." Pp. 177–99 in Gary Tobin, ed., *The Changing Structure of the City.* Beverly Hills, CA: Sage.

Katz, Allen, 1981a. "Giant plan for east New Orleans." New Orleans *Times-Picayune/States-Item,* March 15: 39.

————. 1981b. "Fight that shaped future." New Orleans *Times-Picayune/States-Item,* February 15: 35.

————. 1981c. "Boom isn't coming to New Orleans—It's Here." New Orleans *Times-Picayune,* January 25: 8, 2.

Katznelson, Ira. 1981. *City Trenches: Urban Politics and the Patterning of Class in America.* New York: Pantheon.

Lewis, Pierce F. 1976. *New Orleans: The Making of an Urban Landscape.* Cambridge, MA: Ballinger.

Louisiana, State of. 1977. *Statistical Abstract of Louisiana.*

Massa, Joe. 1979a. "High, low moments at the hall." New Orleans *Times-Picayune,* November 18: 49.

————. 1979b. "City's financial crisis wears on." New Orleans *Times-Picayune,* December 9: 35.

Moore, Molly. 1981. "New Orleans: schools in crisis." New Orleans *Times-Picayune,* May 5: 1; New Orleans *Times-Picayune/States-Item,* May 6–10: 1ff.

Nathan, Richard A., and Charles Adams. 1976. "Understanding central city hardship." *Political Science Quarterly* 91 (Spring): 47–62.

New Orleans, City of. 1980a. "The Dynamics of Growth," *1980 Annual Report.* New Orleans: Supplement to *New Orleans: Times-Picayune,* n.d.: 1–22.

————. 1980b. "Citizen attitude survey, 1979: citywide results." Data Analysis Unit, Office of Analysis and Planning.

New Orleans Office of Policy Planning. 1979. "New Orleans economic development strategy." New Orleans.

New Orleans *States-Item.* 1979. November 29.

————. 1976. July 8.

New Orleans *Times-Picayune.* 1981a. May 3.

————. 1981b. April 26.

————. 1981c. January 25.

————. 1981d. January 11.

————. 1980a. November 2.

————. 1980b. February 15.

————. 1979. November 18.

————. 1978. April 1.

————. 1975a. October 19.

————. 1975b. September 21.

————. 1975c. July 1.

————. 1969. December 12.

New Orleans *Times-Picayune/States-Item.* 1982. March 22: 5.

————. 1981a. June 26.

————. 1981b. June 23.

————. 1981c. February 4.

————. 1981d. January 29.

————. 1980a. October 25.

————. 1980b. August 20.

New York Times. 1963. September 11.

O'Brien, Lawrence. 1981. "Sharing the 'port' barrel." *New York Times,* April 16.

O'Connor, James. 1973. *The Fiscal Crisis of the State.* New York: St. Martin's.

Perry, David C., and Alfred J. Watkins, eds. 1977. *The Rise of the Sunbelt Cities.* Beverly Hills, CA: Sage.

Peterson, Iver. 1982. "Boom and bust overlap in Cleveland." *New York Times,* February 5.

Peterson, Paul E. 1981. *City Limits.* Chicago: University of Chicago Press.

Piore, Michael J. 1976. "The dual labor market: theory and implications." Pp. 93–97 in David
    Gordon, ed., *Problems in Political Economy: An Urban Perspective.* Lexington, MA: Heath.
Preservation Press. 1975a. December.
———. 1975b. August.
———. 1978. February.
Ridenhour, Ron. 1981. "More decline." *Figaro,* May 11: 6–9.
Roper, James. 1978. "Orleans rates high on worst cities list." *New Orleans Times-Picayune,* March
    26: 18.
Ross, John P. 1980. "The impacts of urban aid." Pp. 127–44 in Donald Rosenthal, ed., *Urban
    Revitalization.* Beverly Hills, CA: Sage.
Sale, Kirkpatrick. 1975. *Power Shift.* New York: Random House.
Sanders, Heywood T. 1980. "Urban renewal and the revitalized city: a reconsideration of
    recent history." Pp. 103–26 in Donald Rosenthal, ed., *Urban Revitalization.* Beverly Hills,
    CA: Sage.
Schattschneider, E. E. 1960. *The Semisovereign People.* Hinsdale, IL: Dryden.
Smith, Michael P. 1979. *The City and Social Theory.* New York: St. Martin's.
Smith, Michael P., and Dennis R. Judd. 1982. "Structuralism, elite theory, and urban policy."
    Comparative Urban Research 9 (2).
Statistical Abstract of Louisiana. 1977. James Bobo and Harris Siegal, comps. 6th ed. New Orleans:
    University of New Orleans.
Stone, Clarence N. 1980. "Systemic Power in Community Decision Making," *American Political
    Science Review* (December): 978–990.
Stuart, Reginald. 1982a. "New Orleans mayor to face state lawmaker in runoff." *New York
    Times,* February 8.
———. 1982b. "Deep South's economic surge found slowing." *New York Times,* March 12:
    1, 32.
———. 1982c. "New Orleans mayor elected to 2d term in runoff vote." *New York Times,*
    March 22: 12.
Tomaskovic-Devy, Donald, and S. M. Miller. 1982. "Recapitalization: the basic U.S. urban
    policy of the 1980s." Pp. 23–42 in Norman Fainstein and Susan Fainstein, eds., *Urban
    Policy under Capitalism.* Beverly Hills, CA: Sage.
Therborn, Göran. 1980. *The Ideology of Power and the Power of Ideology.* London: Verso.
U.S. Bureau of the Census. 1981. *Advance Reports.* Washington, D.C.: U.S. Government Printing
    Office.
———. 1980a. *Statistical Abstract of the United States.*
———. 1980b. *Estimates of Populations of Counties and Metropolitan Areas, 1977 and 1978.*
———. 1978. *Statistical Abstract of the United States.*
Watkins, Alfred J., and David C. Perry. 1977. "Regional change and the impact of uneven
    urban development." Pp. 19–52 in David Perry and Alfred Watkins, eds., *The Rise of the
    Sunbelt Cities.* Beverly Hills, CA: Sage.

5

From Cowtown to Sunbelt City: Boosterism and Economic Growth in Denver

Dennis R. Judd

The economic stagnation of the last several years hit hardest the cities already staggered by intractable social problems. Unemployment reached 19.8 percent in Saginaw, Michigan, in June 1980, and stayed over 12 percent all winter. By July of 1981, unemployment levels among the nation's black youth—counting only those who wanted to work but who could not find jobs—hovered around 35 percent and reached more than 50 percent in September. In Detroit, by early summer 1981, unemployment stood at 11.4 percent compared to 7.6 percent in New Orleans, 6.7 percent in New Haven, and 5.5 percent in San Francisco. Throughout Michigan, unemployment stayed above 10 percent for the entire summer (U.S. Department of Labor, 1981a: 110–12; U.S. Department of Labor, 1981b). A September 1981 article in *The Denver Post* quoted an unemployed auto worker: "I think Detroit is dead. I don't see it getting any better" (1981a: 14).

The same day's issue of the *Rocky Mountain News* (1981c: 7, 16) included a long story about how "Former Denver Mayor Marvels at 'New' City." From its opening lines the article described Denver with rhetorical flourish: "J. Quigg Newton, Jr. was standing at his window on the 26th floor of the Colorado National Bank Building, surveying the sunlit city." Newton, who was Denver's mayor from 1947 to 1955, "shook his head in wonder at . . . what he saw—50-story aluminum cylinders shimmering in the late-morning sky, the stolid black fortress of the Park Central complex and Mountain Bell's massive block of corporate ice. . . . Gigantic cranes swooped to and fro . . ." Newton, who had left the city in 1963, described a "sense of amazement": "The city is vibrant and beautiful and new. I feel a little like Rip Van Winkle must have felt."

Indeed, Denver is the sunbelt city personified. Money and people for oil and gas development throughout the West are funnelled through the corporate offices which occupy the new aluminum cylinders.

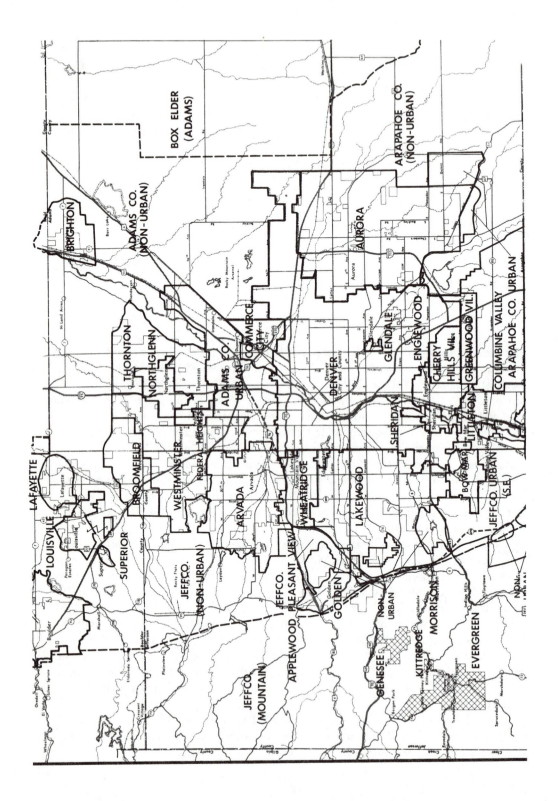

DENVER AS A SUNBELT CITY

Denver is the regional city for an eight-state area. Corporations of all kinds have located their administrative headquarters or regional offices there (*Media Scope,* 1978: 53–66). Petroleum and energy-related companies have constructed or are tenants in more than a third of the skyscrapers built during the 1970s. The climate for investment is ideal: according to Dunn and Bradstreet, Denver has one of the lowest business-failure rates in the country.

Southeast of the city, all around the appropriately named Denver Tech Center, a "silicon valley" second only to California's Bay Area electronics industry is springing up. In the last two decades, hundreds of companies moved to the Front Range, and were in turn surrounded by a corridor of suburban growth sprawling more than a hundred miles along the east face of the Rocky Mountains. Many of the companies are high-tech firms specializing in military production, electronics, and energy development. In 1957, Martin Marietta Aeronautics chose an area a few miles south of Denver to build the new Titan intercontinental ballistics missile. In the next few years, Beech Aircraft, IBM, Hewlett Packard, Johns-Manville, and Honeywell moved major operations to the Front Range. Professional and technical jobs proliferated, exceeded in occupational growth only by openings for clerical and service workers (*The Seven Counties of Denver,* n.d.: 5; Harrison and Hill, 1979: 15–45).

The high-tech industries generated a demand for highly educated people. By 1980, the Denver region had one of the highest educational levels per capita in the United States. In 1970, more than 18 percent of the labor force in Denver's suburbs had completed a college education or received advanced degrees (Rahe, 1974: 18).

And compared to the rest of the country, Denver's population was young and affluent. The fastest growing group was made up of people 25 to 34 years old. Even so, between 1970 and 1976, the proportion of children under 15 years of age declined, showing that an increasing proportion of young adults were unmarried singles or childless couples. Compared to the largest twenty-five urban areas, the Denver Standard Metropolitan Statistical Area (SMSA) ranked fifth in the growth of personal income (*The Seven Counties of Denver,* n.d.: 4–5). Probably because so many people were affluent and childless, Denver took on characteristics often associated with Southern California: a proliferation of health clubs, movie theaters, radio stations (more per capita than in any other metropolitan area in the U.S.), discos and "fern bars," skylight and stained-glass restaurants, and hot tubs. In three decades, Denver shucked its cowtown image, and became "trendy." It became a sunbelt city, in culture and lifestyle as well as in weather.

People flocked to the Denver area by the thousands—averaging more than 3,000 a month during the 1970s. Among the twenty-five largest metropolitan areas, Denver ranked fifth in growth rate during the 1970s, behind Anaheim, Phoenix, San Diego, and Houston (see Table 5.1). In the two decades since 1960, it has grown at 2½ times the national average. All of the growth is now taking place outside the City of Denver. Denver's boundaries were filled by the end of the 1960s, so that in the

TABLE 5.1
Population Growth in Selected Metropolitan Areas, 1950s through 1970s: Percent Increase in Population

Metropolitan Area	1950–60	1960–70	1970–80
Phoenix	100.0	45.8	55.6
Houston	51.6	40.0	44.6
San Diego	85.5	31.4	37.0
Anaheim	225.6	101.8	35.5
Denver	51.8	32.1	30.2
Dallas	43.4	39.0	24.6
San Francisco	24.0	17.4	3.7
Detroit	24.7	11.6	−2.1
St. Louis	19.9	12.3	−2.6
Pittsburgh	8.7	−0.2	−6.0

SOURCE: U.S. Bureau of the Census, *1970 Census of Population,* Vol. 1, *Characteristics of the Population,* Part 1, Table 32, p. 171; and Bureau of the Census, "Population and Housing," *Advance Reports,* 1980.

TABLE 5.2
Population Growth in Seven Cities, 1940–80 (in percent change)

Metropolitan Areas	1950–60 Central City	1950–60 Outside Central City	1960–70 Central City	1960–70 Outside Central City	1970–80 Central City	1970–80 Outside Central City
New York City	− 1.4	75.0	1.5	26.2	−11.0	2.0
Chicago	− 2.0	71.5	− 5.2	35.3	−10.7	13.5
Boston	−13.0	17.7	− 8.1	11.3	−12.2	2.7
St. Louis	−12.5	50.8	−17.0	28.3	−27.5	10.2
Cleveland	− 4.2	67.3	−14.3	27.1	−23.7	1.0
Los Angeles	25.8	66.6	13.6	20.0	5.0	7.0
Denver	18.8	121.8	4.2	63.7	− 4.5	59.3
End-of-decade population in Denver	493,887	435,496	514,678	712,851	491,396	1,128,537[a]

SOURCE: U.S. Bureau of the Census, *1950 Census of Population,* Vol. 1, *Number of Inhabitants,* Part A, Table 27, p. 69; *1970 Census of Population,* Vol. 1, *Characteristics of the Population,* Part 1, Table 34, pp. 1–180 to 1–186; and *Advance Reports,* Tables 1–3, 1980 Census.

[a] Including Boulder, which is a central city of the Denver–Boulder SMSA.

ensuing decade the city actually lost 4.5 percent of its population. Meanwhile, the Denver suburbs (excluding Boulder) grew by 59.3 percent, from 727,000 in 1970 to 1,072,000 in 1980.

Table 5.2 shows population changes in several cities from 1950 to 1980. Older cities like New York City, Chicago, St. Louis, and Cleveland experienced massive declines in central city population. In the 1980s, in these areas, even suburban growth slowed to a crawl, reflecting regional economic stagnation. What Denver shares with these cities is that its boundaries have been filled in. Growth now *has to* take place outside the city. Population losses in Denver do not, however, necessarily indicate economic stagnation in the central city. In fact, part of the city's population loss can be traced to changes in the kinds of people living in the city: as families move out, they are replaced by young singles or childless married couples.

Jobs have kept pace with the population increases in the metropolitan area very well—in fact, in the early 1980s more jobs were created than there were people to fill them. In July 1982, unemployment in the Denver area stood at 6.3 percent, compared to 9.8 percent for the nation (Colorado Division of Employment and Training, 1982). Only during the national recession of 1975 and 1976, when national unemployment rates neared the 8 percent level, did unemployment in Denver exceed 7 percent, by a small margin (Colorado Division of Employment and Training, 1978, 1980).

"Boosterism" and Denver's Growth

A drive through the Los Angeles-type sprawl surrounding Denver could convey the impression that the economic and population boom is a result of "accidental" forces: Denver's sunny weather, the nearness of the mountains, and development of energy resources throughout the West. Newspaper, magazine, and television stories often identify western "lifestyle" as the principal attraction for new residents. But far more is involved.

It is important to understand that Denver's post-World War II growth was carefully sought by business and government leaders. Like every other city in America, "boosterism" has been a central feature of local politics. Growth has never been left to the vagaries of chance.

Denver's postwar business and political leaders exhibited remarkable similarity to their counterparts of a hundred years before. Then, Denver was a struggling frontier outpost, founded when gold was discovered in 1859. What prevented it from becoming another Virginia City, Nevada—a town that died when its gold played out—were aggressive entrepreneurs who wanted to make it the economic center of the Rocky Mountain West. Another city might have fulfilled that role: Cheyenne, for example, was fortunate enough to sit astride the Union Pacific track that joined with the Central Pacific rails at Promontory Point, Utah, in 1869, to complete the transcontinental railroad. In anticipation that Cheyenne would grow and that Denver would fade, several businessmen packed it up and moved to Cheyenne. But some Denver businessmen were not ready to call it quits. In November 1867, they organized the Denver Board of Trade specifically for the purpose of building a rail connection to Cheyenne. Helped by a land grant from Congress and further encouraged by a $280,000 purchase of stock by the Denver business organization, the Union Pacific completed a spur line from Cheyenne to Denver in June 1870 (McKelvey, 1963: 260). By September of the same summer, a link was established with the Kansas Pacific to the east. Left to "chance," Denver might have died on the vine: there is little to distinguish its location on the plains from that of towns a hundred miles to the north or south.

Almost a century later, in the early 1950s, Denver's Chamber of Commerce began an active boosterism crusade which has yet to run its course. The Chamber began to place advertisements in national magazines extolling Colorado's virtues as a vacation spot. Over the years, "Colorful Colorado" has become the mecca for tourists coming west. It is advertised in all the national magazines; a well-organized tourist industry is promoted through the Colorado Bureau on Tourism, founded in 1937.

The ski industry, which helped finance the carefully orchestrated campaign, mushroomed. By 1975, there were more than 30 major ski areas in Colorado. More than three dozen manufacturers and wholesalers of ski equipment were located in Denver, including industry leaders like Lange and Head. A multitude of mountaineering and hiking firms, like Holubar and Gerry, also found the Denver area to their liking.

In 1981, tourism ranked fourth in the economy of Colorado. Its growth, as shown in Table 5.3, has been phenomenal. In 1980, it brought more than $1.6 billion into the state and employed 59,000 people.

But tourism paled in comparison to spending by the federal government. Military spending alone doubled tourism dollars. In 1975, the military spent $1.36 billion in Colorado (Dorsett, 1977: 262). Since the 1940s, Denver leaders have lobbied hard for military installations. For example, in 1950, a 200-page survey of the Denver area was published in an attempt to sell Denver's climate, low land prices, cost of living, housing, and other amenities to military and civilian firms (Dorsett, 1977: 260). Perhaps efforts such as this helped. The Air Force Academy decided to locate near Colorado Springs during the 1950s, at a cost of $250 million. Later, the U.S. Army Corps of Engineers blasted a huge cavern into the mountains south of Denver, at a cost of $66 million, to headquarter the North American Air Defense Command (Nash, 1977: 233). The project was completed in 1965. The Air Force Accounting and Finance Center was also built. With Lowry Air Force Base and Buckley Naval Air Station already in Denver, and the expansion of Fitzsimmons Army Hospital into a major regional medical facility, the groundwork was laid. By 1980, more than 19,000 military personnel were stationed near Denver, and many defense contractors also brought in employees. Denver's economy is intricately tied to the Cold War.

Denver's boosters also worked hard for civilian federal dollars. By the end of World War II, several important federal agencies had adopted Denver as a regional center for administrative offices. To make sure that still more agencies would open offices in Denver, delegations of city officials and businessmen went to Washington to lobby federal bureaucrats. Over a period of several years, the old Denver Arms

TABLE 5.3
Twenty-five Years of Colorado Tourism Statistics

Year	Dollar Volume	% Change	Number of People	% Change
1981 (Projected)	1,996,600,000	+ 20.5	12,931,683	+ 9.2
1980	1,657,200,000	+133.3	11,843,890	+33.2
1975	710,220,000	+ 24.6	8,890,000	+13.2
1970	570,000,000	+ 28.4	7,852,200	+35.7
1965	443,931,000	+ 23.4	5,786,225	+26.7
1960	359,625,000	+ 72.4	4,567,500	+27.5
1956	208,638,000		3,583,000	

SOURCE: *The Colorado Tourism Scene,* Division of Commerce and Development, Office of Economic Planning, Denver, December 1980.

Plant was transformed into the Denver Federal Center. With consolidation of federal programs into nine regions under the Johnson Administration, Denver's status as a federal regional center was assured. In 1948, there had been 10,000 federal civilian employees in Denver. By 1961, the number was 23,000, and by December 1975, it was more than 32,000 (U.S. Civil Service Commission, 1977).

Denver boosters pulled out the stops when President Eisenhower proposed a 40,000-mile interstate highway system in 1956. The original plans, hammered out between the President, Congress, and a horde of special interests representing towns and cities, state and federal highway engineers, highway contractors, and others, specified 299 Colorado miles for I-25, running from Cheyenne south through Denver to Albuquerque, and I-70, a freeway coming from the east coast, but stopping in Denver (Kelly, 1974: 84). This was somewhat like the problem of the transcontinental railroad almost a century earlier. Coast-to-coast truckers would go through Cheyenne, unless a highway could be built across the mountains. Governor Ed Johnson, intent on building such a road, asked the State Highway Department "to prepare an elaborate presentation book. In splashy Madison Avenue fashion, it detailed the many reasons I-70 should not terminate in Denver" (Kelly, 1974: 84).

Together with Denver Mayor Will Nicholson, the Governor flew to Washington to meet with President Eisenhower—ostensibly a ceremonial mission to present Colorado's number 1 fishing license to the President. The Mayor, a friend of Eisenhower's press secretary, described the meeting:

When we got inside, Johnson first gave the President the fishing license. Then Eisenhower asked Ed what he had in the package. The governor, of course, tore the wrappings off the book as fast as he could. Ed explained the entire problem and said Colorado needed help quickly before Congress took final action.

The President asked what he could do to help Colorado. (Kelly, 1974: 85)

Before Congress passed the National Defense Highway Act of 1956, a thousand miles was added, as recommended by President Eisenhower. Three hundred of those miles (a few other deals had also been made) carried I-70 west to Salt Lake City.

Through the 1960s and 1970s, boosterism accelerated. The February 23, 1976, issue of *Business Week* magazine carried a full-page advertisement sponsored by the Forward Metro Denver Group and the Chamber of Commerce. The ad extolled Colorado's climate, scenery, and other amenities, then made its pitch to businessmen who might have tired of the frostbelt:

The strong growing economy of the mile high city: A boom that's been fed by a highly educated, young, hard-working population. A growing market for your products, skilled labor force for your business and a loyal pool of talent that tends to choose lifestyle over dollars when the executive recruiters come sniffing around.

The previous year, even the environmentally conscious Governor Richard Lamm, a frequent advocate of planning and balanced growth, had gotten into the act by commissioning novelist James Michener to do a story on Colorado for *Business Week* (Dorsett, 1977: 270).

It is clear that Denver's growth was not left to chance. While it is true that its climate and general location favored population and economic expansion, a well-organized business and financial coalition took strong measures to ensure that potentially competitive cities, like Cheyenne, Salt Lake, and Albuquerque, would not prove to be as attractive. There is little doubt that the efforts of the progrowth coalition speeded up population and business expansion, and pushed it in certain directions. For example, the successful campaign to have Denver designated as a federal regional center brought thousands of government employees, especially in the 1960s. The very extensive military activity has also shaped the basic economy of the region. All of these developments may have occurred without the efforts of the local coalition—that will always remain an unanswered question—but the fact that decisions about the location of government installations are decided more by political than by administrative considerations argues strongly in favor of the view that the progrowth coalition has wielded strong influence.

Conflicts over Growth

On a September afternoon in 1946, Denver mayor Ben Stapleton looked out of his office at the city:

Traffic sped back and forth on Bannock St. and Broadway. Civic Center was alive with scores of persons converting the mall into a park. The trolley cars were jammed, because the automobile industry was still retooling from war production. These activities, visible from the mayor's office, were symptoms of a boom that would transform Denver from a quiet, conservative, fairly large city into a burgeoning metropolis with mushrooming suburbs and seemingly unsolvable problems.

How to solve the problems? Stapleton had the answer: "If those people would just go back where they came from, we wouldn't have any problems here" (Kelly, 1974: 1).

Over the past thirty years, Stapleton's opinion has been transformed into a catechism for "native" Coloradans, as well as for those who have just arrived and want to shut the door on next month's immigrants. Since 1968, for example, a bumper-sticker war has been waged, started by a firm that did a brisk business selling stickers with the word "Native" embossed against a background of mountain peaks. Fortunately, the war has been met with a fusillade launched by would-be humorists, who countered with stickers announcing *their* status, such as: "Semi-Native," "Restless Native," "Alien," "Who Cares," and "Semi-Naive." But there remains a serious undercurrent in the war: ask Coloradans about Texans, and the talk about "outsiders" turns decidedly deadpan. After all, it has only been ten years since the most popular sticker read, "Don't Californicate Colorado."

There is an inescapable, fundamental contradiction about local attitudes toward growth. Nearly everyone loves the benefits of growth, and they also decry its costs. The key term in this schizophrenia is the "quality of life." With growth has come new cultural amenities, prosperity, and services—and also air pollution, freeway congestion, urban sprawl. The antigrowth point of view was succinctly stated by Lyle Dorsett, the author of the only scholarly book yet written about Denver:

Unquestionably, Denver's quality of life has deteriorated in several important ways since World War II. The beauty of the Rocky Mountains, the delightful climate, the growing popularity of outdoor sports, the untapped natural resources in the midst of an energy crisis, and the colossal success of booster campaigns have inspired a boom of destructive proportions. (Dorsett, 1977: 273)

To Dr. Dorsett, the costs of uncontrolled growth clearly outweigh its advantages—though he, like this author, is an "immigrant."

No controversy so well illustrates the conflict between the boosters and the controlled-growth groups as the fight over the 1976 Winter Olympics. An Olympics for Colorado was a promoter's dream come true: construction of housing, special buildings, ski jumps, bobsled and luge runs would generate profits and jobs. More than 15,000 people would be engaged as timers, judges, athletes, coaches, trainers, and security. Restaurants, bars, ski shops, tourist and souvenir shops, groceries, and other businesses would do a brisk trade. The worldwide publicity—coming especially during the state's centennial and the nation's bicentennial year—would bring more tourists to Colorado, both during the Olympics and for years to come. The Olympics facilities would be turned into a permanent ski resort, with organized winter competitions. To the promoters, Olympic gold encompassed more than the medals draped around the necks of the athletes.

Ski resort entrepreneurs began laying plans for the Olympics in the mid 1960s. In June 1966, with the support of Governor John Love and Denver Mayor Tom Currigan, the group announced their plans to have the United States Olympic Committee (USOC) and the International Olympic Committee (IOC) designate Denver as the site of the 1976 Winter Olympics. On December 18, 1967, after formal presentations and extensive lobbying, the USOC designated Denver as the sole American applicant. Over the next three years, Mayor Currigan and Governor Love went abroad to talk with IOC officials. International Olympic officials, in turn, sent delegations to Colorado to look at possible sites and talk with local committee members. Finally, on May 13, 1970—and despite the international furor raised against the United States for the April 30 bombing and invasion of Cambodia by American and South Vietnamese troops—the IOC selected Denver for the Olympics. Securing the approval was not easy, as indicated in a story about the boosters' efforts published in the *Rocky Mountain News* one day before Denver's selection:

Seven years of work, $750,000 in cost and untold hours of volunteer effort added up here Monday to just 36 minutes—the time for Denver to make its presentation in a final effort to win the 1976 Winter Olympics. (*Rocky Mountain News,* 1970: 1; Kelly, 1974: 242)

Many Coloradans held a vision of the Olympics which was distinctly different from the one presented by the promoters. They saw environmental destruction in the mountains and an invasion by thousands of outsiders. Letters to the editor columns in the *Rocky Mountain News* and *The Denver Post* voiced opposition. Some political leaders expressed reservations. Environmental groups were overwhelmingly opposed. It took a long time for the promoters to recognize the potential power of the opposition. Having enjoyed a virtual monopoly over issues of growth for so long, it was inconceivable to the economic elite that it could be effectively challenged.

In early 1972, opponents presented petitions signed by 20,000 people to the International Olympics Committee in Sapporo, Japan, where the Winter Olympics were being held (Kelly, 1974: 254). During the same month, the newly organized Citizens for Colorado's Future (CCF) initiated a drive to place before the voters a constitutional amendment that would forbid the legislature to spend money on the games.

In response to these actions, the IOC asked members of the Denver Olympics Committee to come to Sapporo to explain the opposition. The delegation was successful in Sapporo, but not at home. As explained in a February 1 editorial on Denver's Channel 7 News:

Despite brave official statements to the contrary, Colorado citizens are divided over the '76 games. Opponents, as well as ardent boosters, deserve to be told the facts and soon: How much will Colorado taxpayers have to underwrite? Specifics on federal government financial support; details on after use of expensive installations for bobsled, luge, and ski jump . . . housing for participants, officials and news media; and guarantees concerning protection of the environment. (Kelly, 1974: 254)

Within a few weeks, CCF had collected 76,000 signatures asking for a November vote on the issue. A separate petition campaign placed a charter amendment before Denver voters designed to forbid the city from spending money for the Olympics.

In the months before the November 7 referendum, thousands volunteered to participate in the out-financed campaign to stop the Olympics. The Denver Olympics Committee and its supporters seemed unstoppable: the Chamber of Commerce, the Governor, the Mayor, and most elected officials, along with nearly all Denver's business and financial elite, poured money and propaganda into the campaign. They outspent their opponents 100 to 1. But the proponents became their own worst enemies when they tried to smear the CCF leaders as meddling outsiders. The strategy was a catastrophic mistake: now it looked like "big money" was trying to "muscle" the voters into approving the Olympics (Kelly, 1974: 256). On November 7, the voters vetoed the Olympics by a 3–2 margin. News media across the country interpreted the election as a victory for environmentalists. And only two years later, State Representative Richard Lamm, who had been one of the leaders of the Olympics revolt, was elected governor.

These events hardly signaled a grand defeat for the promoters of growth. The Olympics were moved to Germany; and in the meantime, business and people continued to pour into Colorado. As before, the proponents of growth held most of the money and leadership. The "antigrowth" or "environmentalist" coalition had no new causes around which to organize. The "war" over growth had been brief, and the results illusory. Measured in terms of staying power, organization, and money, the boosters were in a better position to wage a protracted campaign. Long before the Olympics controversy and long after, they dominated the politics of growth.

THE EFFORT TO RECLAIM THE DOWNTOWN

Like most other cities of the sunbelt, Denver came to central city revitalization a bit late, as compared to some of the older, declined cities of the frostbelt. Pittsburgh organized the Allegheny Conference on Community Development in 1943 to revitalize the Golden Triangle. In Boston, the New Boston Committee, made up of reform politicians and downtown business interests, defeated James Michael Curley's machine in 1951. Subsequently, the new coalition launched a massive urban renewal effort which ultimately involved 10 percent of the city's land area (Mollenkopf, 1978: 138). In the early 1950s, St. Louis's banking and commercial leaders joined with a progrowth mayor to build public housing and to reclaim the downtown (Salisbury, 1960: 501). The instrument for the renewal activity in city after city was the federal urban renewal program, created by the Housing Act of 1949.

Even in the sunbelt, in those cities which had developed significantly before World War II, inner-city decline had occurred. The car culture was busily creating urban sprawl, with its attendant proliferation of suburbs, in the 1950s and after. To capture a share of regional growth—and in competition with each other—sunbelt cities fought to make the downtowns attractive for new investment: "Where nineteenth-century cities had competed to acquire the best railroad connections, those of the twentieth-century worked to provide the facilities for metropolitan activities of regional finance, public administration, business headquarters and distribution, and professional services" (Abbott, 1981: 144). Investment capital flowing to the sunbelt was footloose—businesses moving their operations or corporate headquarters could settle in Houston just as well as in Denver or Phoenix. Local political and economic leaders were aware of this fact. Each sought a competitive edge, and the result was that every city saw the organization of redevelopment committees or downtown improvement associations. The development which resulted tended to be remarkably the same—"Dallas, Los Angeles, Denver, Houston, Atlanta—the fast-growing American cities from one ocean to the other have built interchangeable cores. The uniform environment of high-rise offices, convention centers, sports arenas, and girdling freeways is an expression of shared values among urban leaders in our boom-town cities" (Abbott, 1981: 143). In the same way that Denver did not leave regional growth to chance, its political and financial leaders in the city proper did not leave the fate of the downtown to chance, either. Too much was at stake.

During and after World War II, Denver's population burgeoned, from 332,000 in 1940 to a 1960 population of 493,000. Nevertheless, generalized prosperity did not guarantee that the downtown business district would remain the center of economic activity. By 1950, the fate of the downtown was very much on the minds of civic leaders. Little new investment had been committed since the early 1930s. The downtown had a shabby look: old brick buildings faced with bumpy streets, inadequately lighted at night. Nearby slums encroached upon the downtown, as in many other cities across the country. Many marginal businesses—pawn shops, bars, liquor stores, shoe shops, second-hand stores—sat uncomfortably close to the 17th Street financial district.

In 1947, J. Quigg Newton, a 35-year-old member of Denver's business elite, defeated Ben Stapleton in the mayoral election by a landslide. Unlike Stapleton, Newton was not nervous about outsiders coming to Denver. In fact, the new mayor was eager to attract new investment capital. But promoting growth would not necessarily be easy. Denver's business community had been completely dominated, at least since Stapleton's first election to the mayor's post in 1923, if not before, by a few old-wealth families led by Claude Boettcher, John Evans, and Gerald Hughes. These three men dominated the financial and banking community, and maintained their control through conservative investment policies—as late as 1950, the banks along 17th Street loaned only 20 percent of reserves for investment (Abbott, 1981: 124).

But before long, Newton became the center of a coalition of entrepreneurs who recently had moved to Denver, and who wanted growth. Under new, outside ownership, the Central Bank began pioneering in liberalized loan policies and advertising for new customers. William Zeckendorf, a New York real estate promoter, paid unheard-of prices for land in downtown Denver, defying law suits filed by the old Denver elite. *The Denver Post,* under a new editor, began to lead a crusade for growth. By the mid 1950s, Newton presided over a "postwar generation of bankers, real estate brokers, merchants and small industrialists who, in concert with the Chamber of Commerce, sought growth at any price" (Dorsett, 1977: 251).

At the prodding of the Chamber of Commerce and downtown businessmen, the city appropriated money for new street lighting, adopted stricter zoning regulations, and tried to expand the number of parking spaces. Meanwhile, the first real signs of private activity also showed, when the *Rocky Mountain News* and *The Denver Post* built new plants in the downtown area.

In 1955, 75 downtown businessmen founded Downtown Denver, Incorporated (DDI). Shortly after, DDI and the city brought in an expert panel from the National Urban Land Institute to make recommendations on downtown development. The Institute recommended a coordinated development strategy involving public authority and private funds. The mechanism for this, it said, should be an urban renewal program (Judd and Mushkatel, 1979).

In 1956, the Downtown Denver Improvement Association was organized by 176 business firms. The Association's central goal was very specific—to lobby the legislature for legislation allowing the city to create an Urban Renewal Authority. The state passed enabling legislation creating the Denver Urban Renewal Authority (DURA) in 1958. DURA's initial projects consisted mainly of clearance and rehab/ construction of residential units through categorical grants provided by the federal government. The City of Denver was responsible for paying one-third of the costs of land clearance.

The early DURA housing rehabilitation and redevelopment projects were much like the initial urban renewal programs in other cities. The programs began with a focus upon slums and low-income housing and consisted of clearing slums in run-down residential areas of the city. The Denver residential projects undertaken by DURA included six major areas: Avondale, Whittier, Mitchell, College View, West-side, and Russel Park Manuel. By 1974, DURA had made 247 residential redevelopment grants (DURA, 1978a). In addition, DURA had offered 144 grants for a total of $1,121,000 for emergency home maintenance.

One major project, begun in 1972, involved the razing of 22 square blocks on the west side of the downtown. The area contained a large neighborhood of Victorian homes dating from the late 1880s. Though in need of restoration, these homes comprised some of the most significant architecture in the entire city. On the margins of these residential neighborhoods sat rundown commercial and industrial buildings, along with vacant land.

All of this was cleared to make way for the Auraria Higher Education Center, a newly constructed campus for Metropolitan State College, the Community College of Denver-Auraria, and the University of Colorado, Denver Center. After clearance was completed, in 1974, the land was sold to the State of Colorado. The controversy over the razing of beautiful Victorian homes and the displacement of the Chicano residents was largely ignored by DURA. As a token gesture to the past, one block of homes in the middle of the new campus was restored, to be used as a conference center, administrative offices, and a restaurant.

The centerpiece of Denver's urban renewal, dwarfing every other project in publicity and priority, was the Skyline Project. In 1961, a Downtown Denver Master Plan Committee—made up of both public officials and businessmen—was drawn together, and chaired by the executive director of the Improvement Association. Its purpose was to write and obtain voter approval of an urban renewal plan. In late 1963, the committee's work culminated in the proposed Skyline Project, as proposed in the *Development Guide for Downtown Denver*. Originally the Skyline Project was designated to "encourage development of the area as a balanced residential and business center." In addition, it was expected that the project would eliminate "skid row," an area of several blocks which seemed to threaten the entire downtown (DURA, 1967: B–1).

In 1964, a specially created Forward Metro Denver group campaigned for voter approval of an $8-million bond issue to finance the local contribution of the Skyline Project. Voters rejected the bond issue, though the campaign was well financed and well organized.

The Skyline Project was again placed on the ballot in the city election of May 1967. In the interim, the editor of *The Denver Post* and one of Colorado's congressmen had successfully lobbied the Johnson administration to allow the city's local matching share to take the form of the newly constructed Currigan Exhibition Hall. As a result, the city was not forced to pay its one-third share of the cost of clearance with cash. Not having to approve a bond issue, voters passed the Skyline Project overwhelmingly.

Through 1978, over $600 million of public and private monies had been committed to the Skyline Project in construction that had been completed or was near completion (DURA, 1978b). DURA invested nearly $5 million for the replacement of sewer systems and private utilities. In 1972, an $87-million bond issue was approved by the voters for the construction of new police and fire buildings, a sports arena, libraries, and other public improvements, including the $31-million Denver Center for the Performing Arts. Millions of dollars were, in turn, poured in by private investors. Within a few years, a dozen new buildings were completed: the Mile High Center, Petroleum Club, Denver Club, First National Bank, Hilton Hotel, Brown Palace West, May D & F, Security Life, Western Federal, Colorado State Bank, Lincoln Center, Downtown Holiday Inn and Denver Plaza Hotels. On just 27 acres of land, skyscrapers shot up like a newly planted forest, and development spilled over the boundaries.

Without urban renewal, development probably would have proceeded at about the same pace in the Denver area, but probably not in the downtown. Urban renewal, with the new street lighting, public utilities, and razing of blighted areas, made the downtown attractive to investors.

The scale of the Skyline Project was enormous. Taxes in the Skyline Area prior to urban renewal in 1967 amounted to a little over $181,000. As of 1977, the total taxes received by the city each year were close to $2.5 million as a result of the redevelopment (DURA, 1978c). Little or no neighborhood opposition to the project surfaced because the major redevelopment effort was located in the central business district.

The revitalization of Denver's downtown has been the product of both public and private sector efforts. It is the merging of these two sectors into the Skyline Project which explains the magnitude of construction and revitalization. During the 1950s and early 1960s, urban renewal in Denver was either absent or focused on very small residential rehabilitation efforts. As we have seen with the Skyline proposal, the focus and scope of these projects shifted rather dramatically in 1963. The reason for this shift in policy is found in the wedding of public and private power under the auspices of the Denver Urban Renewal Authority.

Although Downtown Denver, Inc., initially proposed the project, it could not have been accomplished without the approval of DURA's Board of Commissioners. The board, appointed by the mayor, consists of eleven commissioners who serve without pay for staggered 5-year terms. From its inception in 1958, the Board was dominated by representatives from large corporations and Central Business District real estate and merchant interests. As of 1978, the largest law firm in the city was represented by one member of the Board. Other members included the president of the Bank of Denver, the chairman of the First National Denver Manufacturing Company, the president of Civitan (a businessmen's association), a representative of the Potash Company, and a realtor. In the past, commissioners have been architects, representatives of construction enterprises, a former mayor, the president of Denver's School Board, and the president of Denver's Underwriters Association.

It was the close cooperation between private capital and the board of a public authority that led Denver to define urban redevelopment synonymously with downtown redevelopment. The composition of the original planning committee which provided the impetus for downtown revitalization clearly demonstrated the interlocking relationship between business and the public sector. The planning committee included the president of a downtown Denver bank, the president of the largest retail store in Denver, the president of Mountain States Telephone and Telegraph Company, a wealthy realtor, and several business executives. An unbroken theme underlying Denver's rehabilitation history is private enterprise's predominant role not only in DURA's Board of Commissioners but also in setting the entire urban redevelopment agenda for the city.

Despite DURA's commitment to revitalizing the central business district, the banks of Denver still remain relatively small investors in Denver's future. Major funding for the redevelopment effort is out-of-state money from the very largest of corporations. These firms include Prudential Insurance Company of America, Four States Realty, Mountain Bell, Stellar Enterprises, Ltd., Barcel Properties, Inc., Oxford Anschutz Development Company, a Fairmount Hotel, Amoco, Anaconda, and ARCO (DURA, 1978b). According to Governor Lamm, "At least half of the Denver central business district is owned by outsiders, and 99 percent of the long-term financing for downtown office buildings is from out of state" (Lamm and McCarthy, 1982: 5B). By 1982, the total *private* investment in the central business district of Denver since the beginning of Skyline exceeded $2 billion (DURA, 1979; *Empire Magazine,* 1982: 10).

Public financing for all this redevelopment has been provided by federal categorical grants, block grants through the Community Development Program, and urban renewal authority bonds. Local noncash grants to finance DURA's activity through 1977 amounted to over $22.4 million. Local cash grants amounted to about $11.5 million. Federal grants to DURA through 1977 amounted to over $68 million (DURA, 1978c). In addition, in September of 1972, bond issues for projects worth more than $87 million were approved by Denver voters (DURA, 1978a). The total *public* investment in Skyline, as of 1978, was $188.9 million.

Redevelopment in the central business district has consisted largely of office space, commercial centers, and hotels. All of DURA's revitalization activities have been located either in the central business district or very close by with the exception of the residential redevelopment program that DURA has administered for the Community Development Agency (CDA). The major redevelopment effort continues to be the city's core financial and economic center. The degree to which this commercial revitalization dwarfs DURA's efforts at residential revitalization can only be understood by comparing the dollar investments of the two.

Combining all the dollar amounts that DURA has administered for housing rehabilitation up to 1979 yields a figure of just over $11.5 million (DURA, 1979). The total public and private investment in renewal of the central business district was in excess of $1.27 billion for commercial and economic revitalization. The residential rehabilitation expenditures represent less than 1 percent of the amount committed by public and private sectors to revitalizing the downtown central business district (DURA, 1979). Even if we compare the amount of money spent only in the 27-acre Skyline Project ($675 million) to the amount DURA administered for residential rehabilitation ($11.5 million), we find less than 2 percent of the private and public investment was committed to residential development.

In 1979 there were only 794 housing units in the Skyline Project. Of these, 590 were subsidized for the elderly or low income (*Rocky Mountain News,* 1979b: 4). By 1981, DURA planned to construct an additional 297 units for the elderly and physically disabled. Nearly all of the remaining several hundred housing units in the downtown are luxury condominiums which sell for upwards of $150,000. In 1979, DURA approved a development by Writer Corporation of 42 luxury townhouses, each to cost at least $150,000. These were completed in late 1981. Within months of the announcement that they would be constructed, there was a waiting list of 250 people (*Rocky Mountain News,* 1979a: 5, 14). Critics were charging that DURA was subsidizing the construction of office buildings and luxury condominiums at the expense of the city and its low-income residents.

Though DURA's projects frequently met with criticism and controversy, throughout the 1970s the agency had such strong support from city officials that it seemed invincible. Even after the passage of the Housing and Community Development Act in the late summer of 1974, DURA continued in business, despite the fact that all urban renewal programs were folded into a single, annual community-development grant. In other cities urban renewal staffs became part of comprehensive community development agencies. In Denver, because DURA had become so singularly valuable as the coordinator of public and private efforts in the downtown, it took on many activities in cooperation with or instead of the Community Development Agency. The Housing Rehabilitation Grants Program and the citywide Rehabilitation Grant Program were administered through a subcontract with the CDA. Thus DURA became a split agency. With two-thirds of its staff working on housing programs in the neighborhoods, its public focus was still concentrated on the downtown.

Throughout the 1970s, DURA's political status remained secure. It was not entirely dependent upon federal programs for its continued existence. In 1968, the Colorado legislature had passed a tax increment financing bill specifically for Denver. Under the legislation, DURA could create its own funds for renewal activities by floating bond issues based on the increment in taxes anticipated in specific renewal areas. Thus DURA could obtain the up-front money necessary for land acquisition, clearance, and relocation. The bonds would be paid off by the increased taxes generated through the redevelopment process.

On October 15, 1981, DURA made a surprise announcement that it would redevelop a 19-block area just south of the CBD. By using its bonding authority it planned to raze at least 8 blocks, making the land available for condominium development.

DURA officials had not anticipated the reaction which followed. The target area did not fit usual definitions of "blight." It was populated with small, successful businesses and a few homes, whose owners immediately went on the warpath. They quickly organized the Golden Triangle Association, collected petitions, hired lawyers, and lobbied the city council. Protesters claimed that DURA was trying to destroy a viable business area in order to allow a few developers to make big profits. The controversy became very emotional; William Sears, owner of a refrigeration company, threatened to defend his property with a shotgun (*Rocky Mountain News*, 1981b: 4). Sears had been forced to move once before by DURA, when the Auraria campus was developed.

Within a week, DURA announced that it had dropped three parcels from the proposed project, including Sears Refrigeration Company (*Rocky Mountain News*, 1981a: 6). This decision, though designed to reduce protest, only increased the militance of the property owners, and perhaps gave them reason to hope for victory. None of the property owners on the exempted land parcels dropped out of the Association or changed their stand. Several talked in violent terms.

The strength of the opposition was related to their status as businesspeople. DURA was not dealing with the poor, minorities, or the elderly. The small businesses they were threatening were located on valuable land close to the downtown. Part of DURA's motivation was probably its need, or desire, to "protect" the downtown on all sides from possible threat. Another motivation might have been related to its desire to have a project, something to do, as noted by one of the businesswomen in the Golden Triangle: "They say that for DURA to stay in business, it has to keep finding people like us already in business, and drive us out for one reason or another" (*Rocky Mountain News*, 1981a: 12).

City Council members found themselves faced with a white heat of opposition, and potentially expensive litigation. One hundred protesters attended the City Council meeting of November 13, while the only proponent was the DURA director. A month later, the Council voted overwhelmingly to veto the project.

By the spring of 1982, DURA was in trouble. Federal cuts in housing rehabilitation funds threatened to reduce the DURA staff by two-thirds. The Golden Triangle debacle haunted every move of the agency. In desperation, DURA hired a public relations consultant to shore up its image (*The Denver Post*, 1981b: 12A). But it was too little too late. In February 1982, DURA laid off 9 of its 27 staff, and was proposing to reduce the staff to 3 by the end of 1982.

Perhaps DURA had outlived its usefulness even to the downtown business coalition. By 1982 the downtown was not only "saved," but investment was still accelerating. Fifty new buildings were constructed from 1973 to 1982. In only three years from 1979 to 1982, more than $2 billion was invested in the skyscraper boom (*Empire Magazine*, 1982: 10). A substantial proportion of the new investment came from Canada. Of the 50 new buildings constructed between 1973 and 1982, 14 were built entirely by Canadian interests, and 2 by French consortia. The Canadian firms liked Denver. Many of them had long invested in energy growth, as in Calgary and Edmonton, and Denver's economic structure was familiar to them. One Canadian investor said, "I saw in Denver the same situation as in Calgary—natural resources, huge potential, same climate, even chinooks" (*Empire Magazine*, 1982: 11).

Concern over "foreign," and especially Canadian, investments frequently sur-
faces in the Denver and even in the national press. *Newsweek* magazine carried an
article about "Canada's U.S. Land Rush" in September 1981 (Nicholson, 1981: 80).
From mid 1979 to 1982, more than a dozen articles in local newspapers and magazines
prominently featured Canadian investment.

The concern about foreign investment in downtown Denver is only one facet
of a more generalized complaint that "outsiders" control Colorado. Governor Lamm
has often propounded the theme that the West has always been plundered by outside
entrepreneurs. According to the Governor, "The West has never controlled its own
destiny" (Lamm and McCarthy, 1982: 3B). As pointed out by Lamm, all of Colorado's
oil shale, coal, molybdenum, and uranium companies are subsidiaries of out-of-
town corporations. Only 50 of the 147 industrial banks in the state are owned by
investors within the state. Nearly all of the large newspapers and television stations
are owned by "outsiders" (and all of Denver's). The top ten radio stations are controlled from outside (Lamm and McCarthy, 1982: 5B).

Despite the widespread concern about the extent of investment originating from
outside the state or nation, every effort has been made to attract more outside
capital. The earlier discussion of boosterism showed an intense effort to attract
capital to Colorado. A similar effort has been made to attract outside entrepreneurs
to downtown Denver.

For example, urban renewal helped Canadian investments in Denver. J. Robert
Cameron, DURA's executive director, expressed support for all investment, from
whatever the source: "If Canadians want to participate here that's good, but as
far as we're concerned, we'll give everybody a crack at developing here" (Kinsey,
1979: 57). One appreciative Canadian businessman, Steve Dudelzak, moved from
Paris, France, to Calgary in 1969, thence to Denver in 1975. Within the Skyline
Project, he has constructed two skyscrapers, 34 and 24 stories, at One Denver Plaza,
and is constructing Stellar Plaza, which, at a cost of $140 million, will have three
towers. Dudelzak, commenting on his success in Denver, said, "DURA helped me
and the city helped me a lot" (*Empire Magazine,* 1982: 18).

The *combination* of public authority and private investment spurred Denver's
CBD growth during its "takeoff" phase. It remains to be seen whether CBD businessmen are now willing to go it alone, or whether they will revive DURA (or an
equivalent agency) so that valuable land yet "unreclaimed" can be appropriated.

Denver's Neighborhoods in the Political Process

In the Housing and Community Development Act of 1974, Congress consolidated
seven major categorical programs—including model cities, urban renewal, housing
rehabilitation, historical preservation, water and sewer construction, and others—
into the Community Development Block Grant (CDBG) program. When the Community Development Agency was created in Denver to administer the act, it moved
into territory not occupied by DURA. DURA had a lock on the downtown coalition.
As a consequence, the CDA became a neighborhood-oriented institution. With $44.6

million to spend over the first three years, the CDA became the center of considerable attention.

The CDA's neighborhood focus was a natural outgrowth of its programs and its strategies. Funds were available for the rehabilitation and renovation of physical structures like community centers, curbs and gutters, health facilities, and youth centers. Park and recreation funds were available for parks development and maintenance and to develop new parks (six were built by 1982). Wastewater funds were to be used to correct storm and sanitary sewer problems. The largest program was the Housing Assistance Plan, which included housing rehabilitation grants and loans.

The Department of Housing and Urban Development (HUD) required the CDA to submit a three-year plan to maximize the impact of the federal funds in Neighborhood Strategy Areas. This requirement virtually guaranteed a neighborhood focus. This focus was effectuated through the Mayor's Advisory Council (MAC), set up in 1974, whose members were supposed to represent the neighborhoods before the mayor, the council, and the city's agencies. The MAC was also charged with making major policy decisions about the expenditure of Community Development funds. Of 23 members in 1978, 13 were appointed, one by each member of the City Council. Six were appointed by the mayor to represent city departments, and he appointed four more at-large.

After a slow start in which the MAC members found it difficult to question "expert" planners, they became an important, rather central, institution in city politics. The mayor encouraged the MAC to take a leading role in representing the neighborhoods and in making basic decisions about the distribution of CDBG funds and projects to the neighborhoods. For him, it solved the problem of involving himself in controversial allocation decisions. The MAC also fulfilled the citizen participation requirements of the CDBG program.

Nearly all CDA staff and MAC members who were interviewed in a 1979 HUD study rated the MAC very highly. Early in its history, the Mayor's Advisory Council members jockeyed for position with each other and were often distant from community groups. Within a couple of years, however, they became "institutionalized" as the spokespersons for neighborhood groups with the CDA.

Denver's bureaucrats rather than its elected politicians have represented the neighborhoods. Many staff planners working for the Denver Planning Office have provided assistance to neighborhoods in developing proposals made to the Mayor's Advisory Council. The MAC has relied heavily on the CDA and on the Planning Office for technical assistance.

The mayor continues to be closely allied with the downtown coalition. The fact that 11 of the 13 council members are elected by districts might suggest that they would be oriented to the neighborhoods, and thus be a counterbalance to the mayor. Some members of the council are oriented to neighborhoods. But the council rarely, if ever, stands up to the mayor on important policy questions. A *unified* neighborhood perspective does not exist.

It might appear that Denver has achieved a balance between downtown interests and the neighborhoods. MAC hearings have often been quite noisy, making it appear that citizen participation was working. The mayor and council gave virtually final

authority to the MAC over most programs administered through the Community
Development Block Grant program. However, it should be kept in mind that the
total amounts of federal funds available were miniscule in comparison to the *private*
resources in the city. By 1982, the CDA budget had declined to $9 million, down
from the $15.8 million in its first-year, 1975 budget.

URBAN SPRAWL AND THE QUALITY OF LIFE

Even while Denver's downtown was being transformed into a visual symbol of
corporate technology in the two decades after 1960, growth elsewhere in the Denver
area mushroomed. Office space increased in downtown Denver from 8.3 million
square feet in 1975 to a projected 22 million by 1982. Meanwhile, a corridor of
development spread southeast of the city. In the area along I–25 running north to
south from the Denver Tech Center, 7 million square feet of office space was in
place by 1981, with 3 million more under construction. Ten years earlier, there
was less than a million square feet. In the Denver Tech Center itself, about 2.5
million square feet are under one roof, with 28 restaurants and scores of shops.
The major developer's goal is to create 20 million square feet of office space by
the end of 1982—as much as the entire amount in downtown Denver in 1979 (*The
Denver Post*, 1981d: 35).

These developments were unstoppable. In 1979, the Denver Regional Council
of Governments, in its regional master plan, urged, in vain, that development outside
the central business district be "compatible" rather than competitive. "The Central
Business District of Denver will be encouraged as the major high density core of
business, cultural, governmental, commercial and residential activity," and "new
development should be encouraged only in locations contiguous to existing urban
areas" (DRCOG, 1977: 12).

But high-sounding planning principles could not stop the inevitable; in their
search for new office space, corporations now had two "downtowns" from which
to choose. The intensity of the competition increased accordingly. And the new
development was competitive to the downtown in every conceivable way: "Through
four years of activity, a corridor of commercialism has grown, an airport has matured
and a once quiet bedroom suburban county has its own new 'downtown' replete
with highrises—and more on the planning boards—theatres, restaurants, new car
agencies, golf courses surrounded by thousands of square feet of office space and
a sea of residential rooftops stretching into the distance" (*The Denver Post*, 1981d:
35). From 1960 to 1975, the city's share of the area's jobs declined from 63 percent
of the total to 52 percent (DRCOG, 1977: 4).

Denver had attempted to forestall the political fragmentation resulting from
urban sprawl decades earlier. In the 1940s and 1950s, the Denver Water Board,
which represented downtown interests, tried to exert a veto over suburban annexa-
tions and expansion. A serious drought in the 1950s gave the Board a weapon
which it used to try to stop suburban expansion. In 1951 the Board drew a "blue
line" on a map, beyond which it would not supply service (Abbott, 1981: 177).
The Board refused to supply emergency service to communities whose wells ran

dry. The blue line remained Water Board policy until 1960. By then, the large suburban jurisdictions had built their own water systems, one in cooperation with Colorado Springs fifty miles to the south.

The legacy of bitterness left by the water fights doomed most of the subsequent efforts to create regional service districts. In 1965, 1966, and 1967, Denver's attempts to create a regional government to administer six services failed in the state legislature. Sensing time was running out, and that the city was becoming politically isolated, Denver initiated a series of annexation efforts in the late 1960s and early 1970s. Although successful at annexing twenty square miles of land between 1970 and 1974, the "land wars" brought on an overwhelming political reaction. In 1974, voters approved the "Poundstone Amendment," which amended the constitution to require approval by all the voters of a county for annexation of any area of a county (Abbott, 1981: 190).

By 1975, Denver was surrounded by a ring of 26 suburbs. In 1950, two-thirds of the metropolitan area's residents lived in the City of Denver. This fell to 53.1 percent by 1960 and 41.9 percent by 1970. In 1980, 31 percent of the area's residents lived in Denver; the rest in its suburbs (U.S. Bureau of the Census, 1952, 1972, 1981). After the 1970 census, suburban representation in the state House of Representatives and the Senate was within two votes of Denver's. The consequences of political fragmentation would soon be felt. In the 1970s, Denver would be the repeated loser in attempts to articulate "urban" interests. The most bitter political conflicts involved attempts to solve the problems of air pollution and uncontrolled growth.

The Brown Cloud Invades Paradise

Air pollution is especially disturbing to Denver residents because they think of it as the place they came to in order to escape the problems of *other* cities. The "Eden complex" helps explain the degree of anger and disappointment that often colors discussions about the "Brown Cloud." It wasn't supposed to happen here. "For the rest of America, Colorado is a fabled escape hatch; in reality, it's becoming the epitome of what people want to get away from everywhere else" (Gardner, 1974: 18). There is always the comparison, not only with what it is "supposed to be," but with what it allegedly once was. The Rip Van Winkle technique is common in such comparisons. A writer who hadn't seen Denver for twenty years wrote this description for the *Atlantic Monthly:*

I am somewhat dumbfounded to discover that the vast, flat plan that used to stretch before us farther than our eyes could see has been filled in . . . farther than our eyes can see. Because now our eyes can't see very far. Not only has Denver oozed off in every direction like molten lava, it has a smog problem. Air Quality measurements indicate that at times it is the worst in the nation. (Stegner and Stegner, 1978: 83)

Denver does, indeed, have a serious air pollution problem. Like cities throughout the West, it is dependent upon the automobile. Like them, it has not developed an adequate mass transit system. Also like them, it sits in a basin which is prone

to air inversions. But the comparisons stop there, for Denver sets the standards
for all the others. There are more cars per capita than in any other U.S. city, including
Los Angeles. No other U.S. city sits within such a *high* basin: from the mountains
through the plains stretching one hundred miles east, the elevation actually rises
slightly. Denver, a mile high, can only be compared to Mexico City, which is even
higher (7,575) and has more people (more than 10,000,000). Mexico City may be
the most polluted city in the world. In the United States, Denver often has the
highest carbon monoxide levels, and is not far behind in hydrocarbons, ozone, and
particulates.

Altitude makes air pollution worse. Like the tourists who find themselves short
of breath, car engines do not operate efficiently a mile high: there is 18 percent
less oxygen in Denver than in, say, Boston. Cars and trucks emit more pollutants,
and get worse gas milage. Above 4,000 feet, automobiles emit at least 200 percent
more carbon monoxide and 150 percent more hydrocarbons than at sea level (Jones,
1975: 51). At high altitudes, ultraviolet radiation from the sun causes chemical reac-
tions among hydrocarbons and nitrogen oxides, forming ozone—which destroys
lung tissue more efficiently than any other known air pollutant.

Automobile emissions are the most important single source of most pollutants
in the Denver area: 93 percent of ambient carbon monoxide, 85 percent of hydrocarbons, 45 percent of particulates, and 37 percent of nitrogen oxides (Air Quality
Control Commission, 1979: 62–63).

An important psychological element is added to the pollution problem by the
very visible Brown Cloud which gathers over the city. The desertlike climate suspends
tons of sand and dust in the air. Combined with the emissions from autos and
industry, the Brown Cloud sits like an enormous blob, contrasted against the azure
sky highlighting the mountains—if the mountains are visible at all.

A 1976 survey found that metropolitan residents were more concerned about
air pollution than any other problem involving government service (Denver Metropolitan Study, 1976: 25). Considering the high level of public concern about the
pollution problem, one might predict aggressive governmental action, possibly along
the lines of California's strict state laws on auto emissions adopted in the mid-
1960s. Such a prediction would require, however, (1) a serious underestimation of
the influence still exerted by the ideal of Western individualism, (2) a failure to
account for the self-interests of developers and boosters, and (3) an overestimation
of the ability or willingness of governmental leaders to cooperate.

The ideal of Western individualism still wields a big stick in Colorado state
politics. Even though residents of the city of Denver recognized air pollution as a
serious problem by the mid-1970s, they could not get suburban and rural interests
to cooperate in achieving a solution. The pollution problem was worst in the city
and in a few of the northern suburbs. If suburban commuters could drive out of
the Brown Cloud at the end of their working day, they considered the problem
sufficiently contained. In any case, they did not want a "big government" solution—
one requiring regional or state planning. In the suburbs as well as in rural Colorado
there is a hypersensitivity about government, fueled by a desire to escape the com-
plexities which beset the rest of the country. Western individualism is, after all, a

central component of Eden: nobody tells *me* what I can do in my backyard (or lower forty).

Second, the same boosterism that characterized Denver's growth has characterized growth outside the city. Effective car pollution control constitutes a potential threat to expansion and growth. It might require curtailing auto traffic; worse yet, stopping new development altogether. Without people, there is no growth. With people, and their cars, there is pollution. The problem of air pollution is not easily separated from urban sprawl and all its other consequences. Boosterism "equates growth with progress, and finds the concept of expansion the first principle of the American Dream" (Stegner and Stegner, 1978: 86). It also equates growth with profits.

Because air pollution controls were potentially threatening, culturally as well as economically, proposals for effective action were deeply divisive. Environmentalists and urban (read: Denver City) interests were soon locked in a bitter struggle with suburban and rural legislators, who resisted any strong state legislation. When Richard Lamm was elected as Governor in November 1974, the battle was joined.

As a state representative, Lamm had often advocated state planning and environmental controls. Through the 1970s, he pushed the Colorado General Assembly to enact pollution legislation which would require monitoring of exhaust gases emitted by individual automobiles. It was good fodder for the newspapers. The governor would propose, the legislature would dispose. Then, in 1979, the Environmental Protection Agency (EPA) changed the terms of the struggle.

In November of that year, the EPA told state officials that effective air pollution legislation would have to be forthcoming, or the federal government would be forced to impose sanctions (*The Denver Post*, 1979: 1). The EPA had determined that nine counties in the Denver area violated national air quality standards. Under the terms of the 1970 Clean Air Act, states were required to take action to meet the standards.

The legislature moved to counter the threat. Early in December, several legislators sued the EPA, with legal assistance provided by the Mountain States Legal Foundation (the same organization which helped lead the Sagebrush Rebellion, and supplied the Reagan Administration with its Secretary of the Interior) (*The Denver Post*, 1980a: 1). In its brief, the suit claimed that the EPA had overstepped its authority and violated the state's constitutional rights. Two months of confrontation and name-calling followed. A lot was at stake: the EPA was threatening to cut off $300 million in federal water, sewer, and highway funds in nine counties if the legislature did not pass an air pollution bill by March 1, 1980.

Worried about this prospect, a group of local officials formed an Air Quality Coalition to lobby the legislature. The mayor of Denver joined the group, along with other urban-oriented local officials (*The Denver Post*, 1980f: 3). Colorado's Representative Timothy Wirth and Senator Gary Hart urged the legislature to act. Both the *Rocky Mountain News* and *The Denver Post*, the two metropolitan dailies located in downtown Denver, editorialized in favor of legislation. Still the General Assembly stalled.

On March 1, 1980, the EPA set in motion a process to freeze, effective March 14, all federal water, sewer, and highway construction funds in the nine counties. Bitter charges were leveled at the federal government. The EPA held firm. Local environmental and urban-oriented papers petitioned the legislature for action. The pressure was felt: on April 3, the President of the Colorado Senate and the Senate Majority Leader, both Republicans, published a lengthy editorial in *The Denver Post* defending the legislature's record on air pollution (*The Denver Post*, 1980c: 27). But against the loss of federal aid, the legislature finally caved in. On April 7, 1980, a bill was finally approved, in an atmosphere filled with tension: "several senators, angered by recent caustic comments by the regional EPA administrator, switched their positions and opposed the bill, almost defeating it" (*The Denver Post*, 1980b: 1, 26). The final Senate vote was 19 to 16.

The bill was very weak. It required annual tailpipe inspections on all 1968 or later model year cars after January 1, 1981. If a car failed to pass the test, about $15 in adjustments would be required. If it still failed to pass, it would nevertheless receive certification. No constraints on local governments, no traffic controls, but still the bill barely squeaked through. In an act of revenge, possibly, the legislature repealed Colorado's annual auto safety inspection law which had been in effect since the early 1960s.

The air pollution controversy illustrated the extreme difficulty—near impossibility—of achieving a regional or state focus on Colorado's urban problems. The revitalization of Denver's downtown did not require state action of a kind which seemed threatening to suburban or rural interests. The state legislature had lent a hand to Downtown Denver, Inc., by passing urban renewal enabling legislation in 1958, bringing the Denver Urban Renewal Authority into existence. The legislature had also helped by approving tax increment financing powers for the city. These were crucial steps. But everything else took place within the politics of the City of Denver. A business-local government official coalition came together to implement revitalization.

No similar coalition existed with regard to regional urban problems. Obviously, such a coalition would not emerge from a legislature which could not even handle air pollution legislation.

The Failure of State and Regional Planning

Air pollution and runaway sprawl were very much on the minds of Denver residents throughout the 1970s. To many people, growth had run amok. The very qualities which had attracted them to Denver seemed threatened. A *Christian Science Monitor* article published in June 1975 had ranked Denver as one of America's "10 Most Livable Cities." In the January 1975 issue of *Harper's* magazine, Denver had been ranked 7th among the nation's 50 largest cities as a place in which to live (Louis, 1975: 67–71). All of this now seemed in danger. A feature story in the February 9, 1981, issue of *The Denver Post* was headlined "Colo. Front Range Disaster Danger Cited" (*The Denver Post*, 1981c: 3). It referred not to war or natural catastrophe, but to runaway development. A gloomy assessment was offered by Lyle Dorsett in the conclusion to his history of Denver:

The only certainty is that if metropolitan Denver finds the water to continue its financially profitable postwar pace of expansion, overall quality of life will deteriorate. If that happens,

Denver will lose its minority status as one of the remaining livable cities. The Mile High City will become just another sprawling metropolis. (Dorsett, 1977: 288)

When Richard Lamm was elected Governor in 1974, he brought with him a concern about unplanned growth. Lamm had been one of the leaders of the effort to stop the Olympics. As a state representative, he had advocated a state planning role in local development. As a legislator, he found himself at odds with most of his colleagues. When he became governor, a confrontation was more or less inevitable.

He was a Democratic governor, and his victory was widely interpreted as a mandate for the environment and for planned growth. In the same election, Gary Hart was elected to the U.S. Senate. He had received national attention as George McGovern's campaign manager in the 1972 presidential race. Some of the national news media interpreted these election results as an indicator that Colorado was a bastion of liberal politics.

But this was hardly the case. Confronting Lamm was a conservative state legislature in which rural legislators were joined by their suburban colleagues in opposing any state action which threatened local autonomy. There was, in fact, hardly any bloc of urban votes at all: sprawl along the Front Range had created a multitude of independent municipalities which refused to see themselves as confronted by common "urban" problems, as was clearly evident in the battle over air pollution.

In his first years in office, Lamm was repeatedly frustrated in his efforts to get the legislature to take a serious look at urban problems in Colorado. This was nothing new. In 1973, Lamm, as a state legislator, had seen his Republican colleagues defeat a proposed State Policies Act which would have set goals to control urban sprawl, and air and water pollution. It would also have initiated a state planning process.

Frustrated by legislative inaction, by 1979 the governor was ready to use the powers of his office to endrun the General Assembly, if necessary. His attempts to promote state planning oversight of local development immediately led to bitter squabbling.

On September 13, 1979, the Governor signed an executive order adopting a series of "Human Settlement Policies" to guide the "decisions and actions of all boards, commissions, and principal departments of the state government." According to his order, the governor was establishing the policies because:

Colorado has entered a period of rapid population and economic growth without a plan for how that growth can best be accommodated; and . . . failure to plan for growth accommodation will result in the continuation of deteriorating air quality, increased energy scarcity, inflationary governmental expenditures, loss of essential and desirable resources, worsened water quality, escalating housing costs, overtaxed transportation systems, consumptive cost-inefficient lifestyles, and generally deteriorating quality of life. (Executive Order, 1979)

The order went on to say that state agencies would use the Human Settlement Policies to review local projects which applied for state or federal funding, with any inconsistencies to be reviewed by the State Planning Coordinating Council or the Human Services Policy Council.

Colorado's Human Settlement Policies had been printed in a 22-page document distributed by the Colorado Division of Planning on July 20, 1979 (Colorado Department of Local Affairs, 1979). With the Governor's encouragement, the Division had been working on the policies for nearly three years. The Division had enunciated ten separate policy objectives, all bound to arouse the ire of local officials and suburban and rural legislators. The policies proposed: to assist communities to achieve higher standards of health and safety, to help improve regional services, and to "encourage accommodation of anticipated growth" if the local communities fulfilled several criteria, which included (among others) a requirement for adequate housing, adoption of comprehensive plans and regulations, designation of the community as a "growth center in an adopted regional plan," and a willingness of the community to "share the costs of such growth" (Colorado Department of Local Affairs, 1979: 2). Development was to be discouraged if it (among other things) jeopardized air and water quality standards, conflicted with mineral resource development, destroyed wildlife habitat or "heritage" areas, or took prime agricultural land.

These criteria were so inclusive that development became difficult or impossible without, in theory, confronting one of the standards. But the Settlement Policies went still further and promised to promote "clustered, compact development" or development within or connected to existing communities. Priority was put on avoiding "diffused, low density development," "strip or corridor development," and "leap-frog development" (Colorado Department of Local Affairs, 1979: 3).

During the fall of 1979, several proposals by local governments ran afoul of the Human Settlement Policies. For example, on October 12, the Department of Local Affairs declared that a proposed annexation by a sewer district in southwest Colorado violated the policies because the new annexed area was a very low-density (one dwelling per acre) residential addition. Further, the Department said, the sewer district was not charging enough for the proposed new service. On these grounds, the Department recommended against any state or federal funding for the project (Memorandum from Phil Schmuck, 1979).

It took little time for actions such as these to prompt legislators to resist. On March 4, 1980, the Republican members of the House State Affairs Committee approved a resolution asking the governor to withdraw the policies. The Republicans charged that Lamm had tried to "establish through executive order the statewide land-use policies he unsuccessfully pushed both as a legislator and as Governor" (*The Denver Post*, 1980d: 16).

In March, the Senate State Affairs Committee held hearings to consider whether to join its House committee counterpart in adopting a resolution opposing the policies. Local officials complained that their applications for state and federal funds were being short-circuited by Lamm's policies. A Jefferson County Commissioner, whose county is located within the Denver SMSA, testified that the policies "absolutely usurp the power of citizens in voting to elect people to represent them. They totally usurp the local control." In response to testimony from a state official that the policies were only advisory, a local planning consultant said, "It appears to me that they're advisory only if state people happen to agree with what the local people decide. If they disagree, they're in trouble." Some State senators made comparisons to the resettlement policies of Nazi Germany: "Just the title is offensive. It has a dire ring to it" (*Rocky Mountain News*, 1980a: 8).

The word "planning" was alone sufficient to sound the "dire ring." For example, the testimony of County Commissioner Guy Mauk before the House committee:

Mauk, who said he raises hogs and keeps his business very organized, with different kinds of hogs in different pens, told the committee, "I don't think we should handle people the way we do hogs. We should give people the right to make a choice of where they live and under what conditions as long as they can afford to do so." (*The Denver Post,* 1980d: 16)

By the end of March, the Governor and the legislature were at virtual war. The Governor said that he had asked the legislature to act on growth policies in 1976, but had gotten nowhere. He told reporters, "Not only is the Legislature not being constructive, it is being destructive" (*Rocky Mountain News,* 1980b: 3). For its part, the legislature stalled on budget requests made by Lamm, and threatened to give itself more power in administrative decisions. Later, both sides backed off enough to allow the controversy to cool, but the differences were never resolved.

The controversy surrounding the Governor's Human Settlement Policies threatened to paralyze the ability of state agencies to influence local decisions at all. But the Governor was working on another strategy, one which held the prospect of mobilizing political and business leadership without confronting the General Assembly. He wanted to create a semi-official citizen's caucus which could pressure the General Assembly to act—or, if necessary, could bypass it altogether.

In November 1979, Governor Lamm launched a "citizen's crusade"—the Front Range Project—to study problems connected to growth and development. He hoped the project would develop into a coalition of business and political leaders who would be able to flex the muscle necessary to achieve some degree of regional planning.

The Front Range Project was designed to involve hundreds of people in a volunteer effort to preserve the quality of life in urban Colorado. In late 1979 and early 1980, 475 volunteers were recruited to conduct research for nineteen committees, established to study Front Range problems (Welles, 1980: 53). The Governor appointed only 125 of the volunteers, asking counties to appoint the rest. In May, a Front Range Conference was held in Denver to define the basic agenda. During June and July 1980, citizen forums were held in the 13 counties included within the three SMSAs along the Front Range. More than 1,200 people attended. Local media provided extensive coverage to all these events.

In a full-page feature article in the November 16, 1980, *Denver Post,* Governor Lamm compared the Denver Conference with the Constitutional Convention of 1789, on the somewhat shaky ground that "the men and women who assembled in Denver to begin charting a future course for the 13-county Front Range area were contemplating a future for about the same number of citizens that our founding fathers were representing 200 years ago" (Lamm, 1980: 30).

The Governor nearly doomed his brainchild before it got off the ground. Local officials were critical, thinking the Project to be another try by the governor to achieve state land-use planning. They quite naturally tied it to the governor's Human Settlement Policies, which were just then being imposed by (and on) state agencies.

Lamm himself revealed that there was, in his mind, an intimate connection. In his letter to the Chairman of the Coordinating Committee of the Project, he stated his "intention that these [Human Settlement Policies] . . . serve as guiding principles for the Front Range Project during its initial stages. These policies represent a broad consensus of opinion regarding ways in which state government can and should influence the direction of growth and urbanization" (*Rocky Mountain News,* 1980b: 3).

The Chairman disagreed, and thereby almost certainly saved the Project from being embroiled in the bitter struggle between the governor and the legislature. He suggested that the themes of the Project emerge from citizen meetings. He also resisted Lamm's suggestion that the purpose of the project was to recommend solutions on Front Range problems to state government. This, together with the presence on the Coordinating Committee of well-placed business and government leaders, took the Front Range Project out of the fight.

The democratic symbols permeating the Front Range Project were misleading. Governor Lamm wanted a lot more than discussion and study from the project. He was trying to find a way around the Republicans in the state legislature, and perhaps around local political leaders who resisted state planning. The only way to accomplish this would be to use the Project to create coalition of leaders with the stature and resources to overcome opposition.

The 21 members of the Coordinating Committee appointed by the governor to lead the Project heavily represented the business community—at least 10 were identified with corporations or with local business concerns. There was one labor union representative, an "environmentalist" (Colorado Open Space Council), a state senator and representative, and a county commissioner. Later, the Committee was expanded to 25 members in response to complaints that local officials were left out—the latter omission probably revealing Lamm's attitudes toward most local officials.

The Project's agenda soon emphasized such items as "new public and private policy guidelines for Front Range development, incentive mechanisms for guiding growth, and increased technical assistance to various levels of government" (The Colorado Front Range Project, n.d.). Left out were negative, implied threats contained in Lamm's Human Settlement Policies. The first year agenda of the Project emphasized the process of participation, goal-setting, and coordination, and took great pains to avoid specificity.

This was all it could do. Any attempt to recommend actual growth controls would have run into the same problems encountered by the Human Settlement Policies. Most local officials and *all* developers bridled at suggestions of actually imposing regional growth controls. Business and political leaders promoting controls tended to reside in or were identified with Denver City proper: their motivation was to prevent competition with the downtown and to promote "compatible" development outside the city. In contrast, suburban officials and developers were quite anxious to develop their own economic bases, and they cared little if this was compatible or competitive with Denver.

THE UNEVEN BENEFITS OF GROWTH

Nearly everything written about Denver takes as a first premise its status as a boom-town. Urban sprawl, air pollution, downtown redevelopment, and water dominate public discussion. One could easily get the impression that social problems which plague cities elsewhere—racial segregation, poverty, poor housing, high crime—are more or less absent in Denver. The single-minded concern about growth issues provides a perfect setting for a politics of neglect regarding social problems.

It is undoubtedly true that the social problems connected to race and poverty in Denver are less massive than in older, big cities of the Northeast and Midwest. Unemployment rates are lower, the incidence of poverty is less. Nevertheless, Denver exhibits many characteristics associated with declined central cities. Prosperity is not evenly distributed, and the differences between the people in the city of Denver and those in the suburbs have become greater and more obvious. "In recent years, Denver's patterns of population change have begun to closely resemble those of older, urban core cities, increasingly populated by: the poor; the less educated; the minorities; the less easily employed; the elderly, and the working young adult house-holds." The city has become "surrounded by a solid suburban ring populated by: the white majority; the affluent; the better educated; the family households with children and with adults in their most productive years; and the higher skilled and more easily employable" (Rahe, 1974: 26).

Only after the 1960 Census, with the explosion of population in the suburban ring and of the high-tech industries within it, did this description become accurate. Table 5.4 shows that in 1950, Denver City's residents had more education, higher incomes, and higher status occupations than did the people residing in the suburbs. But in the decade of the 1950s, the relationship was reversed. According to the 1960 Census, Denver's residents had lower socioeconomic status than the people living in the suburbs. By 1970, the gap had widened further, especially with regard to income.

Over the past thirty years, the city's share of the SMSA's population and eco-nomic growth has steadily declined. Table 5.5 shows that every sector of the economy has decentralized, with the lion's share of new economic activity being located in the suburbs, rather than in the city of Denver. In 1950, the vast majority of SMSA jobs in all economic categories were located in Denver City—in all sectors of the job market, two-thirds or more. The steady decline to 1977 is remarkable, down to 58 percent of service jobs and 38 percent of retailing jobs left in the city. This development is comparable to older, declined central cities.

Like many of these cities, Denver has undergone a revitalizing process in its central business district and in many of its neighborhoods. Nearly all large cities have gone through a visible renaissance of downtown business districts and of se-lected neighborhoods. San Francisco has its Giardelli Square and Fisherman's Wharf; Salt Lake City, its Trolly Square; Chicago, its Navy Pier. In Atlanta, it is Peachtree Plaza, in Kansas City, Crown Center. St. Louis has Laclede's Landing and the Westend redevelopment. In Denver, Larimar Square has been revitalized, against a backdrop

TABLE 5.4
Differences between Denver and Its Suburbs, 1950–70

Socioeconomic Characteristics		Decennial Census Year		
		1950	*1960*	*1970*
Educational Attainment: % with 13 or more years education in:	*Denver*	23.6	25.8	29.5
	suburbs	19.6	28.9	35.1
Difference, Denver vs. suburbs:		+ 4.0	− 3.1	− 5.6
Occupational status: % Professional or Managerial in:	*Denver*	25.2	23.7	27.3
	suburbs	21.0	27.7	31.2
Difference, Denver vs. suburbs:		+ 3.8	− 4.0	− 3.9
Income: % Families below $6,000 per year in:	*Denver*	78.8	45.7	24.5
	suburbs	85.8	40.5	14.5
Difference, Denver vs. suburbs: (+ means Denver better off)		+ 7.0	− 4.8	−10.0

SOURCE: U.S. Bureau of the Census, *1950 Census of Population, Colorado,* Vol. 1, Part 7, Tables 30–43; *1960 Census of Population, Colorado,* Vol. 1, Part 7, Tables 20–30; *1970 Census of Population, Colorado,* Vol. 1, Part 7, Tables 120–33.

of skyscrapers and new luxury condominiums. And in all of these cities, segregation, poverty, crime, and bad housing persist. Denver is undergoing a boom in downtown construction; many neighborhoods are thriving; new restaurants, bars, ice cream parlors, bookstores open every month. As elsewhere, economic vitality benefits some people—those with sufficient money—but does little but provide low-paying service jobs for those with lower incomes.

TABLE 5.5
Denver City Share of Denver SMSA Employment, 1958–1977

Employment Sector	*1958* Percentage	*1967* Percentage	*1972* Percentage	*1977* Percentage
Retailing	73.9	57.1	44.7	37.9
Manufacturing	67.2	54.6	47.8	NA
Selected Services	81.9	71.2	67.3	58.2

SOURCE: William G. Colman, ed., *Suburbs and States: Governing and Financing Urban America* (New York: Free Press, 1975), pp. 58–59, and the sources cited therein. For 1977 figures: U.S. Bureau of the Census, *Employment and Population Changes—Standard Statistical Areas and Central Cities.*

TABLE 5.6
Socioeconomic Disparities Based on Race, City of Denver, 1970 Census

	Median Income	*Percent below Poverty Level*	*Percent Unemployed*[a]	*Median Years Education*	*Percent High-school Graduates*
All Persons in City	$9,654	9.4	4.4	12.3	61.8
Black Population	$7,287	20.7	6.6	12.1	53.2
Spanish-surname Population	$7,323	21.2	6.6	9.9	31.7

SOURCE: U.S. Department of Commerce, Bureau of Census, *1970 Census of Population, Colorado,* Vol. 1, Part 7, *Characteristics of the Population,* Tables 120–33.
[a] Males, 16 and older.

Those least benefited by economic growth are Denver's Chicano minority. In 1980, Chicanos made up 18.7 percent of Denver's population, and blacks made up 12 percent (U.S. Bureau of the Census, 1980b). Chicanos constitute the most visible minority in Denver because of their numbers and relative poverty. Table 5.6 compares blacks and Chicanos with the entire population of Denver. A popular myth that Denver's blacks are predominantly middle class is obviously contradicted by the data. But the biggest minority in Denver are Chicanos. They occupy a segregated area of Denver in the north and northeast sections of the city, encompassing perhaps a quarter of the city's land area.

Racial tensions exist, primarily in the schools and between the police and the Chicano community. In 1974, a federal court ordered that the Denver schools be desegregated by busing. By 1976, for the first time, minority students outnumbered Anglos in city schools. A 1975 survey revealed one of the reasons for the changing racial balance: 25 percent of people who had moved from the city to the suburbs in the previous two years named busing as the reason for their move (Denver Metropolitan Study and Action Program, 1977: 29).

THE UNCERTAIN EFFECTS OF GROWTH

The important political issues in the Denver region are very similar to those which face frostbelt cities. Within the city of Denver, there is a conflict between downtown and neighborhood interests—and certainly there is a trade-off between downtown and neighborhood development. Urban renewal conflicts have generally revolved around these trade-offs. Despite its low unemployment rate, Denver has periodic conflict between minorities and whites, between the poor and the privileged, just as is the case in frostbelt cities. Neighborhood gentrification is proceeding, as elsewhere, in a pattern which displaces the poor and elderly. Condominium construction and conversions near the downtown are creating a foothold for the truly wealthy. Busing, as elsewhere, is a contentious issue, with the school board trying to implement court orders while minimizing white flight.

The benefits of economic development are unevenly distributed. A large proportion of the jobs created in the service economy of Denver go to highly educated
white-collar workers. But an even larger proportion of jobs connected to the entertainment and tourist sectors of the economy—restaurants, bars, hotels—are at or
near minimum wage.

Denver's downtown redevelopment occurred on land reclaimed from small, marginal businesses or residential areas. In the neighborhoods, the gentrification process
is well under way. Middle-class home-owners have already displaced, or are in
the process of displacing, poor and elderly tenants and home-owners in neighborhoods with significant architectural features. Poor residents in these neighborhoods
are afraid of displacement. One councilperson noted, "Displacement is a political
issue and a coming issue in the city. The city cannot move as fast as the market
can, so we must do something to help existing property owners to stay there and
help people buy their homes" (Interview with Denver City Council Member, 1979).

Gentrification is moving fast into several neighborhoods which have received
Community Development or rehabilitation attention. The Baker neighborhood in
Denver, one of the CDA target areas, has undergone extensive gentrification since
the mid-1970s. The proportion of professional or managerial heads of households
has gone up from 15.8 percent in 1973–74 to 27.9 percent in 1980. Sixty percent
of new in-movers to the neighborhood in 1966–67 were single-person households
(Schill and Nathan, 1982: 162). Federal funds pushed the process along:

As private investment took hold in Baker, both the federal and the city governments began
to play a role in the neighborhood's development. Funds channelled to Baker enhanced the
neighborhood's attractiveness in the eyes of potential in-movers. (Schill and Nathan, 1982:
166)

As rents went up or buildings were bought for renovation, displacement occurred
at a high rate. A recent study comparing displacement in Boston, Cincinnati, Seattle,
Richmond, and Denver found that displacement of Chicanos in Denver exceeded
displacement of residents in all the other cities. Thirty-nine percent of all households
were displaced in Baker in the last decade, compared to a 23 percent average for
neighborhoods studied in the five cities (Schill and Nathan, 1982: 202).

The processes occurring in the central-city neighborhoods of Denver are not
fundamentally different from those characterizing older cities of the Northeast and
Midwest. Racial and social class antagonisms between the "haves" and the "have-
nots" exist. The reclaiming of downtown and the neighborhoods often exacerbate
these antagonisms, and increase the general level of racial and social class segregation.

Denver has become politically isolated over the past thirty years, in a way
which resembles the fate of the nonsunbelt cities. As noted by political scientist
Carl Abbott, this has happened to most cities in the sunbelt:

For the future, sunbelt citizens can expect that increasing political fragmentation of their
metropolitan areas will gradually erode their advantages over older cities, and exacerbate
inequities in the intrametropolitan allocation of the benefits of growth and government. (Abbott, 1981: 254)

Are sunbelt cities like Denver going the way of the nation's older cities? Will the sunbelt cities suffer from the effects of classic urban decay? Certainly, political isolation of the sunbelt central cities, which results from suburban growth, together with a relative concentration of poor and minorities in the core, make it inevitable that these cities will experience *some* of the same problems previously encountered in Northern cities. But sunbelt cities probably will continue to share in many of the benefits of rapid regional growth for some time to come. In the immediate future, political conflicts over growth—such issues as air pollution, water, and regional planning—will dominate. Issues connected with poverty and race will periodically surface, but will continue, for a while at least, to be low on the list of political priorities.

REFERENCES

Abbott, Carl. 1981. *The New Urban America: Growth and Politics in Sunbelt Cities.* Chapel Hill: The University of North Carolina Press.

Air Quality Control Commission. 1979. *Report to the Public, 1979.* Denver: Colorado Department of Health.

Colorado Department of Local Affairs, The Division of Planning. 1979. *Colorado's Human Settlement Policies.* July 20.

Colorado Division of Employment and Training, Research and Analysis. 1982. "Labor market information—September 1982." Estimates for July.

———. 1980. "Resident labor force." March.

———. 1978. "Resident labor force." July.

The Colorado Front Range Project. n.d. (c. 1979). "The Colorado Front Range Project: a summary."

Denver Metropolitan Study and Action Program. 1977. *Final Report.* National Academy of Public Administration.

Denver Metropolitan Study. 1976. *Denver Metropolitan Study, The Denver Region Citizen–Voter: Reported Ideas and Concerns.* National Academy of Public Administration.

The Denver Post. 1981a. September 13.

———. 1981b. March 16.

———. 1981c. February 9.

———. 1981d. January 25.

———. 1980a. December 4.

———. 1980b. May 8.

———. 1980c. April 3.

———. 1980d. March 5.

———. 1980e. March 2.

———. 1980f. January 30.

———. 1979. December 1.

Denver Regional Council of Governments (DRCOG). 1977. *Summary of the Regional Growth and Development Plan for the Denver Region.*

Denver Urban Renewal Authority (DURA). 1979. *DURA's Housing Rehabilitation Program.*

———. 1978a. *Denver Urban Renewal Authority Ten Years Highlights Report.* December.

———. 1978b. *Skyline Urban Renewal Project, Denver, Colorado: Completed Development, Developments Under Contract or Construction.* August.

————. 1978c. *Skyline Project: Summary of Developments.* July.

————. 1967. *Redevelopment Plan: Skyline Urban Renewal Project.* August.

Dorsett, Lyle. 1977. *The Queen City: A History of Denver.* Boulder, CO: Pruett.

Empire Magazine of the Denver Post. 1982. "Dynamic downtown Denver." January 3.

Executive Order: Human Settlement Policies. 1979. State of Colorado, Executive Chambers (No. D0018 79). September 13.

Gardner, Hugh. 1974. "Goodbye, Colorado." *Harper's,* 248 (1487).

Harrison, Bennett, and Edward Hill. 1979. "The changing structure of jobs in older and younger cities." Pp. 15–45 in Benjamin Chinitz, ed., *Central City Economic Development.* Cambridge, MA: Abt.

Interview with Denver City Council Member. 1979. Conducted by staff of HUD study. June 16.

Jones, Charles O. 1975. *Clean Air: The Politics of Pollution.* Pittsburgh: University of Pittsburgh Press.

Judd, Dennis R. 1979. *The Politics of American Cities: Private Power and Public Policy.* Boston: Little, Brown and Co.

Judd, Dennis R., and Alvin H. Mushkatel. 1979. "National policy and redevelopment of the central cities: some lessons from Denver's urban renewal experience." Unpublished paper.

Kelly, George V. 1974. *The Old Gray Mayors of Denver.* Boulder, CO: Pruett.

Kinsey, Gary. 1979. "Canadian connection." *Denver Monthly,* June 1979.

Lamm, Richard D. 1980. "Front Range Project: balancing the future." *Denver Post,* November 16.

Lamm, Richard D., and Mike McCarthy. 1982. "Outside interests continue to milk the West." *Denver Post,* March 28.

Louis, Arthur M. 1975. "The worst American city." *Harper's* 250 (1496).

McKelvey, Blake. 1963. *The Urbanization of America 1860–1915.* New Brunswick, NJ: Rutgers University Press.

Media Scope. 1978. "Denver: a market, a way of life." 12 (8)(August).

Memorandum from Phil Schmuck, Director, Department of Local Affairs, Colorado Division of Planning, to Steve Ellis, Colorado Clearing House. 1979. October 12.

Mollenkopf, John H. 1978. "The post-war politics of urban development." Pp. 134–39 in William K. Tabb and Larry Sawers, eds., *Marxism and the Metropolis.* New York: Oxford University Press.

Nash, Gerald D. 1977. *The American West in the Twentieth Century: A Short History of an Urban Oasis.* Albuquerque: University of New Mexico Press.

Nicholson, Tom. 1981. "Canada's U.S. land use." *Newsweek,* September 28.

Rahe, Charles P. 1974. "The economic base of Denver: implications for Denver's fiscal future and administrative policy." Denver Urban Observatory.

Rocky Mountain News. 1981a. October 28.

————. 1981b. October 18.

————. 1981c. September 13.

————. 1980a. March 25.

————. 1980b. March 5.

————. 1979a. September 5.

————. 1979b. September 2.

————. 1970. May 12.

Salisbury, Robert. 1960. "St. Louis politics: relationships among interests, parties, and government structure." *Western Political Quarterly,* 13 (June).

Schill, Michael H., and Richard P. Nathan. 1981. *Neighborhood Displacement: Causes and Consequences.* Albany: State University of New York Press. Draft manuscript.

The Seven Counties of Denver. n.d. (c. 1978). Denver: Colorado National Bank.

Stegner, Wallace, and Page Stegner. 1978. "Rocky Mountain country." *Atlantic Monthly* 241 (4).

U.S. Bureau of the Census. 1981. *Advance Reports, 1980 Census of Population.* Washington, D.C.: U.S. Government Printing Office.

————. 1972. *1970 Census of Population. Vol. 1. Characteristics of the Population. Part 1,* Table 23, p. 180.

————. 1952. *1950 Census of Population. Vol. 1. Number of Inhabitants. Part 1,* Table 27, p. 69.

U.S. Civil Service Commission. 1977. "Employment trends as of January 1977." *Monthly Release,* March.

U.S. Department of Labor. 1981a. *Employment and Earnings.* "State and area unemployment data." August.

————. 1981b. News release. October 5.

Welles, John G. 1980. "The Colorado Front Range Project: a stumbling starter turns the corner." *Rocky Mountain News,* December 2.

6

San Francisco: Urban Transformation and the Local State

Susan S. Fainstein
Norman I. Fainstein
P. Jefferson Armistead

Residents are trying to cordon off a
chunk of San Francisco for themselves.
Everyone wants to live in San Francisco,
rich and poor. We live on a gold mine
here, and everyone wants to live on top
of it.

COMMUNITY LEADER,
MISSION DISTRICT

Amidst the sorry picture of decline in America's old, ethnically heterogeneous cities, San Francisco appears to offer a stunning example of success. A combination of public and private funds reversed a decaying trend and produced a transformed city with a revitalized core, multitudes of new or rehabilitated buildings, an active street life, lively neighborhoods, ascending property values, and expanding commercial functions. Everybody loves to visit San Francisco. Those lucky enough to live there, whatever their class, remain sensitive to its physical beauty and sophisticated culture. San Francisco, to superficial observation, has adapted remarkably to changed economic circumstances and a series of inconsistent governmental programs aimed at urban redevelopment.

As elsewhere, low-income people, and particularly racial minorities, have been dislocated by redevelopment programs, and even more significantly, by the massive injection of private investment into real estate markets. Unskilled low-income workers have been unable to take advantage of rapid expansion of financial and administrative sectors. But neither have the interests of these groups been totally excluded from consideration. Mobilized community forces have won concessions from city hall and maintained their hold on desirable territory. Evidence of past gains is layered

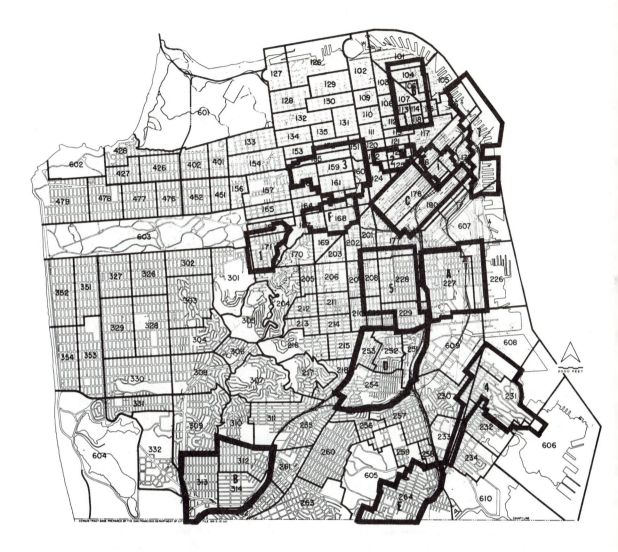

Neighborhood Strategy Areas
1. Upper Ashbury
2. North of Market
3. Western Addition
4. Bayview-Hunters Point
5. Inner Mission
6. Chinatown-North Beach
7. Northeast Waterfront

Neighborhood Improvement Areas
A. Potrero Hill
B. Oceanview-Merced Heights-Ingleside
C. South of Market
D. Bernal Heights
E. Visitacion Valley
F. Hayes Valley

Others
i. Yerba Buena Center Redevelopment Area

SAN FRANCISCO

into the complex set of institutions that comprise the highly pluralistic municipal government.

San Francisco is especially interesting as a case study of urban redevelopment because clearly articulated political conflict has taken place in a milieu of increasing affluence. Whereas New Haven and Detroit represent classic examples of futile governmental efforts in the face of capital withdrawal, San Francisco, like Denver, demonstrates the uneven benefits of growth and the effects of "trickle down" as a mode of social distribution. But its much larger and more diverse ethnic populations make it a more complex political arena than Denver. The city's political battles and their changing nature revolve around manifold and shifting issues—the relationship between neighborhoods and downtown; aesthetic versus financial considerations; opposed cultural definitions of urban life; homeownership against rental status. Despite the dominance of tourist and financial interests in the city's redevelopment pattern, other forces including Latino, black, Asian, and gay communities have demanded routinized shares of public programs. Often under the guidance of professional organizers and advocates, they have won some of their demands. Indeed, San Francisco exceeds most cities in the effectiveness of its urban movements. But, ironically, private investment is so overwhelming that lower-class victories dissipate as neighborhoods which once gained public programs for low-income residents rapidly become transmuted into chic enclaves through private purchase.

This chapter examines the interplay of macroeconomic forces, public programs, private investments, and political struggles that have transformed San Francisco. Once an increasingly, though hardly predominantly, black and Hispanic, economically stagnant central city, it has become a wealthy, multi-ethnic one. Examination of the causal factors, costs, and benefits of this process partially undermines the claims of capital to providing general benefits through growth, even under the most propitious circumstances. But our analysis also illustrates the potential gains for neighborhood and ethnic-based social movements waging their battles within the realm of public consumption. Comparison of San Francisco with the other cities described herein, especially New Haven, indicates the different consequences of extensive grass-roots political activity combined with prominent public intervention in sharply contrasting economic situations. In San Francisco, unlike Detroit or New Haven, the threat to low-income occupancy is investment rather than disinvestment. Our analysis proceeds by first describing the major changes that have taken place in the city in the postwar years, then by examining the specific developmental thrusts and community conflicts that have occurred during each of the periods of this era.[1]

TRANSFORMATION OF THE CITY

Since World War II, San Francisco has experienced a thoroughgoing upheaval in economic function, physical form, and demographic composition. The City by the Bay had throughout its history served as a locus of services and exchange (Wirt, 1974). In the postwar era, however, these functions underwent explosive growth. While the city's manufacturing sector declined, its role as a center of corporate headquarters and financial services for the rapidly growing Pacific Rim trading region expanded sharply. After 1960 huge investment in high-rise office buildings recast the skyline of the central business district. Hotel construction intensified, serving the booming convention and tourist trade. By the mid-seventies, only New York exceeded San Francisco as a center of international commerce and banking (Cohen, 1981: 303).

While corporate decisions were at the core of postwar development, government also played a significant role. Local government, in conjunction with other levels, both regulated and subsidized growth. It determined land use, height and density for office building development; organized and financed major investments in high-speed commuter rail and urban renewal; and expended large sums on antipoverty programs. As development proceeded, local government mediated among groups in conflict over the outcome of particular regulatory, investment, or social-service expenditure decisions.

Simultaneous with the influx of new investment was the arrival of new population groups and the departure of old. The early postwar years saw an in-migration of blacks, Mexicans, and Chinese. In the 1970s these groups were pressed by the drying up of blue-collar jobs and inflation in housing prices. The expansion of headquarters and financial service sectors attracted high-income white professionals eager to take advantage of the city's cultural opportunities. Gay individuals were attracted by the existence of a large, tolerated, politically and culturally strong homosexual community. Central Americans, fleeing economic deprivation and political repression, increasingly settled in the Mission District. Given the small land mass and fully developed character of the city, the growing number of households making claims on its territory could only be accommodated through shifting land uses and increasing structure size.

A closer examination of population characteristics and economic activities reveals the nature of San Francisco's recent transformation. In both categories aggregate statistics are only part of the story—shifts in composition and function of population and economy are the key to the new San Francisco. These, in turn, have caused striking changes in land use and are reflected in political conflict and coalition.

Population Shifts

San Francisco reached its peak decennial census population of 775,357 in 1950, following a decade in which it experienced a growth rate of 22 percent (see Table 6.1). Since then it has been declining, but only slowly. Compared to shrinking cities of the northeast and north central regions, its population loss has been quite mild. While San Francisco lost only 5 percent of its population, New York, Chicago, Detroit, and Cleveland showed declines ranging from 10 to more than 20 percent for the last decade (*Numbers News*, 1981).

The San Francisco standard metropolitan statistical area (SMSA) outpaced the city, experiencing explosive growth during 1940–50 (nearly quadruple the nation's rate) and continued to expand rapidly (30 percent higher than the national rate) in the 1950–70 decades. Although overall totals for the SMSA remained fairly stable

TABLE 6.1
Demographic Characteristics of San Francisco, Oakland, and the San Francisco–Oakland Standard Metropolitan Statistical Area, 1940–80

	1940	% Change 1940–50	1950	% Change 1950–60	1960	% Change 1960–70	1970	% Change 1970–80	1980
San Francisco City									
Population	634,536	+22.2	775,357	−4.5	740,316	−3.3	715,674	−5.1	678,974
Black (%)	0.8		5.6		10.0		13.4		12.7
Chinese and Japanese (%)	3.6		3.9		6.2		9.8		
Filipino (%)					1.7		3.8		
Spanish origin (%)							9.7		12.3
Oakland City									
Population	302,163	+27.3	384,575	−4.4	367,548	−1.6	361,561	−6.2	339,288
Black (%)					22.8		34.5		46.9
Spanish origin (%)							6.7		9.6
San Francisco–Oakland SMSA									
Population	1,461,804	+53.3	2,240,767	+18.2	2,648,762	+17.4	3,109,249	+4.6	3,252,721
Black (%)					8.5		10.6		12.0
Spanish origin (%)							7.4		10.8

SOURCE: U.S. Bureau of the Census, *City and County Data Book*, 1950, 1957, 1967; *1980 Census of Population and Housing: Advance Reports*, March 1981; "1980 Census Population Totals for Racial and Spanish Origin Groups in California Announced by Census Bureau," U.S. *Department of Commerce News* 1981; Frederick M. Wirt, *Power in the City* (Berkeley: University of California Press, 1974), p. 33.

for the 1970–80 decade, important shifts of population occurred between the last two censuses. People have been sorted into San Francisco, Oakland, and the suburban communities according to class, race, and ethnicity. Thus, after San Francisco's black population had grown from about 5,000 (0.8 percent of the city's total) in 1940 to over 43,000 (5.6 percent) in 1950, 75,000 (10 percent) in 1960, and 96,414 (13.4 percent) in 1970, it declined by 10.3 percent to 86,414 in 1980 (12.7 percent of total population) (U.S. Bureau of the Census, 1981a). In contrast, Oakland, the other central city of the metropolitan area, has not shown a similar reduction. Although its total population declined by 6 percent between 1970 and 1980, blacks increased by over 34,000, nearly a 28 percent gain over the previous level, and the city's population shifted from 35 percent to 47 percent black (U.S. Bureau of the Census, 1981). Half the size of San Francisco, Oakland has nearly twice the black population; with just 10 percent of the SMSA's population, Oakland has 41 percent of its black residents.

It is more difficult to track the demographic trends for the Hispanic population of the city. The 1980 Census counted 83,373 "persons of Spanish origin or descent," comprising 12.3 percent of the city's population (U.S. Bureau of the Census, 1981), but the Census Bureau's failure to count Hispanics in earlier censuses precludes precision about trends. The Census Bureau estimates that in 1970 about 9.7 percent of the city's population was of Spanish origin, including about 69,000 persons. Thus the decade was one of growth for the Hispanic population.

Revision of U.S. immigration laws in the late 1960s precipitated a rapid rise in the Asian population. Hong Kong Chinese and Filipinos were the first to take advantage of the revision of country quotas, and they were followed in the middle and late '70s by Southeast Asians. According to preliminary 1980 Census data, the Asian-American population has increased dramatically, both relatively and absolutely. This census enumerated 147,426 Asian and Pacific Islanders (21.7 percent of the population), a 50 percent increase over the estimated 97,349 (13.6 percent) in 1970 (*New York Times,* 1981a: A12). Of this 1970 total, Chinese and Japanese made up 8.2 and 1.6 percent of San Francisco's population, respectively. The China-town area, although a major tourist attraction, has been one of the poorest sections of the city.

The population shift which is most difficult to estimate using census data, but which has had a profound effect on residential development in San Francisco, is the increasing proportion of the population that is homosexual. Using a number of different indicators of gay occupancy, Castells and Murphy (1982: 257–58) estimate that the total gay population of the city in 1980 was 100,000–120,000 (about 17 percent of the whole population); about two-thirds of this number was male.

Overall, then, the population of San Francisco has become increasingly dominated by ethnic groups and the gay community, but not by blacks, who along with whites represent a diminishing proportion of the city's inhabitants. While lack of detailed census data makes estimation hazardous, the white population seems increasingly to contain childless, two-earner couples. As a consequence of reduced household size, the number of households residing in the city increased by an estimated 9,200 (Gellen, 1982: 18) between 1970 and 1980, even while total population declined.[2]

Economic Function

The demographic trends detailed here have occurred while the city was undergoing a change in economic function. Employment has shifted from manufacturing, wholesaling, and port-related activities to finance and service functions, especially business services, which have expanded dramatically (see Tables 6.2, 6.3, and 6.4). Tourism and finance have become the two major industries of San Francisco.

Employment. San Francisco experienced employment growth concurrent with its population decline. Tables 6.2, 6.3, and 6.4 show employment gains and losses by industry over three successive seven-year periods spanning 1958 to 1979. Employment in the city increased 5.5 percent in each of the first two periods, and during 1972–79 nearly 75,000 jobs were added, a 16.5 percent increase. These indicators placed the city in an enviable position—23 of the nation's 57 largest central cities experienced employment loss in the same time span (U.S. Department of Housing and Urban Development [USDHUD], 1980: Section 3). Jobs in the San Francisco SMSA expanded even more rapidly—by 38 percent during 1958–72, and by 21 percent in the 1972–79 period.

These figures on net increases in employment conceal major shifts by industry (Tables 6.2, 6.4). Most striking are the declines in manufacturing and the gains in finance-insurance-real estate and service industries. Nearly 17,000 manufacturing jobs were lost in the city from 1958 to 1972, a decline of 25 percent, while 23,000 jobs were added in finance-insurance-real estate, and over 35,000 jobs in services

TABLE 6.2
**Estimated Nonagricultural Wage and Salary Employment
by Industry, San Francisco (in thousands)**

	1958	*1965*	*1972*	*1979*
Total Workers	421.8	444.7	455.1	529.7
Manufacturing	66.6	58.7	48.6	48.6
Transport, communications, and public utilities	54.1	52.9	53.1	49.1
Wholesale trade	46.7	42.5	36.2	37.7
Retail trade	53.8	54.3	54.3	65.4
Finance, insurance, real estate	43.0	53.5	63.5	82.8
Services	66.3	83.0	97.3	137.3
Government	71.5	81.3	84.9	88.4

SOURCE: State of California, "Estimated Nonagricultural Wage and Salary and Agricultural Employment: San Francisco–Oakland SMSA County Series, 1958–1974," San Francisco, 1974; State of California Health and Welfare Agency, "Wage and Salary Employment by Industry: San Francisco City and County, 1972–1979," San Francisco, 1980.

TABLE 6.3
Percent Distribution of Nonagricultural Wage and Salary Workers by Industry, San Francisco City and County, San Francisco–Oakland SMSA, and United States

	1958 City	1958 SMSA	1958 U.S.	1965 City	1965 SMSA	1965 U.S.	1972 City	1972 SMSA	1972 U.S.	1979 City	1979 SMSA	1979 U.S.
Nonagricultural wage and salary workers	100.0	100.0	100.0	100.0	100.0	100.0	100.0	100.0	100.0	100.0	100.0	100.0
Manufacturing	15.8	20.1	31.1	13.2	18.4	29.7	10.6	14.8	26.0	9.2	13.5	23.4
Transportation, communication and public utilities	12.8	11.5	7.7	11.9	10.2	6.6	11.7	10.2	6.2	9.3	8.2	5.7
Wholesale trade	11.1	7.9	5.8	9.6	7.1	5.7	7.9	6.6	5.6	7.1	6.6	5.8
Retail trade	12.8	14.1	15.1	12.2	14.5	15.2	11.5	15.0	16.1	12.3	16.6	16.8
Finance, insurance, real estate	10.2	6.8	4.8	12.0	7.3	4.9	14.1	8.2	5.3	15.6	9.2	5.5
Services	15.7	13.7	13.2	18.7	16.1	14.9	21.5	18.8	16.7	25.9	21.9	19.0
Government	17.0	18.2	15.3	18.3	20.0	16.6	18.8	21.7	18.1	16.7	18.9	17.7

SOURCE: Calculated from Table 6.2 and State of California Health and Welfare Agency, "Wage and Salary Employment, by Industry: San Francisco–Oakland Metropolitan Area, 1972–1979," San Francisco, 1979; U.S. Department of Labor, Bureau of Labor Statistics, *Employment and Earnings*, May 1981.

TABLE 6.4

Percent Change in Estimated Nonagricultural Wage and Salary Employment, by Industry, San Francisco City and County, San Francisco–Oakland SMSA, and United States

	Percent Change 1958–65			Percent Change 1965–72			Percent Change 1972–79		
	City	SMSA	US	City	SMSA	US	City	SMSA	US
Nonagricultural wage and salary workers	5.4	19.2	18.4	5.6	15.9	21.2	16.4	21.3	22.0
Manufacturing	−11.9	5.1	13.3	−15.2	−6.8	6.0	0.0	11.1	10.0
Transportation, communication and public utilities	−2.2	5.2	1.5	4.2	15.9	12.5	−7.5	0.0	13.2
Wholesale trade	−9.0	7.5	16.3	−13.2	7.5	18.7	4.1	20.3	26.5
Retail trade	0.9	22.8	19.0	−1.7	20.0	28.0	22.5	34.5	27.3
Finance, insurance, real estate	22.4	28.4	20.0	23.6	30.0	31.3	30.4	39.1	27.3
Services	25.2	40.7	33.6	22.3	34.5	35.9	41.1	41.1	39.1
Government	13.7	31.1	28.5	9.1	25.4	32.4	4.1	5.3	19.4

SOURCE: Derived from State of California, "Estimated Nonagricultural Wage and Salary and Agricultural Employment: San Francisco–Oakland SMSA County Series, 1958–1974," San Francisco, 1974; State of California Health and Welfare Agency, "Wage and Salary Employment by Industry: San Francisco City and County, 1972–1979," San Francisco, 1980; State of California Health and Welfare Agency, "Wage and Salary Employment by Industry: San Francisco–Oakland Metropolitan Area, 1972–1979," San Francisco, 1979; U.S. Department of Labor, Bureau of Labor Statistics, *Employment and Earnings*, May 1981.

appeared, each representing gains of over 53 percent. These latter two categories continued to grow at rates of 30 and 41 percent, respectively, in the next seven years. In contrast, while the manufacturing sector had ceased declining, it continued to stagnate. In 1979 manufacturing jobs accounted for only 9 percent of all jobs in San Francisco, down from 16 percent 21 years earlier (Table 6.3). Finance-insurance-real estate jobs were 16 percent of the total, up from 10 percent in 1958; and services accounted for 26 percent of all jobs, rather than the 16 percent share this category held in 1958. These changes far outpaced the shifts in the same direction which characterized the U.S. economy as a whole.

Land Use

The rapid increase in the finance and service sectors manifested itself visually in the concrete, steel, and glass of downtown San Francisco, where a boom in the construction of high-rise office buildings remade the city's landscape. Between the end of World War II and 1979, 52 high-rise office buildings were constructed in the central business district (CBD); 20 more were under construction or projected. This was a startling alteration in a once low-rise city that in 1954 had only five such edifices. The period 1966–75 witnessed a spurt of office construction that added 15 million gross square feet, with an estimated 11 million more to be completed by 1980, a new record (*San Francisco Examiner,* 1979). Afterwards San Francisco could boast the second highest ratio of office space to population—52 square feet per person—in the country. Only Boston, with 68 square feet per person, exceeded this figure (Black, 1980).

Not surprisingly, the drastic revision of San Francisco's physical form stimulated acrimonious debate and bitter struggle between opponents and proponents of the phenomenon. Opponents charged that high-rises destroyed the aesthetic character of the city, increased fiscal strain by costing the city more than they produced in tax revenue, destroyed jobs of resident minority workers and presented an environmental hazard in an earthquake-threatened area (Brugmann and Sletteland, 1971). Defenders rebutted these arguments with studies demonstrating that the city gained net revenue and jobs (Wirt, 1974: 177–83). Opponents unsuccessfully sought to limit heights through ballot initiatives in 1971, 1972, and 1979.

Public and Private

The shifts in population, economic function, and physical form described here comprised the overall trends of the postwar period. They were accompanied by a series of investments which both generated and responded to these macrophenomena. Massive urban renewal projects carried out by the San Francisco Redevelopment Agency (SFRA) in the Western Addition, South of Market Street (Yerba Buena Center), and Financial District areas enlarged the periphery of the CBD, removed low-income residents from proximity to new retail and office enterprises, and introduced upper-income households to these border areas. Urban renewal in Bayview-

Hunters Point, physically isolated although scenically blessed, afforded some new low-income housing and industrial employment. Construction of the 75-mile commuter rail system, the Bay Area Rapid Transit (BART), linked the city, Oakland, and suburban counties. Heightened interest in historic preservation, partly catalyzed by resistance to urban renewal, stimulated enormous reinvestment in rehabilitation of residential housing. Eventually no neighborhood, no matter how seemingly forlorn, was immune to Victorian refurbishment and rising property values, with predictably negative consequences for low-income tenants.

City Government as Orchestrator of Change

During the 1950s and '60s the government actively promoted growth. State-sponsored expansion, however, became increasingly constrained by financial limitations at various levels of government. Fiscal crisis, exacerbated by the passage of California's Proposition 13, which drastically cut property-tax collections, seriously inhibited the city's capacity to provide services. Cutbacks in federal funding, beginning under the Nixon and Ford Administrations, and accelerating thereafter, transmuted the government's role in redevelopment from major actor to facilitator.

The rather unusual institutional structure of San Francisco's government provides a backdrop for the dynamics of redevelopment politics. Arising out of a history of anticorruption reforms, the consolidated city-county government has been characterized as "weak mayor—weak council—weak chief administrator" (Bach, 1976). The short-ballot movement never completely triumphed in the city, and voters directly elect the mayor, the eleven-member Board of Supervisors (city and county council), six financial and legal officials, municipal and superior court judges, and the boards of education and of the community-college system (Wirt, 1974: 118–19). A 1976 initiative, sponsored by community groups, caused a switch from at-large to district-based elections for supervisors; however, subsequent referenda in 1980 restored the at-large status quo ante. In addition to the various independent elected officials, there are appointed fixed-term commissions with powers to review appointments and activities of certain important city agencies, including police, fire, housing, planning, port, and redevelopment. These commissions, while seemingly rather inactive despite their theoretical authority, act as buffers between the various agencies and other centers of control. An appointed Chief Administrative Officer serves for a 10-year term. As one city official commented to us:

The fundamental fact of San Francisco government, its flavor, is that it is the most cumbersomely organized city in the U.S.A. There are some 30 autonomous commissions, cantankerous—there is difficulty in reaching consensus within commissions, let alone between commissions. All of this flows from the City Charter. Read it if you want to understand San Francisco. Chaotic anarchy. . . . There is no centralization of power. You just can't say who is in the driver's seat.

Neither political party nor bureaucracy acts as a unifying force. Party structures are not organized at all at the precinct level as a consequence of San Francisco's nonpartisan government. Most elected officials are Democrats, but this affiliation is primarily important in terms of the city's links to higher levels of government.

A Democratic Party leader contended that neighborhood groups were serving the functions of party, but without the accountability:

If there is the potential for ward politics, it would revolve around those [neighborhood] groups. They provide work for people politically aligned with them, like the Chicago Daley machine. . . . The problem is that they are nonpartisan. . . . I am against this because it is a facade, a social-service facade. I am against an organization with a political philosophy gaining control over a nonpartisan community action group, because later they will engage in political activity. It is a financial base [for political action] at the taxpayers' or churches' expense, while *we* [the Democratic Party] are cut off from the action; we are not allowed to run a district candidate.

In contrast to the party organizations, the civil service has accrued considerable inertial power. It is, however, fractionalized into a number of competing agencies. Within the area of redevelopment, the Department of City Planning, the Bureau of Building Inspection, the Redevelopment Agency, the Economic Development Committee, and the Office of Community Development had seemingly overlapping and uncoordinated activities during the late 1970s.

The power of interest groups to place issues on the ballot further limits governmental control over public programs. Wirt (1974: 57) lists 47 bond issues and 165 charter amendments taken to the electorate between 1958 and 1971. These decisions by the voters, which have endorsed high-rise development and the financing of the Yerba Buena Center, as well as recently defeating a strict rent-control and anti-condominium conversion proposal, can significantly affect the real estate development process. As a consequence, the campaigns preceding them have attracted major financing from real estate and financial interests both in California and across the country.

Superimposed on this congeries of local institutions are the layers of advisory bodies associated with past and present federal programs, all preserved more or less intact. These include poverty program boards, Model Cities boards, and within the redevelopment realm, the following bodies: project area committees in each of the designated redevelopment areas; Model Cities organizations in both former Model Neighborhoods; the citywide Citizens Committee on Community Development (CCCD), an appointed group of citizen representatives; and the Technical Policy Committee, comprised of heads of all city departments and agencies that administer funds related to community development.

Depending on the particular mayor in office and the nature of federal programs during his or her regime, the ability of the mayor to influence the course of events varied. Mayor Joseph Alioto (1968–76) was a strong proponent of the urban renewal program. His support was a significant underpinning of the city's efforts, but in no sense did he organize the coalition promoting the endeavor. Rather, his candidacy was promoted by business and labor groups supporting redevelopment. Direction of the program lay with the Redevelopment Agency, which could "make and implement its own plans, move people from one section of town to another, arrange massive sums for financing, condemn property, and promote all its wonders" (Wirt, 1974: 298).

George Moscone, elected mayor in 1975, built his political base on a wider constituency than did his predecessor. Moscone was the candidate of many neighborhood activists and had substantial support in the homosexual community. Once elected, however, he was criticized by some black leaders as being less accessible than Alioto; other community leaders regarded him as insufficiently forceful. During his administration the termination of the old federal urban renewal program gradually reduced the power of the SFRA relative to the mayor's office. As in New Haven, however, the renewal agency, while weakened, was not eliminated and continued to be the force behind the continued implementation of old renewal plans. Moscone's administration ended abruptly in 1978, when he and Supervisor Harvey Milk were assassinated by Dan White, a former supervisor.

Moscone's death placed in office a previously defeated mayoral candidate, Supervisor Dianne Feinstein. The mode in which she assumed office prevented her from taking strong policy stands or dismissing her predecessor's appointees until she could be elected in her own right. She did manage to centralize more power in her office through reliance on the Office of Community Development as her staff agency for redevelopment. After her election in 1980, she was limited by the different electoral base of the supervisors, who, despite the switch back to at-large voting, have continued to represent the neighborhood constituencies from which the re-elected incumbents originally sprang.

Mobilized Interests

The weakness of the city government allowed private groups to take a leading role in formulating development plans. Wirt (1974) distinguishes between the roles and interests of the "big rich" (the officers of national and international corporations headquartered in San Francisco) and the "little rich" (locally based real estate, hotel, and retail figures) in the life of the city. But he notes that both groups were highly active and visible in promoting redevelopment. One of the supervisors summed up a commonly held view concerning the linkages between the city government and big business, which was the leading force in the Chamber of Commerce:

The mayor's office and administration is more tied to the Chamber of Commerce [than to neighborhood constituencies]. Not just this mayor—this is traditionally true. That one group has been in charge so long that they [city officials] have adopted those viewpoints and attitudes. The anti-high-rise initiative is about this—neighborhood versus downtown. People see a connection between downtown interests and city policies in support of downtown interests.

Counterposed to these "downtown" interests were neighborhood and ethnically based groups. As well as organizing to defend their neighborhoods and cultural interests, they established themselves as clienteles of various city agencies. Thus the Western Addition Project Area Committee (WAPAC) and its counterpart in Bayview-Hunters Point over the years developed close ties with the SFRA. Other community groups, which identified themselves with the "neighborhood movement," worked intimately with the Mayor's Office of Community Development, while yet others depended on relationships with individual supervisors for their access to government. Many of these community elements developed in strident opposition to government policies, and counted individuals with clearly formulated, left ideologies among their leaders. Even those most critical of San Francisco's development, however, seemed eventually to have forged linkages with some part of the governmental apparatus.

The most recent group marshaling its voting strength in order to influence government has been the gay community (Castells and Murphy, 1982). Located in the most important center of gay culture in the United States (and perhaps the world), the San Francisco gay community has significantly influenced both the politics and the life of the city (Becker, 1971). Some of the supervisors, including the assassinated Harvey Milk, were openly homosexual; a number of candidates have directed appeals at this highly educated and well-to-do constituency. Gay individuals occupied a variety of appointed positions in city government. The gay community has succeeded through political pressure in greatly reducing police harassment. After the assassin of Harvey Milk received a light sentence, gays rioted in front of City Hall; the annual Gay Rights Day parade attracts over 100,000 participants and constitutes another show of strength of this highly mobilized group. Whereas the investment practices of large corporations created San Francisco's new downtown, real estate rehabilitation by gays was a principal factor in the physical upgrading of a number of its neighborhoods. A parish priest in one of the city's most heterogeneous districts observed to us:

Gays—they make the neighborhood beautiful by the improvements they make in their houses, but for me they represent the end of parish life. They are forcing the family out of the city. Gays can afford to pay for many services privately. The families here can't.

The politics of community development in San Francisco was thus highly pluralistic. Social and economic groupings interacted with each other within the context of a fragmented political system, a multitude of mobilized interests, and a diverse culture. The systemic bias (Stone, 1976) favoring corporate interests was to some extent checked by community groups demanding specific concessions. They, however, had to deal not only with the impacts of governmental decisions and nondecisions upon their neighborhoods, but also with the overwhelming pressure of private money seeking real estate investment opportunities. The history of redevelopment in San Francisco intertwines private sector initiatives with complex bureaucratic and community politics.

Periodization

While private investment and business expansion have been the dominant factor in San Francisco's economic growth and social transformation, government, despite its highly fragmented, pluralistic character, has played a key role encouraging and shaping redevelopment. Consequently the story of San Francisco's transformation can be conveniently described in terms of three main phases of governmental activity and popular response. We designate these *unopposed clearance, confrontation with continued investment,* and *consolidation.*

The period of *unopposed clearance* extended from 1950 to 1964. Planning commenced for large-scale urban renewal projects requiring wholesale demolition of inhabited structures in several locations adjacent to the CBD. The SFRA began implementation of two of them during these years. The Renewal Agency acted boldly and faced little opposition, either ideological or practical.

The years 1964 to 1974 were ones of *confrontation with continued investment,* reflecting a nationwide trend of resistance to redevelopment. But San Francisco, as one of the centers of urban radicalism in the country, was a progenitor of the national mood. Community organizations, especially among minority groups, became increasingly mobilized. During this conflict-ridden time government was forced to increase its contribution to services in low-income areas as well as rethink its investment priorities.

Private and public investors, however, did not discontinue their redevelopment activity during this period. San Francisco's role as staging ground for the Vietnam War and center for Pacific trade meant that it was also a focus for capital investment. These years marked the beginning of major private office-building construction. Government pressed ahead with even larger renewal projects and sponsored the construction of BART. The physical manifestation of the Bay Area's dominating economic position thus continued to grow, despite the heightened demands and greater political effectiveness of community groups.

The years from 1975 to 1981 represented *consolidation.* Community Development Block Grants (CDBG) replaced categorical federal urban redevelopment programs, partially diffusing federal funding across the city. Although the Redevelopment Agency maintained control of about half the block grant, funds were also allocated to a variety of neighborhood organizations and projects. Different groups staked out particular programs and territories as their own, and their rights were generally acknowledged by other potential claimants. More communities divided fewer resources. The private sector continued to infuse funds into housing and commercial development, though with less reliance on direct governmental sponsorship. Mobilization diminished. The housing crisis became alarmingly acute even as it assumed the more subtle form of displacement and rising costs rather than government-imposed relocation. The role of the city government increasingly became that of mediator instead of initiator.

We look now at the three periods in greater detail.

THE UNOPPOSED-CLEARANCE PERIOD: 1950–64

The creation of the San Francisco Redevelopment Agency, its subsequent amassing of power, and its initiation of two major redevelopment projects—Western Addition A-1 and Golden Gateway—inaugurated San Francisco's period of large-scale transformation. The agency had the active support of business leaders under the auspices of two complementary organizations: the Bay Area Council (BAC), a private, regional planning body, and the San Francisco Planning and Urban Renewal Association (SPUR),[3] a business-financed group which, once federal statute required designation of a citizens advisory panel for urban renewal, was officially named as such by the mayor (Hartman, 1974: 37–38). In conjunction with these two organizations, composed of high-ranking officers of the largest corporations in the nation as well as major real estate interests, the SFRA launched its giant projects aimed at redeveloping and enlarging the boundaries of the CBD (Wirt, 1974: chapters 7, 8, 11). The mayor's office and the Board of Supervisors played a supportive, but on the whole reactive, role. The two major papers, the *Chronicle* and the *Examiner*, as well as the area's television stations, consistently editorialized in favor of major development ventures, both public and private (Wirt, 1974: esp. 168; Hartman, 1974: 68–73).

The SFRA, established as the city's urban renewal authority under the federal Housing Act of 1949, did not always wield the power it was eventually to amass. According to Hartman (1974: 46):

During the 1950s the SFRA's operations were limited, and its relative lack of importance was evident in a small and not very talented staff, generally uninspired appointments to its [five-member] governing board, and frequent squabbles both internally and with federal urban renewal officials.

The rapid ascendancy of the SFRA dates from the 1959 appointment of M. Justin Herman as its executive director. Operating with the style and ambition of Robert Moses, his East Coast counterpart, "until his death in 1971, Justin Herman was official and corporate San Francisco's chief architect, major spokesman, and operations commander for the transformation of whole sections of the city" (Hartman, 1974: 48). According to a former director of the City Planning Department, once Herman headed the SFRA, it "was endowed with massive amounts of federal funds, a large staff, freedom from most city hall red tape, and prestige among the business community and elected officials" (Jacobs, 1978: 108).

The Golden Gateway and Western Addition A-1 projects began before Herman's reign and continued for its duration. The Western Addition project involved the widening of Geary Boulevard into a major east-west expressway connecting the northwestern part of the city with downtown (see Barton, 1979). A long thirty-block corridor along both sides of the expressway was slated for redevelopment, which involved demolition of nearly the entire area. An estimated 4,000 households were displaced, most of them low-income blacks and Japanese-Americans (Hartman, 1974: 50).

The centerpiece of the Western Addition project was the Japanese Cultural and Trade Center, which houses commercial and office space of firms specializing in Japanese-American trade, a Japanese-style luxury hotel, and the Japanese consulate. It symbolizes the new economic ties between the Bay Area and Japan. The replacement of a neighborhood of low-income Japanese residential occupation by a high-rise center of corporate commercial ventures reflects both the changed nature of U.S. relations with Japan and the prominence of San Francisco in ministering to them. No longer functioning as a source of cheap labor, Japan now is an important supplier of capital as well as a major trading partner. While Japanese competition depressed the Detroit economy, the intermediaries located in San Francisco reaped the benefits of Japanese comparative advantage and reinvested some of the proceeds in Bay Area real estate.

In addition to the Japan Center, the A-1 project included new parks and playgrounds, schools, medical facilities, and churches, among them the imposing Saint Mary's Cathedral and Cathedral High School. Of 1,853 units of new housing built in the project area, 65 percent was market rate and 35 percent subsidized for moderate-income families. Virtually no low-income housing was built in the project area, and few of the former residents returned. The A-1 project was completed in 1973 after the expenditure of $8.2 million in federal funds (SFRA, 1979).

The Western Addition A-1 stands as a glaring example of early renewal projects, in which housing for low-income minority groups was removed, usually without relocation payments to the occupants, and replaced by office, commercial, and institutional structures and middle- and upper-income housing. Hartman (1974: 100) observes: "It was from Western Addition A-1 and projects like it around the country that redevelopment and urban renewal became known as 'Negro removal.'" The project was also typical in that it produced little public opposition, although its example was sufficient to generate mistrust of the SFRA's intentions in those neighborhoods scheduled for future renewal. Like most low-income residents in the early days of urban renewal, Western Addition inhabitants did not fully anticipate the consequences of wholesale demolition and rebuilding (cf. Gans, 1962). The civil rights movement and the consciousness and organizing skills that it brought were still to arise. Advocates of the poor were not yet available with legal and technical skills. Redevelopment agencies could move swiftly, and removal battles were over almost before they had been contested. Although these elements were certainly present in San Francisco, some observers have claimed that they were compounded in the Western Addition because many of the relocatees were Japanese-Americans, still traumatized by their World War II experience of relocation (Schoch, 1979: 98).

The Golden Gateway project created a complex of high-rise office buildings, commercial and hotel space, housing, parks and plazas. Located on a prime, underutilized 51-acre site at the foot of Market Street near the financial district, the project required the relocation of the wholesale produce market. The initiative for it came from a group of corporate officers who in 1956 formed the Blythe-Zellerbach Committee. The committee donated nearly $50,000 to the City Planning Commission to prepare a redevelopment plan for the area. In 1959 this group gave birth to SPUR, which became the principal "citizens" group supporting urban renewal (see Hartman, 1974: 37–38).

Begun in 1959, the Golden Gateway project included the five-block Embarcadero Center, with four new high-rise office buildings interconnected by pedestrian walkways and containing 3 million square feet of space; the spectacular 840-room Hyatt Regency Hotel, pioneer of the glass elevator; a movie theatre; and several acres of parks, plazas, and recreational facilities. While the architecture of the buildings themselves was not notable, the site design, landscaping, paving, and ornamental detail reached unusually high standards for contemporary construction. Fourteen hundred units of new luxury housing were constructed, mostly high-rise but including some townhouses. To secure access to high-speed rapid transit for this dense new development, the SFRA issued $13 million in tax allocation bonds to finance a new Embarcadero Station for BART (SFRA, 1979).

While Golden Gateway resembled the Western Addition A-1 in its scale, emphasis on new construction, use of federal funds to transform land use, and subsidies to real estate developers, it provoked little criticism. No major residential relocation was required, although Hartman (1974: 99) notes that it did displace 200 single men and two dozen families. It used $5 million of federal subsidy to attract, as of 1979, $200 million of private investment (SFRA, 1979). Despite its deficiencies in providing for any other public besides the consumers of high-priced office, commercial, residential, and hotel space, it represents an at least palatable case of wholesale urban renewal. Because the area was not in fact a slum, in the sense of a densely inhabited, low-income residential area, "slum clearance" techniques could create amenities and profitable land uses without causing large-scale social distress.

Until 1964 renewal efforts focused exclusively on wholesale transformations of relatively unprofitable areas into ones of "highest and best use." Eventually, however, community protest over forced relocation and demands by low-income groups for public subsidies for housing and social services caused a reevaluation of priorities. But for the initial period of redevelopment planning and implementation, the emphases of the SFRA and its corporate backers went virtually unchallenged.

CONFRONTATION WITH CONTINUED INVESTMENT: 1964–74

Governmental activity and community response between 1964 and 1974 were far more complicated than in the period which preceded it. The government commenced vast new programs of expenditures on community action and social service provision, even while it continued to mount major capital investment programs. Community groups became highly involved in a number of issues, both independently of governmental programs and in response to opportunities or threats that they posed. During this period of high mobilization, community groups managed to extract real, if small, concessions from their adversaries.

Community Action

The year we have chosen to signify the beginning of the confrontation period, 1964, was marked by the eruption of the civil rights movement in the city. The movement attacked the hiring practices of major businesses, particularly hotels, auto dealers, and banks. Demonstrations in front of places of business produced sufficient response that "it was generally conceded by city figures that CORE [the Congress on Racial Equality] and other such groups had 'won' important victories against major employers in the city in a short, sharp campaign" (Wirt, 1974: 256–57). Although conflict emerged between "moderate" and "militant" black leaders over appropriate tactics and targets in this struggle, both factions were highly active in the battle against discrimination and created a situation in which their claims could not be ignored by city officials and business leaders.

The War on Poverty, signaled by the federal Economic Opportunity Act of 1964, came to San Francisco in the same year as these turbulent civil rights protests, and it immediately engendered a bitter struggle over who should speak for the poor:

Although ostensibly the issue was maximum feasible participation, the battle over representation of the poor was in reality a power struggle between the Mayor of San Francisco and a group of young minority-group spokesmen, most of whom had leadership roles in prior civil rights protest activities and in opposing redevelopment in the Western Addition neighborhood of San Francisco. (Kramer, 1969: 25)

While the program did not provide resources sufficient to affect significantly the general condition of the poor, it did offer a limited number of jobs to residents of poverty areas, access to media, and opportunities for organizing a constituency. Control of these benefits was hotly contested, both as between the city and neighborhood leaders, and among community activists themselves.[4]

A coalition calling itself Citizens United Against Poverty (CUAP) challenged the mayor's domination of the Economic Opportunity Council (EOC), the nonprofit organization devised to oversee San Francisco's program. CUAP demanded "the right of target area residents to review and veto programs; employment policies that would not exclude those lacking formal education and professional training; and majority representation of the poor on the executive committee of the EOC" (Kramer, 1969: 29). In a year-long struggle, CUAP and its supporters prevailed. The EOC was reorganized, providing for majority representation by target-area elected representatives on both the EOC and its executive committee. Bylaws granted sweeping independent authority over programs to decentralized target area action boards.

The four target areas—the Western Addition, Hunters Point, the Mission, and Chinatown—differed from each other and produced conflicts and programs in keeping with their varying social base. Western Addition activists strongly articulated an ideology of community empowerment. Their stress on organizing the poor distinguished them from the leaders of other communities who placed a stronger emphasis on service provision.

In contrast, the Hunters Point organizational base developed out of its social service agencies. The area was an isolated black neighborhood characterized by a "lack of civil rights organizations, churches, voluntary associations, and middle class residents" (Kramer, 1969: 49). The neighborhood was the scene of a 1966 riot precipitated by a policeman's shooting of a sixteen-year-old boy (Hippler, 1974). While not particularly large compared to riots that later engulfed other major cities, it left a strong impression on San Francisco. The next year, when Mayor Joseph Alioto took office, he used poverty program jobs to cool off the tense racial situation in Hunters Point and to ensure political support. Subsequently Alioto pushed for the designation of Hunters Point in 1969 as a Model Neighborhood under the federal Model Cities program. The structure of social service agencies employing a staff of neighborhood workers was continued even after the termination of Model Cities in 1974. Indeed, Model Cities programs in Hunters Point continued virtually intact until the present, with CDBG funding replacing the Model Cities grant.

Mobilization spread from the black community to other groups. The Mission

Council on Redevelopment waged a successful battle to keep the Redevelopment Agency out of the Mission in 1966. Spanish-speaking elements in the Mission also participated in the struggle to wrest control of the poverty program from the mayor's office. Subsequently, the Mission Coalition Organization (MCO) was organized, and in five years came to represent over two hundred community organizations in the Mission. The group was influential in having the Mission designated as a Model Neighborhood and recipient of nearly $15 million in Model Cities and CDBG funds from 1971 to 1980.

While the black neighborhoods were unified by a common perception of discrimination and social background, the Mission encompassed a plurality of Spanish-speaking nationalities—Mexican-Americans, Nicaraguans, Salvadorans—as well as Filipinos, blacks, and white ethnic groups. The Hispanic residents spoke different dialects, came from disparate cultures, and had varying political histories. This heterogeneity constituted a major obstacle to the ongoing organization of the community and participation of its residents in the poverty program. A social service agency director explained the political ineffectiveness of the Mission in the following terms:

Lots of people in the Mission think that they represent the community, but for each one there are five who hate him. It is the Latino system of "caudillos"—little leaders in Latin American politics. It is not issue-oriented, it is personality-oriented. That is one reason that there is no one who represents Mission interests. Then the Mexicans don't talk to the Central Americans, who don't talk to the South Americans. There's no ability to organize around issues.

At the same time that the MCO was reaching the height of its influence, Model Cities grants were becoming available. The Mission, with the endorsement of Mayor Alioto, was successful in gaining the second Model Neighborhood designation in the city. Model Cities funds were used to set up a number of social service programs, which were staffed heavily by community residents. As in the Hunters Point Model Neighborhood, they produced a relatively permanent cadre of neighborhood leaders. Meanwhile, the MCO began to decline. When numerous neighborhood activists were interviewed for this study in 1979 and 1980, they almost all attributed the demise of the MCO to the competition for Model Cities funds and jobs. A typical statement was:

There is no organized body of residents in the Mission anymore. The money and staff of Model Cities did it. The MCO leadership was coopted by becoming directors. There is no new leadership, and this leads to isolation and exclusionary practices.

Chinatown, the fourth of the poverty program's target areas, did not participate in much of the controversy surrounding the program. Despite the area's cohesive social base and poverty, organizational leadership has been highly conservative. When the poverty program was first instituted in San Francisco, members of the Chinese community initially opposed naming Chinatown as a poverty area, and there was little pressure for participation of the poor in program operations. Control was quickly taken by the "Six Companies," a long dominant group of family-based firms, and other traditional leadership groups (Wirt, 1974: 241–42). These leaders concentrated on providing a program of social services with little attention to community organizations.

Major Investment Programs

Rising community militance and increased expenditures on social services did not halt the continuing effort to make San Francisco the center of Pacific finance, trade, and tourism. The two major projects directed at this goal were the development of the Bay Area Rapid Transit, a regional commuter rail system, and the construction of the Yerba Buena Center on a site south of Market Street. Two other SFRA projects were primarily residential in scope: Diamond Heights, a wholly new development on vacant land; and Western Addition A-2, which aimed at changing the social composition, property values, and aesthetic qualities of a large tract adjacent to the Civic Center.

BART.   The corporate leaders that promoted BART envisioned San Francisco as a headquarters city dominated by high-rise office buildings. Fulfilment of their vision required a transportation system to move suburban commuters quickly to the dense, downtown business district (see Wirt, 1974; Wolfe, 1971; Hartman, 1974; Zwerling, 1972). Financing of the $1.5-billion system was through general obligation bonds sold by the three-county (San Francisco, Alameda, and Contra Costa) transit district. When the system ran into serious financial difficulties, a rescue in the form of an additional one-half percent sales tax in the three counties was arranged in 1968.

Since its inception detractors of BART have criticized it for the very reasons that its supporters applaud: its role in the transformation of San Francisco into a commuter office center, and its irrelevance to solving the problems of low-income San Franciscans. It has consistently been in financial trouble and has been widely attacked for poor design and poor management (Hall, 1982: 109–37). It has never, however, been seriously threatened by organized opposition, although community pressure did force it to add two stops in the Mission District. The major newspapers of the Bay Area unflaggingly endorsed the system despite its ever more evident deficiencies. In the authorization election the measure received 68 percent of the vote in San Francisco, and successive referenda continued the authorization.

Yerba Buena Center.   Despite intense opposition to urban renewal, the SFRA was at the height of its power, as measured by funding, size of staff, and influence, during this period. Its Yerba Buena Center (YBC) project, the subject of a book-length treatment by Chester Hartman (1974), epitomized its audaciousness and predilection for massive business and tourist-oriented endeavors. The South of Market area designated for the YBC had an estimated population of 4,000 before redevelopment (Hartman, 1974: 96). In addition, 723 businesses and 7,600 jobs were located on the site in 1963 (Hartman, 1974: 178). Although the area was widely perceived as a "Skid Row," it afforded low-rent business space, as well as inexpensive housing, restaurants, and a viable community to a population of single, elderly men of various ethnic backgrounds, living predominantly in residential hotels. The impression that most of these people were derelicts was, in fact, unfounded.

The neighborhood, however, occupied land that was the logical area for downtown expansion, lying as it did just adjacent to the existing, high-intensity CBD. Hotel owner Ben Swig initially mobilized support behind his proposal for redevelopment of the area in 1954; subsequently the plans underwent a number of permutations under the sponsorship of the SFRA. Relying on area-wide demolition, the project centered on the construction of a publicly financed convention center. Surrounding it were hotels, offices, restaurants, shops, and some market-rate housing. The Board of Supervisors approved Yerba Buena in 1966, and demolition and relocation began shortly thereafter. Resistance was fierce, utilizing demonstrations, sit-ins in hotels about to be demolished, and litigation. Residents and student radicals who joined in the protests were pictured in the media being dragged out of hotels in front of the wrecker's ball; advocacy lawyers contributed their services. The residents' organization, Tenants and Owners in Opposition to Redevelopment (TOOR), managed to delay the project ten years in the courts. Ultimately TOOR extracted concessions from the Redevelopment Agency that provided for 1,158 low-income housing units for the elderly within the project boundaries and 1,500 outside the area. Financing of the housing, which was not included in the SFRA plan, was through the earmarking of a portion of the city's hotel tax. By the time the issue of relocation housing was settled, much less built, almost all of the area's residents had been displaced and many were untraceable (Hartman, 1974).

San Francisco's two daily papers mobilized public opinion in favor of the YBC venture. In addition to editorials directly endorsing the project, news articles often reflected the Redevelopment Agency's viewpoint. In this controversy, as in most of the other conflicts surrounding redevelopment, coverage of opposition to programs involving displacement or high-rise construction was left to the "alternative" *Bay Area Guardian* (Hartman, 1974: 68–73).

Federal funds paid for planning and demolition. Public facilities and infrastructure within the project area were financed through revenue bonds based on returns from leasing the convention center and allocation of half of the city's hotel tax (Hartman and Kessler, 1978: 165). Efforts by opponents of the project to block financing were defeated in a ballot referendum. Litigation on the issue did not end until 1979, and completion of the convention center finally occurred in 1981.

Diamond Heights. This large residential project, planned during the 1950s, did not actually get under way until the mid-sixties. Since the land involved was in fact undeveloped, designation of it as an urban renewal project area required a court decision, *SFRA v. Hayes,* to affirm the validity of defining vacant land as blighted under the California Community Redevelopment Law. Working on a very steep and forbidding terrain, the SFRA sponsored the construction of 2,259 new housing units, of which 20 percent were federally subsidized low- and moderate-income dwellings. Many of the market-rate houses and condominiums constructed sold at the upper end of the luxury housing market, for prices in the hundreds of thousands (and were eventually resold for far more). The only federal subsidy involved brought down the interest rate on the assisted housing; some local government grants supported infrastructure and public facilities; the remainder of the financing ($76 million) was raised in the private sector (SFRA, 1979).

In this instance the SFRA acted very similarly to a private developer building a subdivision on vacant land. It did, however, have the advantages of eminent domain and tax-free bonding, making it feasible to mount an operation of a scope beyond the capabilities of private investors. The outcome was a well-planned subdivision which, while designed primarily for the wealthy, did make available more than 400 low-priced housing units. Along with the Golden Gateway project, it reflected the SFRA's great competence at project execution, its emphasis on accomplishments at a grand scale, and its usefulness as a vehicle for generating development with very high initial costs. Since relocation was not an issue here, the venture showed the possibilities for using the state sector for capital accumulation without direct negative consequences to low-income people.

Western Addition A-2.   Implementation of the second phase of the Western Addition project began in 1966. SFRA literature described it as follows:

The program for the Western Addition A-2 includes development of 4,100 new housing units, the rehabilitation and retention of over 3,100 housing units, the revitalization of the Nihonmachi and Fillmore business districts, construction of new commercial buildings and the provision of a new community recreational facility. (SFRA, 1979: 47)

Before this shining vision could be realized, however, a great part of the 277 acres, comprising more than sixty blocks just northeast of the Civic Center, was razed to the ground. In the words of one critic: "On a street [Fillmore] that a short fifteen years ago was the third busiest neighborhood commercial center in San Francisco, not a building stands. The Fillmore center is a wasteland" (Clark, 1981: 7). Estimates of the number of people eventually displaced vary, but Hartman (1974: 99) places the number at 13,500. He believes that about one quarter of the people relocated from A-1 had settled in this area and were forced to move a second time.

Whereas renewal efforts in A-1 met only weak opposition, the case was different in A-2 (see Mollenkopf, 1981). The Western Addition Community Organization (WACO) was started by white organizers from outside the neighborhood but was soon taken over by indigenous leaders. This group, led by a black student at San Francisco State, assisted by the San Francisco Neighborhood Legal Assistance Foundation (SFNLAF), sought a federal injunction blocking relocation, demolition, and federal funding until a relocation plan for the area was developed. The injunction was granted, then withdrawn. By 1971, when the U.S. Department of Housing and Urban Development (HUD) ordered the SFRA to cease relocation until residents could be guaranteed decent housing within the project area, most of the evictions had long since been completed. The project, however, was reformulated to respond better to the needs of the original occupants.

As part of the settlement of the first suit, a new organization, the Western

Addition Project Area Committee (WAPAC), was established and charged with the responsibility for providing residents with input into the program. With funds allocated by the Redevelopment Agency, WAPAC hired staff and organized tenants of the subsidized housing constructed within the project area. WAPAC's career has been uneven, and the group has been variously accused of being too militant, losing touch with its community base, and being coopted by the SFRA.

Fifteen years after the Fillmore Center was demolished, much of the land within the A-2 project remained vacant. The SFRA could, however, claim credit for working closely with local residents on the redevelopment plans for the Nihonmachi and Fillmore Centers and for 2,850 units of new subsidized housing (SFRA, 1979: 47). Two-thirds of the new housing built in the area was reserved for low- and moderate-income families. Compared to the A-1 project, the interests of the area's original residents were certainly better represented, and eventually the neighborhood again became the home of a number of relatively low-income people. Nevertheless most of the black businesses destroyed were not replaced, and the cost to the community fabric resulting from the long time-lag between demolition and reconstruction can never be recompensed.

The Legacy of Confrontation.   In San Francisco, as in most other cities, the decade spanning the late sixties and early seventies opened up the political-administrative system to previously excluded groups and stripped redevelopment projects of their protective technical veneer. The designation of project areas and choice of programs (rehabilitation vs. demolition and new construction; commercial vs. residential development, etc.) came to be seen as highly political and subject to pressure and negotiation. The period left city officials and private capitalists feeling that community-based interests could not be ignored. Government, as well as proceeding more cautiously in its redevelopment projects, began to address the needs of lower-income renters and middle-class home-owners. As will be discussed later in the chapter, a sizable number of new, low-income units were under construction in Hunters Point, and several rehabilitation and code-enforcement programs were started.

Although a new group of leaders and professional advocates now defended neighborhood interests, private developers were no less hopeful of realizing enormous gains through the conversion of land to higher and better uses. As compared to most of the other cities that had witnessed the urban struggles of the late sixties, the stakes were heightened within San Francisco by the influx of new private capital for both residential and commercial purposes. Winners of the redevelopment battles could win big as property values began to shoot upwards. The effectiveness of SFRA projects in enlarging the CBD both vertically and horizontally had by 1974 attracted sufficient autonomous private investment capital and upper-income employment into the city to make government's direct role in encouraging redevelopment far less necessary and central than in the preceding years. Thus, just when community groups had established their entitlement to a share of public renewal endeavors, private redevelopment through the market became the dominant force in the continued transformation of San Francisco.

CONSOLIDATION: 1975–81

The year 1975 marked a turning point in San Francisco. The switch in federal funding from categorical to block grants caused a *restructuring of the decision-making process* for urban redevelopment. The mayor's office began to exert stronger program control, as both the SFRA and Model Neighborhoods lost their independent sources of funding. Changes in the method of electing the Board of Supervisors caused that body to represent more diverse constituencies than formerly.

Heightened demand for office and commercial space set off a real estate investment boom. Although the decline of manufacturing in the city was halted, the relative and absolute growth of the tertiary employment sector accelerated (see Tables 6.2, 6.3, 6.4). Commercial encroachment on residential land and expanded employment caused housing prices to soar and vacancies to disappear. *Cost and availability of housing* became the central political issue of the decade. Economic growth and increased property values, however, did not save the city government from the financial difficulties that plagued declining metropolises. *Fiscal crisis* was suddenly exacerbated by the passage of Proposition 13 in 1978, with its drastic limitation on property tax collection.

All these issues involved conflict over power and resources. Nevertheless, we label this most recent period one of consolidation. While militant protest, in the form of sit-ins and demonstrations, flared up over the Yerba Buena Center, the black and Hispanic communities were largely quiescent. Highly mobilized groups had mainly either vanished or transformed themselves into service delivery organizations. The remaining advocacy groups operated primarily through structured processes of citizen participation. The highly elaborated framework of city agencies and programs, often vestigial remnants of defunct federal legislation, permitted some form of access and share of benefits, however small, to virtually all claimant groups. Thus the rivalry between downtown and the neighborhoods became absorbed in the multiple and conflicting skirmishes over budget allocations and program intentions. One Hispanic leader described the situation thus:

All minority influence relates to federal money. . . . people fight over it, and that weakens doing battle over important issues and [diverts them] from providing services. The fight over federal money diverts attention from the important issues being decided by the all-white, all-business influence.

Another commented similarly:

There is a great deal of ethnic diversity and separatism, which results in fighting for federal crumbs and isolating neighborhoods. . . . Politicians play groups off against each other.

The remainder of this chapter is devoted to an examination of the post-1974 allocation process and the major issues we have just enumerated.

Decision-Making Process

The distribution of federal funds as block grants gave the mayor's office, through its central role in their allocation, the opportunity to coordinate development planning. In response to the 1974 federal Housing and Community Development Act (HCDA), the city established a staff agency, the Office of Community Development (OCD), and the Technical Policy Committee (TPC), consisting of directors of city departments and agencies concerned with redevelopment, to be chaired by the director of OCD. While none of the old agencies was eliminated, all now had to apply to OCD for funds that had previously been granted to them directly by HUD.

An advisory committee to the mayor, the Citizens Committee on Community Development (CCCD), was established to represent the viewpoint of neighborhood residents. From its inception the mayorally appointed CCCD reflected the diversity of the city's racial and ethnic composition: of the sixteen active committee members in June 1979, there were six blacks, two Chinese, five whites, one Japanese, one Filipino, and one Hispanic. (Blacks were therefore overrepresented in relationship to their proportion of the city's population; Hispanics were underrepresented.) All the committee members when interviewed expressed strong allegiance to the HCDA's legislative aim of benefiting primarily low- and moderate-income people. Indeed, observation of CCCD meetings validated their commitment if not their effectiveness.

The CCCD became an important element in the allocation process, as it reviewed proposals submitted by both city agencies and community groups. While the committee would on occasion be overruled by the mayor or Board of Supervisors, for the most part its recommendations prevailed. Members, however, recognized that their role was advisory to the mayor and generally acted in ways they thought compatible with the mayor's general policy directives.

Neighborhood viewpoints were also represented in the Board of Supervisors, which reviewed CCCD recommendations as well as other capital budget expenditures before final enactment. An initiative to elect Supervisors by district succeeded in 1976, was successfully defended in 1977, but was defeated in 1980 referenda. District elections were seen by most low- and moderate-income communities as a key defense against downtown interests which could dominate an at-large board. A number of community leaders devoted considerable effort to the campaign in support of district-based elections. The impact of both the switch to district elections and the switch back remained unclear in 1981. Observers felt that the district-based 1978 election made only marginal changes in the composition of the Board and that some members of the 1980 at-large Board had strong neighborhood constituencies. Neither form of election produced a Board that mirrored the ethnic and racial composition of the city. The pre-1976 Board contained one black and one Hispanic. Although the first district-based board did have an Hispanic and a Chinese, subsequent Boards, elected under both systems, had one black and no other minority group members.

The OCD performed all the technical work on the Community Development (CD) budget. The CCCD lacked an independent source of information on most proposals and thus relied heavily on the OCD. The relationship between the OCD staff and the CCCD thus raised questions concerning the independence and influence of the CCCD. The Feinstein-appointed OCD director, a black man, was seen by committee members as "knowledgeable about the community and with a similar philosophy to us." Community leaders outside the CCCD characterized it as well meaning, but very dependent on its staff and the pleasure of the mayor. A staff attorney for a legal advocacy group summed up the relationship between the CCCD, the mayor, and the OCD in words that echoed a number of informed judgments by community leaders involved with the development process:

I was pleasantly surprised by the operation of the CCCD. But I think part of the problem is the task before them is very narrow—it is not an open slate of deciding how to spend the money. They are hard-working, diligent, and earnest. But there is only a small amount for CCCD to really look at. This is largely the social service component. They are virtually powerless against the city agencies which eat up the bulk of the CD dollars, and they have no political say in that regard.

The mayor has made her position clear to them and to . . . [the OCD director] that they are her committee and it is her program. . . . There is on CCCD a certain amount of respect for the integrity of the program and there is less horse-trading between neighborhoods on it than one might expect. . . . There is a healthy balance between those representing the communities of the city and those representing the low and moderate people of the city as a whole. . . .

The mayor made it clear that the director of OCD was the *mayor's* director of OCD, a representative of the mayor. The mayor holds the director accountable for the behavior of the CCCD to not be too independent or go public or go back to their communities. . . . The CCCD respects him and so they have tempered their own decisions through respect for him, because they wanted to prevent the loss of him, which would be a loss to low- and moderate-income interests.

Two factors were identified by both CCCD members and critics of the citizen participation process as seriously limiting the power of neighborhood representatives to shape San Francisco's priorities. First, the SFRA, now headed by a black, former Western Addition leader Reverend Wilbur Hamilton, continued to play the leading role in government-sponsored redevelopment. While the SFRA no longer received urban renewal funds directly from HUD, it continued to get the bulk of CD funds, controlled the much larger sum raised from bonds, constituted the planning body for the still extant renewal project areas, and, in conjunction with the Housing Authority, disposed of the various subsidies for low- and moderate-income housing.

Nevertheless, the SFRA was no longer the free-wheeling body of former days, and its director no longer played such a strongly entrepreneurial role. He predicted a diminished impact for the agency as it engaged in smaller-scale, quicker projects:

Our demands on the block grants are diminishing rapidly. We see clear completion dates for our [old] projects. The future for the agency is in a different kind of project.

Urban renewal has been costly because of huge landholding and property-management costs. The state legislature has given us a more effective way of doing things called "right of possession"—we don't have to acquire property until we have a developer . . . ; then [when] we do, the new state statute gives us the right of immediate possession and even eviction, if necessary. Smaller projects are the future. We will never have any more Western Additions. There will be a shorter turn-around.

The second serious limitation on the CCCD's effectiveness lay in the restriction of its authority to CDBG funds alone. Unlike the citywide citizens' advisory boards in some other cities, including Denver, the CCCD did not scrutinize any part of the capital budget other than that funded by CDBG. The smallness of the block grant in relation to the size of both community needs and private and bonded investments made the CCCD's input relatively inconsequential. Even in regard to the funds over which it did have jurisdiction, it was hemmed in by the force of past commitments made under the earlier federal programs folded into CDBG. A former CCCD member expressed his frustration at the constraints on the committee:

In the first two or three meetings, I asked, why waste time on the bottom 10 percent of the budget? The $12–14 million for [the] Redevelopment [Agency] was taken for granted. Larger decisions were already in place. We talked about $30–40,000 grants. It was not what I wanted to be doing, so I left it. . . .

CDBG Expenditures. For the first four years of CDBG, funds were used primarily to continue existing programs (Table 6.5). The two largest shares went to SFRA renewal projects—Hunters Point (29 percent) and Western Addition A-2 (18 percent). It is worth noting, however, that Hunters Point, as well as social services in the former Model Neighborhoods (13 percent share), public housing rehabilitation (4 percent), and the India Basin Industrial Park (6 percent), were programs benefiting low- and moderate-income people. These projects did not include downtown commercial or high-income housing uses.

By the 1979 and 1980 program years, however, priorities shifted as India Basin was closed out and Hunters Point received a decreased share of the budget (Table 6.6). Planned housing in Western Addition A-2 was to be three-quarters market rate. The new Northeast Waterfront project of the SFRA was an ambitious proposal to develop hotel, commercial, and recreational facilities, as well as "mixed income"

TABLE 6.5
San Francisco CDBG Program Budgets, 1975–78 (4 program years)

Project Activity[a]	Allocation, 1975–78	Percent of Total Grant, 1975–78
Hunters Point (SFRA)	$ 30,757,330	29
Western Addition A-2 (SFRA)	18,827,422	18
Model Cities continuation	13,690,672	13
Housing rehabilitation (Bureau of Building Inspection)	9,584,169	9
India Basin Industrial Park (SFRA)	5,942,516	6
Public housing rehabilitation (SFRA)	4,702,131	4
Recreational facilities rehabilitation	4,088,300	4
Neighborhood centers	2,540,745	2
Housing site acquisition	2,300,000	2
Miscellaneous, including administrative costs and contingencies	12,945,715	13
Total Grant	$105,379,000	100

SOURCE: Mayor's Office of Community Development, San Francisco, records.
[a] Items are ranked by budget amount. Only items amounting to more than 2 percent of the total, or about $2 million, are listed. Letters in parentheses indicate the administering agency, where the item is under the auspices of a single agency.

TABLE 6.6
San Francisco CDBG Program Budgets, 1979 and 1980 (2 program years)

Project Activity	Allocation, 1979–80	Percent of Total Grant, 1979–80
Western Addition A-2 (SFRA)	$10,503,124	19
Public services (former Model Cities)	6,248,436	11
Hunters Point (SFRA)	5,067,222	9
Housing rehabilitation (Bureau of Building Inspection)	5,050,370	9
Yerba Buena Center (SFRA)	3,469,111	6
Housing finance programs	2,300,000	4
Recreational facilities rehabilitation	2,040,000	4
Neighborhood housing development corporations	2,244,535	4
Neighborhood centers	1,930,500	3
Housing site acquisition	1,750,000	3
Public housing rehabilitation	1,208,500	2
Neighborhood physical improvements	1,126,950	2
Northeast Waterfront (SFRA)	1,087,079	2
Bayview Industrial Triangle (SFRA)	1,016,074	2
Neighborhood commercial districts	1,000,000	2
Miscellaneous, including administrative costs and contingencies	9,670,499	20
Total Grant	$55,713,000	100

SOURCE: Mayor's Office of Community Development, *Community Development Program and Housing Assistance Plan, 1979,* San Francisco, March 1979; *Community Development Program and Housing Assistance Plan, 1980,* San Francisco, February 1980.

housing. The Yerba Buena Center captured a substantial chunk of the freed-up funds; the remainder was dispersed over a large number of projects, as the concentrated activity fostered by the earlier categorical programs faded away.

The more recent activity under CDBG reflected the tendency of that program to lead to a scattering of funds across a variety of projects in order to respond to numerous constituencies. A high-ranking official in the mayor's office described the method by which funds were allocated:

There is only nibbling away at the edges of the $24.2 million. If half a million is shiftable, that's a lot. How do you divvy it up? The politics of that is hard [i.e., physical development] versus soft [i.e., social services]. Everybody is interested in housing and software now. We are forced into a HUD-forced large shift into hard from soft. . . . We had picked up Model Cities service programs in CD. We are trying to maintain those programs which have the best measurable output, but as the pot shrinks, soft will take more of a beating than hard. . . .

Yes, there is consideration to black and Mexican constituencies, but there is as much interest there in housing as in software. There is not so much ethnic rivalry. It is more hard versus soft, economic development versus housing—different constituencies *within* ethnic constituencies. There are no macro constituencies, just hundreds of micro constituencies, and we have to consider them all.

There were no new macro projects either. The demise of the federal urban renewal legislation set in motion a more piecemeal strategy of redevelopment that would not dramatically transform large sections of the city. But by the time this less draconian approach came along, following two decades of urban renewal and additional years of transition, most of the original urban renewal projects either had been completed or were underway. The new decision-making process and funding method insured a more moderate and inclusive future conception of governmental activity. The ongoing test of this approach has been the course of San Francisco's housing crisis.

Housing

In many American cities the housing problem has been less one of availability than of costs. In San Francisco superinflated prices reflected both general increases in real estate values (see Table 6.7) and a shortage of available units throughout the city. The entirety of San Francisco by 1980 had come to resemble Manhattan below 96th Street—that is, low-income households had to compete with upper-income ones for the limited number of units (Berkeley Planning Associates, 1980: 8). Moreover, the continuing success of San Francisco in attracting commercial development constantly added new pressure on the housing market. Using a City Planning Department estimate that every 1,000 additional square feet of new office space created a need for one additional housing unit within the city, the Council of Community

TABLE 6.7
Changes in San Francisco Real Property Base, 1956–78

	1956	*1971*	*1976*	*1978*
Gross assessed value locally assessed real property ($ millions)				
Current dollars	929.4	1,924.4	2,787.1	3,404.4
Constant (1980) dollars[a]	2,799.6	3,886.5	4,009.9	4,272.2
Assessed value as fraction of sales price (median ratio)	.14	.19	.14	n.a.
Estimated value of real property ($ millions)				
Current dollars	6,638.6	10,128.4	19,907.9	n.a.
Constant (1980) dollars[a]	19,997.1	20,455.3	28,642.0	n.a.

SOURCE: US Bureau of the Census, *Statistical Abstract of the United States, 1980,* Table 792; *State and Local Government Special Studies No. 92: Property Values Subject to Local General Property Taxation in the United States: 1978; Census of Governments, Taxable Property Values and Assessment/Sales Price Ratios,* Vol. 2, 1977, 1972; *Census of Governments, Taxable Property Values in the United States,* Vol. 5, 1957; authors' computations.

[a] Based on consumer price index normalized for 1980 current dollar = $1.00 constant.

Housing Organizations (n.d.) contended that between 1970 and 1980 there was a demand for 27,000 new units.

By 1980 there were virtually no uncontested areas left within the city, and Berkeley and Oakland, two other Bay Area centers of low-income occupancy, displayed similar housing shortages. The extremely high purchase price of a housing unit in San Francisco in 1980 ($103,900—see Table 6.8) was exceeded by the even higher price of a suburban dwelling. The Federal Home Loan Bank placed the median price of a dwelling in the San Francisco-Oakland SMSA at $129,000 in May 1981 (*New York Times*, 1981a: A12). Displaced San Francisco residents thus had few alternative locations open to them in the Bay Area.

Two-thirds of San Francisco's residents are renters. Despite increasing numbers of households, the supply of renter-occupied housing has stayed essentially constant since 1970 (Table 6.8).[5] The relatively low rate of increase in median rents did not exceed changes in the Consumer Price Index. Leases, landlord restraint toward sitting tenants, and rent-control ordinances meant that long-term tenants were somewhat protected from exorbitant increases. New entrants to the rental market, however, confronted prices derived from the present set of property values. The magnitude of costs for those who could not gain access to subsidized housing was indicated by the enormous percentage increases in rents for available units: they jumped from a 10.5 percent annual rate of increase in the years 1973–78 to annual growth rates of 29.2 percent between 1978 and 1979 and 30.3 percent in the next year. Thus in 1980 the median rent for available units was $490 (Table 6.8). The HUD valuation of fair market rent in new or substantially rehabilitated construction was $697 per month for a two-bedroom apartment in a walk-up building, or 35 percent of the estimated median income for a family of four (Mayor's Office of Community Development, 1981: 30). The situation was especially acute for households displaced by private upgrading and condominium conversion.

There have been four major modes by which the public sector has addressed

TABLE 6.8
Housing Units in San Francisco: Tenure Status and Value

	Occupied Year–Round Units	Owner-Occupied	Median Value Owner-Occupied	Renter-Occupied	Median Rent	Median Rent, Advertised Available Units
1970	295,174	97,036 (33%)	$ 28,100	198,138 (67%)	$128	$191
1973						191
1978						291
1979						376
1980	298,957	100,786 (34%)	103,900	198,171 (66%)	266	490

SOURCE: U.S. Bureau of the Census, *Housing Characteristics for States, Cities, and Counties,* I:6: California, Table 15 (1970); *Selected Housing Characteristics by States and Counties: 1980,* October 1981; San Francisco City Planning Department Survey of Newspaper Classified Advertisements, reported in *San Francisco Bay Guardian,* January 6, 1982.

the issues of the cost, availability, and quality of housing: direct subsidies for new construction; rehabilitation subsidies; funding of community housing corporations; and regulation. Each of these modes has involved a different distribution of benefits and, accordingly, a different politics.

New Construction. The Hunters Point redevelopment project was the city's largest recent commitment to publicly sponsored low- and moderate-income housing (Table 6.9). Begun in 1969, full implementation really got started only under CDBG. During the first four program years of CDBG, it was the largest recipient of CD funds, as well as a major user of federal subsidies for new construction.

Hunters Point, located on a bluff with stunning views of the Bay, had originally been built up with "temporary" structures to house workers in World War II defense industries. These continued to be occupied by low-income black people. Because much of the site was vacant land, relocation into new dwellings could occur before the demolition of old ones. Eighty-five percent of 1,542 units planned were subsidized for low- and moderate-income households (SFRA, 1979: 5); 929 of these units were completed by 1979. The regional HUD office blocked additional new, low-income Section 8 housing during 1978–80 on the grounds that the area was racially "impacted"; that is, continued construction there of low-income housing would increase ghettoization. While the redevelopment project was distinguished by the quality of its site planning and scenic advantages, it was poorly served by retail establishments and public transit.

The development of Hunters Point, the construction of subsidized housing in the Western Addition A-2, discussed earlier, as well as new construction and rehabilitation for low-income Yerba Buena relocatees in the Market Street area, constituted the fruits of confrontation (Table 6.9). The Western Addition Project Area Committee

TABLE 6.9
New Housing Construction in SFRA Project Areas:
Completed or under Construction, January 1, 1979

Project Area	Low to Moderate Income[a]		Regular Market	
	No. of Units	% of Total	No. of Units	% of Total
West. Add. A-1	654	35	1,199	65
West. Add. A-2	2,525	88	345	12
Diamond Heights	437	20	1,801	80
Hunters Point	929	100	—	—
Yerba Buena Ct.[b]	793	100	—	—
Golden Gateway	—	—	1,304	100
Total	5,338	53	4,649	47

SOURCE: San Francisco Redevelopment Agency, *1979 San Francisco Redevelopment Program: Summary of Project Data and Key Elements.*
[a] The income limit defining a low-income family of four in January 1978 was $9,600; moderate-income—$15,350.
[b] All housing for the elderly.

(WAPAC), the Bayview-Hunters Point (BVHP) Joint Housing Committee (the SFRA's designated project area committee), as well as the BVHP Coordinating Council, a coalition of the various social service agencies originally funded under the poverty program and Model Cities, became important mechanisms connecting black San Francisco to city government. With the integration of community leaders into the city's institutional structure, however, came declining militance and frustration at lack of real influence. As one of the BVHP Council members noted, "We know what we used to do. . . . We would have 300 or more people downtown in no time. Now, nobody." Activists had a strong sense that their gains came in response to their earlier vocal protests. Now, although they routinely received their share of federal funds, the amount was diminishing, and they lacked the clout to improve their position. Moreover, the administrative separation of the Housing Authority and Redevelopment Agency, as well as the division within HUD of housing and community development programs, limited program coordination within project areas and increased the obstacles to political action of residents affected by redevelopment (see Friedland, Piven, and Alford, 1978). HUD's refusal to continue subsidizing public housing construction in Hunters Point illustrates the problem. Its opposition to encouraging segregation through its housing programs blocked the full implementation of earlier concessions made by the Redevelopment Agency to black inhabitants of project areas.

The overall reduction in federal subsidies for new housing construction has meant that the city could not rely on public money alone if it was to increase its housing supply. In a unique move, the Department of City Planning, under heavy political pressure to respond to the housing crisis, decided to require commercial developers to build housing or contribute to a housing fund in order to receive permission to build (*New York Times*, 1981b: Section 8). While the policy had not yet been formally approved by the end of the year, and no set of guidelines determining how the funds should be spent had been established, developers had so far agreed to meet the requirements.

Clearly such a policy could work in few cities besides San Francisco. In most other places, city officials were begging for development and were in no position to put conditions on it. But the privately financed housing fund pointed to a way by which community pressures in highly desirable areas could force concessions from developers rather than waiting for the benefits of growth to trickle down.

Rehabilitation. Although demolition and new construction were the principal targets of opposition to urban redevelopment programs, rehabilitation efforts did not escape controversy. San Francisco has mounted a variety of code enforcement and rehabilitation programs since 1950. They have been sponsored by a number of agencies and have drawn on various funding sources. Continuing through the period of consolidation, they have been applauded for their contributions to neighborhood stabilization and upgrading, castigated for their alleged impetus to displacement. As shown in Tables 6.5 and 6.6, housing rehabilitation programs captured 9 percent of the total CDBG allocation; in addition, the SFRA listed 2,056 housing units, or about 17 percent of the total number of housing units completed or under construction in project areas, as rehabilitation units (SFRA, 1979: 9). Of these about 40 percent were publicly financed by either federal subsidy or SFRA-financed loans, and the remaining 60 percent were privately financed.

The city began its housing rehabilitation sponsorship in the early 1960s, when it set up a concentrated code enforcement program. This was enlarged in 1966 with the addition of Federally Assisted Code Enforcement (FACE) program funds, then operated again under local funding as the Rehabilitation Assistance Program (RAP), when federal funds were discontinued. The basic mechanism of all the programs was inspection, then the provision of either low-interest loans or grants to income-eligible owners to bring the dwelling up to code.

In the early days of urban renewal, preservation was presented as the antithesis to demolition. It had considerable white middle-class support, especially within the gay community, as neighborhood leaders sought to save the city's heritage of Victorian homes. The premium which the middle class placed on historic preservation, however, in contrast to lower-income groups' concerns with decent housing, led to the accusation that rehabilitation used public subsidy to cater to the aesthetic interests of the well-to-do. One CCCD member commented that she had left the Victorian Alliance, a preservationist group, when it became "taken over by an elite group of gays."

A case in point was Alamo Square. This area, perched on a hill with its elaborate Victorian homes silhouetted against the San Francisco skyline, has become a favorite postcard view of the city. Originally considered "blighted" by the SFRA, the neighborhood fought off that designation and succeeded in getting rehabilitation assistance. Houses on the Square became among the most valuable properties in the city. Two other RAP areas, the Upper Ashbury and the Inner Richmond, have been characterized as "overwhelmingly middle class and upper income" (San Francisco Lawyers' Committee 1979: 10–11), despite the designation of these neighborhoods as needing assistance.

Nevertheless, defenders of the program argued that it had a significant effect in conserving housing and preventing deterioration with minimal displacement and little effect on rents (Jacobs, 1978: 117). If FACE and RAP were evaluated primarily for what they were—programs of assistance to moderate-income home-owners—then Jacobs' (1978: 125) conclusion was probably justified. They "worked in the sense of helping people adapt their homes to contemporary standards without significant hardships" (Berkeley Planning Associates, 1980). They were not, however, programs to improve the quality of low-income housing.

Perhaps the greatest failing of the public rehabilitation programs was their lack of attention to the problems of multifamily rental housing. Although two-thirds of San Francisco's households were renters, the city planned to rehabilitate only 15 percent of rental units requiring assistance (11,725 out of 75,165). Moreover, in the years 1975 to 1978 the city had only attained 12 percent (770 of a projected 6,729 units) of its previous rental rehabilitation goal (San Francisco Lawyers' Committee, 1979: 6–7).

Housing Development Corporations. Housing issues were a major—perhaps the major—focus of community activism during the consolidation period. A number of community radicals became the nucleus of a new group in the seventies—the

Council of Community Housing Organizations (CCHO—pronounced choo-choo). This group which managed to attain a $2-million allocation in the 1979 and 1980 CDBG program years, represented an effort by community forces to achieve through small-scale activities the neighborhood stabilization goals that were the ostensible aim of government-sponsored redevelopment.

Three housing development corporations (HDCs) preexisted the formation of CCHO in 1979. They used various public subsidies to attract reduced-interest-rate loans from banks as well as directly assisting home purchasers and owners making improvements. They also were involved in developing housing themselves, obtaining HUD Section 8 commitments, and managing subsidized apartment buildings.

In 1978 the OCD proposed forming a citywide housing development corporation to centralize the tasks performed by the HDCs. The HDCs, in alliance with a number of other community organizations, opposed centralization as being insensitive to neighborhood needs. In the process the coalition that was to become CCHO emerged. The group was successful in defeating OCD's proposal in the CCCD and obtaining CDBG funding for the decentralized bodies. Leaders from outside the original HDC neighborhoods formed new corporations, and by 1980 nine housing development corporations were recipients of CDBG funding, seven of which were associated with CCHO. The executive director of one of the original neighborhood corporations described his organization's reasoning:

We pioneered the Council of Community Housing Organizations. It became important to try to coordinate the activity of all the community development and housing development corporations in the city. Also we had common problems with the OCD. We are all concerned with low- and moderate-income people. . . . We want to make sure that they are getting the benefits [of federal programs]. . . . The development corporations should be doing land banking, and in fact they could do land banking under the regulations. This might have to be done by a citywide HDC. We aren't opposed to certain elements of a citywide HDC. Clearly some administrative costs are being wasted by having decentralized HDCs go, because we don't yet have a confidence that a citywide group would be representative of our interests.[6]

CCHO's objective was the development of housing for low- and moderate-income people without relocation. It sought to achieve this through small-site construction projects and loan packaging that would permit lower-income people to purchase and improve available housing. Despite the opposition of OCD, which continued to favor a single, centralized agency, it succeeded in receiving a CD allocation for administration as well as access to a site acquisition pool totaling over $2 million by 1980. However, except for the HDC in the Mission and those corporations located within SFRA project areas, the HDC's had difficulty spending the money. No financing had been provided for architectural and other technical services, and acquisition funds could not be drawn down until site plans were approved. The Mission HDC, which built upon a preexisting neighborhood economic development corporation, had previously developed plans for the conversion of air space over a city parking garage into a 50-unit housing cooperative, using federal Minority Enterprise Small Business Investment (MESBIC) funds for construction. TODCO, in the Yerba Buena Center area, was able to carry out its program of rehabilitating apartments and residential hotels and operating multifamily buildings through the assignment to it of the portion of the hotel tax dedicated to low-income housing resulting from the YBC settlement (TODCO, 1979). The BVHP corporation was developing new $80,000 homes ($40,000 cheaper than those being built nearby by a private developer) using SFRA planning assistance.

CCHO's success in attracting funding resulted from the considerable organizational sophistication of its leaders. Although the group was representative of the various racial and ethnic constituencies in San Francisco's neighborhoods, the leading roles were played by a few whites with highly articulated political consciousness. A small grant from the National Citizens Monitoring Project of CDBG, funded by the now-defunct federal Community Services Administration (CSA), permitted one organizer to be a full-time activist, redevelopment monitor, and lobbyist. Under his leadership, CCHO could effectively criticize OCD's priorities at the CCCD public hearings. Since CCHO permitted the HDC's to work out in advance their own requests for funds, they did not appear to be competing among themselves over relative shares. When, in 1981, they were unable to persuade the CCCD to continue their allocation, they were successful in pleading their case before the Board of Supervisors. As necessary, the leadership was able to bring out large, noisy groups of supporters for its cause.

CCHO maintained itself, at least until 1982, as an independent outlet of community activism—a synthesis of 1960s consciousness and 1970s service delivery styles. Its political success, however, depended in part on federal funds to pay staff in the various housing development corporations. Whether it could sustain itself in the face of Reagan's cutbacks remained a question, and whether it could raise sufficient funding to finance actual construction on a scale adequate to affect the housing situation remained another. The OCD's criticism of its amateurism and inefficiency was not baseless. Nevertheless CCHO, like the dedicated housing funds now required with new commercial construction, constituted an innovative response to San Francisco's housing crisis. Like the housing construction funds, it was the outcome of intense community pressure on public authorities.

Regulation.   As well as seeking to increase the housing supply, community activists have attempted to limit withdrawal of housing from the stock available to low-income households. Two routes to achieving regulatory legislation have been pursued: ballot initiatives and ordinances passed by the Board of Supervisors.

Community groups seeking to limit private redevelopment of residential land succeeded in 1975 in persuading the Board of Supervisors to approve a new zoning code. This code zoned certain areas exclusively residential that had previously been designated for commercial use, and it placed height and density restrictions in various residential neighborhoods, thereby curtailing the profitability of luxury apartment development. Some critics of this effort have argued, however, that by limiting new development, it primarily benefited present owners, who saw the value of their property increase. One of these detractors, commenting on the prevalence of antigrowth sentiment, remarked: "You couldn't build the Taj Mahal in San Francisco."

In 1979 a group calling itself San Franciscans for Affordable Housing (SFAH) placed a major initiative, Proposition R, on the ballot. Led by Chester Hartman, a nationally known advocacy planner and scholar, and Charles Lamb, head of the Hotel and Restaurant Workers Union Local, SFAH devised a plan that touched on all aspects of rental housing regulation. Proposition R limited rent rises to pass-throughs of increased costs; prohibited evictions except for "just causes"; placed a quota on condominium conversions, as well as protecting the tenure of tenants under conversion; and allocated 25 percent of CDBG funds to neighborhood HDCs (San Franciscans for Affordable Housing, 1979). The proposition was strongly opposed by well-financed real estate and development interests. It lost badly in the November elections, in part because it was preempted by a weak rent control ordinance passed by the Board of Supervisors shortly before the election.

In 1980 the issue came again before the Supervisors, who this time responded to community pressure by strengthening the legislation. Whereas the existing ordinance had placed the burden on tenants of demonstrating excessive rent increases, the new law switched the responsibility of proof to landlords. It also limited rent rises on vacant units. The new ordinance, however, was vetoed by the mayor (*San Francisco Bay Guardian*, 1982: 7–10).

Politics of Housing.   The housing crisis provided the context in which San Francisco's most active community politics took place during the period of consolidation. The city proved more amenable to measures that would increase the housing supply than to ones that would restrict property owners from realizing the new, inflated values of their holdings. Different interests linked to different agencies of government pressed for their particular programs. Black groups, which over the years of opposition had eventually worked out a modus vivendi with the SFRA, tended to work primarily through their client status with that agency. Hispanic and multiethnic neighborhood groups related to the CCCD and the supervisors. The Mayor, through the OCD, responded to some extent to neighborhood pressures but nevertheless maintained her economic development priorities. Given the overwhelming private market pressures for high-income residential investment and continued commercial expansion, the limited space and funds available for low- and moderate-income housing construction, and the absence of strong advocates for subsidized housing within any level of government, the efforts at increasing the housing supply remained modest (see Mollenkopf, 1981: 28–30).

Fiscal Crisis

Attempts by the low-income population to cope with the hardships imposed upon them by San Francisco's economic success became further limited at the end of the decade by sharply decreasing funds. Like many American cities, San Francisco experienced fiscal strain during the 1970s as the costs of providing municipal services rose rapidly. The passage of Proposition 13 in June 1978 severely restricted the city's ability to raise revenues just before the 1980 election of Ronald Reagan was to truncate federal assistance.

Proposition 13 limited local property tax rates to 1 percent of market values, rolled back assessed values to 1975–76 levels, and limited increases for inflation to 2 percent on properties that did not change hands. Finally, Proposition 13 prohibited local government from imposing any new taxes without approval by two-thirds of the electorate. Landlords and businessmen were not required to pass through their tax savings to tenants and customers (Tipps, 1980: 66). The restrictions reduced San Francisco's property tax revenue by 55 percent in 1978 (Coro Foundation, 1979). While most of that difference was initially compensated by state funds, the state surplus ran out in 1980. Over the highly inflationary decade of the seventies, despite the enormous increase in property values and current incomes, there was a 13 percent drop in revenues in *current* dollars raised from local taxes (Table 6.10).

The two-thirds requirement for the imposition of new taxes defeated efforts to improve San Francisco's revenue situation. In 1979 the voters gave a majority to a ballot initiative that would increase business taxes, but the number supporting the measure did not reach the necessary two-thirds. In 1980 the city faced a $126-million budget deficit. Mayor Dianne Feinstein proposed a revenue package raising transit fares, parking fees, and other user charges, as well as $58 million in new taxes. While a two-thirds majority supported raising the hotel tax, increases in business taxes failed. In 1980 a group called the Grass Roots Alliance succeeded in obtaining passage of an initiative stating that "San Francisco must increase the taxes paid by its largest corporations." But the statement made no provisions for its implementation.

Budgetary shortfall meant that San Francisco's neighborhood groups had to devote most of their energies to protecting whatever funding they were receiving rather than pressing for new programs. As a consequence of revenue restraints, the ostensible benefits predicted for the majority of San Francisco's residents from downtown development could not be realized in improved services.[7] The politics of redevelopment switched in the decade of the seventies from conflict over the distribution of costs and benefits of new programs to one of defense. Low-income

TABLE 6.10
General Revenue, San Francisco County

	1961–62	*1966–67*	*1971–72*	*1979–80*
Total general revenue (millions of $)	254.3	464.5	885.6	1,390
Total intergovernmental (millions of $)	65.6	143.9	322.0	707
From federal government (%)	n.a.	n.a.	33.6	38.1
Total from taxes (millions of $)	147.7	242.0	424.3	370.5
Property tax per capita ($)	171	302	448	297

SOURCE: U.S. Bureau of the Census, *County and City Data Book, 1967, 1972, 1977;* U.S. Bureau of the Census, *Local Government Finances in Selected Metropolitan Areas, 1979–80.*

people were no longer hostage to the grandiose visions of the Redevelopment Agency, but neither were they able to command a steady share of new revenues. Despite continual forays onto the ballot and at the level of mayor and supervisors aimed at forcing corporations to contribute more to the general welfare of the population, community effort remained primarily a holding action once social services and neighborhood stabilization became luxury items in the city budget.

CONCLUSION: THE RIGHT TO THE CITY

The complexity of San Francisco's government, the source of its economic prosperity in world shifts in trade, its unusually high levels of community mobilization and business activism—all combine to make explanation of its economic and physical transformation extremely complex. The particular outcome of redevelopment in the city must be seen as resulting from regional and sectoral shifts in the national economy, a facilitating role played by local government using federal funds, and struggle between community groups and financial interests, with government alternating its roles of opponent, cooptive agent, and mediator.

Who benefited from the three decades of postwar activity that created an enlarged central business district, a vastly expanded tourist industry, Victorianized neighborhoods, resident displacement, and subsidized housing construction? The French, when discussing the conflict over who should live in central Paris, have used the phrase "the right to the city." Its application is appropriate to San Francisco, where middle- and low-income groups are competing fiercely to maintain their rights to urban amenities and centrality. The absence, two years after the 1980 Census, of census tract data, however, makes it extremely difficult to estimate which groups have in fact managed to retain that right. One indication of the residential displacement process consequent to the expansion of professional and clerical employment is revealed by figures on in-migration. Gellen (1982: 20–22) shows that 64 percent of the 39,553 in-migrants to San Francisco in 1979 came from outside the Bay Area, implying that long-time residents are being replaced by new employees of the expanding industries, drawn from other parts of the country.

The problem of evaluating the distribution of benefits resulting from redevelopment is further compounded by the existence of horizontal inequities. Thus moderate-income home-owners benefited greatly from rising property values if they escaped demolition. Moderate-income renters who managed to obtain subsidized housing similarly gained. But new entrants into either the renter or owner market, and sitting tenants in buildings undergoing conversion, suffered disproportionately from the rapid escalation in housing prices. Centrally located residents were far more likely to be affected by renewal, both negatively and positively, than ones located in peripheral areas. The reduction in the size of the black population between 1970 and 1980 was undoubtedly in part a consequence of the predominantly black character of the largest renewal areas—Western Addition A-1 and A-2. The elderly tenants of residential hotels were also particularly victimized.

The economic prosperity created by the flourishing finance and tourist industries left a metropolitan area unemployment rate of 5.4 percent in September 1981 compared to a national rate of 7.5 percent (U.S. Department of Labor, 1981: 110). Throughout the decade of the seventies, however, Bay Area unemployment was not much lower than the U.S. rate. The creation within the city of 70,000 new jobs between 1972 and 1979, a 16.4 percent increase (Table 6.2), meant that at least some of the results of business expansion were felt broadly throughout the population. But job expansion occurred mainly in two quite different labor markets: office employment and tourism. It is probable, based on the high in-migration figure from outside the Bay Area, that the upper end of the employment scale was filled by individuals recruited nationally, while the lower-paid, deadend clerical and service jobs went to local residents and foreign immigrants.

The promise of a greatly expanded tax base, despite an enormous increase in real estate values (Table 6.7), was not realized, due partly to the passage of Proposition 13. A combination of revenue limitations, drastic declines in federal assistance, and increased service costs have resulted in service cutbacks despite rising tax rolls.

Community groups have influenced the agenda of city government and, in the years of confrontation, forced concessions to their demands. The California system of ballot initiatives has guaranteed at least a hearing for advocates of strong property market controls. Their failure to win partly reflected the exclusion of advocates from the major media and the vastly superior financial situation of the anti-Proposition R forces. Given the success in passage of strict rent control ordinances in some other California cities and the fact that two-thirds of San Francisco's residents are renters, one may question the continued ability of real estate interests to defeat attempts at regulation.

The adversary of community groups has mostly ceased to be the government and has become instead the impersonal forces of the marketplace. The measure of institutionalized access to government won by these groups became less significant as the local state itself lost resources. Use of the political process to control "private" activity is vastly more difficult than employing it to affect government itself. The most promising strategy for advocates of low-income groups seems to be entering the market themselves through the vehicles of the housing development corporations. But community self-help agencies lack the resources of big property developers; they suffer from inefficiencies due to their limited capacities and low potential given the magnitude of the need.

The years 1974–81 were ones of consolidation in San Francisco. But the dynamics of a new process have been set in motion by national recession and federal cutbacks. Their effects on the economy and level of activism in San Francisco are not yet determined. The city's prosperity may turn out to have been short-lived; its political accommodations temporary. Indeed, the advent of the Reagan Administration's economic and urban policies seems to demarcate the end of one period in San Francisco's redevelopment, while it remains too early to foretell the next.

NOTES

1. Field research for this chapter was conducted in 1978–80 under the auspices of the Community Development Strategies Evaluation, sponsored by the U.S. Department of Housing

and Urban Development through a cooperative agreement with the School of Public and Urban Policy, University of Pennsylvania. The authors of this chapter were part of the project staff during this time period. Findings and conclusions presented here are not an official product of the research supported by the Department. Further documentary research and some telephone follow-up interviews were conducted through January 1982. The information contained herein that is not referenced to specific works was gathered through semi-structured interviews with senior administrators, political officials, members of various citizen boards including all the members of the Citizens Committee on Community Development, neighborhood leaders, and scholars at local universities. Neighborhood leaders were identified through organizational position and reputation. A number of informants have been reinterviewed several times. Altogether 150 individuals have been interviewed.

2. Gellen adjusted the 1980 Census count of 298,957 households upward to include an estimated 5,473 uncounted illegal dwelling units. He lists average household size in 1970 as 2.34 and the number of households as 295,230; the 1980 figures are 2.15 and 304,430.

3. SPUR later changed its name to the San Francisco Planning and Urban Research Association, apparently in response to the growing negative connotations of "urban renewal."

4. Information on the dynamics of the poverty program in San Francisco is drawn primarily from Kramer (1969) and Wirt (1974).

5. Available data provide different indications of San Francisco's housing vacancy rate. The 1980 Census lists an overall vacancy rate of 5.5 percent and a rental vacancy rate of 4.1 percent (U.S. Bureau of the Census, 1981b), a figure considerable higher than the estimates of local observers. The Coro Foundation (1979: 38–39) cites the following estimates: a 2.6 percent figure for apartments in 1979 by the City Planning Commission, an overall 1.4 percent rate and a 2.4 percent apartment vacancy rate for 1975 derived from a U.S. Department of Housing and Urban Development and Postal Service study, and an overall December 1978 figure of 1.7 percent compiled by Pacific Gas and Electric, based on the number of idle meters.

6. This opinion was presented by a man who had previously worked both as a private planning consultant and for the SFRA. Although he therefore came from a quite different, more establishment background than the more radical community activists who were CCHO's driving force, he evaluated the conflict between neighborhoods and city government in similar terms.

7. According to the SFRA, the total increase in yearly property tax revenues in 1978–79 attributable to SFRA-sponsored redevelopment was only $5.8 million, although it predicted an eventual additional $8 million once present projects were closed out (SFRA, 1979: 11). The agency did not list figures showing the loss of revenue while previously built-up tracts were kept vacant pending redevelopment.

REFERENCES

Bach, Victor. 1976. "San Francisco: a CDBG case study." Austin, TX: Lyndon B. Johnson School of Public Affairs, University of Texas, unpublished.

Barton, Stephen E. 1979. *Understanding San Francisco: Social Movements in Headquarters City.* Berkeley: Department of City and Regional Planning, University of California, unpublished.

Becker, Howard S., ed. 1971. *Culture and Civility in San Francisco.* New Brunswick, NJ: Transaction.

Berkeley Planning Associates. 1980. *Displacement in San Francisco.* Prepared for the City of San Francisco. Berkeley: Berkeley Planning Associates.

Black, J. Thomas. 1980. "The changing economic role of central cities and suburbs." Pp. 80–123 in Arthur P. Solomon, ed., *The Prospective City.* Cambridge, MA: MIT Press.

Brugmann, Bruce, and Greggar Sletteland, eds. 1971. *The Ultimate Highrise: San Francisco's Mad Rush toward the Sky.* San Francisco: San Francisco Bay Guardian Books.

Castells, Manuel, and Karen Murphy. 1982. "Cultural identity and urban structure: the spatial organization of San Francisco's gay community." Pp. 237–59 in Norman I. Fainstein and Susan S. Fainstein, eds., *Urban Policy under Capitalism.* Beverly Hills, CA: Sage.

Clark, Marilyn. 1981. "The tragedy of the Fillmore." *San Francisco Bay Guardian,* June 10: 7–9, 21.

Cohen, R. B. 1981. "The new internation division of labor: multinational corporations and urban hierarchy." Pp. 289–315 in Michael Dear and Allen J. Scott, eds., *Urbanization and Urban Planning in Capitalist Society.* New York: Methuen.

Coro Foundation. 1979. *The District Handbook.* San Francisco: Coro Foundation.

Council of Community Housing Organizations. n.d. (c. 1981). *The Community Housing Advocate.* San Francisco: Regional Young Adult Project.

Friedland, Roger, Frances Fox Piven, and Robert R. Alford. 1978. "Political conflict, urban structure, and the fiscal crisis." Pp. 197–225 in Douglas E. Ashford, ed., *Comparing Public Policies.* Beverly Hills, CA: Sage.

Gans, Herbert. 1962. *The Urban Villagers.* New York: Free Press.

Gellen, Martin. 1982. "Migration and urban revitalization: the case of San Francisco." Paper presented at Symposium on the Changing Face of Urban America, School of Planning, University of Cincinnati, April 29.

Hall, Peter. 1982. *Great Planning Disasters.* Berkeley: University of California Press.

Hartman, Chester. 1974. *Yerba Buena: Land Grab and Community Resistance in San Francisco.* San Francisco: Glide Publications.

———, and Rob Kessler. 1978. "The illusion and reality of urban renewal: San Francisco's Yerba Buena Center." Pp. 153–78 in William K. Tabb and Larry Sawers, eds., *Marxism and the Metropolis.* New York: Oxford University Press.

Hippler, Arthur E. 1974. *Hunters Point.* New York: Basic Books.

Jacobs, Allan B. 1978. *Making City Planning Work.* Chicago: American Society of Planning Officials.

Kramer, Ralph M. 1969. *Participation of the Poor.* Englewood Cliffs, NJ: Prentice-Hall.

Mayor's Office of Community Development. 1981. *Community Development and Housing Assistance Plan, 1981. Final Program.* San Francisco, March.

———. 1980. *Community Development Program and Housing Assistance Plan, 1980. Final Program.* San Francisco, February.

———. 1979. *Community Development Program and Housing Assistance Plan, 1979.* San Francisco, March.

Mollenkopf, John. 1981. "Neighborhood political development and the politics of urban growth: Boston and San Francisco, 1958–78," *International Journal of Urban and Regional Research* 5 (1): 15–39.

New York Times. 1981a. June 9.

———. 1981b. May 17.

Numbers News (Supplement to *American Demographics*). 1981. Ithaca, NY: American Demographics, January 15, February 18.

San Franciscans for Affordable Housing. 1979. "Text of Proposition R." San Francisco.

San Francisco Bay Guardian. 1982. June 6.

———. 1981. February 4.

San Francisco Examiner. 1979. January 28.

San Francisco Lawyers' Committee for Urban Affairs. 1979. "Comments on 1979 CDBG application of the City and County of San Francisco." Mimeo, January 26.

San Francisco Redevelopment Agency. 1979. *San Francisco Redevelopment Program: Summary of Project Data and Key Elements.* San Francisco: SFRA.

Schoch, Jim, ed. 1979. *Where Has All the Housing Gone? Readings on the Housing Crisis and What's Being Done about It.* San Francisco: New American Movement.

Stone, Clarence. 1976. *Economic Growth and Neighborhood Discontent.* Chapel Hill, NC: University of North Carolina.

Tipps, Dean D. 1980. "California's great property tax revolt: the origins and impact of Proposition 13." Pp. 68–90 in Dean C. Tipps and Lee Webb, eds., *State and Local Tax Revolt: New Directions for the 80's.* Washington, D.C.: Conference on Alternative State and Local Policy.

TODCO. 1979. "Formal proposal for 1980 Community Development Program." Contained in letter from John Elberling to James Johnson, June 7.

U.S. Bureau of the Census. 1981a. "1980 census population totals for racial and Spanish origins groups in California announced by Census Bureau." *U.S. Department of Commerce News.*

————. 1981b. *Selected Housing Characteristics by States and Counties: 1980.* Washington, D.C.

U.S. Department of Housing and Urban Development. 1980. *The President's National Urban Policy Report.* Washington, D.C.: U.S. Government Printing Office.

U.S. Department of Labor. 1981. *Employment and Earnings* 28 (December).

Wirt, Frederick M. 1974. *Power in the City: Decisionmaking in San Francisco.* Berkeley: University of California Press.

Wolfe, Burton. 1971. "BART's ride to bankruptcy." Pp. 192–204 in Brugmann and Sletteland, 1971.

Zwerling, Stephen. 1972. *The Political Consequences of Technological Choice: Public Transit in the San Francisco Metropolitan Area.* New York: Praeger.

7

Regime Strategies, Communal Resistance, and Economic Forces

Norman I. Fainstein
Susan S. Fainstein

The role of the local state has proved to be variable in its level of interventionism yet consistent in its substance within the five cities of this study. The recent reduction in national sponsorship of redevelopment activity, paralleling the move toward privatization in other policy areas, undermines the assumption of both liberal and Marxist thinkers that the capitalist state will inevitably continue to enlarge its scope (Lebas, 1981). Our analyses of the rise and decline of public intervention in urban redevelopment in five cities permits us to address the question of when state redevelopment activity occurs. In this final chapter we look first at the causes of state inactivity and assertiveness, then at the content and consequences of urban redevelopment efforts.

Our purpose here is to identify areas of determinism and flexibility. We begin with a structuralist model of the state, meaning we assume that the state role will be broadly determined by the relations of production in society (Clark and Dear, 1981). But we also expect that at any particular moment capitalist interests, political organizations, and urban social movements can immediately affect as well as indirectly bias state behavior. While the processes and outcomes of redevelopment are broadly confined by the social relations of capitalism, the resolution of conflicts can differ in different places, with dissimilar results for comparable population groups. In other words we conclude that political pressure matters—that the difference between the condition of low-income people in New Orleans and San Francisco stems in part from the higher levels of mobilization achieved in the latter, not just from the differing economic circumstances of the two cities. Thus we regard the state and capital as the two major initiators of redevelopment activity and think that in some cases a purely instrumentalist explanation of state action, whereby the state acts at the direct bidding of capital, applies. But we also accept a class-struggle model of the state, in which the state incorporates the gains that have been won by popular movements (Holloway and Picciotto, 1977: Chapter 1).[1]

In order to understand the forces creating redevelopment and decline, based on the histories of the five cities described herein, we proceed by first analyzing the factors that gave rise to postwar, state-sponsored renewal programs. We then look at constant and changing aspects of the state role during three major periods. Next we examine the outcomes of regime initiatives and popular resistance under varying political and economic conditions. Finally we relate changes at the urban level to the contradictions of U.S. capitalism. Throughout, we are primarily concerned with the roles and interests of local regimes and political forces, examining national factors only as they provide the political-economic context for particular urban situations.

INTERESTS OF STATE AND CAPITAL IN URBAN REDEVELOPMENT

Most older American cities suffered the much-chronicled symptoms of economic and physical decay during the postwar period. Nevertheless, local political regimes did not consistently sponsor serious efforts to reverse the trend, regardless of the potential benefits to themselves and local capital that might have resulted. Both in the years before the 1954 intensification of the federal urban renewal program and in the post-1974 withdrawal of large-scale federal funding of urban redevelopment, we have witnessed governmental restraint despite perceptions of need. Several factors explain the unwillingness or inability of local forces to mount a serious program to improve the urban economy and physical environment. We initially analyze the forces causing inaction so as better to understand the conditions prompting state intervention.

First, the local state normally contains few offices capable of playing a leading role in directing development. State-sponsored investment activity, just as in the private sector, requires entrepreneurship. During the heyday of urban renewal, federal directives caused the establishment of semi-autonomous renewal agencies with access to sequestered capital funds. Such agencies, however, threaten vested bureaucratic and electoral interests, though their largely uncontrollable activities serve capital well (Friedland, Piven, and Alford, 1978). Even the most powerful of these seemingly insulated agencies have had their influence seriously curtailed (e.g., Denver) or abrogated (as happened to the formerly mighty New Haven Redevelopment Agency) once federal support terminated. In the absence of specially designated and separately funded renewal agencies, city government will proceed incrementally to disperse its resources across various functions and geographic areas. Federal urban-renewal funds constituted "free money" not subject to the routine revenue-raising constraints and allocational processes of local politics. Pre-urban-renewal local financial autonomy and post-Reagan federal cutbacks reveal that except under unusual circumstances municipal governments are incapable of a highly directing role in shaping cities, regardless of the potential profitability that can result.

Second, even when outside funding creates opportunities for state initiatives, local regimes may fail to act because of opposition from established business groups.

Crouch (1979: 27) comments wryly on the difficulty for Marxists in dealing with the "remarkable fact" that within liberal democratic capitalist societies "ruling classes mistrust the state and try to limit its activities." The case of New Orleans illustrates his point well. Economic dominants, integrated into a tightly knit social hierarchy, emphasized preservationism, scorned "new money," and joined with a populist mass to block enactment of local enabling legislation for urban renewal. It was only in the 1970s, with the intrusion of outside capital and significant changes in political leadership, that public sponsorship of redevelopment activity began.

Third, capital does not necessarily require the state in order to reshape the urban environment. In the absence of a national force and without local mobilization of a "progrowth coalition" (Mollenkopf, 1978) of elected officials, development administrators, and business leaders, physical redevelopment may yet transpire. Market factors by themselves can produce a revaluation of inner-city property. Heavy private investment in formerly declining urban centers occurs when the relative *future* value of the core is enhanced. Such a shift in the investment potential of core-area land may result from more intensive use, increased consumption needs, or the imposition of a class-monopoly rent (Harvey, 1974). Downtowns have gained value as a result of the pressure of service industries seeking office space. The absolute population decline that characterizes many cities which have attracted sizable private investment (e.g., Denver, San Francisco, and limited areas of New Orleans) indicates that neighborhood investment may result from the levying of a class-monopoly rent despite declining densities. In this process the domination of a territory by upper-class owners and speculative investors forces up the exchange values of surrounding properties even without expenditures in rehabilitation to make them intrinsically more valuable; where rehabilitation investment does occur, the new price far exceeds the cost of improvement.

New Orleans offers the clearest example of redevelopment without either state action or a major business coalition. Its first large central-city endeavor, the Superdome, was a private initiative, not involving federal funds, with capitalization coming from outside the city and from a disguised state subsidy. In the French Quarter, as in San Francisco and other cities, opposition to growth by middle-class conservationists provided the setting for massive private investment in housing rehabilitation. Once the initial pattern of upper-income occupancy was set, inflated land prices, condominium conversion, speculative site development, transformation of low-rent units into luxury apartments, and upper-class retailing rapidly followed. These areas of snowballing private reinvestment were often either ignored by the city's development office or originally named as targets for publicly funded demolition.

The absence of governmental activity in New Orleans, and its sharp increase there during the 1970s, a period of withdrawal in most other cities, illustrates the contingent nature of local state involvement. State-sponsored redevelopment requires the conjunction of both internal and external economic and political forces. While geographical shifts of investment across the country and between city and suburb can be traced to important changes in the capitalist economic structure, the extent of state intervention is less determined (Harloe, 1979: 134).

In the United States generally, conservative business groups opposed housing and renewal legislation at its inception, just as they were eventually to be responsible for its demise. The basis for opposition derived from the absence of an étatist or corporatist tradition that could justify an interventionist state (Hartz, 1955). While direct state subsidy of business has been a long-accepted American mode, intrusion of the government into the private sector through planning and investment policies has always been resisted (Fainstein and Fainstein, 1982a: 13–16).

Three factors were necessary to create the setting in which the local state became a potent force for urban transformation. These were national funding and the federal imposition of an administrative structure capable of pursuing renewal goals; the changing economic and racial composition of urban populations; and popular perceptions of the causes of urban decline. While these factors could not by themselves cause local action, they were nevertheless prerequisites to it and profound determinants of the character of redevelopment programs.

National Programs and Local Activity

The national political force that created the 1949 and 1954 urban renewal legislation consisted of a temporary and uneasy coalition of liberals and conservatives, business, labor, and city officials (Gelfand, 1975: 151–56, 175–76; Farkas, 1971). The impetus behind these national enabling programs lay in circumstances somewhat similar to those that prevailed in postwar Western Europe at the same time. Severe housing shortages, fear of depression, and the hiatus in domestic investment caused by the war, combined with wartime habits of governmental activism, led national governments in both places to mount programs aimed at rebuilding cities. But the difference in political configurations on the two continents produced quite different paths of development (see Fainstein and Fainstein, 1978).

The key element of the 1949 and 1954 federal acts that were to shape urban redevelopment in the United States was the separation of social expenditures (i.e., public housing) from renewal programs. When liberals supported the legislation because of its promise of rehousing the working-class inhabitants of the inner city, they failed to foresee the extent to which its clearance provisions would in fact produce unhousing. The newly granted power of eminent domain for private development gave public and private entrepreneurs in various cities a tool for remaking their central business districts. Once development administrators like Edward Logue in New Haven and Justin Herman in San Francisco produced the model of massive clearance followed by new construction of high-rise commercial and expensive residential development, numerous local regimes rushed to follow suit.

Effect of Population Change

Municipalities were not required to replace the housing units demolished under renewal programs. During the 1950s and 1960s the tide of black migration into northern cities was met by governmental attempts to buffer city centers from inundation by minority groups. At the national level the Democratic Party sought to maintain black allegiance, and urban legislation was ostensibly aimed at assisting black groups. But at the local level this legislation along with highway programs was used to remove minority communities from areas adjoining the central business district (CBD). In Detroit, which became a black-majority city and eventually elected a black mayor, urban renewal protected the commercial district from minority encroachment. No public housing was even built in Detroit between 1957 and 1970. Despite the profits that public-housing construction offered to contractors and associated groups, normally urban government's most influential constituencies, local housing authorities were extremely, and increasingly, reluctant to build units that would provide for black habitation. Consequently the lesser willingness to accept public activity in housing markets that differentiated the United States from, for example, England at the beginning of the postwar period became markedly exacerbated.

Urban renewal ironically acted as both the cement and the undoing of interventionist coalitions within cities. For the depredations of the program, in combination with the colonialist qualities of social service and control agencies, helped provoke the riots and popular movements that ultimately improved the political status of urban blacks (Cloward and Piven, 1974). Once minorities threatened social stability, the state could not wholly disregard their interests when intervening in urban development. Government, using condemnation powers, had prevented undesired population groups from impinging on valuable, or potentially valuable, real estate. In response to pressures from below, however, federal legislation became increasingly stringent in protecting the rights of affected residents. The ultimate consequence was a lessened use of urban renewal and its eventual merger into Community Development Block Grants (CDBG). During the interim, spatially targeted programs (Community Action, Model Cities, Neighborhood Development) directed at low-income people became a major component of federal urban efforts.

Local Perceptions

The advent, reformulation, then curtailment of redevelopment programs reflect local as well as national regime responses to economic and racial forces. The local situational factors of economic decline and racial change shaped perceptions within cities concerning the nature of their problems and the appropriate remedies. Recollections of more vibrant days and failure to grasp the ultimate implications of uncontrolled suburban growth led planners to seek to restore the downtown of yesteryear. The competitive disadvantage of core retailing was perceived as the result of shabbiness and traffic congestion, rather than of a major shift in the uses of space across the country. Re-creation of the CBD as a mecca for middle-class shoppers and white-collar (and presumably white-skinned) workers became the implicit renewal goal. Middle-class residences near the center and peripheralization of its former occupants were further objectives. The enormous emphasis on retailing in the redevelopment plans for Detroit and New Haven can only be understood in this context. These perceptions of problems and solutions, reinforced by the absence of national policy concerning the location of people and industry, constituted the third element, in addition to federal subsidy and changing social composition, creating the local circumstances surrounding redevelopment activity.

But this set of circumstances alone did not produce the dynamic that created large-scale, state-sponsored redevelopment. Needed also was a political force to press for growth and an acquiescent population that would not stand in its way (see Molotch, 1980). The former only existed at certain times; the latter largely disappeared during the 1960s.

In all five cities of this study, state redevelopment activity was initiated either by the mayor or an organized business group. The San Francisco Planning and Urban Renewal Association (SPUR) provided the initial thrust for state intervention, and its corporate members supported the successful candidacy of a mayor who would promote its plans. The mayor, in turn, encouraged the growth and power of the renewal agency (SFRA), which then acted as an autonomous force to further publicly sponsored redevelopment. Similarly, the New Detroit Committee and subsequently the Detroit Renaissance provided the impetus for that city's development strategy. In New Haven, New Orleans, and Denver the mayors used their offices to organize supportive business coalitions. In all five cases a symbiotic relationship developed between the mayor's office and the business community, cemented on the one side by the city's access to federal funding and on the other by the commitment of business to invest if redevelopment plans conformed to its perception of an appropriate strategy.

Support from the local media usually constituted an additional component of this redevelopment coalition. But even in the exceptional case of New Haven, where the local newspapers opposed government intervention on conservative principle, local electoral majorities continued to perceive the redevelopment program as positive. Certainly the absence in the daily press and television of any left-oriented critique of urban programs was enormously important in legitimating the political force behind them.

The setting for heightened intervention in its physical environment did not, *per se*, force the local state to take action. But that setting did in many ways determine the nature of action when it did take place. While the extent of state intervention may vary, its content is seriously constrained by the structure of social relations in which it occurs. State-sponsored redevelopment efforts in different locales with varying economic conditions share significant commonalities. Although their character changes over time, the direction of change is likewise similar in disparate places.

THE CHARACTER OF STATE-SPONSORED REDEVELOPMENT

The character of state action is produced by the interplay of a set of relatively constant elements with a set of dynamic ones. The former encompasses the systemic biases of the local state—a dialectical product of institutional arrangements and class-defined politics—its strategic aims in redevelopment, and the operational issues associated with governmental programs. The latter includes the national transformations in public policy, political alignments, and investment patterns which have affected municipalities since World War II. These external forces combine with the outcomes of city politics and programs to produce a succession of typical urban regimes with varying roles in redevelopment and responsiveness to the interests of lower-income and minority populations. We designate the different regimes as *directive, concessionary,* and *conserving.* The discussion to follow begins with the constant elements in state-sponsored redevelopment, then treats dynamic factors and the differences among regimes.

Constant Elements: The Local State, Its Strategic Objectives, and the Conflicts of Redevelopment

Several mutually reinforcing factors give the local state a consistent bias towards redevelopment which favors the interests of business firms, elite institutions (hospitals, universities), and middle-class residents. The first stems from organizational interests in fiscal solvency. U.S. cities raise the majority of their revenue locally, with property taxes the most important source. While municipalities differ considerably in the per-capita magnitude of their expenditures, the system of finance compels every local state at least to maintain its revenue base by attracting investment which contributes to the market value of real property. Moreover, because lower-income populations contribute much less to revenue than they do to expenditures, local states (even those with majorities of poor people) have an interest in excluding such households; conversely, they strongly desire to attract upper-income residents. Reinforcing these fiscal interests of the state are, of course, the economic interests of local property owners in keeping high the ratio of governmental expenditures received by them to the tax rates they must pay (Peterson, 1981: Chapter 2). Because property owners have disproportionately great electoral strength, governmental regimes almost automatically integrate their concerns with the fiscal needs of the state itself. The result is a deeply rooted system of municipal mercantilism biased against the lower classes.

The second factor stems from the structural position of the state in relation to private economic institutions. Capital effectively controls production of most goods and services. Its domination establishes a social dependency on private investment and profit (i.e., accumulation) for the provision of employment on the one side, and the built environment on the other. But only the state takes collective responsibility for the functioning and outcomes of the urban economy. The state is therefore placed in the position of having to facilitate accumulation in order to advance the material interests of its citizens. It must attract new private investment and retain what already exists. Municipalities accomplish these ends through various combinations of direct subsidies, allocations to business firms of desirable land and locations, and tax relief. Sometimes capital uses its advantaged position openly to coerce the local state into making concessions, as when a large firm threatens to leave town if it is not provided with public subsidy. But such conflicts usually do not arise because of a third factor underlying state orientation toward redevelopment.

This is the political power of capital and the class character it establishes for the state. Business dominates the political system. It finances candidates in both major political parties. It acts as a powerful interest group affecting elections and referenda. It controls the mass media. And the business class fills most top state administrative positions and elective offices. The ensuing class character of the local state is expressed concretely in the overarching objective of all public policy affecting business and development: to maximize the size and profitability of the private sphere; to prevent public production from reducing opportunities for profit.

"The main job of government," Edward Koch stated two months after his inauguration as mayor of New York, "is to create a climate in which private business can expand in the city to provide jobs and profit. It's not the function of government to create jobs on the public payroll." (*New York Times,* March 4, 1978, as quoted in Katznelson, 1981: 4)

Business domination also manifests itself in a more diffuse, yet no less important, way. Put simply, public policies embody the bourgeois vision of the good city, and public officials propagandize bourgeois cultural values throughout the population. The "better city" is clean, orderly, new, and expanding, with lower classes that are hidden, quiescent, and shrinking. In many respects little has changed since Engels (1968: 54–56) described the bourgeois vision in Manchester. The middle and upper classes see their city in the downtown, in cultural amenities, big buildings, and manicured residential neighborhoods. The condition of territory occupied by the lower classes and the welfare of the entire urban population are not equated with the quality of urban life. A better city is a more middle-class city even when the majority of citizens are poor and working-class people.

State Objectives.   The strategic aims of the state in urban redevelopment are expressed in common policies and programs across cities and over time; they are to be found in the topography of state actions, rather than in explicit plans, projects, and issues. State objectives may be disaggregated along three vectors: economic, sociospatial, and political. Together, these establish the basic direction of public action, which is the operational expression of the systemic biases of the local state.

The economic objective of state action is to facilitate accumulation: in general terms, to implement programs which produce new investment in the built environment capable of generating private profit and of expanding the market value of real estate. Yet because each local state represents—and is confined by—a particular business class, its freedom of action is always limited. Thus the local state does not act in the interest of capital in general (much less, of economic efficiency), but, instead, of specific fractions of local capital along with ancillary private institutions. Since capitalists are mutually competitive and often oppose entrepreneurship and new industries, specific state strategies for accumulation may vary as they reflect the changing balances of power within the local business community. The state's overall aims are to (a) maintain the position of leading local firms in the changing national economy and competitive system of cities; (b) eliminate economic "blight," meaning those firms and activities devalued by powerful economic actors; (c) pursue firms drawn from expanding industry sectors which have the capability of restructuring the functions and advantages of the local economy in the system of cities. The first two of these objectives enhance the position of leading resident firms; however, they do not necessarily constitute the optimum state strategy for accumulation, since some of these firms (e.g., auto manufacturers in Detroit, big department stores in New Haven) represent industries with a declining regional or national competitive advantage.

The problem for the state in seeking to restructure its economy stems from the presence of obsolete business elements, the unpredictability of national economic trends, and the uncertain possibilities of taking advantage of these trends locally. Even in cities which do not face Detroit's acute dilemma over further investment in auto production, there may be confusion and disagreement in identifying "growth" industries (which are sometimes mistaken for "marginal enterprises" and extirpated as "blight"). By the time a new consensus has emerged, the competitive advantage of a particular city may have been lost.

During the fifties and sixties local states showed incoherence in the forms of investment and sectoral expansion they wanted. By the mid-seventies, however, a more integrated vision had emerged, though by no means one every city could realize. Accumulation priorities now included expansion of white-collar industries, high-technology manufacturing, and bourgeois consumption services. Every city wanted to be a world (or national, or at least regional) corporate headquarters center, with a central business district of office buildings, specialized shops and restaurants, hotels and luxury apartments—the restructured Denvers and San Franciscos (see McGrath, 1982).

Although there have been reformulations by cities of their accumulation objectives, there has been remarkable consistency in the sociospatial aim of redevelopment policies: to reestablish business and middle-class control of urban territory. This objective is realized through a set of interlocking efforts:

- *"Bring back" the white middle class.* In the post-World War II period, no developed city has ever sought to attract proletarian, minority, or poor households. Every city has advertised its advantages to "desirable" population groups.
- *Remove lower-income and minority households* from the central business district, the territorial ring surrounding it, and close proximity to important institutions like museums, medical complexes, universities, sports arenas, and convention centers. In general, the state aims to make available to private firms, developers, and elite institutions land with aesthetic and transportation advantages once "undesirable" populations are removed.
- *Maintain and reestablish racial and class territorial segregation* through locational decisions involving clearance, zoning, public facilities (especially schools), transportation routes, and publicly subsidized housing.
- *Encapsulate the lower classes in peripheral locations:* construct public housing in remote areas of the city or on land with no apparent market value.

The first of these efforts is widely covered in the media and is officially documented. The others, for obvious reasons, are never discussed and usually run counter to official policies. Nevertheless, they enable the local state to use territory as an instrument for maintaining social control over the still-existing lower-class population.

The political vector of state strategy points toward the objective of insulating redevelopment decision-making from popular influence, as well as, whenever possible, using redevelopment itself to enhance the power of state officials. Many modes of redevelopment (e.g., urban renewal, code enforcement, highway construction) place the local state in direct confrontation with lower-income households and small businesses. For this reason, the state aims to segment off the administrative apparatus of redevelopment from democratic representative mechanisms, to keep decision-making bottled up among a small circle of technocrats, developers, and elite public officials sharing common interests. Popular legitimation is provided by "citizen boards," which, when the development issue is CBD renewal, are comprised of the business elite. For example, the business coalition which first sponsored urban renewal in San Francisco (SPUR) was designated as the official vehicle for citizen participation; the mayor of New Haven appointed a citizens advisory commission comprised mainly of big business and university leaders. When participation is required by federal regulations or forced by mobilized local opposition (as in San Francisco's Western Addition renewal projects), the state attempts to achieve outcomes which are mainly cooptive or symbolic. Although local states have sometimes found it necessary to cede real power to representatives of lower-income and minority groups, this has never been a desired objective, only a tactical concession.

If redevelopment is politically destabilizing, it also can bolster political power, and regimes seek to capitalize upon these potentialities. The continuous mobility imposed on lower-income people minimizes their ability to pressure city officials through electoral mechanisms, as was the case in New Haven where the Democratic party machine could ignore displaced blacks for more than a decade. Moreover, by visibly uprooting racial minorities from proximity to white, moderate-income neighborhoods, the state gains popular support for the redevelopment process. Finally, if economic forces are favorable and redevelopment proceeds sufficiently far, much of the population from which opposition might arise is removed from within municipal boundaries (a tendency well along in San Francisco), thereby facilitating a new period of political stability in some jurisdictions, even while others (like Daly City and Oakland) must now deal with households displaced in their direction.

Fault Lines and Conflicts. The politics of redevelopment rarely centers on the strategic aims of the state. The counterstrategies of major economic redistribution, social integration, and political democratization become local political issues only during periods of extreme popular mobilization. Conflicts over redevelopment do not drastically alter its overall course for several reasons: the decision-making agenda is almost always framed by the state in collaboration with capital; the areas of discretion relative to the entire redevelopment effort are small; and outcomes of individual decisions, even if some are inconsistent, cumulatively favor the interests of capital.

The substantive character of redevelopment policy creates a relatively constant set of fault lines by which conflicts may be logically defined. While the visibility and outcomes of these divisions differ across cities and historical periods, the same fault lines continually reappear and become the "urban trenches" (Katznelson, 1981) about which redevelopment skirmishes are fought.

A brief listing of the fault lines which have remained relatively unchanged since the 1950s, and of the conflicts associated with each, looks as follows:

1. *Divisions within the business and middle classes.*
    a. Uncontrolled growth and investment *versus* historic preservation, aesthetic virtue, or environmental quality.
    b. Public tax expenditures to benefit commercial investment *versus* lower tax rates for households.
    c. Maintenance of manufacturing plants and related facilities employing blue-collar workers *versus* emphasis on development of office buildings, commercial and tourist facilities employing mainly white-collar workers (with some lower-class service workers in the case of hotels and restaurants).
    d. Large, profitable firms (e.g., banks, major corporations) *versus* small, marginal businesses (e.g., small manufacturing establishments, auto parts stores—the labor-intensive economic infrastructure of "blighted" areas).
    e. Capital investment by financial institutions within the municipal CBD *versus* more profitable investments in the region, but outside the political jurisdiction of the city (e.g., in a suburban shopping center).
2. *Allocation of public investment as between core and peripheral areas.*
    a. Subsidized maintenance or expansion of CBD functions catering to commuters and tourists combined with public neglect or elimination of neighborhood businesses *versus* a balanced strategy or one which emphasizes neighborhood economic infrastructure.
    b. Downtown housing construction and rehabilitation, often at luxury prices, *versus* neighborhood housing improvements.
3. *Allocation of state expenditures for capital accumulation* versus *social consumption* (each of the accumulation alternatives here are claimed to benefit the whole city through their contribution to growth and long run fiscal solvency; the social consumption alternatives, while very important, are said to benefit only particular social groups, strain municipal fiscal capacity, and do nothing for the local economy).
    a. State subsidies for "market rate" housing and profitable commercial ventures *versus* publicly owned or assisted housing.
    b. Investment in physical infrastructure such as roads, sewers, and redevelopment site preparation *versus* funding of social services (e.g., health care, child care, and job training).
    c. Public capital investment and tax expenditures for downtown businesses (termed "economic development") *versus* publicly subsidized housing and public facilities in low- and moderate-income neighborhoods.
    d. Encapsulation of tax yields from state-sponsored development for further development ventures (employing such mechanisms as tax-increment financing, special development districts, and self-financed public authorities) *versus* inclusion of yields in general municipal revenues (it should

be mentioned that legal restrictions strongly encourage the local state to pursue the former alternative by making it much easier and cheaper to float bonds with segregated revenue streams than general obligation bonds).

4. *Treatment modalities and resource allocation between and within lower-income neighborhoods.*

   a. Choice of neighborhoods for housing, public services, and development expenditures: emphasis on neighborhoods likely to be most responsive to treatment (the "triage" approach) *versus* those most in need.

   b. Treatments which benefit home-owners, such as rehabilitation loans and grants, *versus* those which directly benefit renters, such as Section 8 rent subsidies for low-income households.

   c. Clearance and construction of new housing *versus* rehabilitation of existing housing.

   d. Choice of which lower-income groups will be provided with public and publicly assisted housing: elderly households *versus* families with children.

Municipal redevelopment policy is the resultant of outcomes along this whole set of fault lines. Policy choices, however, are made incrementally, frequently by decision-makers in mutual isolation, with long implementation lags and inertial tendencies. Accordingly, public officials do not necessarily perceive an overarching redevelopment policy, much less a rational connection between strategic objectives and the mix of operational program elements. Yet precisely because of the "market" character of decision-making, redevelopment programs in the aggregate reflect the systemic biases and strategic aims of the state. For these impose a constant pressure at every decision point toward "realism," in other words, toward policies which further economic health (private accumulation), recognize and reinforce the hostilities among income and racial groups (sociospatial segregation), and maintain the political capacity of the state to govern rationally (social control).

Structurally determined systemic biases and strategic objectives establish consistency in the activities of the local state. But municipalities are also extremely dependent entities of the national political and economic system. Changing external factors strongly affect local state resources, the political capacity of oppositional forces, and, as a result, the ways in which conflicting social interests are represented in different regimes and modes of state programs. It is these dynamic elements which we next examine.

Changing Elements: Typical Regimes and Their Programmatic Choices

Analysis of change in state activities requires that we distinguish between the state as a whole, and that part of it responsible for setting policy and susceptible to electoral forces. The contours and structural position of the local state are far more stable than the circle of powerful elected officials and top administrators who move in and out of office. The latter comprise what we call in everyday language the administration or the government. It is what we mean by the local regime.

Regimes, Class Conflict, and Local Politics. Regimes make a difference in how the strategic objectives of the state are translated into action. Not only do they determine choice along the fault lines previously enumerated, they help establish which lines will be politically salient, i.e., they set the agendas for political conflict over state activity. In doing so they directly or indirectly mobilize both business and communal interests. The role of the regime is especially critical in establishing the collective programmatic interests of the business class in redevelopment (see Stone's [1976: esp. 89] discussion of Atlanta). It may do so by directly translating the program of a powerful business interest group (e.g., SPUR in San Francisco) into state policy, by establishing such a group (Downtown Council in New Haven), or by siding with one set of business interests over another (as in New Orleans where the regime favored tourist over industrial uses of the waterfront). Regimes also organize some working-class groups politically and divide others. Depending on both their ideology and programs, regimes can make specific class and racial interests politically relevant categories (as in the ethnic politics of political machines or in affirmative action programs), thereby raising group consciousness, solidarity, and political capacity. Finally, regimes do not simply depend upon the state, they shape it through the creation or elimination of specific agencies (e.g., urban renewal, community action) and mechanisms for political representation (e.g., citizen boards).

The systemic biases of the local state mean that the interests of capital, and to a lesser extent those of the middle class, though varying in specific definition, are directly incorporated into the regime. In contrast, lower- and working-class interests are external to it. In some cities a few elected officials (usually on the council) support particular lower-income neighborhoods, organizations, and government programs. But these "representatives" rarely have a coherent ideology or program counter to the strategic objectives of the local state. They are identical to trade union officials making economist, not class demands. And their effectiveness, in any event, depends upon popular pressure external to the state. Therborn (1980: 181) defines the situation when he says that the regime *represents* the ruling class (i.e., capital), but *mediates* between it and under classes and strata.

For this reason, regimes significantly advance lower- and working-class interests in redevelopment only when compelled to do so by political movements, protest, and social disorder.[2] Electoral representation, by itself, is never adequate. Class mobilization (even by only racially defined elements) changes the way in which local capital defines its interests, and thereby the programmatic objectives incorporated into the regime. Most broadly, confronted with a threat to the social relations of production, capital comes to see various state-sponsored legitimation efforts and collective-consumption programs as functional to its long-term interests (see Wright, 1979: 230).

Under attack, capital does not, however, sit back passively; it mobilizes its own very considerable institutionalized power to threaten the fiscal solvency of the state, determine its economic environment, and influence public perceptions. Business interest groups spent untold millions on influencing electoral decisions with regard to municipal rent control, development bond referenda (e.g., for the Bay Area Rapid Transit [BART] and Yerba Buena in San Francisco), the Superdome in New Orleans, and similar issues associated with accumulation. When antagonized by local regimes which tilted towards working-class interests, business organized to throw the dangerous elements out of office. (See Swanstrom's account [1981] of the fate of the Kucinich regime in Cleveland.) During both the Depression and the urban fiscal crises of 1975, capital went one step further and insisted upon reforms in state structure which would guarantee direct business authority over the program choices of urban regimes (David and Kantor, 1979). The imposition of the business-dominated Emergency Financial Control Board to control the New York City budget is a case in point which presented a nationwide warning of what capital could do to any municipality.

Regimes maintain control of state power by dint of winning elections. The interaction between regime activities and mobilized class and racial elements strongly influences the character of electoral politics. Regimes which appeal to lower-income constituencies encourage them to vote, and thereby to provide support. But since liberal regimes ultimately pursue the class objectives of the state, they are never willing to lose business and middle-class constituencies by actually implementing a program rooted in working-class interests. Thus, when popular mobilization abates, or is countered, regimes which previously made concessions to some working- and lower-class demands must turn around or be thrown out of office (see Morris [1980] on the change in course of the Lindsay regime in New York City after 1969).

Together these factors establish a dynamic element at the municipal level in the political situation of regimes and in the ways they translate state strategic objectives into operational program choices. Figure 7.1 illustrates some of the interrelationships we have described. It also shows that municipal politics is highly dependent on national political forces, governmental programs, and economic conditions. These influence the fiscal resources available to regimes, the structure of the local state (as in the change from segmented urban renewal agencies to integrated offices of community and economic development), and the mobilizing capacities of different racial and class actors. At the cost of simplification, we periodize local politics into three stages, each established by a particular type of regime and resulting mix of program choices for urban redevelopment.

Successive Types of Regimes: Directive, Concessionary, Conserving. The class character and strategic objectives of the local state have been relatively constant elements of American urban development. But its activities have changed with time, in part as a consequence of the rise and ebb of class struggle within big cities. The greater or lesser necessity for regimes to mediate among classes thus also helped define their character. Faced with mass mobilization, typical regimes had to operationalize the aims of capital under duress, and they were willing to make some tangible concessions to lower-income interests as the price for political stability.

U.S. postwar history has involved only a single interlude of mobilization by the lower classes, extending from about the mid-sixties to the mid-seventies (Huntington [1981] calls this time the Sixes and Sevens). Before 1965 urban regimes planned large-scale redevelopment, which initially was directly sponsored by the state. These governments, which we call *directive,* operated with little effective opposition. These

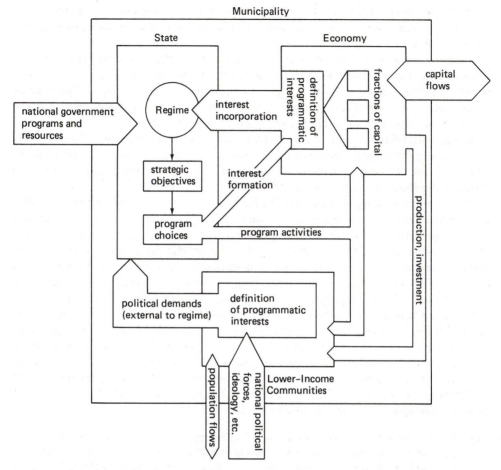

FIGURE 7.1   Interactive Elements in the Politics of Redevelopment.

were succeeded by *concessionary* regimes, which were forced by the uprisings of the sixties to be more responsive to lower-class interests than before or afterwards.

The most recent period, marked by both the counterattack of capital at all levels of the state and by the acquiesence of underclasses, witnessed the emergence of yet a third type of regime, one which better reflected lower-income interests than the governments of the 1950s, but like them was again clearly under the hegemony of capital. By now, however, the political interests of local capital had changed. It no longer sought state-directed redevelopment, in part because that process had already achieved its objectives of making the CBD suitable for investment. Rather it asked the local regime to subsidize private-market actors without involving itself in land acquisition. At the same time regimes were to maintain relations with the lower class so as to prevent another period of mobilization. This last regime type, extending from 1975 to 1981 (and perhaps beyond), was neither directive, nor concessionary, but *conserving*—conserving in the senses of being politically conservative, of trying to preserve the fiscal stability of the local state given stagnation in the national economy, and of keeping poltical arrangements which maintained social control without costing capital very much.

Table 7.1 presents a comparison of regimes employing the categories we have discussed in this section: the collective interests of the business class, popular demands, and the manner in which regimes operationalize the strategic objectives of accumulation, sociospatial segregation, and social control. Without repeating the details, it is important to discuss several aspects of the typology.

First, with relatively minor variations in dating, most larger cities with a significant minority presence fit well into the typology. Thus New Haven, Detroit, Denver, and San Francisco each had major, state-sponsored urban renewal programs which began in the 1950s, went through a period of turmoil when they became "ungovernable" in a politics Douglas Yates (1976) has called "street-fighting pluralism," and then settled down into a conserving mode in which initiative shifted to the private sector. New Orleans is the major exception among our case studies, and it is typical of some other old cities concentrated primarily in the South and Southwest. In this part of the country urban renewal was sometimes blocked either by traditional business elites (as in New Orleans), and/or by state governments opposed to the "confiscation" of private property (Texas being a case in point). Concessionary regimes proved unnecessary when the lower classes, through a combination of conservative ideological hegemony and repression, remained politically deferential (see Lupsha and Siembieda, 1977). But even in these regions the typology works more often than not. Thus the most important city of the Southeast, Atlanta, conformed quite well to our schema. Clarence Stone's description of redevelopment politics under what we would call the *directive* administration of Mayor Hartfield could just as well have applied to Detroit or San Francisco:

City officials acted, not as brokers among competing interests, but as fairly consistent promoters of CAIA [Central Atlanta Improvement Association] objectives. . . . Coalition formation, bargaining, and negotiation—far from indicating official responsiveness to the full range of citizen interests—were the very practices whereby business interests secured extraordinary control over the renewal process. (1976: 89)

In the case of blacks, city actions not only failed to encourage solidarity, they explicitly discouraged it. . . . Policy measures and administrative practices . . . were used to afford *particular benefits* to the black community in order to fragment opposition to the city's renewal program. (1976: 40, emphasis in original)

Second, common national factors external in origin to particular municipalities functioned to produce similar changes in many cities at about the same time. These account for the point of transition from directive to concessionary and finally to conserving regimes.

1. Black mobilization in the mid-sixties and retreat in the mid-seventies changed the character of political pressure and thereby of the accommodations regimes made.
2. There was a rapid expansion between 1964 and 1966 in federal programs

TABLE 7.1

Political Situation of the Local State under Typical Regimes, 1950–81

	Directive (1950–64)	Concessionary (1965–74)	Conserving (1975–81)
Collective programmatic interest of business class	Direct state intervention in built environment: expanded state activity to preserve market value and reestablish functional importance of CBD	– – – – – (continues) Protection of business from popular attack by minority groups through public/private ventures in "social responsibility" Expanded state provision of collective consumption for lower class and minority population	Functional conversion of land use and local economy through private means; state subsidies to enhance private accumulation Reduced state provision of collective consumption: reduced social outlays and privatization of services which can be profitably recommodified
Popular demands on regimes:	Political parties, interest groups, elections	– – – – – (continues)	– – – – – (continues)
Modes of expression		Political movements, protest activity, social disorder	

261

TABLE 7.1 (continued)

	Directive (1950–64)	Concessionary (1965–74)	Conserving (1975–81)
		Bureaucratic enfranchisement (citizen participation, neighborhood organizations, etc.), professional advocacy groups (legal services, welfare rights)	- - - - - - (continues)
	Emerging unions of state workers	Collective bargaining with frequent strikes	Collective bargaining with infrequent strikes
Substance of demands	Disaggregated and weak demands for improved services (especially schools) with taxpayers groups resisting	Collective and strong demands by minority groups for state jobs, social expenditures, and control over bureaucracies - - - - -	(continues, but greatly weakened, with reduced expectations; approach becomes defensive, to protect resources, conserve organizational capacities)
	Some conservative and business opposition to urban renewal	White opposition to government jobs for minorities, racial integration, and bureaucratic enfranchisement	

262

Programmatic choices for implementation of state strategic objectives:			
	Emerging minority-group pressure for racial integration	(continues, much stronger)	Taxpayer revolts (expressed through elections and referenda) become common
		Communal resistance to state-sponsored redevelopment; advocate planners challenge state schemes	Community groups, tenants press for state mediation with private developers and landlords; antigentrification, rent-control demands
		Emerging middle-class concerns for historic preservation and environmental quality	(continues, stronger)
		State workers demand expanded employment in social welfare agencies	State workers resist contraction in public employment, wage cuts
Accumulation	Urban renewal: large scale clearance of central territory; rebuild CBD as retail/office/cultural center (no coherent economic strategy); major role for state planning	(continues, but with ideas emerging late in period of urban functional conversion, corporate headquarters center, new kinds of retailing, households; emphasis still on physical environment)	Privatized physical redevelopment

Shift in programs to economic development using direct subsidies to private firms (e.g., UDAGs); limited role for state planning; |

TABLE 7.1 (continued)

Directive (1950–64)	*Concessionary* (1965–74)	*Conserving* (1975–81)
		emphasis on "public–private partnership," development coalitions, etc.
Construction of urban highways - - - - - -	(continues, but balanced by mass transit projects) - - - - - -	(transit projects continued)
	rehabilitation and neighborhood preservation - - - - - -	(continues)
		New development tools: self-contained and segregated mechanisms for financing accumulation subsidies (revenue bonds; tax increment financing; special development districts, "enterprise zones," etc.)
		Contraction of state expenditures for collective consumption; recommodification of public programs

Sociospatial segregation	State-directed displacement of lower-income and minority groups from core areas Encourages racial segregation through location of publicly supported housing, its patterns of occupancy, location of schools	– – – – (continues) State efforts to limit private housing discrimination, integrate schools, disperse publicly supported housing; most pressure on white working-class neighborhoods; many contradictions in programs, as some continue to reproduce racial segregation	– – – – Permit market forces to displace and resegregate lower-income and minority households Weakening of programs to integrate neighborhoods and schools
Social Control	Use of traditional individual material benefits, symbolic representation of class and ethnicity in regimes	– – – – (continues with better symbolic representation of minority groups) elaboration of mechanisms for bureaucratic enfranchisement: emergence of politics of bureaucratic clientelism Sharp expansion of expenditures for social consumption Publicly subsidized housing programs; some aimed at increasing home ownership among low-income and minority groups	– – – – (continues) (continues, but with more effective state domination of passive clienteles) Ideological counterattack, imposition of "fiscal crisis" definition; direct mechanisms for class control outside of regime (financial control boards)

265

TABLE 7.1 (continued)

Directive (1950–64)	*Concessionary* (1965–74)	*Conserving* (1975–81)
	Provision of state jobs to minority groups	Disciplining of state workers through layoffs
	Repression: expansion of police capabilities, penetration of radical groups - - - - -	(continues, but public visibility reduced)
		Co-production, self-help, voluntarism and tenant ownership/management substituted for state social expenditures

for social consumption (welfare, education, manpower training, housing, health care), bureaucratic enfranchisement, and racial integration (see Haveman, 1977). The sharp conservative reorientation of the national government just a decade later resulted in the imposition of block grants, reduced levels of funding, and the effective redirection of political power from racial minorities and community organizations into the hands of local regimes.

3. In the mid sixties, during a period of super economic growth and minority rebellion, relatively liberal elements in the business class established a conciliatory corporate response. By 1975, however, with stagflation and profit squeeze limiting accumulations and political order taken for granted, conservative business leaders reoriented the political stance of capital. The new, hard line worked in producing municipal fiscal crises and retrenchment by local regimes.

Third, reinforced by the continuity in federal accumulation programs, business interests in urban redevelopment remained basically the same under both directive and concessionary regimes. The emphasis was on restructuring land use through state planning and orchestration of development. While the concessionary period saw the emergence of program mixes involving more preservation and less clearance, as well as coherent strategies for the functional conversion of old cities, the role of the state remained active and central. Thus, what distinguished concessionary from directive regimes was not the mode by which accumulation objectives were operationalized, but rather the superimposition of programs offering benefits to the lower classes.

Fourth, there was a sharp break in accumulation strategies around 1975. The completion of most CBD clearance efforts, combined with the new national emphasis on enhancing the conditions of profitability, resulted in the primacy of economic development over land-use strategies. This shift had some major ramifications.

1. Capital pressed successfully for contraction in collective consumption as a prerequisite to development, realizing its dual payoffs in reducing the tax squeeze on profits and, perhaps more important, in privatizing control over land uses.

2. Within the realm of economic development the local state has relatively weak planning capacity. Economic planning is difficult at the municipal level since regional economies are fragmented by many—sometimes hundreds—of political jurisdictions. Business plays municipalities off against each other for subsidies and concessions, thereby increasing the average public subsidy to private accumulation while severely limiting the ability of even large municipalities to direct investment for socially desirable purposes. Moreover, there is little ideological and institutional support for economic planning at any level of the state. Economic development agencies function almost entirely to facilitate market-defined investment decisions, rather than to demarcate the parameters of market behavior.

3. Program mechanisms designed to facilitate development through enhanced private profitability (e.g., revenue bonds, tax-increment financing) kept the

benefits of private investment bottled up within either particular firms or within a self-contained budgetary segment devoted solely to further subsidy and accumulation. Fiscal strain on the local state remained high or increased, thereby lending support to business demands for contraction of the public sector.

4. Representation of lower-class interests in the state, won through the class struggles of the concessionary period, became limited in potential payoff as the basic conditions of material existence were increasingly determined directly by capital through market processes.

Fifth, and related to this last point, conserving regimes marked the reversal of the postwar trend of the politicization of class conflict. As the state ceased to be the direct agent of redevelopment, it became a less important target for class conflict over use of the city. This conflict was now played out in a disaggregated manner between landlords and tenants, working-class residents and gentrifiers, small shop-keepers and big developers. Even where popular forces were strongest, local regimes could claim correctly that they had only limited control over private-market actors.

Finally, the typology of regimes explicates general tendencies in the whole system of cities under evolving historical conditions. It does not in itself account for variations among cities in redevelopment outcomes at a given point in time. The next section examines how economic and political factors specific to particular cities interact to influence the program choices of local regimes and the character of urban development.

POLITICAL REPRESENTATION AND REDEVELOPMENT OUTCOMES

Regimes are limited by the specific economic context in which they find themselves, since, regardless of their aims and composition, they remain hostage to general economic forces. This is particularly true during the present period when reduced revenues limit the state sector mainly to facilitating private investment. As a consequence, political success in penetrating the regime and formulating its programs does not guarantee that represented groups will achieve desired redevelopment outcomes. While regimes can reinforce tendencies, they cannot determine their economic environment. In order, then, to spell out the logic by which the benefits of redevelopment are distributed, we must specify the components of the urban economy which affect redevelopment, then relate the economic to the political situation. By redevelopment outcomes we refer to the restructuring of the city's economy, the transformation of its physical form, and the reallocation of its population ensuing on efforts to reconstitute its built environment.

The single most important factor determining the redevelopment potential of a city is its position in the national system of cities (Harvey, 1973). As capital flows throughout the country, it seeks industries generating the highest levels of profitability. Metropolitan areas which offer the greatest investment opportunities by dint of their current economic base and labor force composition will attract investment almost regardless of local governmental efforts. Places such as San Francisco and Denver, which are centers for high-technology industry, financial and corporate headquarters, and tourism can achieve an inflow of investment capital with relative ease (Table 7.2). Cities like Detroit and New Haven, which have relied preponderantly on manufacturing and retailing for their past economic prosperity, lose heavily in the competition to attract new funds. The phenomenal difference between Detroit and Denver, reflected by a 49 percent drop in Detroit's property values and a 97 percent increase in Denver's between 1956 and 1976, reflects the respective fortunes of the automotive and energy industries. While the role of these industries in the national, and international economy, is certainly affected by state policy at the national level, it is out of the control of local regimes (See Tomaskovic-Devey and Miller, 1982).

Endogenous factors do, however, affect the relative balance of investment within metropolitan economies. The capacity of local business, as in Denver and San Francisco, to organize itself to attract outside capital and renew the downtown determines

TABLE 7.2
Changes in Estimated Value[a] of Real Property Subjected to Local Taxation, Five Cities, 1956–76

	Millions of dollars			Percentage change
	1956	*1971*	*1976*	*1956–76*
New Haven				
Current dollars	802	1,135	1,556	
Constant dollars[b]	2,414	2,298	2,240	−7
Detroit				
Current dollars	8,011	9,275	8,594	
Constant dollars[b]	24,134	18,736	12,375	−49
New Orleans				
Current dollars	1,856	3,772	6,056	
Constant dollars[b]	5,591	7,619	8,720	+56
Denver				
Current dollars	2,207	4,801	9,101	
Constant dollars[b]	6,648	9,696	13,105	+97
San Francisco				
Current dollars	6,638	10,128	19,908	
Constant dollars[b]	19,997	20,455	28,668	+43

SOURCE: Derived from U.S. Bureau of the Census, *Statistical Abstract of the United States, 1980,* Table 792; *State and Local Government Special Studies No. 92: Property Values Subject to Local General Property Taxation in the United States: 1978; Census of Governments, Taxable Property Values and Assessment/Sales Price Ratios,* Vol. 2, 1977, 1972; *Census of Governments, Taxable Property Values in the United States,* Vol. 5, 1957.

[a] Computed using assessment/price ratios for single-family housing; ratios for all property produce very similar results.
[b] Based on consumer price index normalized for 1980 current dollar = $1.00 constant.

whether investors locate within or outside the central city. New Orleans failed to take full advantage of the petro-boom that brought enormous wealth into adjacent parishes (counties) as a consequence of the traditional nature of its economic elite. New Haven, despite the presence of Yale, lacked national corporate leaders with a commitment to the city. Thus the initial existence or absence of a rooted business elite and its mobilizing capacity accounts for significant *intraregional* differences. This is particularly evident in the Northeast, where cities like Boston and Pittsburgh, in contrast to Hartford, New Haven, and Buffalo, have had considerable success in retaining corporate investment and attracting new financial and service headquarters.

A second endogenous factor which influences the attractiveness of central cities to private investment is racial and ethnic composition. Seemingly, the prerequisite for escalating investment in city centers is the absence, either preexisting or forced, of low-income inhabitants. This argument is consistent with a recent study of ten gentrifying cities, which showed a considerable reduction in the proportion of black occupancy within the "revitalizing" urban core (Spain, 1981: 19). Black-majority cities have particular difficulty in competing for private capital. Those like New Orleans that have had some success in doing so evidence extreme internal uneven development.

The local political situation constitutes a third internal factor contributing to redevelopment, even though that situation is itself dependent on outside forces. Cities which are sites for rapid inflows of private capital have a different politics from those experiencing disinvestment. Political issues in rising cities center on a class struggle for territory and control over the cost and availability of housing. Even in cities with considerable private market-created displacement, a substantial low- and moderate-income population remains. For them the level of private investment determines the potential payoff of access to the local political regime. Low-investment cities, on the other hand, are faced with a shrinking tax base, the strain of serving large lower-income areas, and the necessity to attract capital investment at any cost. Capture of the government of such a city yields relatively few rewards. The main political battles come to revolve around whose programs will be cut back first. Thus the market situation of a particular city will affect its physical development dually: directly through private investment, and indirectly through the types of political conflicts it creates and the redevelopment choices made by local government.

Potential for Counterstrategies

Our examination of regime strategies showed a number of constant elements, despite popular resistance to accumulation aims and varying degrees of success in achieving concessions. Even in the late sixties, at the peak of the concessionary model, the state pursued a redevelopment strategy that gave first priority to growth and elite domination rather than social welfare and participation. Legitimation crisis constrained state efforts to promote accumulation, but it did not transform the local state into a vehicle for neighborhood-based, bottom-up (as opposed to trickle-down) redevelopment. Potentially, however, counterstrategies exist, although they would only be adopted in the event of lower- and working-class incorporation into the regime.

An analysis of the relationship between degrees of lower- and working-class representation and levels of investment in the built environment provides an understanding of the situations which produce varying redevelopment outcomes. This approach reveals the effects of a potential counterstrategy, even though, as we have argued, clear cases of such do not exist at present in the United States. Using the dimensions of private investment and political representation, we can construct a "space" which encompasses extant and potential cases of redevelopment (Figure 7.2). For the sake of simplicity we have dichotomized market forces into extreme cases and assumed a single continuum of political representation. (The measure of representation thus includes both electoral and bureaucratic [i.e., citizen participation] components [see Fainstein and Fainstein, 1982b]). Figure 7.2 suggests how redevelopment is affected by increasingly powerful representation of lower- and working-class interests in governmental policy under conditions of weak versus strong private investment.

When representation is low, local regimes play the redevelopment game by simply equating private accumulation with the public interest. They seek to restructure central space for a service economy and new middle class. Cities in stagnant or deteriorating market situations, however, can only partially realize these objectives. The physical expression of their failure is extreme uneven development. High levels of private investment, however, do not necessarily produce greater benefits for working people, as New Orleans shows. Frequently city governments plow back the tax benefits of accumulation in new development schemes, or severely restrict tax receipts through

FIGURE 7.2   Redevelopment Tendencies and Possibilities.

Net private investment in the built environment	Low	Medium	High
High	Rebuilt and secured core area; functional conversion; displacement and gentrification; limited taxes on new development (New Orleans)	Some lower-income neighborhoods protected; services and public investment for extant population; governmental clientelism (Denver, San Francisco)	Strict controls on developers and landlords; mandated contributions as tax on development; housing and jobs programs
Low	Extreme uneven development; islands of investment in core, disintegration of lower-income neighborhoods; low services and public investment outside core	Mitigated uneven development; segment of expenditures for decaying lower-income areas; governmental clientelism (Detroit, New Haven)	Neighborhood emphasis; redistributive taxes on capital; maximum provision of public housing and services

Representation of the Interests of Low- and Moderate-Income Neighborhoods

abatements and revenue caps. They provide limited services to lower-income people and allow economic factors to play themselves out in real estate markets, as new middle-income workers bid up housing prices. When private investment is sufficiently great, uneven development disappears within an entire city, only to reappear on a metropolitan level as other jurisdictions become the recipients of displaced households.

As lower- and working-class interests are better represented, government takes a more active role in protecting neighborhoods and population groups from the ravages of either limited or large-scale private investment. In low-investment cities like New Haven and Detroit, governments, while pursuing the typical downtown-accumulation strategy, also seek to mitigate the effects of class stratification and uneven development. They create clientele systems of social-service provision whereby the resident lower classes receive tangible benefits in exchange for political acquiescence. Efforts are made at neighborhood rehabilitation, especially aimed at helping lower-income home-owners, and construction of subsidized housing. The limited fiscal capacity of these cities means, however, that all the lower classes can hope for is a regular share of a fixed or shrinking pie. The bitterly ironic result of territorial domination for low-income, minority groups is that their numbers, which permit electoral control, preclude economic growth. In Detroit and New Haven the extensiveness of the needs of the population undercuts the potential for government to attract capital to address those needs.

But if low-income populations are a principal obstacle to redevelopment in declining cities, their invisibility becomes the barrier to benefits in high-investment municipalities. Without electoral strength, low-income and minority communities are not usually able to convert even high levels of private investment into a commensurately expanded fiscal capacity and level of service expenditures. In growth cities like Denver the minority population is largely ignored; in San Francisco, where it is more politically potent, it is still too weak and divided to regulate massive private investment to its advantage. What prosperity offers low-income people in cities where they have some political and administrative representation is a degree of protection and a share of customary benefits. The government channels public investment with the objective of preserving some parts of the city as working-class neighborhoods. In San Francisco, where the conserving regime is more responsive to demands for limits on private-market activity, it controls rents, imposes taxes on business to finance lower-income housing, and regulates real estate speculation through land-use controls. But the results of partial representation resemble the effects of trade unionism on the economy: in exchange for security and material gains for a fraction of the working class, capital is allowed to have its way with the rest. And as in the case of trade unionism, if development shrinks the protected enclaves sufficiently, the loss of political power may eventually result in the end of protection altogether.

The case of high working-class representation according to the model of the socialist city (Hill, 1978: 232–37) is wholly hypothetical in the United States. It is presented to indicate the kinds of alternative regime strategies that would occcur if city government were not dominated by business interests. For declining cities the most that such a government could hope to do would be to use whatever resources it had to improve the quality of its neighborhoods, attempting as far as possible to mitigate uneven development. Such cities undoubtedly would face a bleak future, but the costs of decline would be distributed more equitably throughout the population.

In rising cities the potential is twofold. First, private investment is realized by the public sector in expanded fiscal capacity, which, in turn, makes possible a consciously redistributive pattern of public expenditures. Second, low- and moderate-income residents are strictly protected from "natural" market forces which would expel them from town. In these ways the benefits of growth can be realized not only by capital but also by the extant population of a municipality. While the combination of prosperity and working-class political dominance appears anomalous, its existence, even if unstable, in a number of European cities demonstrates that it is not a logical impossibility.

Limits on Working-Class Representation in the United States

The United States lacks regimes dominated by working-class groups with a consciously transforming ideology. There is no working-class-based political force at either the national or local level able to use electoral politics to achieve social transformation. Even in Detroit, where organized labor wields more political power than in any other American city and a black man occupies the mayor's office, redevelopment strategy conforms to the general accumulationist model, with heavy investment in downtown and residential displacement for the sake of economic development. The ability of social movements to transform urban regimes is narrow despite the highly visible increase in community mobilization that has characterized the last twenty years. In fact, certain aspects of this mobilization have proved virtually self-limiting, thereby reducing the potential effectiveness of heightened activism. Built-in limitations derive from the racial foundation of the movements of the sixties (Fainstein and Fainstein, 1974) and the neighborhood basis characterizing the "backyard revolution" (Boyte, 1980) of the seventies.

Race is an essentially divisive base on which to build a political movement. The identification of the movement for community control with black power delegitimized that movement among white people (Fainstein and Fainstein, 1976), rather than providing a common bond for equally powerless black and white communities. Friction as a consequence of racially based demands is particularly great among black and white groups that share similar economic positions (see Katznelson, 1981: 130–34). As a consequence, black-white alliances tend to be across class lines, producing coalitions between white business interests and black elected officials. These have recently occurred in Detroit, New Orleans, and other cities with black mayors (see Eisenger, 1980). Furthermore, the high proportion of Hispanics found in poor neighborhoods of many American cities does not tend to bolster minority power. In both Denver and San Francisco, despite a major Latino presence and some visible leaders drawn from this group, the Hispanic population tends to be quiescent. The brief ascendancy of the Mission Coalition Organization in San Francisco did show the potential for organizing based on Latin American ethnicity, but the organization proved to be easily coopted by the granting of jobs and funds to its leadership.

While the 1970s witnessed the decline of militant protest movements, they also encompassed the proliferation of an extensive network of community organizations that has been called the neighborhood movement. These groups fuse community organizing tactics and a participatory ideology with issue-based objectives ranging from utility-rate regulation to neighborhood revitalization. To some degree they have institutionalized themselves as a reference group for municipal regimes. But their essential pragmatism and commitment to small-scale organization (see Boyte, 1980: 97, 199) seriously limit their scope.

The European left parties, originating in the realm of economic production, are capable of linking urban social movements with electorally based administrative and legislative power. The extent to which they have actually done so varies considerably from country to country. But in the United States the highly fragmented, nonideological party system offers few possibilities for articulating the demands of locally based movements at any level of government (see Wright, 1979: 232–33). The weakness of left parties, and the bourgeois ideological hegemony that accompanies it, reduces the strategic potential of the neighborhood movement to defensive action. Vulnerable to cooptation, highly disaggregated, leadership-dominated, and episodic in intensity, neighborhood groups nevertheless remain the principal mechanism by which ordinary citizens seek to direct the trends of redevelopment. Their inability either to capture local regimes or to command investment capital, however, means that they will never be the formulators of state policy but can only react to it.

URBAN REDEVELOPMENT AND CAPITALIST CRISIS

Our analysis of urban redevelopment has sought to root local processes in both immediate circumstances and broad social forces. The theoretical approach we have employed treats the urban question—that is, the social relations defining urban life—as a focal point for the expression of certain of the contradictions of advanced capitalism (Castells, 1977). Especially as these contradictions work themselves out in uses of space, they become the factors determining redevelopment and the struggles around it. Three principal contradictions particularly affect the character of cities and the strategies used by capital and municipal regimes to cope with crises arising within the urban system.

1. Uneven development within cities, regions, and the entire country produces the economic and demographic character of particular metropolitan areas (Harvey, 1973; Perry and Watkins, 1981). The internal segregation of cities, suburban growth, and interregional competition for investment all result from the tendency of capital to seek the highest return on new investment, regardless of the impact on use values or future exchange values of already fixed investments. While uneven development profits owners of investment capital, its impact is negative for the holders of illiquid urban property and failing businesses. It is disastrous for those whose employment depends on obsolete industries or whose social benefits are supplied by the depleted fiscs of declining areas. The opportunities for speculative gain afforded by centrally located, devalorized property can redeem the fates of property owners and business

managers, but they only heighten the difficulties of low-income populations already injured by earlier disinvestment. Uneven development thus is the contradictory product of capitalist accumulation, which provides economic growth at the expense of particular places, fractions of capital, and populations.

2. Urban areas are sites for both production and consumption. Both these functions involve state intervention to provide support that capital is unwilling or unable to supply autonomously yet requires for the continuation of the accumulation process (see Hirsch, 1978). On the production side, capital requires physical infrastructure to transport goods and workers and sustain its workplaces. It needs public facilities like sports arenas and convention centers in order to create a market for its products. The character of these necessities is such that they cannot be produced by individual firms.

The reproduction and acquiescence of the labor force are likewise prerequisites for capital accumulation and realization. Since the profitability of capital depends on the rate at which it can exploit labor, wages are lower than the level needed to maintain the entire population. Individual workers cannot obtain directly from their employers wages sufficient to support themselves and dependent population groups. As a consequence of the pressure on capital to provide a higher level of social maintenance, the state intervenes and provides public services:

The process of continuous displacement of the response to class struggle by state intervention in collective consumption seems a central feature [of capitalism]. One must understand that, although displaced, this response has to do with class struggle, but also that, even if there is some response, it is not necessarily a victory in terms of working-class needs and demands. At some moments, the balance of forces may be such that the working class is able to obtain forms of socialization of consumption more adequate to its demands, but the general tendency of the capitalist state will be to displace and reshape the demand according to the dominant interests of the capitalist class, in terms of its economic interests and in terms of the search for social control. (Preteceille, 1981: 7–8; see also Gough, 1979)

State intervention does not permanently solve for capital the problem of dealing with popular demands for a higher standard of living. Whether the state is used cooptively to provide direct benefits to low-income people or as an agent of economic interest and social control, as was the case for urban renewal, it still tends to politicize questions of distribution. Once market forces no longer determine the allocation of the economic surplus, then political decision-makers become vulnerable to mass pressure within the political realm. While political mobilization of lower social strata demanding more state benefits can be tolerated by capital during expansionary times, economic difficulties reduce the leeway for concessions. The current crisis in production and the fiscal crisis of the state (O'Connor, 1973) makes collective consumption too expensive from the point of view of capital (Preteceille, 1981: 9). Indeed, high levels of collective consumption are one of the causes of present capitalist crisis (Szelenyi, 1981: 570).

3. The provision by the state of a social wage displaces class conflict from the workplace into the realm of consumption. As the specific content of controversy changes from wages and working conditions to demands for territory and services, urban social movements become the vehicle for the articulation of popular interests:

Local governments are, at the same time, the most decentralized level of the state apparatus, the most sensitive to the institutional form of class struggle, and the most receptive to the local hegemony of class segments which are in a subordinate position within the power bloc at the national level [i.e., the middle class and small business]. This explains why major social and political conflicts in advanced capitalist societies are increasingly expressed in the field of local politics. (Castells, 1981: 7)

Thus the mode by which capital seeks to disarm the working class gives rise to a new set of conflicts and new kinds of political mobilizations (Hirsch, 1981). Because urban social movements are based in the community rather than the workshop, "they permit the progressive formulation of an anti-capitalist alliance upon a much broader objective base" (Castells, 1978: 36).

While the contradictions of capitalist social relations are played out through the entire state sector, their specifically urban formulation manifests itself within the domain of the local state. The local state is embedded in the state structure of the country as a whole, but it nevertheless responds to a segmented set of interests which does not perfectly correspond to the grouping of interests at the national level. As a result, while the local state is both constrained by underlying capitalist social relations and dependent on the national state for resources, local regimes vary. Variation shows itself in the same city over time, among cities, and in the differences between the character of specific urban regimes and the national administration; it gives urban politics a particular indeterminacy. The processes of group mobilization, pressure, bargaining, and fragmented decision-making, so evident to both pluralist scholars and political actors, define the arena in which city officials interact with segments of the public. But the pluralism of regime activity is always— and heavily—restricted by the balance of class forces embodied in the overall state structure. Thus we see the phenomenon, in cities like New Haven and San Francisco, of enormously proliferated and permeable governmental institutions, multiple points of access, hyperactivity by community groups, yet predictable and biased outcomes.

Stages of Postwar Capitalism and Their Effect on Urban Redevelopment

The local state mediated the aforementioned contradictions of capital through redevelopment policies that affected the realms of both production and consumption. During the period of national economic expansion (1949–73), extreme uneven development created the plight of central cities that has come to seem the norm. The policy response was two-pronged. Cities would be made competitive with suburbs through subsidies to accumulation. Social control would be achieved through the expulsion and encapsulation of the lower classes. When population shifts and urban uprisings made ineffective social control based on territorial isolation, the still expanding economic surplus was increasingly used for cooptive social programs. The switch we described from directive to concessionary regimes could occur relatively easily because the demands of the urban poor were being made during a period of economic expansion. When the surplus was growing rapidly, provision of collective consumption was not an unbearable tax on capital. Accordingly, the transition between the first two periods of postwar redevelopment did not reflect, as did the move to the next one, a change in the general economic situation. Rather it could occur precisely because the economy had remained on the same upward trajectory.

After 1973, economic stagnation made the previous approach too costly for capital. The slump affected both government programs and productive sectors. Capital responded to diminished profits and increased international competition through a major effort to reduce the costs of production. This involved a reduction in taxation used to support state programs and a restructuring of production. The latter produced a new international division of labor based on integration through multinational corporations of production sites throughout the world (i.e., global sourcing) and rapid shifts of capital among sites (Cohen, 1981). The impact on American cities was to improve the economies of international and financial corporate centers like San Francisco while hastening the decline of manufacturing centers like Detroit.

To the extent that state policy continues significantly to affect cities, it is national economic policy that is key (Tomaskovic-Devey and Miller, 1982). Efforts to control inflation through monetarism and consequent high interest rates have stifled most major property development schemes, limiting the ability of both private and public sectors to affect the urban built environment. Tax and defense policies have rewarded those areas fortunate enough to harbor expanding high-technology industry or weapons manufacturers. Drastic cutting of the federal domestic budget has particularly injured the urban working poor and community-based, nonprofit organizations (Nathan, Dearborn, and Goldman, 1982).

Republican domination of the federal government has meant that older urban areas, tied to the Democratic Party and trade unions, do not have their interests represented in the national regime. The fractions of capital such as the construction and real estate industries that actively supported programs for urban redevelopment are not part of the coalition currently in power. Therefore, both the accumulation demands of capital in older cities and the consumption needs of the population are easily sacrificed in national policymaking.

General economic stagnation has undermined the interpretation of capitalist crisis in terms of legitimation, i.e., the threat to stability posed by lower-class uprisings. Indeed the absence of growth is more potentially threatening to regime legitimacy than unequal distribution of the surplus. For the voting majority of the population it was a decline in absolute standard of living rather than relative shares which, under the Carter administration, provoked wrath against officeholders. The remarkable success of the current regime in blaming failures of capitalist accumulation not on capitalists themselves but on low-income people permits the government to sustain its legitimacy while increasing the inequity of the tax system and cutting urban programs.[3] Thus the changed definition of capitalist crisis from legitimation to accumulation results not just from the economic failures of the system but also from the success of conservative elements in promulgating their interpretation of the situation through political leaders and having it accepted by a large part of the electorate.

At the urban level the redefined crisis has been viewed in terms of fiscal strain. Well before the Reagan administration took office, problems of cities were increasingly attributed to poor management and fiscal profligacy. The concessions of the previous period were denigrated as wasted money which had failed to erase the symptoms of low income at which they were addressed. Rather than public policy being viewed as a means to relieve poverty, it became identified as the source of difficulty:

A preliminary report by staff members of the [U.S.] Department of Housing and Urban Development . . . said Government help had contributed to urban decline and transformed local officials 'from bold leaders of self-reliant cities to wily stalkers of aid.' The report said even those cities with the worst fiscal problems could muddle through without that aid. (*New York Times*, 1982: 4E)

Implications for Urban Movements

Urban social movements, as we indicated above, have arisen in response to state intervention in the realm of consumption. Privatization (recommodification) of state activity diminishes the possibilities for these movements to form (Saunders, 1979: 125). The struggle between capital and labor is no longer displaced onto the local state but rather occurs in such inaccessible locations as the Federal Reserve Board. The prizes which can be obtained through local mobilization and the local state actions that provoked resistance both diminish.

Institutionally the consequence of the termination of many of the categorical federal programs is to return urban government to an earlier period of centralized decision-making. Block grants place responsibility for revenue allocations with the mayor and council; increased reliance on locally raised funds means a return of the city to basic housekeeping functions. The reduction in points of access as decentralized programs are terminated makes targets for neighborhood struggles highly elusive. On the other hand, the continued separation of residence from work, the low level of labor militance, and the global character of production make a revival of workplace militancy no more likely.

Cities will nevertheless continue to be centers of low-income residence with strong tendencies toward instability. Downtown redevelopment and neighborhood gentrification have created valuable new investments hostage to urban unrest. Home-ownership, long a bulwark of political equilibrium (Agnew, 1981; Harloe, 1981), is priced out of the reach of many. Thus new factors are rising from present modes of dealing with crisis that furnish the basis for further contradictions and threats to system legitimacy (Bowles and Gintis, 1982: 89).

The political situation is now indeterminate. While the national regime has so far been successful in maintaining its political support, it has been far less effective in achieving its economic ends. The state may wholly fail in its effort to redirect the economy toward greater profitability (O'Connor, 1981). The outcomes for cities of such a failure are not at all clear. The worst possibility is increasing inequality, insulation of the wealthy through heightened security measures, and the use of space to intensify a system of reservations for the poor and protected enclaves for the well-to-do. A national reversion to a Democratic regime might produce a move toward the corporatist model—more state planning, political determination of relative shares, stabilization of urban programs embodying both accumulationist and collective consumption tendencies. A resurgence of major attempts to manipulate urban space under governmental auspices seems extremely unlikely in either event.

The efforts chronicled in the redevelopment histories of the five cities described here are therefore unlikely to be repeated. While the underlying processes that have created contemporary American cities—shifts of capital, employment, and populations—continue, concerted public policy aimed at directing those processes has lapsed and shows few signs of resurgence. Since, as we have shown, much of this policy was highly biased toward capital accumulation at heavy cost to low-income people, its termination is not necessarily to be lamented. But the continuation of conserving regimes, without renewed mobilization of urban social movements, will also result in a bias against the interests of low-income people. Unregulated real estate markets and the absence of new social housing mean that renter households will face increasingly severe difficulties in finding places to live. The reduction of both governmental and nonprofit service organizations caused by contracted federal funding means that the low-income clienteles which had been routinely served by conserving regimes will fade away as organized entities, eventually losing their claims on revenues. To show that former policies were harmful does not indicate that their termination will prove beneficial. The economic and political interactions which produced urban redevelopment over the past thirty years have changed in content. Their results, however, will continue to favor the interests of capital and upper-income residents until there is an effective political force that can connect the interests of workers and urban communities in a class-conscious electoral majority.

NOTES

1. The literature on the relative autonomy of the state tends to separate the three models— structural, instrumental, and class struggle—while to us the latter two appear to be subsets of the structuralist formulation. Even if the state only does capital's bidding, it still carries out functions that capital cannot do by itself and can affect transformations that change the nature of social relations.
2. The Italian cases of municipal government under communist or socialist regimes offer the clearest instances of incorporation of oppositional elements into the state structure. In response to a decade of very high grass-roots activism and intense struggle, the two major parties of the left absorbed various aims of the extrapolitical movements. With success in municipal elections they introduced greater democracy in decision-making, a broader definition of social problems, and an active local governmental role in addressing these problems (Ceccarelli, 1982: 269).

   Within the United States there are no cities with such regimes. In Santa Monica (Shearer, 1982) an avowedly radical group of elected officials adopted strict rent-control measures and forced substantial concessions from developers. For a period the Cleveland City Planning Commission (Krumholz et al., 1975; Krumholz, 1982) explicitly promulgated a neighborhood strategy that favored redistribution over growth. In both these cases, representatives of working-class strata constituted part of the political regime rather than simply pressing on it from outside. Nevertheless, the scope of their programs and the extent to which their stands became institutionalized into the governmental structure are minimal as compared to European examples.

3. A public opinion poll conducted for *Time* magazine among a sample of registered voters found that "70% said Reagan has the right idea in trying to decrease the cost of Government" (Stacks, 1982: 38).

REFERENCES

Agnew, J. A. 1981. "Homeownership and the capitalist social order." Pp. 457–80 in Dear and Scott, 1981.

Bowles, Samuel, and Herbert Gintis. 1982. "The crisis of liberal democratic capitalism: the case of the United States." *Politics and Society* 11: 51–93.

Boyte, Harry C. 1980. *The Backyard Revolution.* Philadelphia: Temple University Press.

Castells, Manuel. 1981. "Local government, crisis, and political change." *Political Power and Social Theory* 2: 1–19.

———. 1978. *City, Class, and Power.* London: Macmillan.

———. 1977. *The Urban Question: A Marxist Approach.* Cambridge, MA: MIT Press.

Ceccarelli, Paolo. 1982. "Politics, parties, and urban movements: Western Europe." Pp. 261–76 in Fainstein and Fainstein, 1982a.

Clark, Gordon, and Michael Dear. 1981. "The state in capitalism and the capitalist state." Pp. 45–61 in Dear and Scott, 1981.

Cloward, Richard A., and Frances Fox Piven. 1974. *The Politics of Turmoil.* New York: Pantheon.

Cohen, R. B. 1981. "The new international division of labor: multinational corporations and urban hierarchy." Pp. 287–315 in Dear and Scott, 1981.

Crouch, Colin, ed. 1979. *State and Economy in Contemporary Capitalism.* New York: Saint Martin's.

David, Stephen, and Paul Kantor. 1979. "Political theory and transformations in urban budgetary arenas: the case of New York City." Pp. 183–220 in Dale Rogers Marshall, ed., *Urban Policy Making.* Beverly Hills, CA: Sage.

Dear, Michael, and Allen J. Scott, eds. 1981. *Urbanization and Urban Planning in Capitalist Society.* New York: Methuen.

Eisenger, Peter K. 1980. *The Politics of Displacement: Racial and Ethnic Transition in Three American Cities.* New York: Academic Press.

Engels, Friedrich. 1968. *The Condition of the Working Class in England.* Stanford, CA: Stanford University Press.

Fainstein, Norman I., and Susan S. Fainstein, eds. 1982a. *Urban Policy under Capitalism.* (*Urban Affairs Annual Reviews* 22.) Beverly Hills, CA: Sage.

———. 1982b. "Neighborhood enfranchisement and urban redevelopment." *Journal of Planning Education and Research,* Summer.

———. 1978. "National policy and urban development." *Social Problems* 26 (December): 125–46.

———. 1976. "The future of community control." *American Political Science Review* 70 (September): 905–23.

———. 1974. *Urban Political Movements.* Englewood Cliffs, NJ: Prentice-Hall.

Farkas, Suzanne. 1971. *Urban Lobbying.* New York: New York University Press.

Friedland, Roger, Frances Piven, and Robert Alford. 1978. "Political conflict, urban structure, and the fiscal crisis." Pp. 197–225 in D.E. Ashford, ed., *Comparing Public Policies.* Beverly Hills, CA: Sage.

Gelfand, Mark. 1975. *A Nation of Cities: The Federal Government and Urban America, 1933–1965.* New York: Oxford University Press.

Gough, Ian. 1979. *The Political Economy of the Welfare State.* London: Macmillan.

Harloe, Michael. 1981. "The recommodification of housing." Pp. 17–50 in Harloe and Lebas, 1981.

———. 1979. "Marxism, the state, and the urban question: critical notes on two recent French theories." Pp. 122–56 in Crouch, 1979.

Harloe, Michael, and Elizabeth Lebas. 1981. *City, Class, and Capital.* London: E. Arnold.

Hartz, Louis. 1955. *The Liberal Tradition in America.* New York: Harcourt, Brace and World.

Harvey, David. 1974. "Class-monopoly rent, finance capital, and the urban revolution." *Regional Studies* 8: 239–55.

———. 1973. *Social Justice and the City.* Baltimore: Johns Hopkins University Press.

Haveman, Robert. 1977. *A Decade of Federal Anti-Poverty Programs.* New York: Academic Press.

Hill, Richard Child. 1978. "Fiscal collapse and political struggle in decaying central cities in the United States." Pp. 213–40 in William K. Tabb and Larry Sawers, eds., *Marxism and the Metropolis.* New York: Oxford University Press.

Hirsch, Joachim. 1981. "The apparatus of the state, the reproduction of capital, and urban conflicts." Pp. 593–607 in Dear and Scott, 1981.

———. 1978. "The state apparatus and social reproduction: elements of a theory of the bourgeois state." Pp. 57–107 in Holloway and Picciotto, 1978.

Holloway, John, and Sol Picciotto, eds. 1978. *State and Capital: A Marxist Debate.* Austin: University of Texas Press.

Huntington, Samuel P. 1981. *American Politics: The Promise of Disharmony.* Cambridge, MA: Harvard University Press.

Katznelson, Ira. 1981. *City Trenches.* New York: Pantheon.

Krumholz, Norman. 1982. "A retrospective view of equity planning: Cleveland 1969–1979." *Journal of the American Planning Association* 48 (Spring): 163–74.

Krumholz, Norman, J. M. Cogger, and J. H. Lenner. 1975. "The Cleveland policy planning report." *Journal of the American Institute of Planners* 41 (September): 298–304.

Lebas, Elizabeth. 1981. "The new school of urban and regional research: into the second decade." Pp. ix–xxiii in Harloe and Lebas, 1981.

Lupsha, Peter, and William Siembieda. 1977. "The poverty of public services in the land of plenty." Pp. 169–90 in David Perry and Alfred Watkins, eds., *The Rise of the Sunbelt Cities.* Beverly Hills, CA: Sage.

McGrath, Dennis. 1982. "Who must leave? Alternative images of urban revitalization." *Journal of the American Planning Association* 48 (Spring): 196–204.

Mollenkopf, John. 1978. "The postwar politics of urban development." Pp. 117–52 in William K. Tabb and Larry Sawers, eds., *Marxism and the Metropolis.* New York: Oxford University Press.

Molotch, Harvey. 1980. "The city as a growth machine: toward a political economy of place." Pp. 129–50 in Harlan Hahn and Charles Levine, eds., *Urban Politics: Past, Present, and Future.* New York: Longman.

Morris, Charles. 1980. *The Cost of Good Intentions.* New York: Basic Books.

Nathan, Richard, Philip Dearborn, and Clifford Goldman. 1982. "Initial effects of the fiscal year 1982 reductions in federal domestic spending." Princeton University, mimeo, May 17.

New York Times. 1982. June 27.

O'Connor, James. 1981. "The meaning of crisis." *International Journal of Urban and Regional Research* 5 (September): 301–29.

————. 1973. *The Fiscal Crisis of the State.* New York: St. Martin's.

Perry, David D., and Alfred J. Watkins. 1981. "Contemporary dimensions of uneven development in the USA." Pp. 115–42 in Harloe and Lebas, 1981.

Peterson, Paul. 1981. *City Limits.* Chicago: University of Chicago.

Preteceille, Edmond. "Collective consumption, the state, and the crisis of capitalist society." Pp. 1–16 in Harloe and Lebas, 1981.

Saunders, Peter. 1979. *Urban Politics.* Harmondsworth, England: Penguin.

Shearer, Derek. 1982. "How the progressives won in Santa Monica." *Social Policy* 12 (Winter): 7–14.

Spain, Daphne. 1981. "A gentrification scorecard." *American Demographics,* November: 14–19.

Stacks, John F. 1982. "Reagan: looking better." *Time* 119 (June 28).

Stone, Clarence. 1976. *Economic Growth and Neighborhood Discontent.* Chapel Hill: University of North Carolina Press.

Swanstrom, Todd. 1981. "The crisis of growth politics: Cleveland, Kucinich, and the limits of local democracy." Ph.D. dissertation, Princeton University.

Szelenyi, Ivan. 1981. "The relative autonomy of the State or state mode of production?" Pp. 565–92 in Dear and Scott, 1981.

Therborn, Göran. 1980. *What Does the Ruling Class Do When It Rules?* London: Verso.

Tomaskovic-Devey, Donald, and S. M. Miller. 1982. "Recapitalization: the basic U.S. urban policy of the 1980s." Pp. 23–42 in Fainstein and Fainstein, 1982a.

Wright, Erik Olin. 1979. *Class, Crisis, and the State.* London: Verso.

Yates, Douglas. 1976. "Urban government as a policy-making system." Pp. 235–64 in Louis Masotti and Robert Lineberry, eds., *The New Urban Politics.* Cambridge, MA: Ballinger.

Epilogue

Susan S. Fainstein ·
Norman I. Fainstein

The first half of the 1980s was marked by dramatic changes in the American economy and government. The stagnant economy again entered a period of growth. At the same time, national politics and federal programs moved sharply toward the right. How should we view these events from an urban perspective? In this epilogue, we address this question briefly and in general terms. Limitations in space and in the availability of data preclude detailed examination of developments in each of our five cities. Nonetheless, the evidence leads us to believe that the trajectories we identified in 1983 have changed little, in large part because the five cities have maintained their previous positions—for better or worse—in the national economy.

CHANGE IN THE U.S. ECONOMY DURING THE 1980s

Following a severe recession during the first two Reagan years, the economy entered a period of substantial growth. Declines in GNP, real income, and employment in 1981–1982 were followed by a strong recovery, which continued into 1985. Real gross national product increased by 3.7 percent in 1983 and 6.8 percent in 1984. Per capita income in constant dollars reached an historic high in 1984, having grown 9 percent during the decade. Five million jobs were added to the economy in 1984. Although there was no way to predict whether the recovery of 1983 to 1985 was temporary, its effects on aggregate American prosperity, not to mention public opinion, were substantial. Economic growth was again viewed as a normal condition. At the local level, the growing economy produced balanced budgets and even surpluses for many state and city governments. Taxes were cut, some jobs added, and long-postponed capital improvements finally made. But growth proved unable to solve the problem of unemployment. By mid-1985, the aggregate unemployment rate still hung at around 7 percent, with much higher percentages for minority groups and central city residents. It had become apparent that the restructuring of the economy which produced growth also established a surplus labor force of considerable size concentrated in urban areas. (Data from USCEA, 1985a: tables B-2, B-24, B-29; USDHUD, 1984: 20; and USBLS, 1985: 31.)

The changing shape of the economy was expressed along several interactive dimensions. These reflected (1) shifts in production and investment among industrial sectors, (2) changes in spatial patterns, (3) reorganization of work, and (4) redistribution of jobs and income among class, race, and gender groups. During the 1980s the position of the United States in the world capitalist economy continued to move away from manufacturing production. Increasingly, its international comparative advantage lay in services, finance, and agriculture. As of June 1985, employment in manufacturing industries stood at about 19.4 million (or 20 percent of nonagricultural employment), down about 1.6 million jobs since 1979. Over the same period, service employment increased by 4.8 million jobs, while the finance, insurance, and real estate (FIRE) industries added another million (USCEA, 1985b, 1985: 14). Between 1965 and 1983, the share of national income contributed by the manufacturing sector declined by 27 percent (USBC, 1984: table 727). The United States had clearly entered a new system of production based on information processing and human interaction.

The spatial effects of sectoral transformation were felt in convergence among most regions but also in continued and probably increased inequality within regions and metropolitan areas. Except for the north central states (including especially our study city of Detroit), which continued in a nose dive, pulled down by their base in metalcrafting industries, the remainder of the Snow Belt exhibited strong signs of economic revival. Services, FIRE, and new "high-tech" manufacturing industries expanded in older manufacturing regions. Thus, between 1978 and 1983, New England showed the most growth in per capita personal income, with the Middle Atlantic states in a tie with the Southwest for second place (Conference Board, 1984). At the metropolitan level, however, economic growth was uneven. Most older cities were unable to replace their old manufacturing bases. New manufacturing employment and the expanding service economy remained suburban phenomena. Even in places like New York—the quintessential "converting," postindustrial city—commuters got a disproportionate share of the new jobs (Tobier & Stafford, 1985). Economic transformation and growth may have stabilized urban finances, but the "new economy" was not reducing the inequality between central city and suburb or among social groups.

Economic transformation and growth were associated with an increasing polarization of jobs. The new economy was one of relatively well-paid managers and poorly paid white-collar proletarians. Women and minorities fell disproportionately into the latter category. Although the causes of this distribution in job quality remain open, its existence has been widely recognized (see Lawrence, 1984). If we divide jobs into three categories according to their wage level (controlled for inflation), we find that about half the jobs added to the economy between 1970 and 1983 paid low wages. About three-quarters of these "poor" jobs went to women (Fainstein, 1985: 17). In fact, it was the inclusion of large numbers of women in the work force as low wage earners that kept America competitive with Japan and the Third World after 1970.

Growing inequality within the world of work was inevitably reflected in the distribution of income. The Gini coefficient, which measures inequality in the distribution of income, increased by almost 9 percent between 1970 and 1983. Over the same period, the income share of the poorest fifth of the population declined 13 percent (USBC, 1985: table 17). Data on poverty showed a similar trend. According to the restrictive official government definition, the percentage of Americans below the poverty line increased from 11.4 percent in 1978 to 15.2 percent in 1983, at which time 36 percent of blacks and 29 percent of Hispanics were in poverty (USBC, 1984: table 758). Significantly, rapid economic growth in 1984 only minimally affected poverty, reducing the rate by about one percentage point.

Interracial inequality also grew worse. In mid-1985, black adult unemployment stood at 13 percent, 8 points higher than the white rate, compared with a 3-point difference in 1972. An astounding 40 percent of black teenagers were unemployed, compared to 17 percent of white youths (USBLS, 1985: 31; Fainstein, 1985: table 4). The ratio of black to white median family income declined from an already low 62 percent in 1975 to 56 percent in 1983 (USBC, 1984: 743). Because about three-quarters of all black people were concentrated in central cities and adjacent suburbs, the continued economic hardships of black Americans meant that economic benefits failed to reach much of the urban population, even in cities where economic "rebirth" and urban professional life-styles were hyped by business leaders and elected officials.

From the perspective of mid-decade, the economic situation of lower-income and minority groups looks, if anything, somewhat bleaker than it did a few years earlier. It is now apparent that the urban impacts of a growing national economy correspond to those of the economy in stagnation—as it was in the seventies. Growth seems to be predicated upon the generation of new inequalities that exacerbate the already large differences among classes and races. When previously declining cities undergo conversion to a service economy, upper-income gentrifiers inevitably cut into what is usually an inadequate supply of housing. Instead of expanded fiscal resources being channeled into low-cost housing and better schools for the resident population, these resources are largely used to subsidize further private investment. As a result, poor people in economically "successful" cities find themselves squeezed in the housing market and unable to capture their share of good new jobs. For most of them, the alternatives to the unemployment of economic recessions and declining cities are usually poorly paid jobs in glamorous industries—orderlies in hospitals, maids in hotels, CRT operators in world-renowned banks. Economic growth, even while calming the political nerves, has exacerbated inequalities. Central cities have continued to be the exploiters of the poor, especially of minority and female-headed households.

If the expansionary period that began in 1983 proves short-lived, the economic inequality that has increased during relatively good ti nes may contribute to significant urban political conflict when the economy turns sour. Durir.g the sixties, active federal intervention in cities established a template that shaped local conflict in similar ways everywhere but the Deep South. Now regional economic diversity has declined sharply. But at the same time, national urban programs under Reagan have been sharply curtailed. As a result, local and national politics have become increasingly disconnected, and local political situations have become more diverse within all regions of the country. To the extent that local political determinants take on greater importance in structuring conflict, the next period of upheaval will be less clearly patterned than the last, yet perhaps no less severe.

THE POLITICAL CHARACTER OF THE PRESENT PERIOD

Under the Reagan administration, governmental intervention in urban redevelopment became more and more dependent on state and local initiatives, as the federal government increasingly reduced its level of activity. The administration explicitly stated that programs aimed directly at improving the urban condition were ineffective and had to be replaced by general efforts at economic development:

The foundation for the Administration's urban policy is the Economic Recovery Program . . . comprising tax cuts, reduction in the rate of government spending, regulatory relief, and monetary restraint . . . . Urban areas and the people living there will benefit from a healthy national economy that provides jobs and leads to an adequate local tax base. (USDHUD, 1982: 1)

Economic crisis, and urban crisis along with it, came to be defined entirely as a failure of growth. To the extent that the distribution of resources was seen as undesirable, it was because the tax system took away too much income from potential investors. Neither class nor regional inequalities were regarded as problems requiring federal remedy. Rather, overcoming economic stagnation demanded the transfer of additional resources to those economic sectors that would contribute to economic expansion. In conformity with this diagnosis, the administration sought to enlarge private sector profitability, and thereby economic growth, through a set of interrelated measures: (1) restructuring of public finance and expenditure to increase regressivity on both sides of the ledger; (2) direct governmental mobilization of capital through vastly increased defense budgets; (3) lowering of social welfare benefits with a consequent downward pressure on private sector wages; and (4) reduction of regulatory costs to business.

The funding of the Community Development Block Grant (CDBG) and federal housing assistance programs demonstrated the extent to which the federal government moved away from urban-oriented activities. While Congress successfully resisted the administration's efforts to curtail these programs even more drastically, they nevertheless fell to virtually inconsequential levels. In constant (1984) dollars, CDBG was reduced from $4.9 billion in 1980 to $3.9 billion in 1984 (USBC, 1984: table 443). The number of newly assisted households receiving a federal housing subsidy fell from an annual average of about 300,000 for the 1976 to 1980 period to 100,000 for the 1981 to 1984 period (Palmer & Sawhill, 372). New construction under Section 8 of the Housing Act was eliminated. Reagan's major urban initiative, the enterprise zone, did not receive congressional approval. Because the enterprise zone would provide federal tax benefits to investors in depressed urban areas, it contradicted the administration's tax restructuring program, which aimed at eliminating tax subsidies for local real estate investments. For this reason, it was never pushed very hard by the president.

The reduction in federal programs caused cities with active redevelopment programs to rely ever more heavily on private sector financing for redevelopment. This meant greater resort to revenue bonds, tax abatement, and tax increment financing, thereby restraining future state and local fiscal capacity. Reduced fiscal support and the termination of detailed guidelines and reporting requirements under CDBG meant that federal programs largely ceased to determine the character of local development efforts. Consequently, we can presume an increase in intercity variation in the allocation of redevelopment funding between downtown and neighborhoods, rehabilitation and new construction, poor and middle-income people, industry and housing. The lack of federal reporting requirements, however, means that the data necessary to map these variations is largely lacking.

It is therefore difficult to determine whether the Reagan administration has been midwife of a conservative period in American urban politics qualitatively distinct from the one that preceded it. Historically, the character of local regimes has been closely linked to national politics and programs: the concessionary period, although precipitated by urban social movements, occurred when there was a liberal regime in Washington; the conserving period began during a national administration that sought to roll back the Great Society programs. Although Reagan's intention of limiting federal urban programs did not represent a sharp change of direction from preceding administrations, the scale of his efforts considerably exceeded past endeavors.

Nevertheless, it is not clear that the transformation of the federal role has greatly influenced the nature of local regimes. Four of the five cities studied (New Haven, Detroit, New Orleans, and San Francisco) have reelected the same liberal mayors, who have changed little in their policy directions. In fact, in San Francisco, Mayor Feinstein, in part to block passage of even more radical legislation, sponsored an ordinance drastically limiting new commercial construction. The fifth city (Denver) chose a Hispanic candidate over the incumbent in its most recent election. Philadelphia replaced its white, "law and order" chief executive with a black man; and Boston selected a mayor with overtly progressive leanings who campaigned on his commitment to residential neighborhoods. Only New York, of the country's major cities, continued to be led by a mayor who did not rely on minority groups as a major element of his electoral coalition. He presided, nevertheless, over a governmental system with a heavy commitment to public expenditures, active redevelopment and rehabilitation programs, and a tax foreclosure program (the "in rem housing program") that continually added housing units to the publicly owned stock.

The stability of relatively liberal local regimes, along with Congress's refusal to cut grant-in-aid programs as extensively as the administration desired, has protected preexisting social and community development efforts. In addition, state governments have increased their urban development activities. They have assumed the role of sponsoring construction activity through extensive use of industrial revenue bonds, providing a de facto national industrial policy in the absence of federal initiatives. The benefits of these programs, which depend on federal tax exemption for their reduced interest rate, have been distributed indiscriminately and do not specifically benefit urban residents. Nevertheless, while most state programs constitute pure subsidies to industry and developers, some have been dedicated to improving neighborhood and minority business opportunities and providing low-income housing. For example, New York State has supported neighborhood economic development corporations that frequently play a low-keyed advocacy role on behalf of residents and small businesses and have produced visible improvements in the quality of neighborhood shopping areas.

Perhaps surprisingly, neither the sharp economic downturn of the early Reagan years nor the economic surge that began in 1983 produced much political turbulence among mass constituencies within American cities. If the recession of 1981–1982 created lassitude, the subsequent recovery did not raise expectations and foment militant consciousness. Nor so far has the restructuring of the economy generated new social movements. While recent shifts in the economy have produced new potential action groups, several factors have prevented them from identifying and acting on their common interests.

1. The massive entry of women into the labor force masked male unemployment and reduced wages by maintaining family incomes. Moreover, the reduction of male blue-collar employment and increase in female white-collar work meant that an increasing proportion of the workforce was in occupational categories traditionally hard to mobilize.

2. As has been the case throughout the century, ethnic and racial divisions have restricted working-class solidarity. New immigration, particularly the recruitment of illegal immigrants into the worst jobs, has made mobilizing low-income people more difficult.

3. Conservatives have succeeded in developing an ideology in which individuals are seen as the victims of clumsy and misguided governmental programs who are to be saved by private-sector initiatives. Their opponents have not been able to generate a counter-ideology that specifies a villain and offers a path of redemption.

While neighborhood organizations have continued to be an important basis for collective mobilization, they nevertheless suffer from their isolation and limited resources. Without an overarching ideology, as was black power during the concessionary period, or a national left political party, as exists in Europe, they are unable to call forth major concessions from government. But they still provide the constituencies that keep conserving (as opposed to conservative) local regimes in office.

Consequently, we have witnessed a shift from the situation that prevailed from the beginning of the New Deal to the end of the Johnson administration, when the federal government was tied to more liberal constituencies than were local regimes. Then the importance of the union movement and other welfare-oriented, nationally organized interest groups caused liberals to urge federal intervention in local policies. Now, as economic restructuring has further weakened labor and right-wing political action committees have become increasingly influential nationally, the locality has become the locus of resistance to sweeping cutbacks and the source of what few policy initiatives exist toward redistribution in favor of those least well off. Thus, while the process of urban restructuring proved very costly to low-income people, they nevertheless managed to retain a political influence within the transformed city that has allowed them to hold on to some of the concessions granted them earlier and to use urban regimes to buffer them from the full impact of national policies.

REFERENCES

The Conference Board. 1984. "Regional and state personal income." *Economic Road Maps* 1982–1983, October.

Fainstein, Norman. 1985. "The continued significance of race in the economic situation of black Americans." Paper presented at a conference on Racial Minorities, Economic Restructuring, and Urban Decline, sponsored by the Centre for Research in Ethnic Relations, University of Warwick, Coventry, England, September.

Lawrence, Robert. 1984. "Sectoral shifts and the size of the middle class." *The Brookings Review* (fall): 3–11.

Palmer, John L., and Isabel V. Sawhill, eds. 1984. *The Reagan Record*. Cambridge, MA: Ballinger.

Tobier, Emanuel, with Walter Stafford. 1986. "People and income." Pp. 54–86 in Charles Brecher and Raymond Horton, eds., *Setting Municipal Priorities*. New York: New York University Press.

United States Bureau of Labor Statistics (USBLS). 1985. *Employment and Earnings*, June.

United States Bureau of the Census (USBC). 1985. *Current Population Reports*, series P-60, no. 146. Washington, D.C.: U.S. Government Printing Office.

———. 1984. *Statistical Abstract of the United States, 1985*. Washington, D.C.: U.S. Government Printing Office.

United States Council of Economic Advisers (USCEA). 1985a. *Annual Report* (included in the *Economic Report of the President*).

———. 1985b. *Economic Indicators*. Prepared for the Joint Economic Committee of the U.S. Congress, July.

United States Department of Housing and Urban Development (USDHUD). 1984. *The President's National Urban Policy Report, 1984*. Washington, D.C.: U.S. Government Printing Office.

———. 1982. *The President's National Urban Policy Report, 1982*. Washington, D.C.: U.S. Government Printing Office.

Index

Abbott, Carl, 198
Abravanel, Martin D., 131
Adams, Melvin, 46
AFRA (Anti-Recession Fiscal Assistance), 152–153
Air pollution (Denver, Colorado), 187–190
Alamo Square project (San Francisco, California), 235
Albuquerque, New Mexico, 173, 174
Alioto, Joseph, 213, 214, 220, 221
Almonaster Industrial District (New Orleans, Louisiana), 148, 158
American Independence Movement, 53
Anti-Recession Fiscal Assistance (see AFRA)
Appleby, L. Thomas, 27
Astrodome (Houston, Texas), 135
Atlanta, Georgia, 142, 151, 152, 153, 177, 195, 260
Automobile industry, 83–85, 113–116, 121 (also see name of individual automobile corporation)

BAC (Bay Area Council) (San Francisco, California), 216
Barbieri, Arthur, 37, 54
BART (Bay Area Rapid Transit), 211, 216, 218, 222, 257
Baton Rouge, Louisiana, 129, 162
Battered Women, Project for (New Haven, Connecticut), 70

Bay Area Council (see BAC)
Bay Area Rapid Transit (see BART)
Bayview-Hunters Point (BVHP) Joint Housing Committee (San Francisco, California), 234, 237
Beckham, William, 107
Belle Isle Regional Arts Center (Detroit, Michigan), 112
Big Three (see name of individual automobile corporation)
Black Coalition (New Haven, Connecticut), 53
Black Panther Party, 53
Blumenthal, Michael, 107
Blythe-Zellerbach Committee (San Francisco, California), 218
Boettcher, Claude, 178
Boggs, Hale, 137
Bombach, Richard O., 137
"Boosterism" (see Denver, Colorado)
Borah, William E., 137
Boston, Massachusetts, 32, 177, 188, 198, 211, 270
Breckenfeld, Curney, 148
Bridgeport, Connecticut, 30, 32
Brookings Institution, 131
Brown Cloud (see air pollution)
Buffalo, New York, 131, 270
Bureaucratic enfranchisement (see enfranchisement, bureaucratic)
Burroughs Corporation, 104

CAC (Citizens Action Commission) (New Haven, Connecticut), 38–39
CADD (core area development district) (New Orleans, Louisiana), 139, 141, 142
Cadillac Center (Detroit, Michigan), 104, 121
California Community Redevelopment Law, 223
Calogero, Pascal, 136
Cameron, J. Robert, 184
Canadian interests in Denver, 183–184
Canal Place project (New Orleans, Louisiana), 141–142
Canizaro, Joseph, 141
Capitalism, 21–22, 80, 97, 109, 148, 160, 245, 247, 252, 257, 258, 267
    stages of and implications for urban development, 274–279
    (also see government, role of, in urban development; and institutions, role of)
CAPs (Community Action Programs), 18, 21–22, 23, 56
Carter (Jimmy) administration, 18–19, 36, 56, 64, 107–108, 145, 156, 212, 277
Castells, Manuel, 148, 207
Cavanagh, Jerome, 95
CBD (central business district), 19, 248, 249, 253, 254, 255, 259, 267 (also see names of individual cities)
CCs (central cities), 2–3, 16, 208, 270
    demography of, 5–13
    social economy of, 4–5, 6
    (also see CBD; and name of individual city)
CCCD (Citizens Committee on Community Development (San Francisco, California), 213, 227–229, 235, 236, 237, 238, 242
CCF (Citizens for Colorado's Future), 176
CCHO (Council of Community Housing Organizations), 232, 236–237, 242
CD (community development program), 64–65, 181, 185, 198, 249 (also see name of individual city)
CDA (see Community Development Agency, Denver, Colorado)
CDBG (Community Development Block Grant), 18, 19, 21–22, 66, 67, 104, 249, 278 (also see HCDA; and name of individual city)
CDCs (community development corporations), 20
    (also see name of individual corporation)
Celentano administration (New Haven, Connecticut), 37
Central Area Committee (New Orleans, Louisiana), 137
Central Functions Area project (Detroit, Michigan), 104, 113, 116, 120

Central Industrial Park project (Detroit, Michigan), 111
Central Pacific Railroad, 172
CETA (Comprehensive Employment Training Act), 56, 67, 121
    New Orleans, Louisiana, and the, 152–153, 157
Cheyenne, Wyoming, 171–172, 173, 174
Chicago, Illinois, 171, 195, 205, 213
Chinatown project (San Francisco, California), 221
Chronicle (San Francisco, California), 217, 223
Chrysler Corporation, 82, 85, 92, 97, 99, 109, 110
Church Street project (New Haven, Connecticut), 39–40, 41–44
Cincinnati, Ohio, 198
Cisler, Walker, 119
Citizens Action Commission (see CAC)
Citizens Committee on Community Development (see CCCD)
Citizens for Colorado's Future (see CCF)
Citizens United Against Poverty (CUAP) (San Francisco, California), 220
Civic Center (New Orleans, Louisiana), 134
Class conflict, 257–258 (also see community participation in urban development; displacement; gentrification; minorities; racial unrest; and names of individual cities)
Clean Air Act (1970), 189
Cleveland, Ohio, 75, 131, 171, 205, 258, 279
Coalition of Concerned Citizens (New Haven, Connecticut), 55
Cockrel, Ken, 112, 113
Collins, Margaret, 161
Community Action Program (see CAPs)
Community Development Agency (CDA) (Denver, Colorado), 182, 184–185, 198
Community Development Block Grant (see CDBG)
Community development corporations (see CDCs)
Community Development, Office of (New Haven, Connecticut), 66
Community Development, Office of (OCD) (San Francisco, California), 213, 214, 227–228, 236, 237, 238
Community Improvement Agency (New Orleans, Louisiana), 139
Community participation in urban development, 21–22, 56, 254, 271 (also see name of individual city and development project)
Community Progress, Incorporated (see CPI)
Community Renewal Program (Detroit, Michigan), 95

Community Services Administration (*see* CSA)
Comprehensive Employment and Training Act (*see* CETA)
Congress of Racial Equality (*see* CORE)
"Conserving clientelism," 36, 55–75
Convention and Exhibition Center, New Orleans, 144
Coplin, Sherman, 136
CORE (Congress of Racial Equality), 53, 219
Core area development district (*see* CADD)
Corktown (Detroit, Michigan), 94
Corporate center strategy (Detroit, Michigan), 102–113, 116, 117
Council of Community Housing Organizations (*see* CCHO)
CPI (Community Progress, Incorporated) (New Haven, Connecticut), 27–29, 50–52, 53–54, 56
Crouch, Colin, 247
CSA (Community Services Administration), 237
CUAP (*see* Citizens United Against Poverty)
Currigan, Tom, 175

Dahl, Robert, 29, 34–35, 40, 72
Dallas, Texas, 131, 132, 177
DARE (Detroit Alliance for a Rational Economy), 112–113, 118
Day, William, 119
DDI (*see* Downtown Denver, Incorporated)
Dearborn, Michigan, 85, 86, 92, 93
Democrataic Party, 36, 37, 67, 96, 107, 212–213, 248–249, 254, 277, 278–279 (*also see* name of individual president)
Demography in central cities, 5–13 (*also see* names of individual cities)
Demonstration Cities Act (1966) (*see* Model Cities program)
Denver, Colorado, 61, 66, 131, 132, Chapter 5 *passim* (167–201), 204, 228, 247, 250, 269
air pollution in, 187–190
CBD (downtown) of, 171, 177–186, 195–196
community participation in decisions about urban renewal in, 184–186
demography of, 169–171, 187, 195
displacement in, 179, 183, 198
employment in, 169, 171, 186
gentrification in, 197–198
growth of, 169–177, 190–194, 195–199
housing in, 181–182
minorities in, 196, 198, 260, 272, 273
social economy of, 6–13, 32
suburbanization and, 169, 186–187, 190–194, 195

tourism in, 172 (*also see* Olympics, Winter)
transportation in, 171–172, 173 (*also see* air pollution)
(*also see* Lamm, Richard; DURA; Western individualism; and name of individual development project)
Denver Federal Center, 172–173
Denver Post, 176, 178, 180, 189, 190, 193
Denver Regional Council of Governments, 186
Denver Tech Center, 169, 186
Denver Urban Renewal Authority (*see* DURA)
Denver Water Board, 186–187
Detroit, Michigan, Chapter 2 *passim* (80–125), 131, 153, 204, 217, 252, 269, 272, 273, 277
automobile industry in, 83–85, 113–116, 121, 253
CBD of, 82, 88, 91, 104, 115, 116, 120
community participation in decisions about urban renewal in, 91–98 (*also see* DARE)
corporate-center strategy in, 102–113, 116, 117
demography of, 80, 83, 88, 91, 93, 98–99, 116, 205
displacement in, 94–95, 113, 273
economic/fiscal policies of, 99–102, 109, 110
employment in, 83, 92–94, 98–102, 108–109, 111, 113, 115, 120, 121, 167 (*also see* automobile industry and name of individual automobile corporation)
gentrification in, 116–117
housing in, 95, 249
HUD and, 102, 107–108, 110
minorities in, 22, 92–93, 96, 106–107, 108–109, 249, 260
public services in, 111–113
social economy of, 6–13
suburbanization and, 85–89, 91, 92–94, 115
transportation in, 80, 88
UDAG and, 102, 110, 121
(*also see* New Detroit Committee; Young, Coleman; Chrysler Corporation; General Motors Corporation, Ford Motor Corporation; and name of individual redevelopment project)
Detroit Alliance for a Rational Economy (*see* DARE)
Detroit Plan, 94, 119
Detroit, Port of, project, 104
Detroit Renaissance, 98, 105, 112, 113, 116–117, 250
Diamond Heights project (San Francisco, California), 222, 223–224
Dilieto administration (New Haven, Connecticut), 44, 67

Displacement, federal urban renewal policies
    about, 17, 18, 20 (*also see* name of individ-
    ual city)
Dixwell project (New Haven, Connecticut), 41,
    46–47, 48–49, 52, 70, 77
Dock Board, New Orleans, 143, 144
Domhoff, William, 39
Dorsett, Lyle, 175, 190
Downs, Anthony, 66
Downtown area (*see* CBD; CCs; and name of
    individual city)
Downtown Council in New Haven, 257
Downtown Denver Improvement Association,
    178–179
Downtown Denver, Incorporated (DDI), 178,
    180, 190
Downtown Development Authority (Detroit,
    Michigan), 110
Downtown New Haven, 73
Dudelzak, Steve, 184
DURA (Denver Urban Renewal Authority),
    178–179, 180–184, 185, 190
Dwight neighborhood (New Haven, Connecti-
    cut), 41, 47, 48–49, 53, 77

Economic Development Administration
    (EDA), 19, 102, 118, 145, 154
Economic Development Corporation of Great-
    er Detroit, 97, 103, 110, 120, 121
Economic development corporations (*see* EDCs
    and name of individual corporation)
Economic Development Planning Unit (New
    Orleans, Louisiana), 145
Economic Development, Office of (New Ha-
    ven, Connecticut), 62
Economic Development, Office of (New Orle-
    ans, Louisiana), 147–148, 154
Economic/fiscal policies (*see* government, role
    of, in urban development; and names of
    individual cities)
Economic Growth Corporation (Detroit, Michi-
    gan), 110, 121
Economic Opportunity Act (1964), 17–18, 219–
    220
Economic Opportunity Council (EOC) (San
    Francisco, California), 220
Economic Opportunity, Office of, (OEO), 52,
    54
EDA (*see* Economic Development Administra-
    tion)
EDCs (economic development corporations),
    20, 103, 118 (*also see* name of individual
    corporation)
Educational crisis in New Orleans, Louisiana,
    131, 148–150, 157

Edwards, Edwin, 135, 136
Eisenhower (Dwight D.) administration,
    173
Employment (*see* name of individual city)
Enfranchisement, bureaucratic, 21–22, 23, 53–
    55, 66, 67, 75, 76
Engels, Friedrich, 252
Enterprise zones, 20, 118
Environmentalism (*see* air pollution)
Environmental Protection Agency (EPA), 189–
    190
Equal Opportunity Act (1964), 21
Evans, John, 178
Examiner (San Francisco, California), 217,
    223
Executive-centered coalition (New Haven,
    Connecticut), 35, 36–52, 54, 72

FACE (Federally Assisted Code Enforcement),
    235
Fair Haven (New Haven, Connecticut), 47, 55,
    60, 77
Fair Haven Project Area Committee (*see*
    FHPAC)
Faucheux, Ronald, 158, 159
Federal Home Loan Bank, 232
Federal Housing Administration (*see* FHA)
Federally Assisted Code Enforcement (*see*
    FACE)
Federal Reserve Board, 278
Feinstein, Dianne, 214, 239
FHA (Federal Housing Authority), mortgage
    guarantee programs of the, 15–16
FHPAC (Fair Haven Project Area Committee)
    (New Haven, Connecticut), 60, 66
Fiscal/economic policies (*see* government, role
    of, in urban development; and names of
    individual cities)
Fisher, Max, 98, 119
Fitch, Robert, 121
Ford Foundation, 50, 54
Ford (Gerald R.) administration, 18, 36, 212
Ford Motor Company, 82, 85, 121, 122
Ford, Henry II, 98, 104, 106, 108, 119, 120,
    122
Forward Metro Denver Group, 174, 179
Fraser, Douglas, 107
French Quarter (New Orleans, Louisiana),
    132, 133, 134, 137, 138, 139, 140, 141, 142–
    143, 161, 247
Front Range (Denver, Colorado), 169, 191,
    193–194

G & O Manufacturing, 74, 76
Gellen, Martin, 240, 242

General Motors Corporation, 82, 85, 97, 104, 109, 110–11, 113, 121

General Revenue Sharing (*see* GRS)

General Services Administration (federal), 46, 154

Gentrification, 61, 197–198 (*also see* names of individual cities)

Giaimo, Robert, 46, 54

GM (*see* General Motors)

Goals for New Haven, 73

Golden Gateway project (San Francisco, California), 216, 217, 218, 219, 224

Golden Triangle Association, 183

Government Research, Bureau of (New Orleans, Louisiana), 152

Government (federal), role of, in urban development, 118–119, 131 Chapter 7 *passim* (245–282)
    conflict with local/state governments, 248, 249–250, 251–256
    regimes, types of, 258–268

Grass Roots Alliance (San Francisco, California), 239

Gratiot (Detroit, Michigan), 94

"Growth management program" (New Orleans, Louisiana), 139–140

GRS (General Revenue Sharing), 152–153

Guida administration (New Haven, Connecticut), 66

"Halcyon Report" (1978), 73–74

Haley, Orthea, 138

Hallman, Howard, 50

Hamden, Connecticut, 30, 33, 34

Hamilton, Wilbur, 228

Hampton Roads, Virginia, 147

Hamtramck, Michigan, 86, 91

Hannan, Philip, 137

HAP (*see* Housing Assistance Plan)

Harris, Fred, 53, 54

Hart, Gary, 189, 191

Hartford, Connecticut, 32, 270

Hartman, Chester, 218, 219, 222, 224, 238

HCDA (Housing and Community Development Act, 1974), 16, 18, 19, 55, 57, 58, 182, 184, 227 (*also see* Section 8)

HDCs (housing development corporations) (San Francisco, California), 236, 237, 238

HEAL (Louisiana State Health Educational Authority, 140

Health Educational Authority, Louisiana State (*see* HEAL)

Herman, M. Justin, 217, 248

Higgs, Barton, 147

Highland Park, Michigan, 85, 86, 91

Highways (*see* transportation)

Highway Act, National Defense (1956), 13, 173

Highway Act, (1975), 14

Hill project (New Haven, Connecticut), 47, 48–49, 52, 53, 54, 55, 61, 70, 76–77

Hispanic Junta for Progressive Action (New Haven, Connecticut), 54

Historic Preservation, President's Advisory Council on, 141–142

Home Maintenance Corporation (New Haven, Connecticut), 70

Housing, federal policies about, 15–16, 18–19 (*also see* displacement; and names of individual cities)

Housing Act (1937), 15

Housing Act (1949), 15, 16, 119, 177, 248

Housing Act (1954), 17, 37, 248

Housing and Community Development Act (1974) (*see* HCDA)

Housing and Neighborhoods project (Detroit, Michigan), 104–105

Housing and Urban Development, Department of (*see* HUD)

Housing Assistance Plan (HAP), 57, 60, 185

Housing Commission (Detroit, Michigan), 94, 95

Housing development corporations (*see* HDCs)

Housing Rehabilitation Grants Program, 182

Houston, Texas, 128, 131, 132, 138, 150, 169, 177

HUD (Housing and Urban Development, Department of), 18, 19, 64–65, 185, 278 (*also see* names of individual cities)

Hudson, Cornelius, 107

Hudson, Joseph L., Jr., 96, 119

Hughes, Gerald, 178

Human Settlement Policies (Colorado), 191–192, 193–194

Hunters Point project (San Francisco, California), 220, 221, 225, 229, 233, 234

Hyatt Corporation, 136

ICBIF (Inner City Business Improvement Forum) (Detroit, Michigan), 97

Illinois Central Railroad, 136

India Basin Industrial Park, 229

Industrial Corridors project (Detroit, Michigan), 104, 120

Inner City Business Improvement Forum (*see* ICBIF)

Institutions, role of,
    in New Haven, Connecticut, urban development, 36, 37, 55, 67
    in San Francisco, California, urban development, 211–214, 226, 231, 241

Jacobs, Allan B., 235
James, Franklin, 5
Japanese Cultural and Trade Center (San Francisco, California), 217, 218
Jefferson Parish, Louisiana, 128, 133
Johnson (Lyndon B.) administration, 17–18, 76, 173, 180
Johnson, Ed, 173
Jones, James, 134–135, 136
Judd, Dennis R., 161, 163

Kabacoff, Lester, 143
Kansas City, Kansas, 195
Kansas Pacific Railroad, 172
Kemp-Garcia urban enterprise zone proposal, 118
Kennedy (John F.) administration, 50
    antipoverty programs and the, 17–18, 94–95
    New Haven, Connecticut, and the, 38, 76
Koch, Edward, 252
Krumholz, Norman, 75

Lafayette, Louisiana, 128
Lamb, Charles, 238
Lamm, Richard, 174, 177, 181, 184, 189, 191, 192, 193
Landrieu, Moon, Chapter 4 passim (126–166)
Lasalle Properties, 136
Latino Youth Development (New Haven, Connecticut), 70
Lee, Richard, Chapter 2 passim (27–79)
    CPI and, 50–51, 54
    executive-centered coalition, 36–52
Legal Assistance (New Haven, Connecticut), 70
Livonia, Michigan, 92, 93
Local Community Action Programs (see CAPs)
Local Public Works Program (LPW), 152–153
Logue, Edward, 27, 37–38, 41, 46, 50, 248
Logue, Frank, 53, 56, 66, 67, 70
Long Wharf project (New Haven, Connecticut), 44–46
Los Angeles, California, 177, 188
Love, John, 175
Lowry Air Force Base, 172
Luria, Dan, 119

MAC [see Mayor's Advisory Council (Denver, Colorado)]
Macomb County, Michigan, 115
"Managed growth" (see New Orleans, Louisiana)
Mancini, Paul K., 131
Mandell, Lewis, 120
Mardi Gras (New Orleans, Louisiana), 132–133, 158

Martin Marietta Aerospace Center (New Orleans, Louisiana), 147
Mauk, Guy, 193
Mayor's Advisory Council (MAC) (Denver, Colorado), 185–186
McElvenny, Ralph, 119–120
MCO (Mission Coalition Organization) (San Francisco, California), 221, 273
MESBIC (Minority Enterprise Small Business Investment), 236
Metropolitan Fund, Inc. (Detroit, Michigan), 96
Mexico City, Mexico, 188
Miami, Florida, 160
Michener, James, 174
Milford, Connecticut, 33
Military and Denver, Colorado, 172
Milk, Harvey, 214, 215
Millender Center (Detroit, Michigan), 110
Minorities, 14, 248–249, 253, 260, 270, 272, 273
    (also see displacement; community participation in urban development; demography; and names of individual cities)
Minority Enterprise Small Business Investment (see MESBIC)
Mission Coalition Organization (see MCO)
Mission Council on Redevelopment (San Francisco, California), 220–221
Mission District project, 220–221, 222, 236
Mobile, Alabama, 147
Model Cities program (Demonstration Cities Act of 1966), 18, 20, 21–22, 95, 249
    New Haven, Connecticut, and the, 49, 52, 53–55, 57, 63, 77
    San Francisco, California, and the, 213, 220–221, 230, 234
Model Neighborhoods (San Francisco, California), 213, 220, 221, 226, 229 (also see Hunters Point project; Mission District project)
Morial, Ernest, Chapter 4 passim (126–166)
Morrison, deLesseps (Chep), 134–135
Moscone, George, 214
Moses, Robert, 137, 217
Mountain States Legal Foundation, 189
Murchinson, Clinton, 147

"National center strategy," 121
National Citizens Monitoring Project, 237
National Urban Coalition, 119
Neighborhood Corporation (New Haven, Connecticut), 66
Neighborhood Development, 249
Neighborhood Housing Inc. (New Haven, Connecticut), 66
Neighborhood Improvement (New Haven, Connecticut), 50

Neighborhood Planning Team (New Haven, Connecticut), 66
New Detroit Committee, 96–97, 98, 119, 120, 250
New Haven, Connecticut, Chapter 2 *passim* (27–79), 132, 204, 214, 249, 250, 252–253, 254, 269, 270, 272, 276
 bureaucratic enfranchisement in, 21–22, 23, 53–55, 66, 67, 75, 76
 CBD of, 3, 14, 29, 33, 40–41, 44, 46, 47, 73
 CDBG and, 35–36, 55–66, 71, 74
 community development programs of, 21–22, 57, 58–66, 67, 70–71
 community participation in urban development of, 38, 41, 49, 51, 53–54, 66–75
 "conserving clientelism" in, 36, 55–75
 demography of, 30–32
 displacement in, 39–40, 41, 44, 45, 46, 49, 51, 254
 employment in, 33, 38, 167
 executive-centered coalition in, 35, 36–52, 54, 72
 financial impacts of urban development in, 49–50
 housing in, 47–49, 56–57, 60–61 (*also see* displacement; Dixwell project; Dwight project)
 HUD and, 54, 57, 60, 64, 71, 76
 institutions, role of, in urban development in, 66–75
 minorities in, 29, 30–32, 48–49, 52–53, 67, 260
 public services in, 63–64
 social economy of, 6–13, 32–34, 63
 "street fighting pluralism" in, 35–36, 52–55, 66, 260
 transportation in, 37, 39, 44–45 (*also see* Oak Street connector project; and Church Street project)
 (*also see* Model Cities program; CPI; Redevelopment Agency; Yale University; Lee, Richard; and names of individual redevelopment projects)
New Haven Register, 54, 74
New Orleans, Louisiana, Chapter 4 *passim* (126–166), 245, 247, 250, 257, 260, 271, 273
 CBD (downtown) of, 130–134, 135, 138, 139–144, 150, 154, 159, 161–162
 CDBG and, 152–153, 157
 community participation in urban redevelopment in, 158–159 (*also see* names of individual project)
 crime in, 126, 158–159, 161
 demography of, 128–129, 144–145
 displacement in, 138, 156, 161
 economic/fiscal policies of, 145–148, 150–154

 employment in, 129–130, 144–148, 160, 162–163, 167
 gentrification in, 156–157, 161
 housing in, 247
 HUD and, 141–142, 145
 minorities in, 22, 130–131, 136, 138, 143, 158–159, 160, 270 (*also see* educational crisis)
 petrochemical industry in, 129, 130, 142–143, 270
 public services in, 154–156, 157
 Reagan administration and, 150, 156, 157, 160, 162
 social economy of, 6–13
 suburbanization and, 128–132
 tourism in, 126, 159–161 (*also see* Superdome; and World's Fair, 1984)
 transportation in (*see* Riverfront Expressway and Bridge Controversy)
 UDAG and, 144, 152, 154 (*also see* French Quarter; educational crisis; Landrieu, Moon; Morial, Ernest; and names of individual redevelopment projects)
New Orleans Citywide Development Corporation (*see* NOCDC)
New Orleans, University of, 150
New York, New York, 5, 147, 171, 205, 258
Newark, New Jersey, 131, 153
Newhallville (New Haven, Connecticut), 47, 48–49, 52, 55, 77
Newton, J. Quigg, Jr., 167, 178
Nicholson, Will, 173
Nixon (Richard) administration, 16, 18, 23, 56–57, 76, 137, 212

Oakland, California, 207, 211, 232, 254 (*also see* San Francisco, California)
Oak Street Connector project (New Haven, Connecticut), 29, 37, 39, 40–41, 46, 53
OCD [*see* Community Development, Office of (San Francisco, California)]
O'Connor, James, 63
OEO (*see* Economic Opportunity, Office of)
Oil companies (*see* New Orleans, Louisiana)
Olympics, Winter (1976), 175–177, 191
Orleans Parish, Louisiana, 128, 129, 162
"Overall Economic Development Program" (Detroit, Michigan), 103–104

Parker, Henry, 53, 67
People-Mover System (Detroit, Michigan), 105
Petrochemical industry (*see* New Orleans, Louisiana)
Phoenix, Arizona, 169, 177
Pittsburgh, Pennsylvania, 83, 177, 270
"Poundstone Amendment," 187

Preservationists (*see* New Orleans, Louisiana, and San Francisco, California)
Private sector (*see* capitalism; executive-centered coalition; corporate center strategy; community participation in urban development; and government, role of, in urban development)
Proposition R (California), 238, 241
Proposition 13 (California), 212, 226, 238–239, 241
Public Act 87 (Michigan) (*see* "quick-take law")

"Quick-take law," 120

RA [*see* Redevelopment Agency (New Haven, Connecticut)]
Racial unrest, 2–3, 18, 22, 29, 48–49, 52–53 (*also see* minorities; and names of individual cities)
Ravitz, Justin, 113
Ravitz, Mel, 107
Reagan (Ronald) administration, 16, 18–19, 118, 237, 241, 246, 278, 279
    New Orleans, Louisiana, and the, 150, 156, 157, 160, 162
Redevelopment Agency (New Haven, Connecticut), Chapter 2 *passim* (27–79), 246
    CDBG and the, 55–66
    cost of urban renewal and the, 49–50
    discussion of, 34–37, 71–72
    enfranchisement and the, 53–55
    minority demands and the, 52
    redevelopment projects and, 40, 44, 46–49, 55
Redevelopment Agency (San Francisco, California) (*see* SFRA)
Regimes, types of, 258–268
Renaissance Center (Detroit, Michigan), 82, 104, 110, 122
Representation, political, 268–274 (*also see* community participation in urban development; and institutions, role of)
Republican Party, 36, 277 (*also see* names of individual presidents)
Ring area projects (New Haven, Connecticut), 46–49
Riverfront Expressway and Bridge project (New Orleans, Louisiana), 134, 137–139
Riverfront project (Detroit, Michigan), 104, 108, 110, 116, 120
Rocky Mountain News (Denver, Colorado), 176, 178, 189
Rohatyn, Felix, 115–116
Rotival, Maurice, 37, 39

Sagebrush Rebellion, 189
St. Louis, Missouri, 131, 171, 177, 195
Salt Lake City, Utah, 174, 195
San Franciscans for Affordable Housing (*see* SFAH)
San Francisco, California, 61, 66, 132, 139, 161, 195, Chapter 6 *passim* (202–244), 245, 247, 269, 276, 277
    Asians in, 207, 217, 218, 221
    CBD of, 211, 216, 217, 223, 225
    CDBG and, 216, 220, 221, 228, 231, 233, 234, 236, 237, 238
    community development programs of, 219–221, 227–228, 230, 233, 236
    community participation in urban renewal decisions in, 214–215, 216, 219–225, 226–231, 234, 237–238, 242, 254 (*also see* CCHO)
    demography of, 205–207
    displacement in, 217, 218, 223, 224, 225, 232, 240
    economic/fiscal policies of, 219–225, 239–240
    employment in, 167, 208, 211, 240, 241
    Hispanics in, 207, 221, 238, 273
    homosexuals in, 207, 215, 235
    housing in, 216, 218, 223, 224–225, 226, 231–238, 240, 242
    HUD and, 227, 228, 230, 232, 233, 234
    institutions, role of, in urban development in, 211–214, 226–231, 241
    minorities in, 207, 216, 219, 220–221, 226, 227, 230, 233–234, 238 (*also see* CCHO)
    social economy of, 6–13, 32
    transportation in, 217 (*also see* BART)
    (*also see* Model Cities program; and name of individual redevelopment projects)
San Francisco Planning and Urban Renewal Association (*see* SPUR)
San Francisco Redevelopment Agency (*see* SFRA)
Saputo, Albert, 151
SBA (*see* Small Business Administration)
Sears, William, 183
Section 8 housing, 16, 19, 57, 60, 233, 236 (*also see* HCDA)
SFAH (San Franciscans for Affordable Housing), 238
SFRA (San Francisco Redevelopment Agency), 211, 213, 214, 215, 216–219, 221, 222, 223–224, 225, 226, 228, 229, 234–235, 236, 237, 238, 239, 242, 250
SFRA v. Hayes, 223
Shubert Square (New Haven, Connecticut), 23
"Six Companies" (San Francisco, California), 221